Love + affection —

Reigns & Geraldine

22nd August 1980

DUBLIN MADE ME

An Autobiography

C. S. ANDREWS

THE MERCIER PRESS
Dublin and Cork

THE MERCIER PRESS LIMITED
25 Lr Abbey Street, Dublin 1.
4 Bridge Street, Cork.

Dublin Made Me
ISBN 0 85342 606 6
© C. S. Andrews, 1979

Printed in the Republic of Ireland by *The Leinster Leader*, Naas.

CONTENTS

I disclaim all fertile meadows, all tilled land
The evil that grows from it and the good,
But the Dublin of old statutes, this arrogant city,
Stirs proudly and secretly in my blood.

From 'Dublin Made Me'
by Donagh MacDonagh.

FOREWORD

This is an account of my childhood, boyhood and early manhood as recollected by me in my seventies.

It has been written largely, though not wholly, from memory. I am aware of the fallibility of memory. I am particularly aware of that phenomenon of memory known to psychologists as paramnesia, where events as they really occurred are distorted, telescoped, transposed or otherwise confused. Hence I disclaim any intention of writing a historical account of these years, even of the public events from 1917 until 1923 in which I played a most minor of minor roles.

Writing in my old age of the happenings of my early years I am conscious that my reactions to these happenings were based mainly on emotionalism and enthusiasm. I rarely thought; I felt. But I am not too critical of what I felt or did. Most of my feelings seem to me in my maturity to have been justified by events.

Despite the tribulations which affected the nation over the years, especially in the years of my youth, I reckon myself lucky to have been one of that fortunate generation which lived to see Irishmen in control of the greater part of the country.

ACKNOWLEDGEMENTS

I wish to thank my wife, Joyce, for her encouragement to me to persist with this book when so often I felt like abandoning it. She typed my manuscript, inserting verbs which I had omitted and limiting my colloquialisms.

I am particularly indebted to my old friend and former colleague, C. B. Murphy, for having devoted so much time and energy to reading the typescript and for making so many suggestions, principally aimed at eliminating the repetitiousness which, in writing and conversation, afflicts old age. I am most grateful to him.

I am grateful, too, to Dr Brian Inglis for his kindness to me when I was writing the book.

I wish to acknowledge to Mr Alf MacLochlainn, Director of the National Library, the help he so readily gave me whenever I requested it.

Childhood

In 1901 — the year I was born — Queen Victoria died to be succeeded by Edward VII, called 'the Peacemaker'. The Boer War was still in progress although no one realised that it was a cloud no bigger than a man's hand presaging the destruction of the British Empire.

Ireland was at peace. The Nationalist Parliamentary Party under the leadership of John Redmond was slowly beginning to recover from the blight of the Parnell split. Arthur Griffith, founder of Sinn Féin, was a voice crying in the wilderness of national apathy. He had not yet written *The Resurrection of Hungary*. The injection of national spirit from the Gaelic League and the Irish Literary Revival had, as yet, little effect in restoring national pride.

Dublin still retained the beautiful buildings, monuments, parks, streets and squares which it had inherited from the Anglo-Irish Ascendancy. But it had lost the consciousness of a separate identity which, despite their intense loyalty to the Crown, had been characteristic of the Anglo-Irish.

Dublin was a British city and accepted itself as one. Its way of life, its standard of values, its customs were identical with those of, say, Birmingham or Manchester except to the extent that they were modified by one great difference: religion. In Dublin at the turn of the century the population was divided into two classes: the rulers and the ruled. The rulers were mainly Protestants, the Catholics the ruled. The Catholics at whatever income level they had attained were second-class citizens.

From childhood I was aware that there were two separate and immiscible kinds of citizens: the Catholics, of whom I was one, and the Protestants, who were as remote and different from us as if they had been blacks and we whites. We were not acquainted with Protestants but we knew that they were there — a hostile element in the community, vaguely menacing us with such horrors as Mrs Smylie's homes for orphans where children might be brought and turned into Protestants. We Catholics varied socially among ourselves but we all had the common bond, whatever our economic condition, of being second-class citizens.

At the top of the Catholic heap — in terms of worldly goods and social status — were the medical specialists, fashionable dentists, barristers, solicitors, wholesale tea and wine merchants, owners of large drapery stores and a· very few owners or directors of large business firms. These were the Catholic upper middle class; they were the Castle Catholics (the Castle being the seat of Government). Their accents were undistinguishable from those of the Dublin Protestants, who held the flattering belief that they spoke the best English in the world. The Castle Catholics played golf, rugby, cricket, tennis, hockey and croquet and dressed as these games required. They lived cheek by jowl with the Protestants on Mountjoy Square, Fitzwilliam Square and Merrion Square or in Foxrock, Dalkey or Kingstown. They owned carriages and were among the first to own motor cars. The Church's ban on Catholics attending Trinity College did not prevent them from sending their brighter children there. They entertained one another and any Protestant who would accept their invitations. They had dinner in the evening, and dressed for it. They had many servants: butlers, housekeepers, cooks, housemaids, tweenies, nannies and coachmen. They sent their sons to the English Catholic public schools at Ampleforth, Stonyhurst and Downside or, as a compromise, to Clongowes which was the top Jesuit school in Ireland. Their daughters went to school to the Sacred Heart Nuns at Mount Anville and were 'finished' at Vienna and Dusseldorf. For their spiritual needs, they preferred the urbane ministrations of the Jesuits to the cruder rituals of the parochial clergy or the unsophisticated pieties of the Franciscans. An invitation to a garden party at the Vice-Regal Lodge or to a reception at Dublin Castle was the realisation of their social ambitions. From time to time they received knighthoods or judgeships, but even such hallmarks of gentility did not equate them with the top Protestants who regarded them as Uncle Toms. The Castle Catholics had annual holidays at Brighton or Bournemouth. In politics they supported the union with Britain. To most of their fellow Catholics they were John Mitchel's 'genteel dastards' and were detribalised.

In the social scale below the Castle Catholics were the Catholic middle middle class. They were the general medical practitioners, less successful solicitors, grocers, publicans, butchers, tobacconists who did not live over their shops (when they moved from over their shops they ascended in the social scale), as well as corn merchants, civil servants, journalists, coal merchants and bank managers. In politics these people were Nationalist and from them came the municipal politicians, chiefly from among the publicans. They sent their children to be educated by the Jesuits at Belvedere College, to the Holy Ghost Fathers in St Mary's or the Marist Catholic University School and their daughters to the Sacred Heart Convent in Leeson Street or to Loreto Convent on the Green. They would usually have three maid servants, referred to as the cook, the maid and the nurse. They had dinner in the middle of the day and entertained themselves at musical evenings where the guests brought their music and sang 'The Heart Bowed Down' or 'The Last Rose of Summer'. They took holidays in Bray or Skerries. They played rugby, cricket and tennis, but not golf or croquet. Their social lives were conducted on the assumption that, if their businesses prospered, their children at least would rise into the circle of Castle Catholics even if they themselves never could. They could hope to be made Justices of the Peace. The letters J.P. after their names was unquestionable evidence of respectability; to be accepted as 'respectable' was the aspiration of all Catholics. They were strong and ostentatious supporters of the Church. They said the family rosary and went to Mass and Communion as a family unit. Their simple creed was faith and fatherland, priests and people, grace and gear. They provided the social milieu for the priests of the parish, whom they entertained generously. They left money in their wills for Masses, gave themselves grand funerals and erected fine monuments to their families in Glasnevin Cemetery. Their lapidary inscriptions clearly were not on oath. Their attitude to death and survival had in it something of the beliefs and practices of the ancient Egyptians.

Lower down in the scale were the shopkeepers and publicans who lived over their shops, as well as clerks, shop assistants, lower grade civil servants, and skilled tradesmen. They ate mid-day dinner, wore nightshirts rather than pyjamas and slept on feather beds. They took no holidays and seldom entertained. They swam in the Clontarf and Merrion Baths. Their children played soccer football and cricket on vacant lots, frequently with makeshift equipment. Their principal recreation was following Bohemians or Shelbourne soccer teams, with occasional visits to the Queen's Theatre to see melodrama or to the Empire Theatre for variety shows. Golf, tennis and croquet they regarded as effeminate games and rugby as the preserve of Protestants and Castle Catholics. Gaelic football and hurling they regarded as fit only for country 'goms'. They sent their sons to

11

Christian Brothers' Schools and, if they could afford it, they sent their daughters to the Dominican Nuns. They had no capital resources. They rented their shops and houses. If those in business prospered they might accumulate some money, move from over their shops and with luck acquire middle middle-class status. If they were merely employees, the limit of their expectations was to own their house at death. Their hopes for the economic improvement of the family lay in providing a good education for their children, leading to a good job. The idea of sending their sons to the University never occurred to them.

A 'good job' meant a secure job, because insecurity was the bugbear of their lives. The Christian Brothers provided the necessary education and fostered the necessary ambition. For some reason, this section of the Dublin Catholic community never formed close links with the clergy — possibly a hangover from the anti-clericalism of the Parnellite days. Priests visited them only when they were sent for to administer the sacraments to the sick or the dying. They seemed to act on the Gaelic proverb: 'Don't be too close to or too distant from the clergy'. These were the lower middle classes.

At the bottom of the heap were the have-nots of the city, consisting of labourers, dockers, coal heavers, shop attendants, messenger boys and domestic servants. Even those who had regular work were seldom far above the poverty line and very many were below it. There was no security of employment and great numbers of them had no work at all. They sent their children to the National Schools for as short a time as possible and a great many emerged from these schools illiterate and remained so. Their housing conditions were as bad as the worst in Western Europe. They had scarcely any amusements outside the pubs or an occasional soccer match at Dalymount Park or Shelbourne Park. In Summer they walked to the strands at Dollymount, the Shelly Banks, Sandymount and Merrion to bathe and sometimes went to Howth by tram or train on Sundays. Sometimes they went to the Phoenix Park to hear the band playing in the 'Hollow'. They could not afford the price of entrance to the Zoo. They supplied the rank and file of the Dublin Fusiliers, known in the British Army as 'the Dubs', and kept Artane Industrial School supplied with pupils. They had no interest in and took no part in politics. Their main concern was to provide food and lodging for their children; they frequently failed to do either. Among them trachoma and rickets were endemic. They were religious on Sundays, and no matter how small their possessions there was always a statue of the Blessed Virgin, the Sacred Heart and perhaps the Infant of Prague on the mantelpiece. They accepted their misery as the will of God and in the certainty that their fortitude would be rewarded in the next life. They had abandoned hope in the here and now until Larkin, the great Labour leader and agitator, emerged to proclaim the dignity of the working man. This was the working class and there were among them subsects of destitution terminating in the 'lumpen proletariat' whose sign manual was rags.

Unlike the English or any other European class structure, the class structure of the Dublin Catholics was not based on birth. Few families were more than a couple of generations removed from peasant origins; even the rich Castle Catholics had country cousins and brothers tilling the soil and uncles and aunts milking the cows and feeding the hens. At any level, Dublin in the first decade of the century was probably the most·pathetic and apathetic city in Europe. The slums kept on increasing and the poor got poorer and more degraded.

The effects, in cynicism and bitterness, of the Parnell split when the Catholic community was torn asunder had not wholly died and whatever little excitement the Boer War had provided diminished as the war drew to a close. The politicians had transferred their interest to the 'floor of the house' at Westminster and had succumbed to its absorptive qualities. Dublin became a very secondary place in which to seek power or prestige. The mass of the Catholics were as yet untouched by the Gaelic League or Sinn Féin; the voice of D. P. Moran, editor of the famous weekly nationalist paper *The Leader* with its cry of 'Irish Ireland', was only beginning to be heard. There was no significant social consciousness in the community. The time had yet to come when the Lord Mayor of Dublin would say to a St Vincent de Paul Conference 'Someone has said "the poor always you have with you" but we know better'. The better-off people at the top and in the middle of the heap regarded their prosperity as an outward sign of inward grace and were totally preoccupied with holding on to what they had.

I was born into the lower middle class of the Catholic population in number 42 Summerhill, in the Parish of St Mary, of which the Pro-Cathedral was the parish church. My mother had been born in the same house twenty-eight years earlier and my father in a house on George's Quay, across the river. There were only two children in our family: myself and a brother who was five years younger. Summerhill was a street of decaying Georgian houses, dating from the 1780s. It must have been a beautiful thoroughfare at the time of the Union with Britain in 1801. The ground on which it was built was elevated

13

and from the top windows of the house there was a fine view of the city over to Ballsbridge and Killiney. Immediately below the house was Joyce's famous 'Nighttown', known locally as 'Monto' or 'the digs'. It was the red light quarter, except that there were no red lights.

Number 42 was a typical Georgian house of five storeys. The basement held the kitchens and pantries and tiny rooms where the maids slept. The 'area', on the same level, had a cellar under the foot-path containing a coal store. The coal was delivered through a hole in the footpath which was normally covered with a heavy cast-iron lid flush with the pavement. There were stables at the back. On the ground floor was a back and front parlour and return room, and on the first floor a back and front drawing room. Above the drawing rooms were two bedrooms known as the 'two-pair back' and the 'two-pair front' and at the very top were another two rooms known as the 'top-back' and the 'top-front'.

At this time Summerhill was quickly sinking into slums but the houses on either side of us were still occupied by families living over their shops. On the one side was a publican family named Byrne and on the other side was a grocer named Kavanagh. There were no children in either family and I saw little of them. In our house the return room had been made into a bathroom, although there was only a cold tap fitted to the bath. Hot water had to be brought up in pots from the kitchen. There was only one indoor lavatory, called the water closet, which served the whole house. Children were washed in a bath tub in the kitchen. Buildings such as this had once housed the legendary spacious life of Georgian Dublin, but that day had long since passed when I was born.

My grandfather, Christopher Moran, had been an Inspector in the Dublin Metropolitan Police. He married late in life and he and my grandmother rented number 42 Summerhill, where he died soon after his retirement, leaving four young children. My mother, Mary known always as Polly, then aged fifteen, was the eldest and there were three younger boys, Christy, Paddy and Simon. Faced with the prospect of bringing up a young family, my grandmother turned the front parlour into a dairy shop. The extensive yard and stables became a dairy yard where she kept cows, a horse and a delivery gig and a couple of pigs to dispose of the swill. My grandmother's own people had been dairymen in Ballsbridge, so she knew the business well. My uncles, young as they were, started a milk round and milked and looked after the cows and churned the butter. They sup-plemented the milk supply by purchase at the lairage of Messrs Cuddy at the North Wall. In summer they rented pasturage for the

14

cows at Raheny.

My grandmother was the moving force behind everything that happened in Summerhill. In appearance she was frail and slightly stooped, with wisps of greying hair about her face. She had prominent blue eyes which always seemed to be looking into the distance and gave her a worried and very sad expression. She had plenty to worry and to be sad about. She rarely smiled but was never angry.

She also took in lodgers, but the lodgers were all uncles or cousins or aunts from Wicklow or Wexford or, from time to time, nieces and nephews from Longford where her only sister had married and produced a large family. She kept up intimate contacts with her relations and those of her husband. She believed in the principle and the practical merits of the extended family, the old Irish idea of the *deirbhfhine*.

My father, Christopher Andrews, was a neighbour's child, and he and his brother, Matthew, spent much of their boyhood and young manhood in Summerhill. They were motherless and their father, who was a house builder in a small way, was a violent, tyrannical man and his sons escaped from the harshness of their own home to the warmth and affection of Mrs Moran, my mother's mother. In due course my father, Christopher, the older of the two Andrews boys, married Polly Moran. Later, the younger boy, Mattie, moved in as a lodger. In practice, the marriage and Mattie's arrival meant only that there were two additional members of the Moran family and the routine of number 42 Summerhill remained undisturbed. The young married couple used the two-pair front — one enormous room — for their bedroom; for reading or sometimes entertaining their friends they used the drawing room which was also shared by any other member of the family who felt like using it. My parents and Uncle Mattie had their meals with the rest of the family in the kitchen. I shared my parents' room until I was five, when my brother was born and I was moved up to the top back room.

In retrospect, life in Summerhill remains in my mind as something like a scaled-down version of Zöe Oldenburg's account of daily life in the castle of an impoverished mediaeval baron. There was the same kind of comings and goings, of something constantly happening, of shortage of money, of the rough talk of men, of women sewing and stitching and cooking, of abundant food and continuous meals, of laughing and shouting and quarrelling, of horses, cattle, dogs and cats. Life was abundant and improvident.

When my father married into the family, the star lodger was a

15

character known as 'ould O'Brien'. He was a retired and wealthy publican and a bachelor. He was a first cousin of my grandmother and was a pillar of the Church. He left most of his money for Masses and the rest to his nephews and nieces, disappointing the expectations of my mother and my grandmother. My mother was supposed to be a great favourite of his but he left her nothing; the beneficiaries of the will, being decent Wexford people named Culleton, clubbed together and gave my mother a few hundred pounds. Several times later this money saved Summerhill from disaster and the bailiffs. In addition to 'ould O'Brien' and an old aunt, Aunt Anne Moran, there were always nephews and nieces and cousins staying in the house for longer or shorter periods.

Just before I was born 'ould O'Brien' had died, well into his nineties, but Aunt Anne Moran was still there, as indeed she was when I had grown up. She was a first cousin of my grandfather Moran and her brother was Bishop of Dunedin in New Zealand. This latter connection gave her a special status in the household. She was a gloomy old lady and everyone had to keep quiet while she was around. This was seldom enough, as she had her meals in her room which was the back parlour. For the rest of the tribe the kitchen was the heart of the house. It was a very big kitchen with a great raised open fire, an oven and a wide hob. There were pot hooks and hangers and there was always a kettle on the boil. Tea was as readily available as water. There was a screen in the kitchen on which were pasted cut-out illustrations from magazines depicting scenes from sporting life, mainly racing and boxing. My Uncle Simon had the instincts of a Corinthian and eventually made a moderately successful career as a professional punter. He was understood to be 'delicate', although in fact he was not, but he had not been required to go to school or to exert himself around the dairy.

On the kitchen walls was a graduated set of pewter dish covers, ranging from one large enough to cover a turkey to tiny ones for savouries. The small ones were never used because there never were any savouries. The meals were cooked before our eyes and there was always 'lashins and lavins'. There was plenty of variety because all the country cousins brought us chickens and geese and at Easter there were eggs galore: hen eggs, duck eggs, goose eggs and turkey eggs.

At Christmas, the whole house was decorated with masses of holly and preparations began weeks in advance on the making of the pudding. It was a very big pudding and always made in a great black shining crock. My grandmother presided over the grating of the

16

bread, the cleaning and stoning of the fruit, the chopping up of candied peel and the pouring of the stout. The pudding had to be mixed for days and everyone in the house took a turn in mixing — for luck. The pudding was cooked in a cloth and when it was finished had a thick skin coating. There was ham and spiced beef, turkey and goose for Christmas dinner. The turkey was stuffed with bread crumbs and sage and the goose was stuffed with potatoes. The turkey was roasted on a spit in front of the kitchen fire while the pudding was boiling on top of the fire and the goose cooking in the oven. The spit was set into a tall concave pewter-like stand and everyone helped to turn the spit and baste the turkey. The dairy boys and the servants ate in the kitchen when the family had finished and shared the same food.

The dairy boys and girls all seemed to be good humoured in their work and acted like typical Dublin characters. When years afterwards my mother saw *The Plough and the Stars* she said that Fluther Good had worked in '42' as we always called it. Being, until I was nearly five years old, an only child, they made a pet of me in the dairy, letting me sit on the horse or feed the cows and pigs. The dairy boys made great play with the maid servants amid much giggling and tittering. I once found one of them with his hand up a girl's skirt and it was not until he warned me not to mention what I had seen that I wondered what it was all about. If he had said nothing, I would not have noticed or remembered the incident. It was my first introduction to sex.

The servant girls, and there were always two or three around the place, were paid almost nothing because there was nothing to pay with, but they were well fed and could have food for their families.

It was around the yard that I acquired my first lessons in the use of the four or even five letter words, all of which I picked up without conscious effort, together with that commonest of Dublin swear words 'Jaysus'. Like the Catechism, all the swearing was meaningless to me but I never forgot it. Brendan Behan, who was born many years later a few streets away, realised the full potential of the unchanging local argot as an art form and exploited it to shock or amuse the bourgeoisie. I too knew the argot well and in later years on many a boring and formal occasion I wished I had the nerve to follow my inclinations and do the same as Behan.

My grandmother was not a Dublin woman by birth. Her parents had originally been small farmers on the estate of the famous eighteenth century buck, 'Buck' Whaley, near Wicklow. The family was evicted from their holding and it was said that her sister, Kate, had been born on the roadside as the family moved up to Dublin. They settled for a while in a basement in Harry Street, off Grafton Street, and started buying milk and re-selling it from door to door.

When they went to Ballsbridge their fortunes seemed to have improved somewhat because my grandmother and her sister had an education and a refinement of manner and speech and a vocabulary not usually found in people of their circumstance. They got something more than a primary education at the local Sisters of Charity and later attended an institution known as Paddy Mack's Academy. It was run in a private house in Sandymount and, according to the family legend, the kitchen was the girls' and the front parlour the boys' classroom. Just before she married, my grandmother had intended to enter a convent but changed her mind, or her mind was changed for her by family pressure. I think she must always have had an unusually strong vocation and tried to live it out in the world. She was far too other-worldly to bring up a family successfully without a husband.

Despite her frail appearance, my grandmother had limitless physical energy. She rose every morning at 5.30 and went to six o'clock Mass at the Jesuit church in Gardiner Street. She worked unceasingly until bedtime, organising meals, supervising the scalding of the crocks and churns for the butter-making, keeping accounts. Monday was washday and the washing was done in great pots and tubs with everyone lending a hand at stirring the clothes and spreading them out on the line in the yard. Any spare moment she had was devoted to making patchwork quilts. Every bed in the house had one. She plucked fowl and kept the feathers for pillows and mattresses. She was the family doctor, with remedies for all ailments: Friars' Balsam, Zambuk for cuts, horehound and honey for sore throats, Elliman's Embrocation for sprains, bread and oatmeal poultices for boils and swellings, quinine for colds and camphorated oil and mustard baths after wettings, syrup of squills and senna tea for constipation, or Epsom salts in severe cases, and beef tea and calf's foot jelly for convalescence.

When I was a child, every mother of young children lived in constant dread and sometimes real terror of illness. If a child showed any sign of sickness, there were horrible imaginings of death from meningitis, pneumonia, lockjaw (tetanus), hydrophobia (rabies), scarlet fever and, above all, diphtheria. A sore throat threw the whole house into a panic that the child would be sent to the dreaded fever hospital in Cork Street. There was every reason for parental terror, because the mortality rate for children in the city was very high. In young manhood there was an equally well-founded fear of 'consumption' which, in addition to being deadly, was regarded as a rather shameful disease. Consumptives were concealed from the neighbours as much as possible, the concealment adding to the dangers of infection in the home.

My grandmother did not esteem doctors. Nutritious food (all food she described as 'most nutritious') in abundance, and prayer and miraculous medals and scapulars and holy water were for her the basic safeguards for good health.

Indeed, doctors no less than priests counted very little in the day to day life of the family, not because we were unusually healthy but unless the illness appeared to be obviously fatal, my grandmother's prescription together with the continuous family nursing was usually sufficient. Even if the illness was clearly terminal, the family rather than the doctor consoled and comforted the dying patient, making death less difficult to accept. Death itself brought the family closer and was not regarded as the end in any ultimate sense. The corpse was treated with as much respect and ceremony as if it were living.

If it is possible for one human being to possess the theological virtues of faith, hope, charity, and the cardinal virtues of justice, prudence, temperance and fortitude, my grandmother possessed them. Outstandingly, she possessed charity, faith and fortitude. The loss of her husband and the death after prolonged illness of one of her sons, together with the many family disappointments which she had to endure, were borne without complaint and accepted as the will of God. To her the will of God was not an empty phrase, but the dominant reality to which she submitted in the certainty that she would be fully rewarded in the next life for her patient endurance of the vicissitudes and tribulations of this. She lived until she was eighty-six and in her seventies she survived a bad bout of pneumonia, then usually a fatal complaint for old people. When she was convalescing she told me how disappointed she was at her recovery. She said that she thought Almighty God was at last going to call her to her eternal reward, but she supposed 'He had his own designs and we had to be patient'.

The only books I ever saw her reading were her missal and the *Imitation of Christ*. She lived out the advice of Thomas à Kempis by placing such complete trust in God that she had no need for the comfort of men. One of her favourite sayings was from the *Imitation*: 'Would to God that we might spend a single day really well'. She knew her Scriptures well and had many favourite quotations from them: 'Every idle word that men shall speak they shall give an account of them'. Not that there was any shortage of idle words in Summerhill. Another was 'Wide is the gate and broad the way that leadeth to destruction'. This was applied as a mild rebuke to some of the alcoholic excesses which were only too common in Summerhill. But her great virtue was charity. She was kind to everyone. My father and his brother, as young and motherless neighbours, were given the run of the house and were mothered and virtually reared by my grandmother. The Longford nephews and nieces and the Wicklow and Tullow cousins were always made more than welcome and there was neither fuss nor restraint on their comings and goings. She was uncensorious and for her they had no defects, only foibles. They loved coming to stay in Summerhill where living was so relaxed compared with the rigid and narrow life of the country where respectability was everything and people were constantly under the surveillance of their neighbours.

Except for going to the Chapel, my grandmother seldom left the house. We always spoke of the 'chapel' never the 'church', however grand the edifice. The use of the phrase 'going to church' would immediately identify the speaker as a Protestant, or at least as a Castle Catholic. My grandmother did, however, take me on my first visit to the zoo and she had great difficulty in keeping me out of the bear pit. I was only four years old at the time but I remember getting off the tram at Parkgate Street and seeing the soldiers in their red coats outside the Soldiers' Home.

Considering that I rarely met and never mingled with Protestants and only saw them when they paraded on Sunday mornings in great style to Findlaters' Church — the Presbyterian Church in Rutland Square — it is strange that from earliest childhood I seem to have been aware of their presence and influence in the community. I certainly did not get any of this feeling from my grandmother. She was incapable of expressing unkind feelings about anyone. There was only one Protestant couple living in Summerhill. They lived in the front and back parlour of one of the houses and the husband, who was a self-employed engraver, had his workshop in the basement. They were not very well off, but they were far above the poverty line; the Protestant charities saw to that. There were many poor Protestants in Dublin but never destitute Protestants.

* * * * *

I know very few details about my father's parents or grandparents but I know that my grandfather Andrews came from a small farming family at Ardcath, a village near Garristown on the Dublin-Meath border. In that locality, and indeed all over north Dublin and south Meath, Andrews is a common name. As soon as I could ride a bicycle, my father took me once or twice a year to see a Mrs Rath who had once kept house for John Andrews, my grandfather, and my father and his brother. We used to cycle up to Adamstown on Saturday, stay the night with Mrs Rath, go to Mass in Garristown and then we always paid a visit to the cemetery in Ardcath where there are many Andrews' gravestones. Christopher was the predominant Christian name among them. My father pointed out to me two tombstones close together in the corner of the ruined Church at Ardcath. They both belonged, he told me, to our particular branch of the family. The datings on them brought the family back to the turn of the seventeenth century. The Andrews were certainly a long time in the area.

A friend of mine doing mediaeval research, came across the following entry in the Irish Cartuleries of Llanthony:

Place: Ardcath.   Date c. 1194-1210.

Name: Willelmus Andreas.

Grant of Osbertus de Butterley — 9 acres arable land lying between the land held by Willelmus Andreas and Ricardus Reffus.

Butterly, too, is still a common name in North Dublin.

My father, two brothers and a sister were born in number 16 George's Quay, near Butt Bridge. The sister and one of the brothers died young. When the mother died, my grandfather moved across the Liffey to Empress Place, where he carried on a small business as a building contractor. He died a few months after I was born and, as far as I could learn, was not deeply regretted by his sons. Apparently he was a very rough and harsh man. He once hit and hurt my father and was never forgiven for it. When he died, my grandfather left a number of houses which he built and owned in Clontarf but they were all mortgaged to the bank and the only thing my father seems to have inherited was a 'Garde de vin'.

It was to escape from the harshness of Empress Place, which was just around the corner from Summerhill, that my father as a young man sought refuge with Grandmother Moran. All his life he was devoted to her and she to him. He made up to her for so many of the disappointments of her own family. They had an unusually close relationship for a son-in-law and mother-in-law. When he moved to

Terenure he visited her every Monday of his life bringing some small gift of fruit or cakes.

Uncle Mattie Andrews was like Esau, red and hairy. He was a bachelor and a man of regular and limited habits. Although a draughtsman by training (he was trained at Harland and Wolff's in Belfast) he worked as a timekeeper in T. & C. Martin's where he had the reputation of never being late or sick for the thirty years he was there. The Martins were different from the usual run of Dublin employers of their time. They took a personal interest in their employees and, when eventually Uncle Mattie fell ill and was unable to work for two years before he died, they continued to pay his wages.

Mattie was a gruff, rough man, who never spoke much and when he did, shouted. His only hobby was drinking, pursued exclusively at weekends. He paid my grandmother for his lodgings every Friday evening and between Friday and Monday he spent all that was left on drink. From Monday to Friday he was penniless and drinkless. His only exercise was to walk every morning to Martin's at the North Wall and back again in the evening. He always went up to his room after his evening meal and I don't know what he did there because, like Aunt Anne in the back parlour, he liked his privacy.

My father had been indentured to the auctioneering business for a five-year period of apprenticeship at Mr Bentley's of Capel Street. Mr Bentley was what was known as a divisional auctioneer. His patent from the Lord Lieutenant authorised him to sell unredeemed pledges from pawnbrokers. There were only two others who had this authority: the City Swordbearer and the City Macebearer. These offices were sinecures and the holders farmed them out to working auctioneers. All pawnbrokers had to sell unredeemed pledges by virtue of these authorisations.

When Mr Bentley died my father applied to the Lord Lieutenant for the patent but, not being a Protestant, he had no chance of getting it; it was given to a Protestant fellow-worker in the office. For a time, my father continued to work for Bentley's successor. In his will, Bentley left my father a legacy of £100 in recognition of his services. It was this small capital which enabled my father to leave Summerhill which, despite his affection for my grandmother, he found distasteful because of the drinking, disorder and general fecklessness there.

I was eight and a half years old when we left Summerhill and those early years left a lasting impression on me. It gave me a basis on which was built an awareness of the problems of poverty and the harsh constraints of working-class life in Dublin. It also gave me a deep attachment to the very stones of the city. I have travelled abroad a good deal and, invariably, after a few weeks' absence from Dublin, I begin to hanker after it and when on returning from abroad I reach College Green, I always get a sense of security and a feeling of being surrounded by friendly neighbours. All my life, it has been a pleasure for me to walk through the city — particularly on Sunday mornings.

I have only a few bad memories of my childhood in Summerhill. There often seemed to be a money crisis, particularly about the quarterly rent payments. Although I never met him, I knew the rent collector's name was Mr Fenton. His coming on gale days always produced an argument between my mother and my Uncle Christy, who often spent the money reserved for the rent on something else. He would want her to dip into her little legacy and this she always did after a feeble resistance. I understood the argument well enough to know that, if the rent was not paid, we might possibly be evicted and, young as I was, I knew what that meant. The dread of eviction was in the very bones of every Irish Catholic child from the famine days and indeed evictions were the common lot of the tenement dwellers around Summerhill. In Britain Street, Gardiner Street, Rutland Street or Cumberland Street on any day you were almost certain to see an eviction taking place, with all the household goods piled pitifully on the pavement and women and children crying amidst their sticks of furniture, their pots and pans and their mattresses. The bailiffs looked as miserable as the people they were evicting.

Despite the difficulties of raising the rent, there was seldom a Sunday evening in Summerhill that my uncles had not an impromptu party — men only — playing cards, poker or twenty-five, singing and, of course, drinking. I was always sent to bed on these occasions, but this did not prevent me hearing the snatches of songs from operas and 'come-all-ye's', or seeing on a Monday morning the drawing room with empty stout bottles and whiskey glasses and spittoons full to overflowing and smelling the stale smell of beer and tobacco smoke. Spitting seemed to be a necessary adjunct to smoking and a full spittoon was a particularly unpleasant sight. Sometimes drinking or card parties were held in the kitchen and now and again an unfortunate 'whiskey priest', who appeared to be a crony of my Uncle Christy, would be seen with a glass in his hand, his back to the fire, singing 'On Carrig Donn, the heath is brown'. To me priests were very remote beings and to see one at close quarters behaving in such an unbecoming manner left me with a permanent memory of the incident, song and all.

The front drawing room, where the parties were held, was a big room with two tall windows. It was a well-lighted room and had a great marble mantelpiece with two brass candelabra on the mantel shelf and over it a tall gilt mirror reaching nearly to the ceiling. On each side of the mirror were gas brackets with ornamental globes over the gas mantels. A brass fender, a brass coal bucket and long brass fire irons brightened the room when, on special occasions, they were polished and the fire surround was blackleaded. There were heavy red velour curtains on the windows hung from wooden rails with wooden rings. They were very easy to swing to and fro and provided part of my childish amusement. There was an upright Collard and Collard piano with a swivelling piano stool in one corner of the room; in another a black horsehair-stuffed sofa and at either side of the fireplace were horsehair armchairs to match the sofa. The carpet was flowered and rather worn but the outstanding feature of the room, from a child's point of view, was a lionskin hearth rug with its maned head and yellow eyes and wide-open snarling mouth. Odd chairs, a glass chandelier and a what-not full of china, ivory ornaments and bric-a-brac, a heavy mahogany sideboard covered with odd pieces of electro-plate and what might or might not have been silver salvers and trays completed the furnishing of the room.

My parents kept aloof from my uncles' parties and the noisy, but generally light-hearted life in Summerhill. My mother looked on the life there with patient detachment and found her satisfaction in my father, myself and my brother and in an absorbing interest in clothes and a milder interest in music.

My mother was a tall woman with a Gibson-girl figure, of which I think she was very proud. She was not beautiful or even good-looking and her skin was far from perfect. There was no remedy to be found in cosmetics then. To use rouge or lipstick would have been regarded as the practice of a whore. But she had a great mass of light brown hair. I remember the colour because when I was old enough to be sent on messages I used to go to Clery's store in O'Connell Street to buy her the light brown fringe nets which she always wore. She had beautiful hands and knew it, because she was always careful of them. She never went out in the street with ungloved hands (she would regard it as not respectable to be seen without gloves) and she had a great many pairs of gloves which she kept in a special drawer under tissue paper as well as glove stretchers which I used as toys. She had eyes that varied from light to very dark blue. When they were very light and fixed on you, you knew she was annoyed. It was the only sign she ever gave of anger. She never raised her voice for any reason and her usual mode of speech was as monosyllabic as was possible to convey her meaning. When she wanted to express disapproval or disgust, the inevitable exclamation was 'sicken you'.

My mother approached everyone and everything with a not so gentle scepticism and she had little belief in the goodness of humanity. She had a disconcerting capacity to perceive people's foibles and I never found it worth while telling her a lie as she could always spot it immediately. She had a macabre sense of humour and all the funeral rites and customs associated with death were to her a constant source of amused and sceptical comment. Her favourite speculation was as to the destiny of the late departed and how he would appear at the judgement seat to answer for some weakness she might have observed in him. She had none of the charity of her mother and even less of her mother's spirituality. Her religious practices were the minimum necessary to retain her membership of the Church. She was not interested in politics and barely read the papers which, in our house, was difficult to avoid doing. She never read books. Her only reading was fashion magazines of which she bought many. She had exceptional taste in clothes and a talent for making her own and wearing them with style.

In summer my mother went up town in 'full fig'. As a child, I was unable to understand the expression, as I knew a fig was something you ate like a date. She had a feather boa which I enjoyed running through my fingers but it was the muff and fur ties which she wore in winter that I most loved to touch. It was a big red muff lined with blue satin and, in addition to the pleasure I got from rubbing my face against it, the muff gave out the lovely smell of the scent which she always carried in a small bottle encased in a gold filigree cover.

My mother had no jewellery of any value, which is perhaps why she was not very interested in jewellery, but she had a collection of lockets and brooches, gold chains, cameos and a particularly beautiful half-hunter lady's watch which is now being worn by her great-grand-daughter.

She was meticulous in regard to the cleanliness of the house. She had a good sense of decoration. She liked music and played the piano fairly well and played it often. She still played at eighty years of age. At moments of crisis in the family she used say she got 'sick in the stomach' but never sick enough to be unable to cope. Her predominant passion was the welfare of myself and my brother and on our comfort and convenience she concentrated the major efforts of her life. For our benefit she willingly deprived herself and my father of holidays, amusements or any possible luxury. She had never been further from Dublin than Wicklow and Tullow. Despite her closeness to her Longford aunts and cousins, she never got that far abroad. After her marriage she never left Dublin at all. She had one close woman friend, a milliner named Julia Forde, who visited her regularly, but for the rest, cousins and relatives were the only people she welcomed uncritically. I have never seen any affectionate exchanges between her and my father; yet they were always together and she attended on him, as she did on us children, hand and foot. I never saw her show any emotion except once, when she realised that my father was about to die.

In Summerhill my mother would from time to time have a few friends in to a party, but it was a very different type of entertainment from the conviviality of my uncles. The day before the party was taken up with making cakes; my mother was an excellent pastry cook. The drawing room was polished, which was no small task because of all the bits and pieces. I was allowed to join the party for a while before bed time, but was always glad enough to leave as nobody paid any attention to me, being mostly preoccupied with whatever song they were about to sing: 'The moon hath raised', the 'Soldiers' Chorus' or, for the comics, 'At Trinity Church I met my doom'. My mother played the accompaniment for all the numbers.

The parties were always very genteel, with the best china out and no drinking or smoking and no spittoon. They broke up well in time for the last tram home. My mother had very high notions of gentility. Before her father died, when still only a child, she had been sent to the famous Academy of dancing and deportment in North Great George's Street, run by a well-known 'character', Professor Maginni. Even by the standards of the time, Maginni was both egregious and ludicrous. Every afternoon he strolled up O'Connell Street in silk hat, morning coat, lavender waistcoat, striped trousers, silvertopped malacca cane and gold watch chain. Added to this was his special way of walking. He slid along the pavements and all his body seemed to be in motion and in different directions, except his head. Any lady, and she had to be a lady or at least look like a lady, who caught his eye earned a wonderful salute, with the hat swept off and a bow from the waist. Professor Maginni was a great subject of Dublin 'jeers', and his eccentricities made him easy prey for popular derision. He was a 'fantastic' if ever there was one. In her pursuit of gentility, I expect my mother was an example of the common people of Ireland pulling themselves out of the gutter. I once asked her why she had not got any training which would enable her to earn an independent living and she told me that her father held the view that three brothers should be well able to support one sister.

Dublin has always given itself a reputation for wit. In fact the wit, as practised in Dublin, was and is essentially no better than 'jeering' and has its basis in envy and a desire to denigrate.

> Twas Irish humour wet and dry
> Threw quicklime in Parnell's eye.

Anyone who stands out from the crowd in the matter of behaviour, dress, interests and, above all, achievement, is fair game for the jeer. Visiting literary journalists are taken to McDaid's, Davy Byrne's or Neary's and, with perception heightened by alcohol, they hear what they want to hear and the myth of Dublin wit is perpetuated. O'Casey's 'Young Covey' on 'Uncle Peter', Joyce's Citizen on Bloom and George Moore on Edward Martin and Yeats are good examples of the genre. I have lived all my life in Dublin and I have heard only two examples of genuine verbal wit, both from a well-known Dublin character. It is said that asked by his wife how they should celebrate their wedding anniversary he suggested two minutes silence and it is to the same character that the description of the Gate and Abbey Theatres as 'Sodom and Begorrah' is attributed.

From time to time my Uncle Christy took me on his milk round which extended out to Glasnevin. As far as the north side of the city went, he could have acted as a very successful courier if there had been any tourists in those days. From these trips I got to know the architectural landmarks of the north city. He was very proud of the buildings, particularly St George's Church and the Rotunda Hospital, which he described as the best maternity hospital in the world. I don't think his information as to the origin and style of the buildings was very accurate but it was sufficiently relevant to make a child feel that Dublin was a great city and that Mountjoy Square and Rutland Square were the loveliest squares and O'Connell Street was the widest street in the world — a claim frequently made in those days. I seem to have been born, too, with the belief that the Phoenix Park was the largest park in the world. It was from Uncle Christy that I got the information that Irish horses were the best in the world and that our soldiers, i.e. the Dublin Fusiliers, had won the Boer War. We always raised our caps passing Catholic churches, but when we passed Protestant churches, my uncle would invariably make some offensive remark about Protestants. The Black Church was particularly frightening to me for no other reason than that its stonework had turned black with city grime, suggesting the abode of the devil.

Gypsies, as distinct from tinkers, were to be found around the city and my uncle told me that they stole children although why this was done was never explained; they seemed to have plenty of their own. The Parnell Monument was being built at the time and for the first time I heard his name and that of Kitty O'Shea and about some ill the English had done to him. A poorly dressed old man passed the time of day with my uncle and I was told, as if it was a great secret, that the man was 'Skin the Goat', the jarvey who drove the Park murderers, when the Chief Secretary for Ireland and Burke, the Under-Secretary, were stabbed to death in Phoenix Park. I got a confused picture of Carey the Informer, Joe Brady, and a knife. 'Skin the Goat', whose real name was Fitzharris, lived in lower Rutland Street and whenever he passed, people nudged one another and said 'there's Skin the Goat'. I don't think he was ostracised, but people were not too anxious to be seen talking to him. Despite all the hysterical public denunciation of the Park murders, the common people of Dublin hated the memory of Carey the Informer, who betrayed the conspirators, and had a not so sneaking admiration for Joe Brady, the youngest of the conspirators. My tribal prejudices were being created and the tribal folklore absorbed.

On these trips, too, I picked up some of the more respectable slang of the city. At every street corner, where public houses were nearly always located, there was a group of idlers — idlers because there was no work available — who were known as corner boys. When they got drunk or quarrelled, they were called 'bowsies'. Every street had its groups of ragamuffins who never let anyone pass without making some jeering remark. 'Eh, mister, where did you get the hat'. My uncle referred to them as 'towrags' or 'little gets'.

One day my Uncle Paddy was persuaded to take me to a relative in Drumcondra who was an amateur photographer. He had offered my mother to do a portrait of me. I did not want to go but nevertheless I was sent, whining and protesting all the way to Drumcondra bridge where I made my final stand, throwing myself on the ground in a violent tantrum. Trying to mollify such a brat in public must have been a very humiliating experience for Uncle Paddy. In a final effort to placate me, he offered me the only coin in his pocket, and probably the only coin he had in the world, which happened to be half a crown. I took the coin and threw it into the canal shouting that I did not want his 'white money'. Fifteen pints or fifteen half whiskeys was what half a crown meant to my uncle. He must have had great restraint not to throw me in after the half crown. Nor did he drag me home to face an indignant mother but eventually persuaded me to go on and have the photograph taken. I have it still: a portrait of a surly, bad-tempered child. The story became part of the family folklore and I am sure my uncle recovered some of the lost pints and half-ones as he told the tale because he was a good story teller.

Any Dubliner will be familiar with the expression 'We always kept ourselves to ourselves', meaning that the family is a cut above the neighbours and does not mix with them. In the first decade of the century every family that my parents were acquainted with seemed to have adopted that attitude; as a result I had no youngsters of my own age to play with. I spent my childhood almost entirely with my parents or uncles around the cow sheds or with the girls my mother employed to take me for walks around Mountjoy Square or sometimes as far as St Stephen's Green to feed the ducks.

In the years I lived in Summerhill I knew only two boys of the neighbourhood who were regarded as suitable companions. One was the son of a porter in the Bank of Ireland whose family was the very essence of respectability, his mother having been a lady's maid. The second boy was the son of a cabinet maker who lived nearby. These were the only children whose homes I visited. I acquired a particularly strong Dublin accent as well as the dialect of the neighbourhood which, if somewhat modified by time, I have never quite lost.

When I was nearly seven I was sent to school. I sensed some disagreement between my parents as to where I was to go. My father wanted me to go to the National School at North William Street, but my mother did not think this was good enough and I was sent to the Holy Faith nuns in Dominick Street. School was my first real contact with other children. I was soon very conscious that I was different from most of the other pupils who came from the families of the middle middle class. They were sons and daughters of prosperous butchers, grocers, publicans and junior civil servants. To them and to the nuns my accent sounded utterly of the pavement, the more so because the parents of the children and the nuns were mostly from rural areas. Accent has never been a caste mark in Ireland to the same extent as in England, but there are limits and apparently I was below the limit.

There were two nuns in charge of our classes. They taught us the three Rs and religion and drill. One of the nuns, Sister Josepha, was a sharp-faced tall woman, anaemic, with a coarse skin which was disfigured by pimples. She took a dislike to me and continually mocked my accent, giving me to understand that I was not up to the standards of the Holy Faith Convent. I spoke of 'skuel' instead of 'school' and 'Dubbelin' instead of 'Dublin'.

Apart from my accent, I differed from the other children in that I was a very big boy for my age and was therefore immune from bullying. I had no timidities and I also had the advantage that I read very early, thanks to my mother who taught me from nursery books and to my own efforts to follow the illustrated sporting papers which formed my Uncle Simon's pabulum. I could also add up and write so that I was well ahead of the other children, which always seemed to annoy rather than to please Sister Josepha.

The other nun, Sister Monica, was a warm person and more than made up to me by her kindness for the niggling attitude of Sister Josepha, so that on the whole I enjoyed Dominick Street for the years I was there and, by the time I left, I was quite well prepared for the Christian Brothers. Religious instruction at the Convent was of the simplest kind and consisted of memorising the halfpenny catechism; it was not thought necessary to understand it. I had the minor intellectual equipment which enabled me to learn anything by rote and I never had any problem in memorising lessons.

Most of the children were called for after school by their parents, sometimes in pony and traps, or by nannies, although the word nannies was not used then even amongst the prosperous butchers. I was not called for. In spite of being a very sheltered child, my mother saw no difficulty in letting me come home from school by myself. There were of course no traffic dangers in Dublin in 1908 except perhaps from a runaway horse. A motor car was a rare sight. The first one I sat in was on a run from a charity bazaar at North William Street to Nelson's Pillar and back, a distance of about one mile. It cost the not inconsiderable sum of 6d. and was regarded as an adventure to be talked about for days.

I made my way home via Britain Street (now Parnell Street) with occasional digressions through Moore Street, Henry Street, Sackville Street, Gloucester Street and Gardiner Street. With all the curiosity of a child I explored the neighbourhood and absorbed its sights and sounds and smells. I got a closer and more intimate view of the city which I already knew at a distance from my trips with Uncle Christy on his milk rounds. Except for Dominick Street, the buildings in that area have changed very little basically since my childhood, but there are now no ice-cream carts and no summons by a brass horn to come and buy what seems in retrospect to have been the best ice cream ever made. There are no organ grinders trundling out 'O sole mio' with their trained monkeys collecting halfpennies and even farthings — a farthing bought many small things then. The Punch and Judy shows are gone and the wonderful sweet shops at the corner of Dominick

Street and Britain Street where the women who served were so kind to children and often gave more bullseyes than a halfpenny was worth. There was a waxworks in Henry Street where Woolworths is now, with its chamber of horrors. The Princes in the Tower was one of the prime exhibits and later on, Crippen, who was the first criminal to be apprehended by the aid of trans-Atlantic wireless. There was a rhyme about the unfortunate Crippen:

Hawley Harvey Crippen,
Poisoned his wife with drippin'
Went without leave,
To marry Le Neave.
Hawley Harvey Crippen.

Opposite the waxworks was the Penny Bazaar where nothing cost more than one penny and looking around the shop was a pleasant diversion, even if you hadn't a penny to spend.

Coming home from school there always seemed to be some excitement afoot in the streets. Policemen taking some snatch thief or drunk to the station always drew a crowd of children. Military brass bands with scarlet and gold uniforms and busbys marching through O'Connell Street always had a following of children and loafers. There were recruiting marches for the British army and many a corner boy whose curiosity or thirst led him into taking the 'King's Shilling' found himself eventually in India, Egypt or Afghanistan. Each recruit got an immediate payment of a shilling, which represented six pints or six half glasses of whiskey; it was a very considerable temptation.

Drunken men and women fighting on the streets was quite a common sight even in the day time. One sickening scene affected me deeply and created in me a permanent hatred of public drunks and drunken brawls. I saw in Middle Gardiner Street two women fighting, their blouses torn to the waist, their hair about their shoulders and their breasts and faces streaming with blood from nail scratches. They were young women and very drunk. A crowd, mostly men, made a ring around them but did not interfere one way or another, as if accepting the violence as part of the daily experience, as indeed it was.

Even in winter the children of the poor were mainly without boots. They were ragged and frozen looking and sometimes had newspapers tied round their legs with string, in the manner of puttees. Sacking was commonly used instead of overcoats; all the coalmen wore it over their shoulders. Smells are very evocative of places and times past, and of all the unpleasant smells I recall the worst was that of a slum tenement. One of the girls who looked after me often brought me home with her. She lived with her parents in one room in Gardiner Street. The stench of the house when you entered the hall was disgusting. Urine and excrement (visible as well as smelling) mingled with all the stinks that the human body can exude. There was no indoor lavatory and only one outdoor lavatory and one outdoor tap for the whole building. The room where the girl lived with her father, mother and two sisters, had two beds with old rags for bed clothes and no other furnishings except a table, a few chairs, a china dog, and statues of the Blessed Virgin and the Sacred Heart.

These conditions were widespread in the city which had the highest death rate in Europe. James Connolly, the Labour leader and patriot who was executed by the British in 1916, blamed this state of affairs on the Dublin City Council, which was controlled at the time by the Irish Nationalist Party at its most decadent. It had a bad name for corruption and nepotism. The City Councillors hated and feared Jim Larkin because he tried to rouse the slum dwellers and the workers from their lethargy and helplessness.

Larkin had that quality of leadership which evokes either love or hate. At that time nobody in Dublin had heard the word 'charism'; it could well be applied to Larkin. Apart from his natural enemies, the employers who hated him from fear, Larkin evoked in his later career a hatred from his colleagues or ex-colleagues in the Irish Transport and General Workers' Union as obsessional as the hatred one met with in the Civil War. I have heard them accuse him of vanity, peculation, treachery and cowardice and indeed one of them claimed to be writing a book on the subject of his turpitude. Larkin's major task — and a major task it was — was to give dignity to the working class and the slum dwellers who were the social pariahs of that time. After that perhaps he should have retired, his work accomplished. But this he did not do. He was less adapted by talent or temperament to running a trade union than to creating one. Larkin's achievement in restoring self-respect to the working class of Dublin should have earned for him the freedom of the city, but in fact he never achieved respectability, not even in the minds of the Sinn Féin councillors who, when they got control, eventually cleaned up the administration.

I looked forward to coming home from school through Moore Street market with its colour and bustle. There was always chat and banter between the women at the stalls and the passers by. They were kind to us children and sometimes if we stared long enough they would give us an apple or a pear for nothing with a 'Here son, it'll do you good'. They always called us 'son' or 'young fella' and referred to us, as indeed did everyone else, as 'chiselers'. I was friendly with one of the children at school — a butcher's son — who lived in Moore Street. Sometimes on Thursdays, when the butchers did their slaughtering, he took me into the slaughterhouse to see the sheep and cattle being killed. There were no humane killers in those days. I never told my mother of these visits.

Sometimes on our way home I would walk into the Pro-Cathedral more from curiosity than piety. The half-moon gallery, the two Cardinals' hats hanging from the dome, the crucifix the feet of which were almost worn away from pious kisses, were the principal foci of interest. At that time, the centre aisle, referred to always as the Sanctuary, was used by the 'quality' and the working class used what was known as the body of the church, the Gospel side of the aisle for the women and the Epistle side for the men. The body was distinguished, particularly on the women's side, by the smell of unclean human beings not made any pleasanter by the aroma of incense used in large quantities.

Horses were a feature of the main city streets and from time to time great excitement was caused by a runaway horse. The crowds would scatter and then all the idlers and children would run to see the efforts made to stop him. Great courage was sometimes displayed by bystanders in grabbing the berserk animal's reins or clinging to the shafts of the cart in an effort to bring it to a standstill. I once saw a horse career right through the window of a shop in Britain Street. A fallen horse was another cause of excitement. The animal had to be unharnessed while on the ground. It would get to its feet only after great effort, encouraged by the pulling and shoving of the spectators.

On warm summer days the women from the tenements used to sit on the steps to enjoy the pleasant street smells, made up of dust, hay, straw and horse droppings. The women nursed their babies at their breasts without any sense of shame. Lovely was the smell of the city in summer and not even the stink of the Liffey could detract from it. Equally pleasant was the smell of the hucksters' shops where they sold bread and paraffin oil and kindling sticks and coal and hot boiled peas. I suppose the pervading smell was of paraffin oil, but it did not seem to do any harm to the flavour of the peas. There was another smell to compete with the Liffey which I got every day; it came from a shop at the corner of Marlboro Street where tripe and crubeens and puddings were made. In the process the entire contents of the animals' intestines must have been thrown into the back yard and left there to decay for weeks. The Corporation Inspectors seemed unable to do anything to prevent it.

The hucksters' shops sold spinning tops and marbles. Without a word being said and without advertisement or notice, every spring the pavements and the school yard became alive with children playing with tops and marbles. Lashing tops with whips was the most usual method and was quite uncomplicated. The pegging top, an inverted cone with threads for the twine and a spike at the end, was regarded as dangerous, principally because a mistake in throwing it could mean a broken window.

The marble games were called 'dab-out' and 'hole 'n thaw'. With 'dab out', the players each put an agreed number of marbles in a ring drawn with chalk on the pavement, or more often in the dust of a lane. A 'thaw' was thrown by each player in turn and each marble knocked out of the ring belonged to the thrower. At that time there was what would now be known as a king-size marble and this was called a 'buckin' thaw'.

'Hole 'n thaw' required three holes in the ground and the idea was to put your 'thaw' into them and to prevent the opposition getting theirs in. It was played on the principle of croquet but this version was not as popular as 'dab out'. If a policeman saw you playing football on the road you would be chased away, but although tops and marbles caused more inconvenience to the passing public they were by custom permitted. The tops and marbles vanished in April as quickly as they had appeared in March.

Coming home from school one day I saw firemen and policemen and the usual crowd of gapers in Cumberland Street, off Britain Street. One of the tenements had collapsed and a man had been killed and several people injured. I was very frightened and when I was sent to sleep on my own in the top back room of 42 Summerhill, I always had the fear that the house might collapse. The top room was indeed at a great height, as the ground at the back sloped steeply away to Gloucester Street and 'the digs'. There was a very good view from the top of the house over the city and during the Exhibition of 1907 we had a wonderful sight of the illuminations and of the fireworks.

The Exhibition was held at Ballsbridge and our beautiful Herbert Park is the legacy from it. For children not interested in the trade exhibits, the main attractions were the waterchute and the Somali village. All Dublin adopted, of course, the British Imperial attitudes towards the lesser breeds and in the Somali village the natives were exhibited much as are zoo animals. To my disappointment, my mother would not allow me to go on the waterchute because it was too dangerous.

34

For all its poverty Dublin in the years before the First World War was, for a child, a colourful and exciting place. On my trips down to Clery's to buy my mother's fringe nets, I often continued on up to O'Connell Bridge to look at the Bovril flashing-light advertisement over Cook's Tourist Office opposite Trinity College. It was the first of the illuminated advertisements in Dublin and was regarded as one of the sights of the city.

When I was smaller, we employed a girl called Kate who used to bring me to St Stephen's Green to feed the ducks. Passing Clarendon Street Church she took me to the holy water font and made me drink the water from it. It was tepid and dirty and I got sick all over myself and the poor girl. We often passed St George's Protestant Church and Kate, who had strong religious prejudices, would spit out as she passed. I followed suit and one day, passing Findlater's Presbyterian Church with my parents, I repeated the gesture. My parents thought I was being merely bad mannered but when they found out the real motive my father gave me a long lecture, the nature of which I did not understand, but I stopped spitting at Protestant churches from then on.

At that time I don't suppose my father earned more than 50/- or 60/- a week but my mother was determined that, at whatever parental sacrifice, my brother and myself were going to be well cared for. She certainly did not spare money on our clothes. I had the misfortune to have had my boots made to measure (in Winstanleys of Earl Street). Of course the boots never wore out but neither did my feet stop growing and the consequences were disastrous from the point of view of foot formation.

My parents seemed to have had a passion for having the family photographed and many of the pictures are still extant. My father was an amateur photographer and he had a huge camera, standing on a tripod, with a black hood. Taking a photograph with it was a major operation.

My mother helped in all the domestic tasks, but her own private amusement and hobby was dressmaking. She was a good needle-woman, dressmaker and milliner. She spent a good deal of her time cutting out dresses for herself from Butterick patterns and making them up. She did all the sock mending for the house and all the ironing, which was no small job. She knitted a good deal and I was often conscripted to hold the skein of wool while she rolled it into a ball. It was a tiring job holding out one's arms for so long, and very boring. It must have awakened in me some rudimentary interest in time and motion study because I was always inquiring why she didn't

35

buy the wool made up in balls.

Apart from occasional parties, my mother's only other recreation was the theatre, and while we lived in Summerhill my parents went there fairly often. My mother greatly enjoyed the opera, particularly when the Carl Rosa Company came to the Gaiety. Tunes from *Carmen, Rigoletto* and *Il Trovatore* were constantly being hammered out on the piano after these visits. She loved to dress for the theatre. Henry Irving in *The Bells* and Martin Harvey in *The Only Way* were her great favourites and photographs of them in these roles were kept on the piano.

Apart from the Gaiety, there were the Queen's Theatre, the Royal and the Empire, which my father always called Dan Lowry's. My parents never went to the Tivoli or the Abbey. They would not be interested in the Abbey plays and the Tivoli was regarded as the haunt of soldiers (who were considered very low in the social scale) and their 'mots' (the word invariably applied to girls who did not come into the category of 'young ladies'). Every year I was taken to the pantomime in the Gaiety, but I never liked it. It was associated in my mind with 'growing pains', from which I suffered as a child, and an unpleasant smell of oranges which I did not like. Occasionally I was taken to the Queen's and the Royal. At the Queen's I shouted with the rest of the audience to warn the rebels that the Redcoats were coming. I remember a piece of doggerel at the time composed of the titles of the plays in the Queen's repertoire. It began:

Along the line the signal ran,
Sure there's no play like man to man.
He went on the 10.30 down express
To meet the girl who went astray
And saw her face at the window
Playing with her only son.

The shows at the Royal always had a soprano act which I disliked so much that, despite the conjurers and acrobats which were featured there, I always tried to avoid going.

There were occasional visits to the Rotunda to see a circus or the 'living pictures', which were a novelty at that time. The Royal Italian Circus had performing lions and tigers and girls standing on galloping horses and plenty of noise and colour and clowns, but above all I looked forward to seeing a troupe of monkeys dressed as soldiers who took military orders and formed a firing squad and actually discharged their toy guns at a monkey victim. The 'living pictures' came very seldom and they were really no better than animated photographs. There was no story line, just characters chasing one another.

This was before Theda Bara, the Keystone Cops and other heroes of the silent movies, but to the children of 1906 they were a great thrill.

Every Monday afternoon, when the washing had been done, my mother went 'up town' to Grafton Street or Henry Street and took me with her. Monday afternoon was, by custom, the housewife's day out. Sometimes we went to Arnotts in Henry Street to buy clothes for me. We were always attended to by Mr O'Callaghan who, over the years, became a friend. He was a fine tall country man from Clare. He was said to be an 'Irish-Irelander', i.e. someone who wanted to speak Irish, buy Irish goods and play Irish games. My mother regarded holders of such ideas with mildly sardonic amusement.

More often, however, we took the tram to Grafton Street where we visited a milliner's, the Misses Carolan of Wicklow Street, with whom my mother was friendly. This visit seemed to last for hours, while my mother tried on innumerable hats. After this there was window shopping and a visit to Switzer's for handkerchiefs or to Bewley's Oriental Café for cakes. Bewley's was the biggest coffee house in the city. There was always a coffee roasting machine in operation in the window and the lovely smell of coffee filled the street outside. Inside were comfortable seats, like the seats of a railway carriage, set in secluded nooks where private conversations could remain private. There were stained glass windows with pictures of tropical birds. Bewley's was much used as a place of rendezvous by business men and lovers. The afternoon trip would end with a visit to Clarendon Street Church and lighting a candle to the Sacred Heart as was the general custom.

In those days the Lord Mayor gave an Annual Ball for children and, through the good offices of the local tobacconist and newsagent who was on the City Council, my uncle got an invitation for me. My mother was delighted and thought it a lift in the social scale, as indeed for the family it really was, so that she made quite an event of the Ball. As parents were invited too, it gave her a chance to do herself up 'to the nines' and to dress me up to fit the occasion. Father, mother and myself went to the Mansion House in a cab, which was much of a novelty for us all. My memories of the Ball are unhappy. I was uncomfortable in the unusual surroundings and could not take part in the dancing and spilling a raspberry ice cream on my coat and wide white collar ruined the party for me. I had never seen raspberry ice cream before and I thought it was not anything like as good as the yellowish ice cream we bought from the Italian push cart which was my usual source of supply.

My father worked in the morning and late at night in the Auction

Room and he had the afternoons off. Every day he brought home some cakes or fruit or a toy to us. The cakes were bought in the pastry shop of the Misses Edwards at the corner of Cavendish Row and Britain Street. The Misses Edwards were ladies of great refinement and they dressed in the clothes of the previous century. Their speciality was sponge cakes and eccles cakes, which we called 'crushed flies'. They also had calf's foot jelly. They gave the impression of honouring the customers with their service, although they had no use for small boys.

When my father was at home, especially at weekends, he kept me very close to him and resented what he rightly regarded as the bad example of my uncles. He was very angry when one Sunday my mother allowed me to go with my Uncle Christy on an excursion to the Strawberry Beds, a beauty spot on the Liffey between the Phoenix Park and Lucan. This place was always crowded in summer with trippers from the city who went out to eat the strawberries grown by small holders. Excursions were organised by some benevolent society and they set off in 'drags', a kind of long car drawn by two horses and seating about twelve people sitting face to face. Only men travelled on our outing and they loaded bottles of stout into the car and began to drink the moment we left Rutland Square and continued drinking inside and outside the Wren's Nest (a very ancient thatched pub at the Strawberry Beds alongside the Liffey) and again all the way home. Even I recognised it as a disreputable performance and not in any way improved by the drunken songs which were 'rendered' as inspiration seized the singer. Two singers might simultaneously be inspired to sing different songs, but this did not matter. I got little attention, no food and certainly no strawberries.

I had a similar adventure when Uncle Christy took me to the funeral of one of his many friends. We travelled in a carriage from the Pro-Cathedral to Glasnevin cemetery. All was solemnity and decorum. The four horses drawing the hearse were plumed black, as the deceased was married. Grey plumes were used for the unmarried, and the number of horses depended on what the family was prepared to pay. The usual chat went on in the carriage on the way to the cemetery — mainly about the merits of the dead man who was a dairyman from Marlboro Street — and there was much reminiscing about drinking and other adventures. They carried the coffin down to the grave, all sorrow and gloom. The solemnity and gloom only lasted as far as the Brian Boru pub at the Cross Guns' Bridge on the way home. Here it was 'all out' including the jarvey, and they remained in the pub for the whole afternoon, sending out bottles of minerals and biscuits to keep me quiet. We were late back for dinner and my mother was really annoyed. After that, I was never allowed to go with my uncle to social functions.

My father's disgust at all these incidents and at the whole way of life of my uncles in Summerhill, and his refusal to participate in it, made him an object of continual derision by them and their friends. On Saturday afternoons and on Sundays he spent all his time with my mother and my brother and me. As soon as I was old enough I was given a bicycle and taught to ride along Rutland Street, Fitzgibbon Street and Mountjoy Square, still a relatively undecayed neighbourhood at that time. On Saturdays in the summer he took me along with a friend of his to the Phoenix Park to see the Phoenix Club play cricket. He followed the fortunes of the club and was very knowledgeable about the game, but for me it was a bore. I thought that when a wicket fell and a man returned to the pavilion it was the same player who came out again to take up position at the wicket. They all looked alike to me. On a few occasions my father took me to Trinity College to see a match there. This was a strange world because in the ordinary way no one of our class visited Trinity, any more than they entered the nearby Bank of Ireland which at that time was guarded by red-coated British soldiers. The nearest you got to the Bank was to stand at the railings watching the soldiers changing guard. To the ordinary citizen both places were fortresses of the Ascendancy.

In winter my father often took me to Dalymount Park to see the great amateur soccer club, Bohemians, play and at a very early age I had become an addict of soccer and a fan of Bohemians. Sometimes he took me to Clonturk Park where all sorts of games, except rugby, were played — hurling, soccer, Gaelic football and, in summer, cricket. Gaelic football was played almost exclusively by denizens of the city and principally by drapers' assistants and grocers' curates. In the summer my father would get up very early to take me cycling to Clontarf for a swim in the Baths. On Sundays we went to Mass, usually in Gardiner Street, and afterwards visited the Botanic Gardens or the Zoo or Glasnevin cemetery.

Coming home from Mass on one St Patrick's Day I first became conscious of my Irishness. My father and I were stopped in Mountjoy Square by a man shaking a collection box and saying 'pingin más é do thoil é' and when my father gave him a coin he said 'go raibh maith agat'. I asked my father what the man was saying and he told me he was speaking Irish and collecting for the Gaelic League. I then asked what language we were speaking and could not understand why, if we were Irish, we should be speaking English.

39

Glasnevin cemetery was an ever present feature in the consciousness of Dubliners. Nearly every family had close relatives buried there and it was accepted that this was where you would end your days, passing the 'long corner' as Doyle's Corner on the way to the cemetery was generally known then. Visiting family graves was much more a regularly accepted practice then than nowadays and people did not seem dead in quite such a final way as they do now. They were constantly referred to in conversation as if they were still living — a reference that always evoked a prayer. Death did not seem such a disaster that it could not be joked about. There was a sense of continuity between this life and the hereafter that took a lot of the fear out of the act of dying. In Dublin wakes were still a social occasion, if not of conviviality, at least of togetherness, far from being sunk in gloom. All the neighbours crowded in and stayed up all night to keep the family company and people told stories and laughed a lot.

Visits to Glasnevin were really outings. Apart from visits to the graves of national heroes like Parnell and O'Connell, there were family burial plots with all sorts of names familiar to Dubliners and all sorts of tales to be told about them — mainly scandalous. My father took a masochistic pleasure in reading out aloud to me inscriptions on the graves of the families of wealthy Dublin publicans. He had grown up along the quays and had seen the dockers being paid their wages in the pubs. He had seen the slate system whereby during the week when they had no money the dockers got drink on credit and the price was marked up on the slates. When they were paid their wages at the end of the week they cleared off their debts and as often as not they had little or no money left to take home. He used to describe the scenes as wives waited outside the pubs, often with infants at the breast, trying to save something from the weekly wreck. The misery and degradation of the dockside dwellers cut deeply into his mind and he conceived a loathing for publicans whom he regarded as the destroyers of the bodies and souls of the poor. It was probably an oversimplification of cause and effect, but it was a loathing he carried with him to the grave. He read the *Leader*, principally because of the campaign by the editor, D. P. Moran, against the 'Bungs' as Moran always referred to publicans.

The publicans who had risen into the middle of the Catholic class structure certainly distinguished themselves by the grand style of their graveyard monuments, principally lofty Celtic crosses, but occasionally saints and angels surmounting lengthily inscribed plinths. My father considered that these monuments had been built on profits derived from the misery and corruption of the poor and that they were a despicable form of vanity. He seemed to enjoy himself thoroughly in denouncing them. One of the first successes of Larkin's agitation was to stop the payment of the dockers in pubs and Larkin became my father's hero as a consequence. My father identified himself always with the working class and had a total dislike and distrust of anyone aiming at 'respectability'. His dislike of respectability did not in any way prevent him from behaving like the most respectable of men. He was the complete dandy in his dress, if in rather a discreet way; he was very polite, especially to women, with whom he was exceptionally popular, and he had a particular dislike of rowdyism in any form or indeed any kind of violence. To him respectability denoted humbug, pretentiousness and ostentation.

He took no part in politics. He would, of course, support the Nationalist party and he revered the memory of Parnell and always attended with an ivy leaf in his buttonhole the Ivy Day remembrance celebrations of the dead leader. His Parnellite sympathies left him with a distrust of the clergy. His religious observance was minimal. He attended Mass on Sundays with my mother, both dressed to the nines, and on Holy Days he went to the short 12 o'clock Mass in the Pro-Cathedral which only required that you came in one door and moved slowly round the back of the altar and left by another door. On Good Friday he always went to Gardiner Street Church to hear the three hours sermon, as it was called, a sermon on the last words of Christ on the Cross.

With the small legacy left to him by his employer, and what remained of my mother's few hundred, my parents decided to leave Summerhill and rent a shop with living accommodation above it in Terenure on the outskirts of the city. There my mother set up a creamery and sweet shop and at the same time my father and an intimate friend of his, named Rafter, who had some capital, established their own auctioneering business in Capel Street, paying the City Swordbearer for the use of his patent to sell unredeemed pledges.

We moved to our new life early in 1910. I was nearly nine years of age.

* * * * *

The family's removal to Terenure was the end of a very happy period in my young life.

Terenure, in 1910, was a village with a row of thatched cottages where a Bank now stands, and a little semi-circle of cottages, on the opposite side of the cross roads, which gave it its second name of Roundtown. It was only three miles from the General Post Office, which was reckoned to be the centre of the city, but after Summerhill, O'Connell Street and Moore Street, it appeared to me to be in deep countryside. The shop and the house we went to live in was equally in contrast to 42 Summerhill. It was in a terrace of five newly-built shops. The personal relationships of the occupants of these five shops, living cheek by jowl with one another, were determined by their religion or politics.

On the corner was a painter and decorator, a Northern Protestant called Martin, who had no family. Our family creamery was the second shop. No. 3 was a greengrocer's occupied by two old maiden ladies. No. 4 was a family of butchers named Fagan and in No. 5 was a German family of pork butchers named Lang. Lang was interned as an enemy alien at the beginning of the 1914 war. The Fagans, whom we knew well, had been fairly near neighbours of ours in Summerhill. The Misses Bannon in No. 3 were virtual recluses, but we had good neighbourly relations with them.

My parents and the Martins were distantly polite to one another when they met on the street — until after 1916. I had had my bicycle mudguards painted green, white and orange and had a Sinn Féin (i.e. tricolour) flag flying from my lamp holder. Mr Martin took exception to this display and called on my mother to complain of such an exhibition of disloyalty when 'our boys were out in France'. He explained to my mother that he was a Liberal Unionist and that he believed in freedom of expression for all. My mother did not know what a Liberal Unionist was. I interpreted the label as denoting a bloody West Briton and a 'blue-gut' and without delay I went into Martin's shop, for the first and only time in my life, and told him what I thought of his impudence in criticising me or my politics. After that, we ceased to be even on nodding terms.

The shops were well designed and well built. Our shop had two counters facing one another, from one of which was dispensed butter, eggs, bread, cheese, tea and sugar, and from the other, sweets. Behind the shop was a parlour which we used as a living and dining room and behind that again a kitchen and a maid's room. Outside was a coal shed, lavatory and stables which were used as a playroom and to store bicycles, and a small garden used only as a playground. Upstairs were a bathroom, a lavatory and five other rooms, one of which was furnished as a drawing room but was seldom used except by my mother who played the piano there. It was a very comfortable and quite spacious house, but seemed at first tiny compared with the high Georgian rooms of Summerhill. When we went there first my mother suffered from both insomnia and claustrophobia because of the absence of street noises.

My mother was a very good housekeeper so we quickly settled in to our new and strange surroundings. For me it was the end of my childhood. I was big for my age and I had an independent temperament so that I was soon able to get round the village on my own and began to make my own acquaintances. My mother gave me a great deal of liberty as long as I was back for meals on time and she had a rule against ever being out after dark.

Terenure was a mixed community — the village proper consisted mainly of cottages and small houses. These terraces were rented by manual workers or workers employed by the Dublin United Tramway Company or the Dublin and Blessington Steam Tramway Company. The Companies owned the houses. The residents constituted the bulk of the Catholic community but the area had begun to develop and semi-detached houses were being built in rows and squares and occupied mainly by Protestant employees of the big city firms. The Protestants did not impinge on the life of the village and played their bowls and tennis in Eaton Square and their hockey or rugby in the fields in the Green Lanes which, as well as being a sports centre, was the recognised meeting place for courting couples.

I continued to go into the Dominick Street Convent School by tram until the summer holidays and I spent the summer exploring the neighbourhood by myself at weekends, or further afield with my father on bicycles. I discovered that there was a forge, a wheelwright's, a joinery shop, the tram sheds, the steam tram yard and a shoemaker's. I was just getting in on the ways of the village and getting to know the local children when the holidays ended but, instead of going back to Dominick Street, it was decided that I be sent as a day boarder to St Enda's School which Patrick Pearse had just transferred to the 'Hermitage' in Rathfarnham. My parents were persuaded to this improbable decision by a cousin of my mother's, a civil servant who had been transferred from London to Dublin and came to live near us with his young English wife. He had always been close to my mother and father; he had lived with them in Summerhill while he was studying for his civil service examination. He was one of the Wilson cousins from Longford and he and his two brothers and four of his five sisters were either civil servants or school teachers and all of them were Gaelic Leaguers and amongst the early Sinn Féiners.

Patrick Ewart Wilson was the dominant influence of my early

years and when I grew up, my lifelong friend. But his first impact on me — the St Enda's adventure — was not a success. The only reason I can think why my mother agreed to my going to St Enda's was the cachet of a boarding school, even as a day boarder. She had not the remotest interest in the Gaelic League or the Irish revival. My father had quite a different point of view. He was positively hostile to anything that appeared to him 'bourgeois', although I don't think he ever used the word or knew its connotations. St Enda's was, to him, a bourgeois institution although in this assessment he was most certainly wrong.

Patrick Pearse must have appeared to my parents as a slightly eccentric schoolmaster; to most ordinary people who met him or even heard of him he might have been described as a 'mad Irishman', meaning not that he was in any way insane but that he was an enthusiast for the Irish language, Irish products and Irish games. It was a common term less of abuse than of amused, even affectionate, tolerance to those generally called at the time 'Irish Irelanders' or sometimes 'Sinn Féiners'. Pearse conceived St Enda's as a school which would be an antidote to the Anglicisation to which the country, and particularly Dublin, had succumbed.

It was the only school in Ireland which had not as its primary object the preparation of boys to get jobs or to pursue religious vocations. An additional objection from my father's point of view was the cost of the fees. They were not very high but put quite a strain on the family finances which he conducted on the basis that, if you did not have the money to pay for something, you did without. But the family affairs were operated according to the proverb 'Ce que la femme veut, Dieu le veut' ('What the woman wants, God wants') and I was sent to St Enda's. As Patrick Pearse sat in our parlour discussing with my parents my school fees and the equipment I would need I have often thought how honoured a family we should have felt to have entertained under our roof, even for a short period, the Man of Destiny of modern Ireland. We could not foresee that he was the man who would lead the Easter 1916 Rising and, based on the conception of the blood sacrifice and at the cost of his life, lay the foundations of our independence.

If I had been sent to a high class English public school I would not have found myself in an environment more alien to me than that which I encountered in St Enda's. My predicament was, at the low level, a paradigm of the historic conflict of Gael and Gaul. While children like me were vaguely aware that we were Irish and not English, we were much more aware of being Catholics and not

Protestants. The soldiers we saw, with their red coats, their reviews, their trooping of the colour outside the Bank of Ireland were accepted by us as our soldiers. We did not look on them as foreigners. Many of the lads we knew around Summerhill had been at Colenso or Mafeking but they were 'us'. From the comics we read, *Chips, Comic Cuts* and later the *Magnet* and the *Gem* and the *Union Jack,* we absorbed the correct British imperial attitudes to the 'Fuzzy Wuzzies', the 'Niggers' and the Indian Nabobs. If we had read the *Diary of a Nobody* we would have seen ourselves and our social values reflected in every page. We never heard a word of Irish spoken except on St Patrick's Day, although Gaelic words persisted in the common speech of the people much more than they do today. Words like 'flaithiúlach', 'gob', 'amadán', 'a stór', 'óinseach', 'strap' and 'praiscín' were quite usual.

The Union Jack was to be seen everywhere. Irish-Irelanders were looked on as a joke. Off Summerhill was Langrishe Place and the headquarters of the National Foresters. On special occasions the Foresters arrayed themselves in the costume of the great national hero, Robert Emmet, but merely provided the onlookers with a target for derision and jeering.

From childhood, soccer football was the game talked of and played everywhere on the vacant lots in the city and it was, at that time, purely an English game, as was cricket. In cricket we followed the fortunes of Surrey and Kent, Hobbs and Hayward. Cricket too was played with improvised bats and wickets often made from flattened tin cans.

Our nursery rhymes were English and we knew all about Dick Whittington, Robin Hood and Alice in Wonderland, but we never heard of Fionn or Cuchulainn. Portraits of the King and Queen were often on display in shop windows and when Edward the Peacemaker died Dublin went into mourning and the newspapers carried deep black mourning bands. At school in Dominick Street our teaching was confined to the three Rs and to learning by rote the halfpenny catechism and innumerable aspirations and ejaculations. Irish was never mentioned. The only distinctively Irish threads in my consciousness before I went to St Enda's were the faint ones derived from my grandmother's references to the Famine and the evictions, and my father's Ivy Day references to Parnell. When my grandmother wanted to protest against the waste of food in the house she would say 'You will follow a crow a mile for that yet' — an echo of the Famine.

St Enda's was a bilingual school and that meant what it said. Irish dominated the place. For many of the boys it was their mother tongue and many more knew it well and used it enthusiastically. Nearly all the boys knew some Irish but to me, who did not know a single word, its all-pervasiveness was an embarrassment. Even the English spoken by the boys, most of whom were from the country, differed so much from the accent and argot of the Parish of St Mary's in the centre of the city that it seemed a different language. From the beginning I felt an outsider in the place and behaved as one and was treated as one by the boys. My situation was not helped by my expressed contempt for Gaelic football, which to me appeared as a game where all the players were goalkeepers, and hurling which seemed little better than an organised faction fight.

A number of the boys in St Enda's wore kilts. This they probably hated doing and for that reason were all the more ready to resent derogatory remarks about them — remarks which no Dublin boy could resist making and I made them. Between the language, the games and the kilts, I seemed to be always involved in quarrels and was thoroughly unhappy in a situation for which I had no remedy. It would never have occurred to me to complain to the teacher.

In the beginning of the school term a brake was used to pick up the day boarders. It picked me up at Terenure. I was the only one from there. As soon as I got on board, the boys coming from Rathmines who had been pupils of the school when St Enda's was located there began to bully me. Two of my worse tormentors were the brothers Dowling, both a few years older than I and both wearing kilts. They had one particularly unpleasant form of inflicting pain; they pressed a knuckle under my ear. I have never forgotten it for them. As it happened, years afterwards I met the Dowlings again in the IRA and became an intimate friend of themselves and their families. John, the older of the two, was the O/C of the Fourth Battalion of the Dublin Brigade and had a powerful influence on developing my tastes in literature, painting and history. Frank, the younger brother, died in 1973. I still go with John to the meetings of the Irish Historical Society and we still meet to exchange and discuss books and to talk politics.

All schoolboys not accepted by the group are unhappy. My problem was that I did not want to be accepted by the group. I despised them and, from their point of view, I was a 'stinker'. I did not want to talk Irish, I did not want to play hurling or Gaelic football and I thought kilts were funny. I had only one friend, a London-Irish boy who did not know or want to know Irish any more than I did, who disliked all games and tried to avoid them, and who thought that kilts should be worn only by Scots Highlanders.

The scholastic side of St Enda's presented no problems as the instruction in the three Rs and religion was a continuation of what I had been learning at the Convent School. Indeed the fact that I was above average standard in these subjects bolstered my sense of superiority, widening the gap between me and my schoolmates. The only subjects new to me were Irish, drawing and nature study. Irish was taught by the direct method and was painless and easy at the elementary stage, at which we were. Teachers varied from time to time and I do not remember any of them. Willie Pearse, Patrick Pearse's brother, also executed in 1916, taught drawing but all I can recall of him is seeing him once in a smock and carrying a chisel — he was a sculptor. One of Pearse's sisters, Miss Margaret Pearse, taught religion. She looked, and was, very cross.

I have a better recollection of Patrick Pearse at that time. When he came to our house to talk to my parents he was only another adult to me and made no impression on me. When at St Enda's I was caught bringing in cigarettes to my London-Irish friend, I was reported to Pearse. He sent for me and gave me a mild lecture and four not very hurtful slaps with a cane. Corporal punishment was not excluded from his theories of education.

Pearse told us younger pupils about the ancient Celtic legends of Cúchulainn and the Red Branch knights and of Fionn and the Fianna. Whatever it was he said about the Fianna produced some response in my imagination and created in me the first glimmer of interest in the world of the Gael. This interest was increased by what was supposed to be nature study. Nature study meant that the class was taken on a tour of the grounds of the Hermitage by Pearse. He talked less about trees and shrubs than about Fionn and Cúchulainn and about the Priory, the estate opposite the Hermitage, where Robert Emmet courted Sarah Curran. We had several of these excursions. They were the most pleasant experiences I had in St Enda's.

Except for the few months I had lived in Terenure, I had never been outside the city limits and never further on the south side of Dublin than St Stephen's Green. The Hermitage was therefore a revelation to me. It was set in a beautifully planned small estate with open fields, gardens, woodlands, a stream, waterfalls and a lake. Here and there were 'ruins' with which the eighteenth century owners dotted the grounds, as was the custom of the day. They added to the interest of the place and doubtless served as 'interesting subjects' for the young ladies of the time to sketch. Pearse once remarked that it was better that they should spend their money on ruins than on the motor cars which were being bought by his rich contemporaries.

The principal ruin was a hermitage — really a folly. There was also a small castellated building sometimes called Cromwell's Fort and sometimes Emmet's Fort. The whole place was a fairyland to me and in some way became associated in my mind with the Fianna and the high deeds of Fionn. As I knew nothing very concrete about them I had to imagine them, an exercise which, with the lively imagination of a boy of nine, I found easy. With my London friend I often wandered through the woods, playing at warriors or chasing rabbits. Once we saw an otter, which we thought was a large rat, at the lake.

I loved the autumn smell of the woods, especially the smell of the cedars, the firs and the decaying leaves of beeches and elms and the needles of the larches. It was one of these excursions indeed that ended my eight month's schooling at St Enda's. My friend and I had a row with some bigger boys over a punt which we were playing with on the lake. In the course of the quarrel I got a cut over the eye and was pushed into the lake. I felt I had had enough of St Enda's. Soaked and muddy I cycled the two miles home to an indignant and sympathetic mother who quite agreed that I should not go back there. My father took the 'I told you so' line and was probably relieved at not having to pay the fees.

To finish the school year and to prepare for confirmation, I was sent back to the Holy Faith in Dominick Street. Confirmation in the Pro-Cathedral was a tiring and boring ceremony and it was very much of an anti-climax when, after all the instruction in the truths of religion in anticipation of an oral examination by the Archbishop, he asked no questions at all. We were all ready to roll off the precepts of the Church and the seven deadly sins but he never asked us. Anyway, on the great day, my mind was more preoccupied with football than with religion because my father had promised to take me to a cup match that afternoon between Bohemians and Shelbourne at Dalymount Park and I was afraid that the ceremony would not be finished in time.

There were only two senior soccer clubs in Dublin — Bohemians and Shelbourne — and the people on the south side followed Shelbourne. These clubs played in the Irish League. There being no partition then, an Irish Football Association which had its headquarters in Belfast controlled the game. Outside the North and Dublin, soccer was scarcely played in Ireland. The supporters and players of the game were exclusively of the lower middle and working classes. Every Saturday either Bohemians or Shelbourne had a match in Dublin against one of the Northern clubs and every Saturday train loads of working-class men visited Belfast following Bohemians or Shelbourne, or came down to Dublin supporting Linfield, Belfast Celtic, Glentoran, Distillery or Cliftonville. The only club outside these cities was in Derry — Derry Celtic. The team to represent Ireland was picked from these teams or from Irishmen playing for teams in Britain. There was only one Irish international soccer team.

At the end of the school term my mother took me to be interviewed by the Christian Brothers in Synge Street. We met the head of the school, Brother Hayes. He was a very old man and seemed kind and benevolent. He gave me some tests in spelling and arithmetic and endeared himself to me by telling my mother how well I answered. Like everyone else, I had heard of the savagery of the Christian Brothers in the matter of corporal punishment, but my interview with Brother Hayes made me rather look forward to going to school at the end of the summer and so it was arranged. I started with the proper disposition.

In the meantime, I filled the long summer days continuing my explorations of Terenure and I began to make friends with the boys of the neighbourhood. Nearly all of them were from working-class families. Their fathers were conductors, drivers or, in some cases, inspectors with the Dublin United Tramway Company. Some were tradesmen, cobblers, carpenters or mechanics. Others were labourers working on the estates and farms around the village. Some were dairy men and coal men. It was with the sons of these families that I spent the ample leisure time of my formative years, playing football and handball against the gables of houses, playing hockey and cricket, bird-nesting, collecting nuts, playing according to the season marbles, conkers, whipping tops, playing 'Billy rump sticks', 'Jack, Jack, show the light', 'Ball in the decker', swimming in the Dodder river, cycling to Merrion Baths.

Cricket was played on a vacant lot known as the paddock and it was always single wicket, because we never had more than three stumps and one bat; bails were unnecessary. The stony pitch made the bowling unpredictable and dangerous. Hockey was very popular. There was a local team called Olney which played in the Green Lanes; we were enthusiastic followers of it. They played in a lower league and never won a match, but they were heroes to us and we tried to imitate them. We had no hockey sticks but we got branches of trees shaped at least vaguely like a hockey stick and we bullied and dribbled and took corners and penalty corners as if we had the most expensive equipment. We certainly got as much fun from it.

Football we played at any odd time. There was nearly always a

ball of some kind close at hand and we hopped or dribbled it along
the pathway wherever we were going. Usually we played with a tennis
ball (always called a 'shammier') and if there were a few of us together
we tried all the tricks — dodging, trapping, passing, shoulder charging. Street football was an all the year round performance but in
winter we had a real football and a real pitch. With all the sports
grounds along the Green Lanes we never had any difficulty choosing
one. Nobody ever minded us playing and no one taught us how to
play — we just picked up the game naturally. I am sure that is the
only way to learn football and I would be surprised if the skills of
Pele, Puskas, Best and Eusebio had any other kind of foundation.

We were never at a loss for something to do either in winter or
summer. For boys like us, Terenure and its surroundings was a
wonderful playground. As well as the sports grounds, there was
Shaw's Wood and the lake in Terenure College, which sometimes
froze over and became a skating rink. It was surprising how many
people had ice skates and were good at skating because it was seldom
cold enough for the lakes and canals to freeze solid. We had no skates
but we made 'slides' on the ice and enjoyed ourselves thoroughly.

But Shaw's Wood and the River Dodder was our great stamping
ground. Bushy Park was a large walled estate owned by an Anglo-
Irish family named Shaw. They had been there for several
generations and Sir Frederick, his wife and daughter, lived there when
I was growing up. The estate was a great parkland bounded by Rathfarnham and Templeogue and by a bluff which sloped down to a
swamp and the Dodder River. There were beautiful trees, chestnuts,
horse chestnuts, elms, oaks, walnuts and hawthorns; there were
broad acres where in summer cows grazed up to their bellies in lush
grass and where as you walked your shoes were yellowed by
buttercups. There were primroses and cowslips, and down in a
swamp, which was known to us as The Hollow, there were all kinds of
wild flowers, especially in the spring when it was covered with primroses and bluebells which we used to collect and take to school for the
May Altar. A low wall separated The Hollow from the river. The river
bank was lined with sallies and alders and we fished there for trout
and eels, using improvised equipment, i.e. a string, a 'chandler' and a
bamboo cane. The chandler was a deadly bait which we collected
from a butcher's yard in Terenure. We learned about the riverside
birds — kingfishers, wagtails and water hens — but we never found
the nest of a kingfisher. From time to time we saw otters.

The greatest pleasure of all was swimming in the Dodder. It is a
shallow, stony and narrow stream and very clear. Beginning in

Kippure and running down through Glen na Smol, past Templeogue, Terenure and Donnybrook it joins the Liffey at Ringsend. At the time of which I write, the Dodder was inaccessible to the public for a mile of its length, between the bridges at Rathfarnham and Templeogue. We children approached it over a wall or by a ledge under the big bridge which was too small for adults to use. It was all ours. The only adults we ever saw there were a couple of fly fishermen from Terenure who fished in the evenings and as often as not caught as many bats as trout. An occasional dairyman would come looking for a beast that had strayed down the river.

In the ordinary way, the river was far too shallow for swimming. Here and there were holes which were perhaps three feet deep and at these holes we built dams with rocks and sods raising the level sometimes to as much as five feet and forming a pool which might stretch back twenty yards. We had three of these holes between Rathfarnham and Templeogue: the Mollies, the Gudgeon and the Bottoms. When floods came the dams were destroyed but then it was fun to walk maybe 200 yards back up the bank and dive in; coming down with the flood was like riding the rapids. We were a mass of brown bodies all summer long, splashing, floating and sunbathing and it was surprising how adept we became at swimming and diving. Of course we were never taught.

We swam nude. For most of the lads there was no money for bathing costumes; anyway they were unnecessary. When boys are in their pelts it is impossible to tell what class they come from. There was no feeling of shame and indeed there were few inhibitions amongst the bathers.

A curious feature of my Terenure life was the fact that nearly all the boys and many of the men had nicknames — Tipp Dwyer, Nauch McGrath, Giller Guilfoyle, Monkey Donovan — and in due course I acquired my own nickname, Todd. It was derived from a character in the *Magnet* who was called Alonzo Todd whom I resembled in appearance. 'Todd' stuck to me so firmly that it became my Christian name, even amongst my own family; my mother was the only one who called me Christy until the end of her long life. The significance of some of the more picturesque nicknames were hard to interpret: Hockey Mary Hudson, Klocksey Mannering, Gick English.

The trees and hedgerows in our locality housed all the common varieties of bird life: blackbirds, thrushes, wrens and robins. We were very careful not to damage the nests and did not collect eggs. I think this was because whoever found the nest owned it and it became 'my nest'. We got to know the names of the trees and the birds without conscious effort and that was, I think, because Terenure was still more rural than suburban.The boys absorbed the traditions of the country from their elder brothers and their fathers, many of whom worked in the fields or in the estates where gardeners were still commonly employed.

On the second Sunday in August, Frochan Sunday, we used go up to Glendhu to collect frochans. I loved the hills and trees up there in the pine forests. The trees were ruthlessly cut down during the First World War and the whole landscape ruined. Sometimes on Sundays we walked up to the Hell Fire Club which had in fact been turned into a cow byre; it was hard to believe that the romantic stories of the hard drinking eighteenth century bucks who used to frequent it could possibly be true. Often we took the steam tram to Saggart to savour the view over the plains of Dublin and Meath where on clear days it was possible to see Slieve Gullion in Armagh. There were always wonderful sunsets to be seen from the Slade of Saggart. I loved the great panoramic landscape and all my life I wondered what the Normans thought when they first saw these great broad acres stretched before them. Or were they perhaps covered with forest at that time?

Collecting cigarette pictures was for a time a popular hobby. We played cards for them — twenty-five, pontoon and banker — and there was always much rivalry and swapping to complete sets. The sets covered a great variety of subjects and there were either twenty-five or fifty cards in each set. There were Views of Ireland in black and white glossy print (known as 'glossiers'). There were sets made up of the colours of all the English and Scottish football teams, regiments of the British Army, Products of the World, Battleships, Flags of the Nations. They were a wonderfully painless way of communicating information, all of it interesting to youngsters. I first heard of Killarney and the Giants' Causeway from cigarette pictures and I travelled from Assam and its tea to Brazil and its coffee with them. They certainly stimulated my childish curiousity; I was always interested to learn more about strange places and strange people.

Many of the Terenure boys came from very poor homes. I often went into their houses and, apart from poorly furnished and untidy rooms, it was clear that frequently there was not enough to eat. In the houses in the tram terraces, where there was a steady income, there was order and tidiness and a frugal sufficiency of food. In an odd house the housewife was fond of her 'sup' and neighbours would laugh when she came in with her 'message' under her cloak — a pint of plain porter in a tin can. Some of the boys were ragged, some had to go without shoes in the summer but in Shaw's Wood and the Green Lanes or Terenure College grounds that did not matter. Our amusements were all free. No one was expected to have money.

In the village itself we had no difficulty passing the time. Everyone seemed to be tolerant of children. The shoemaker let us watch him working and showed us how to draw wax ends, and sometimes let us hammer nails into a heel. There was a wheelwright's yard and on a couple of days in the week wheels were shod. The wheel was laid on a fixed axle and the metal tyre was heated to white heat. At first they used a kind of circular open wood-pyre but later they got a wood-fired furnace. It was exciting to see the white-hot tyre being lifted onto the wheel and hammered down, with sparks flying like fireworks, and then the great sizzle and the clouds of steam as buckets of water were thrown on the tyre to make it contract and grip the wheel. We spent hours watching the wheelwrights shaping the timber for the wheels and making the axle blocks. There was no machinery and no mass production.

Beside the wheelwright's arch was a barber's shop which had a bagatelle table in the back room. Watching or playing bagatelle was an agreeable way of passing the time for the men in the village — all too many — who had nothing much to do. Bagatelle is a cross between billiards and snooker but the table has only two pockets and most of the scoring is done in cups at the bottom half of the table, furthest from the player. It required no great skill, so any one with three pence to spare could take a hand. The bagatelle room was the centre of the male gossip of the village and the clearing house for dirty stories and a centre of sex education for the young.

I had heard most of the four-letter words before coming to Terenure but they meant nothing to me. Enlightenment set in and in the course of a year my sex vocabulary was complete, even if the words still had little concrete significance. Indeed I heard words and phrases that I thought were mere gobblydegook until many years afterwards I came across Kraft-Ebbing, Havelock Ellis and Kinsey. There must have been a very long underground tradition of sex erudition where boys of fourteen could talk of soixante neuf and of wezels (merkins) and of cunnilingus and fellatio. I confess that now, though I assure the reader that I have heard or read of all erotic possibilities, my taboos and inhibitions are too inbuilt to use simple.English slang terms in this context, even in this age when such knowledge is commonplace. I feel like the editor of an English edition of Bocaccio who leaves out the story of 'How the devil was put in hell' because the technicalities of that mysterious art are supposed to be impossible to explain in English.

There was always activity at Vaughan's public house on one corner of the cross roads, opposite the barber's shop. Vaughan's corner was reserved for illicit bookmaking and moneylending. A Jew from Latvia, always known as 'the Sheenie', or Jack Matowski, was the moneylender and his main clients were tram men. He was at the tram stop every Friday to collect and to loan. He was a very tall swarthy and handsome man. His English was imperfect and he was regarded as a figure of fun but seemed well liked and possibly he provided a necessary service at that time. The bookie's business was very small-time, but it is said that its operator became one of the leading and richest bookies in the city. There was always a group of corner boys standing lounging against one pub or another. They were the unemployed of the day, but there was no dole and no unemployment assistance and the most they could hope for was odd jobs with shopkeepers or getting a few pence or a pint for holding a horse while its owner was having a 'jar'.

Many people came in from the country on horseback to Terenure and the best known was 'The Bird' Flanagan. His father was an extensive market gardener with a considerable acreage of land around Dolphin's Barn and Crumlin. The farm gave extensive seasonal employment to women, who were known as Flanagan's Fusiliers. Alderman Flanagan was actively engaged in municipal politics but his son, 'The Bird', eschewed the serious things of life and his escapades earned him an affectionate if not honoured place among Dublin's characters. He was a practical joker and was supposed to be capable of doing anything for a bet. It is said that he bought a ham in George's Street and left it behind on the counter, coming back in a few minutes to grab it and run away. He ran the length of the street, followed by a crowd shouting 'stop thief'. He was supposed, on a bet, to have ridden a horse into the Gresham Hotel and up the stairs to the first floor. When I saw him, he was a little Toby Jug of a man with a broken nose and an exceptionally florid face. He always arrived outside Flood's pub at speed and pulled up the horse, called Crazy Kate, with such a flourish that she reared up like a circus animal. His arrival never failed to disturb the lethargy of the corner boys and there was always a rush to get the chance of holding Crazy Kate who was a mettlesome nag. 'The Bird' was generous with his tips. After a session in Flood's pub there was no lack of kindly hands to help him on to his horse.

The two tram termini in Terenure provided a source of interest for

small boys. The steam tram, which ran for sixteen miles to Blessington, had its head office at Terenure but its workshops were at
Templeogue. As the service was very infrequent there was not much
to be seen at the terminus, although with surprising frequency some
one got killed along the line and the remains were brought back to the
waiting room before being taken to the morgue. Our curiosity to see
the corpse, half fearful, half morbid, was never satisfied as it was
always covered with a blanket. The line between Terenure and
Blessington was said to be the longest graveyard in the world because
of the number of plaques and crosses commemorating the various
fatalities, nearly all attributable to drink. Apart from humans, delays
constantly occurred in the service caused by cows, donkeys, sheep
and goats being knocked over by the trams. I think the Dublin and
Blessington Steam Tram must have been the origin of the phrase 'a
cow on the line'.

The Dublin United Tramway Company depot was far more
interesting for us boys. Locally it retained the name of the tram
stables since the days of the horse-drawn trams. All watches were set
by the depot clock. We played round the trams and the conductors or
drivers sometimes allowed us, when shunting, to change the trolley
from one electric wire to the next. The trolley had heavy springs
which nearly pulled you off the ground. The men had a room where
they ate their lunches and made up their money collections before
handing them in to the office. Sometimes there was great consterna-
tion because they found themselves short of perhaps a shilling. They
had to make up the missing amount themselves and in those days a
shilling represented nearly 5% of the weekly wage packet. Nearly all
the men employed by the DUTC came from the country because it
was against Company policy to recruit Dublin men as conductors or
drivers. Those attached to the Terenure depot came mainly from
Westmeath.

They were subject to a very severe inspectorial system and
discipline was rigid. In winter the work involved real physical hardship. Despite the disadvantages and the very low pay, it was a
sought-after job because it gave continuity of employment and, if the
regulations of the Company were observed, it offered a reasonable
permanency. But at all times the men looked anxiously over their
shoulders for the inspector. They were also subjected to a hidden
form of inspection from the Company shareholders who thought they
should get special treatment when using the tramway. I heard men in
bitter conversation about some such shareholders. It was the first
time I had heard the word and, with the literal-mindedness of the

child, I wondered for a long time how a number of people could have a share in a tram. A lot of tension was building up amongst the tram employees and the big strike of 1913, with all its bitterness, was largely the result of these accumulated tensions.

At school I had no problem except that in my very early days at Synge Street the music teacher discovered that I could not reproduce a note — not even the tonic solfa — and I was put out of the singing class and never got into a choir. At that time, I was very glad to forego the singing class because the teacher was a cross little man called Daddy Cullen and his grimaces as he sang gave me the giggles. But the incident had quite unfortunate long term consequences for me. It was accepted that not merely could I not reproduce a note but that I was also tone deaf. This was not so, although the hearing in one of my ears had been seriously impaired by the measles. This same attack of measles had affected my whole respiratory system, although I was not aware of this until much later in my life. From this time onwards, I regarded myself as being excluded from music in all its forms; I avoided the occasions of music rather as one was expected to avoid the occasions of sin. Even my mother accepted that, musically speaking, I was retarded. She did not attempt to have me taught the piano. I was thus deprived, or deprived myself, of one of the major pleasures in life. I have never ceased to regret this, especially as it happened that I had during my life exceptional opportunities for enjoying good music. For varying reasons and on varying occasions I have attended operas, ballets and concerts in Dublin, Leningrad, Berlin, Moscow, New York, Munich, Stockholm, Paris, Brussels and Milan and almost invariably I have been bored and, even worse, I have often fallen asleep during these wonderful entertainments.

Music was my only set back in the junior schools at Synge Street. In addition to the three Rs and Christian Doctrine, we began to learn geography, Irish history and elementary Irish. The discipline of the school was strict. When the Brother said go, you went; when he said come, you came. Punctuality had a high priority and telling lies was a major crime. Home work was easy but it had to be done. Discipline was enforced by slaps — 'biffs' as they were called — with a stiff leather strap on the hand, or by a tongue lashing. I think the boys preferred the biffs to the tongue; biffs were much less humiliating and there is nothing more offensive to human dignity in man or boy than public humiliation. Sometimes an exasperated Brother struck a boy on the face with his hand. This kind of punishment was particularly hurtful mentally no less than physically to nervous youngsters. It created tensions and general unpleasantness which might last for days in the classroom.

Only once had I experience of physical assault. A Brother gave me a box on the ear because I could not point out on the map the relative positions of Buenos Aires and Rio de Janeiro. I was not a nervous child and I picked up my atlas and walked out of the schoolroom, leaving my cap and bag behind, and went home refusing to go back unless my father came with me. He came quite willingly. He had been to the Model Schools in Marlboro Street and had, according to himself, both witnessed and endured physical punishment. He was not going to have it inflicted on me. My father's protest to the Headmaster, Mr Hayes — the Brothers were always called 'mister' in Synge Street — was effective. No Brother ever struck me again.

Nor did I see any savage beatings with the hand or the cane while I was in Synge Street although there was a class in the pass stream of the early secondary school which had the reputation of being little better than a slaughter house. The stories told about these beatings were quite frightening and boys in the class lived in terror from day to day. It was always a surprise to us that there was not more violent protest. On a few occasions boys, stung beyond endurance, threw books or rulers at the offending master. In these cases the boys usually left school, never to return. It was unfortunate that this particular master was not removed from teaching duties sooner. Several generations of boys conceived, thanks to him, a hatred of the Christian Brothers and would not, whatever their circumstances, send their own children to a Christian Brothers school. The man in question was quite unsuited to teaching, although he had many other merits. He was in charge of the school library which was a very good one and he ran it well, collecting the weekly penny which it cost to take out a book. He was not used to bending rules and I, who was his most regular customer, thought I would like to borrow two books a week for which I proffered two pennies. The poor man had never had this kind of request before and he told me to take one book and give him one penny. When I said that if I could not have two books I would do without either, he was so nonplussed that he gave me the two books and declined the second penny but he complained to my class master that I was a very odd fellow. In fact, from that time on, he was quite pleasant and helpful to me and I could get as many books in the week as I wanted — all for the same penny. Nobody could ever accuse the Christian Brothers of being avaricious!

Until I was thirteen years old my school life, my home life and my leisure life around Terenure were compartmentalised. All my outside activities were with the boys in the village. In the house I had no visitors and I amused myself. When I got out of school in the afternoon, I left my classmates at the tram stop and did not see them again until next morning. It was curious that I was the only Terenure boy who went to Synge Street except for one, a few years older than I was. He was a cobbler's son name Jack Maguire and of course he was always known as 'Waxy'. At that time I saw very little of him except to notice him amongst the swimmers in the Dodder. I had little contact with my schoolmates and was usually in a hurry to get back to football practice in the Green Lanes or to my swimming and the pleasures of Shaw's Wood. There were no organised games in Synge Street — life was too serious for that — and our only recreation was playing football with a shammier, that is to say a tennis ball. As there were about 200 boys playing in a concrete yard a little more than 200 yards square we received an early lesson in the survival of the fittest.

Recreation time was also the time we ate our lunches. Lunch was bread and butter or jam and a bottle of milk which we brought in our satchels. After a football session, the bread was mashed and the milk so churned up that it was almost impossible to drink. We continued the game with the shammier along the footpath after school, varying it with the usual boyish horseplay of grabbing one another's caps and throwing them into areas or shops. At Portobello or Leonard's Corner I caught my tram and parted from my companions. If I went home by Portobello, I always spent some time playing on the barges in the harbour. Some winters it was possible to skate, or rather slide, on the canal. On these occasions I was always late home for dinner. Dinner was the main meal and, as it was usually a quarter to four when I arrived home in winter, it was as often as not taken standing up and gulped down in an effort to get in the short daylight hours for football and hockey. There were very few rules in the household: there being only two children, one very young, I suppose there was no need for them.

Having come in from football I did not go out again. I read until tea time, did my lessons without difficulty, and amused myself with whatever happened to be my current hobby until bed time which was 9 p.m. in winter and 10 p.m. in summer. After that, I read by candlelight until late in the night. Although she encouraged my reading, my mother always took away my candle before she went to bed. The room was freezing in wintertime but I developed a technique of covering everything except my nose and eyes and turning the pages of my book with my fingertips outside the bed clothes. It required something of the same technique as playing the violin.

I was never at a loss for something to do around the house, so I was never bored at home. My father was very generous and gave me money to buy all sorts of hobby equipment. I always had a paint box and I learned to mix colours but my painting never got further than doing mountains and endless sunsets on the back of envelopes. I would have loved to have been taught painting but, while we got cursory lessons in drawing, no one even mentioned painting at school. There were equally cursory lessons in woodwork which we all looked forward to but they only lasted during one school term.

I had conjuring outfits and found that I was hopelessly maladroit. I tried disguises with false beards and grease paint. I tried Meccano and could never find the right piece or the right wheel at the right time. For a long time I persevered with fretwork and thought I was quite successful with it but, after making some dozens of brackets and other odds and ends for my mother, I noticed that she was not using them, so I gave that up.

I had more success with a box camera. I turned the bathroom into a dark room where I developed my own films. It was a major thrill to see for the first time a picture appearing on the negative. I did so well at photography that my father gave me a 2A folding Brownie which is still taking photographs after nearly 70 years. To avoid having the bathroom immobilised for hours, my father bought me a developing tank. I took photographs all over the place. I was especially successful with snow scenes and got my first lesson in aesthetics in the process. In the middle of a beautiful river scene was a broken bucket. On showing it to my cousin, Ewart Wilson, he pointed out to me how the bucket ruined the picture. In future, I took much greater care of the selection of my subjects. Trivial as was the incident, it was a lesson I remembered and I began to look on landscapes and indeed pictures in general with a better informed eye. Possibly nowadays a broken bucket might well be an acceptable element in any landscape painting, as a reflection of the anti-romanticism of the age.

I was a very indulged boy. I was given great liberty by my parents. As long as they knew where I was and who I was with, I could come and go as I liked. For my part, I must say that I never kept anything from them — I had no secrets to keep and I always did what I said I would do. I am sure my mother's shop never made very much profit but it made enough to provide a rent-free house and abundant food for the family especially later at a time of great wartime scarcity. My father's business was moderately prosperous and between the two incomes the family was comfortably off. Added to this was the fact that there were only two children to be provided for and that my parents had no further aspirations to improve their social position. Indeed my father was determined to remain in the lower middle class.

I never had any difficulty in getting money for football matches, the pictures or, a little later on, for the Abbey Theatre. If I wanted a wrist watch, a new fountain pen, a bicycle, a fishing rod or a cricket bat or football, my father got them for me but things like that never cost him very much because he picked them up for little or nothing in the auction sale rooms. I think one of the very good permanent effects this indulgence had on me was that I never cared very much for owning or collecting items that had no utility for me. The only things I ever really wanted to own were books and to a lesser extent paintings.

Apart from my interest in games and the adventures of Shaw's Wood, my main hobby was reading. I graduated through Grimm, Aesop, Gulliver, Alice, *Comic Cuts, Chips* and the other children's comics to the *Magnet* and the *Gem* where Harry Wharton, Billy Bunter, Alonzo Todd and Tom Merry played their way through school to shouts of 'Hello, hello, hello' and 'Ouch'. The *Union Jack* was a popular weekly, where Jack, Sam and Pete carried the burden of Empire and Pete, being black, did the cooking. The basic assumption of these publications was that the good Englishmen were doing a wonderful job killing 'Fuzzy Wuzzies', taming black savages with rings in their noses and ears who had a taste for the flesh of missionaries, or outwitting slit-eyed Chinese opium smokers who spent all their day dicing preparatory to stabbing the white police inspector in the evening. The Redskins were left to the Americans to kill. The Americans were not sufficiently different from their English cousins to have a separate visual identity in the comics. The French, on the other hand, were readily recognised: they had sleek hair, raised eyebrows and up-pointed moustaches and they ate frogs. The Italians lived on ice cream and the Germans on thick sausage and there was always a German spy lurking around. All this meant that we Irish boys had our minds as much saturated with the British imperial myths as with the teachings of the Catholic religion.

The idea of the German menace to 'our Empire' was being carefully fostered by the English newspapers; Germans were looked at with suspicion. German brass bands — groups of about eight or ten men in uniform — played music on street corners and made collections. They were very good musicians and apparently got a large amount of money. There were two versions of the motives behind their itinerant activities. One, the most widely held, was that they were spies, possibly seeking out secret bases in preparation for a

German invasion when the war came. The other and more probable version was that they were refugees from German conscription and were trying to collect money to pay their passage to America. They often performed around Terenure and always gathered an appreciative audience; the people there were not too worried about menaces to the Empire.

At the Christian Brothers another influence began to operate. We were taught much about the saints and scholars and the wonderful Book of Kells but we also began to hear of Dermot MacMurrough and the perfidies of Strongbow. He was the first iniquitous Englishman we encountered. We met many more cases of English treachery, from Silken Thomas to the Earls who took flight, to Sarsfield, Emmet and O'Connell. We heard rather less about Tone and not much about the Fenians. Parnell was not long enough dead and Kitty O'Shea was still living. It was very simplistic history.

One schoolbook illustration, a great cliché of Irish history, showed Patrick Sarsfield, the Irish hero of the Williamite wars, wounded and dying on the field of Landen, catching his life blood in his hands and exclaiming 'O that this were for Ireland'. We began to look at the soldiers in the streets differently — to think of them as Englishmen rather than Irishmen. The Union Jack and portraits of the King and Queen were no longer accepted as 'ours', nor were the Redcoats. While there was no attempt made to ban the *Magnet* and *Gem* at school; when some boy was caught with one of them in class the Brother heaped scorn on him for reading 'foreign trash'. I began to feel ashamed of my reading matter, more because of the 'trash' than the 'foreign'. I was rapidly outgrowing the comics stage.

The school library provided as much reading as any normal boy could reasonably want and very exciting it was to swim in a South Sea lagoon and shoot the Canadian rapids with Ballantyne or wander through India with Henty or through Mexico with Mayne Reid. There were plenty of travel books in the library. We met Pathans in Afghanistan and Lamas in Tibet. The Lamas had Prayer Wheels and chanted 'O mane padme hum — O jewel of the lotus flower'. Naked Indians in the Amazon chewed cocoa leaf and shot poisoned darts from blowpipes.

Another reading experience took me away for a while from the great world of adventure, tropical forests and frozen steppes. I was given a present of a book about Fionn, the mythical Irish hero, and his companions written by Standish O'Grady. It awakened some latent memory of the Fianna legends carried over from my brief days at St Enda's. I had no trouble in peopling Shaw's Wood and the banks of the Dodder with Fionn, Ossian, Diarmuid, Caoilte, Conan Maol and all their hounds. I suppose one of the great joys that children have in pre-adolescence is the ability to suspend disbelief very easily and to play Walter Mitty in many lands, in an illimitable number of roles. From the school library I got Canon Sheehan's *Graves of Kilmorna* and was charmed by an Ireland of which I knew nothing, described in Kickham's *Knocknagow*.

Knocknagow describes in great detail life in a small Tipperary village at the end of the last century. I had never been in rural Ireland and it was a world even more remote from me than any African country described by Rider Haggard. The only places I had visited outside of Dublin were for summer holidays spent with my relatives — members of the extended family — in Wicklow and Tullow. Always I was in the family circle and never met anyone outside its immediate borders, so that the romance of rural life described in *Knocknagow* had as much effect in exciting my imagination as ever Rider Haggard had. It also predisposed me to an affection for Tipperary and Tipperary people which I retained all my life.

Boyhood

I was growing up physically and mentally and I had had the good fortune to fall under the influence of Ewart Wilson — a man with a mind of great refinement, of considerable learning and sensitivity. He was one to whom Ireland really was Cathleen Ní Houlihan, and surely she had the walk of a Queen!

Ewart and my father discussed the affairs of the country and sometimes of the world every Saturday evening and I listened delightedly. Ewart was a Gaelic Leaguer typical of his period; he always wore Irish tweeds and bought nothing that was not of Irish manufacture. He neither drank nor smoked, for a reason common enough at that time, because alcohol and tobacco contributed to the British revenues. His principal recreation was going for long walks on Sundays to the Pine Forest, Glen na Smol and Glencree. He was a devout Catholic but mildly critical of the clergy. He was totally anti-British and the only time he showed anger was in the face of British turpitude, of which he had no difficulty in finding examples. He was a Sinn Féiner long before the words ever had a general currency. He loved painting and books, and for a junior civil servant he had collected a good library. He had no worldly ambitions beyond that of rearing his family in the fear and love of God and devotion to Ireland. He had an exceptional ability to communicate with young people making them feel that they were to be taken seriously. He was my earliest mentor, encouraging me to read, taking me to the Gaelic League classes and bringing me to see paintings in the National Gallery. I remember him with affection and gratitude.

Under his influence, I joined the Fianna in Oakley Road in 1912 but we got a new headmaster in Synge Street, a very kindly old man named Brother Burgess, who preached so much against secret societies that I became conscience stricken and consulted a priest in Terenure parish. He was horrified at my involvement in what he considered a secret society. He spoke to my mother who was only too anxious that I should not get mixed up in anything that might get me into trouble, so that was the end of my Fianna connection. I should not have heeded Brother Burgess and his denunciation because he was not really referring to Ireland at all. He had spent most of his life teaching in Gibraltar and his idea of secret societies was Grand Orient Masons, Socialists, Anarchists, and perhaps Trades Unionists, all of whom he constantly denounced, in a slightly foreign accent, as 'thoroughly bad men'.

My father was not a reader of books. Jules Verne and Arnold Bennett were the only writers I heard him talk about but he made up for any deficiencies in this regard by his enthusiasm for newspapers. The *Independent* (before 1916), *The Freeman's Journal,* were bought every morning, but never *The Irish Times*; *The Irish Times* simply did not appear in Nationalist households any more than did the *Independent* in Republican households after 1916. People's religion always, and their politics often, were clearly displayed in the trams by the newspapers they read.

On the way to work my father bought an English paper and in the evening the *Evening Telegraph* and sometimes *The Herald*. He bought the *New Statesman* from the day it was published and on Sundays he bought *The Observer*. He took *The Irish Worker* and *The Leader* as well as Griffith's *Nationality*. The newspapers never went to waste as they were used for wrapping parcels in my mother's shop. My father's addiction to newspapers was a household joke, but for him it was a drug. At Christmas, when no newspapers were published he showed pronounced withdrawal symptoms, being restless and fidgety and glum until the papers reappeared. With all that reading matter at his disposal he was well informed on current affairs, but was quite uninvolved in them except to the extent that he admired Jim Larkin and hated all middle-class values and all that he termed 'show-off' and what would now be called status symbols and conspicuous waste. Nevertheless, he liked good clothes and, as soon as he could afford it, he went to a very good merchant tailor in Dame Street to have his suits made. Indeed I went there also because from the age of fourteen I could not get a suit off the peg that would fit me, so awkwardly built was I. At fifteen years of age I was 6′3″ tall and very thin.

A visit to the tailor was always something of an event. Our tailor was Conway and Swann, beside the Olympia Theatre. Swann was the senior partner and he was a very big-boned Scotsman with an accent you could cut with a knife. He was high in the Councils of the Free Church of Scotland. When you went into the establishment (it was not exactly a shop), something of a ritual began. Old Swann, as we called him, put aside whatever work he was doing and began a discussion on the state of our family, how and what they were doing. Then he told us about his rheumatism and there were many references in his conversation to 'the good Lord', employed with a familiarity which no Catholic could aspire to. There followed a discussion about the state of the cloth market and how he had just got in a lovely piece of stuff and finally rolls of cloth would be set out to choose from and he would suggest this and that. At last the suit, or probably in my father's case two suits, would be ordered but in all the chit-chat the one thing which was never mentioned was the price of the suit, or money in any shape. Bills did not appear until about six months after the suits were delivered and you were expected to pay before you ordered the next, but there was never any hurry. Swann died a very rich man and left almost all his money to the Scottish Free Church. His nephew, who succeeded him, died shortly afterwards and the firm died with him. For me they formed part of Dublin and, Scots Presbyterians though they were, they had become my friends.

Current affairs aside, Ewart Wilson was much better informed about Irish history than was my father and much more emotionally involved in Home Rule. The Saturday night discussions were nearly always concerned with Irish affairs, which meant Home Rule. I only half understood what was being talked about and heard words like 'devolution', 'fiscal reform', 'on principle' and 'anarchist', which were meaningless to me. I also heard the names of people of whom there was little mention in school: Meagher, Fintan Lawlor, Tone. There was much talk of Dillon, Redmond, Parnell and Griffith, D. P. Moran, Castle Catholics, Ascendancy and the Garrison. These words and names began to take on reality when I extended my reading of the newspapers from the football page to the general news columns.

I began to take a more general interest in the newspaper reports about happenings outside as well as inside Ireland. Prominent events that dominated the newspapers of this time were the Durbar at Delhi for King George V and the Balkan Wars of 1912 and the taking over of Tripoli by the Italians. I made my first acquaintance with a dictionary in pursuit of the word 'Durbar' and thereby started a life-long practice of looking up in a dictionary the meaning of any word I did not understand. I also started to look at maps to see where the

65

Balkans were and where Tripoli was and I heard of towns called Adrianople, Scutari and Monastir, all of which increased my curiosity about the world at large.

My interest in history and political events was increased by two books my father picked up for me. One was a history of the Franco-Prussian War and the other an account of the Boer War. They were beautifully illustrated with drawings and oleographs and I was continually thumbing through them, so that the names of places like Ems, Gavelotte, Sedan, Colenso, Spion-Kop, Stellenbosch, the Cape, Johannesburg stuck in my mind, as did characters like Kruger, Buller, Roberts, Bismarck and Thiers. Bits of information acquired like this made it much easier to understand the sequence of events leading up to the catastrophe of 1914, by which time I had acquired an unusually precocious knowledge of public affairs.

During the Saturday night discussions I began to ask questions, much to my father's amusement. He pretended to take the line that children should be seen and not heard but really he was very glad to see me taking an interest in the events of the world around me. One lesson I could have learned, but did not, was the difference between discussion and argument. All the conversation took the form of an exchange of views and information. It was quite devoid of assertiveness or emotionalism, except when the British were at issue, when Ewart Wilson could never suppress his antipathy. From a very early stage in my life I had not the capacity to contain two divergent points of view at once. Everything I thought, or rather felt, was right and everything else was error. I would have had no problem, if I had lived at the time of the Inquisition, in accepting employment at the Holy Office.

The only other time I saw feeling enter into the fireside chats was during the 1913 strike. My father thought William Martin Murphy was a blackguard intent on starving not only the strikers but their children into submission. Larkin arranged that some of the children should be taken into the homes of English workers to be fed while the strike lasted. A group of Catholic fanatics under the auspices of an organisation called the Leo Guild, led by the parish priest of Westland Row, organised demonstrations and physically tried to prevent the children being put on the boats for England. In this they largely succeeded. The Guild felt that the children's faith would be endangered. My father believed the Leo Guild to be a gang of crawthumping hypocrites and lickspittles of the Church and the employers and he became very emotional on the subject. He thought it was much more important to save the children's bodies than to worry about their souls. Ewart, on the other hand, accepted Arthur Griffith's view that Larkinism was disastrous to national progress. On the subject of the sending of children to England he too became emotional but for the reason opposite to my father's; he feared for the faith of the children. Like so many people, Faith and Fatherland were synonomous for him and anyway he loathed the idea of our children being beholden to the English.

My mother never entered into any of these exchanges, although she was nearly always present in the parlour. She just knitted or sewed and mended socks. I don't think she even listened to the conversations because politics and public affairs bored her. She worked from morning till night in the shop or in the kitchen, dressmaking or housekeeping. When she washed her hair no one could get near the fire for an hour because she had to dry it at the fireplace. There were no hair dryers and it would never have occurred to her to go to a hairdresser. She was not very articulate, but she had the type of personality which evokes confidences and this made for easy relationships with the customers of the shop who, to a large extent, made up her world.

From the shop she knew everything that was happening in the village, but she never participated in any of the village activities and never had anyone from the neighbourhood in for even a cup of tea. In fact, since we had left Summerhill, she never did any entertaining, except for her cousins, and she never went on a holiday. I think she found the comings and goings of the shop rather a source of relaxation than hard work. She knew all the customers and all about their families, their difficulties and their small triumphs, mainly associated with their children's successes in school. My father never took any interest in the shop and normally did not interfere, except that he would not allow my mother to sell cigarettes. He regarded smoking cigarettes, as did many others, rather as people now regard smoking 'pot'. For young people to be caught smoking was a major offence; boys were threatened with expulsion from school and many a Maynooth student would have been ordained priest if he had not been caught in the act.

My father also interfered in the shop during the strike in 1913 when he insisted on my mother continuing to supply bread, butter and milk to her customers whose husbands were on strike, even though they could not pay. He also insisted on her sending parcels of food to some of the neighbourhood strikers with large families. My mother had no sympathy with the strike and indeed many of the strikers' wives had just as little. When the strikers were forced to capitulate there was great bitterness in the village and some of the militants refused to go back to the tramways; others were victimised and had to take labouring jobs if they could get them.

It was through the shop that I first began to notice social distinctions and became aware of being a second-class citizen. Among my mother's customers there were, in addition to the wives of the tramway men, wives of small-time employees of the great Dublin commercial firms, together with solicitors' clerks and the like. They were all Protestants and very respectable. I noticed that they never recognised me when passing in the street although they knew who I was, and that their children never mixed with the village children. I noticed too that they and their children always travelled inside the trams — never on top — that their daily newspaper was *The Irish Times*. On Sundays they seemed to walk in convoy on the same side of the street with their bibles and their hymnals clutched in gloved hands under their oxters. We always rode on top of the trams, unless it was very wet, and we children went to Mass separately from our parents with our prayer books, if we brought one, stuck in our pockets. It was 'we' and 'they' from an early age.

I took a dislike to nearly all the Protestant customers coming to the shop and often was very critical of them to my mother. I denounced them because they were 'swanks', or more often because they were 'West Britons' or 'Shoneens'. No other word in my extensive scatological vocabulary could express for me the intense contempt contained in the terms 'West Briton' and 'Shoneen'. I inherited more than my share of emotions and was constantly in need of having them purged. My hostility to the shop and its customers probably derived from a subconscious sense of shame that my mother was compelled to play a menial role. I felt that I knew more about almost everything than she did and was in some sense superior to her customers. It was in itself, of course, a form of snobbery. What I did not know was that to my mother I had a 'glass forehead'. She knew very well that I was wrestling with the problems of adolescence and that my violent talk and assertive opinions were part of that phase. She also knew that I was utterly dependent on her not merely for food, clothing and shelter, but for a sense of security and a feeling of protection which emanates from motherhood. No matter how I behaved to her, she knew she was indispensable to me. It took me many years to realise all that. Even when I was grown up and had a family of my own, I found myself thinking, when I had difficulties in my personal or business life, that it was a long time since I had been to see my mother — though it was never more than a few weeks at a time —

so I would go to see her and allow myself to be irritated, as usual, by her excessive concern for my welfare.

In Synge Street the bulk of the pupils were from the lower middle and working classes but, when the Secondary School stage was reached, a great number of the working class boys dropped out. Their family circumstances required that they should contribute to the family budget. Such was the temper of the times that the waste of so much talent to the individual or to the community was accepted, like so many other defects in our society, as the Will of God.

The boys who remained to finish the course usually came from homes above the poverty line or where parents had the will to make the sacrifices necessary to keep their children at school. These were the boys who were my constant companions at school; it was from this group that most of my life-long friends came. I was with some of them in the university, some of them in the Volunteers. In quieter times we spent many a long weekend on walking trips over the Dublin and Wicklow Mountains. It was a sister of one of these boys whom I married.

It has added greatly to my sense of security to have lived my life in such a stable society as these schoolday friends provided. A very few of them left the city, only one of them emigrated. They were always at hand to advise, abuse, amuse or help in difficulties. When I was about fourteen years of age, I established with one of them a particularly enduring relationship.

Hubert Earle was in a higher class in school. I had only a nodding acquaintance with him until, having outgrown the school library, I joined the Rathmines public library where I saw him from time to time. He was as interested in books as I but had more sophisticated literary tastes acquired from books borrowed from the library for his mother and sister who were dedicated readers. One of the first books he recommended to me was *Anna Karenina*. Compared with it all the earlier books which I had read seemed mere fairy tales. The passions of Anna and Vronsky, the dissolute, cruel society in which they lived combined with the kaleidoscope of the Russian scene — the peasants, the nobles, the palaces, the countryside — enthralled me. The significance of the novel as a reflection of life as led by real flesh and blood people was revealed to me.

Earle was unusually clever at his books; he was, too, unusually arrogant and irascible, with the added disadvantage of being a lonely boy. Inevitably his sarcasm offended another boy to the point where satisfaction could only be got by a formal fight with bare knuckles arranged for 'the lane' after school. Earle asked me to be his second.

He took a very bad beating, both his eyes being closed, his lips split, a nasty cut on the ear and a bleeding nose, which made him look more badly hurt than he really was. I took him home, cleaning him up as best I could in the washroom of Rathmines library. We told his mother that he had had an accident which, such is the credulity of doting mothers, she believed. When after a few days he returned to school, the same tale was told to the teachers who did not believe it but made no comment, as was the custom.

Almost imperceptibly I began to find Earle attaching himself to me on all occasions. He waited after school to walk home with me, he made appointments with me in the library, helped me with my homework and invited me to his house. At first I was impatient with this attention but I found it convenient when he undertook to save me the trouble of going to the library by getting my books for me. Gradually I began to accept him and eventually we became inseparable companions and most of his afternoons were spent rambling round Terenure with me or in my house. Together we looked incongruous, I being lanky and thin while he was rather below middle height and chubby. In temperament we could hardly have been more different. Earle had a beautifully modulated speaking voice, he sang in a deep baritone the popular airs from Gilbert and Sullivan and he knew all the arias from the operas. Apart from reading, his only hobby was playing the piano which he did by ear, never having learned to read music. Although he had no interest in the Movement, when I joined the Volunteers he begged me to get him recruited into the local Company. As no one knew him and no seconder was available I had difficulty in persuading the Company to accept him. Only my plea that he lived over the telephone exchange where his mother was caretaker and might, therefore, serve a useful purpose persuaded Coughlan, the Company Captain, to do so. He also joined the Sinn Féin Club where he at once became popular for his singing and piano playing. In the Club too he discovered in himself a quality not heretofore suspected — an unusual attraction for women which was often reciprocated. Between the Volunteers, the Sinn Féin Club and the women, life became very full for him. In due course he got a scholarship to the University and when I went there a year later we joined the Soccer Club together.

When I went to Synge Street, and for quite a while afterwards, I did not regard the Brothers as human beings—as ordinary men and women. They were something separate, a third version of humanity and I was amazed and rather shocked one day to see a Brother urinating in the boys' toilet. Even when I did realise they were human, they always seemed remote from the ordinary life of the city. They arrived at the school at 9 a.m. and disappeared at 3 p.m. and if they had an existence outside the school we knew nothing of it. I suppose it is not in the nature of schoolboys to think much about the private lives of their teachers. The Brothers had a life of their own; it scarcely impinged on the world outside their monasteries. 'The object of the Institute is' to quote from the Rule of the Irish Christian Brothers, 'that all its members labour, in the first place for their own perfection and in the second place for that of their neighbour, by serious application to the instruction of male children, especially the poor, in the principles of religion and Christian piety'. To that end, they led a severe, disciplined and frugal life, deprived of even the most meagre comforts and diversions.

The Brother was expected to 'divest himself of all carnal affections for his relations and change them into spiritual ones, loving them only with that love which well-ordered charity requires; thus, to live only for Christ, whom he receives instead of father, mother, brothers and sisters'. They were enjoined to 'abhor, and not in part, all those things which the world loves and embraces'.

Every moment of their day was prescribed for them, from just before 5 a.m. when they arose until 10 p.m. when they went to bed. At 5 a.m. they meditated together in the Oratory until 6 a.m. Then they said the Angelus, the Litany of Jesus and a few Paters and Aves, not exceeding seven, for particular intentions; then they heard Mass at 8 a.m., had breakfast and prepared for school which began at 9 a.m. For recreation they were allowed only to spend time 'either walking, sitting or in any innocent amusement becoming persons of their profession', and in recreation there 'should be at least two together'. Their reading matter was subject to the approval of their superiors and their letters, coming or going, were subject to censorship.

They were not permitted to visit people's houses, even of their own parents, and in conversations with people outside the Institute they were expected to be as brief as was compatible with civility and never to discuss the internal affairs of the Order. It was no wonder they appeared so remote from the pupils once the school day was over.

Even the pace at which they walked in the street was provided for in their regulations and they were enjoined to show cheerfulness rather than gloom upon their countenances and 'when necessity obliged them to look back they should do so with becoming gravity and without any appearance of curiosity'. Special emphasis was laid on regularity and punctuality and discipline. The Brothers took the

71

vows of Poverty, Obedience and Chastity and they also vowed to teach the poor gratuitously.

There have been many changes and modifications in the severity of these rules in recent years, but the Brothers who taught my generation in Synge Street were the product of the regimen I have described. A formation of that kind produced an exceptional man. They were noticeably indifferent to either physical comfort or public esteem. They had not free access to literature and the world of theatre and music was denied them. No sporting facilities were available to them and even, if there were, the rigid rules of non-participation in activities outside their Order would have made competitive sport impossible. They believed in authority and in the order and discipline that authority produced. Women did not exist for them, or if they did it was as a source of temptation to be avoided as much as possible. Any activity that did not conduce to their own perfection in the sight of God was equally to be avoided. But what distinguished them from any other male religious order was that they were essentially Irish in character; they were the Culdees of our time.

Most of the Brothers were apolitical and indeed, except for matters of Faith and Morals, they held no strong views. They accepted, as did the country at large, that Ireland owed allegiance to the British Crown. Even Griffith, with his idea of a dual monarchy, recognised that. Separation was the policy of a minority. It was unusual for any of the Brothers to display political partisanship although in Synge Street in my time there was one who did. Brother Crane was a Waterford man, a native Irish speaker and the son of evicted tenants. He did not seem to have any settled function and was to be seen moving through the school, always with a number of tomes under his arm. He was known to all the boys as 'Bang' — why nobody knew. It was surprising that he was not called Friar Tuck; because of his stature, hair style, jovial smile, he looked like every picture of Friar Tuck that ever was. When we came across him in the first year of the 1914 war he was in his late fifties and the story quickly spread through the school that he had the ear of Dublin Castle and was the Brothers' contact with the authorities, via the backstairs. He was certainly very pro-British in sympathy and gave us a lecture illustrated with lantern slides on 'Little Belgium' describing how the Germans burned Louvain University and Library — deliberately of course! The lecture led to howls of protest and because I was vociferous and, being so very tall, was more conspicuous than the others, I was sent for by Bang to 'the parlour'.

The parlour was a frighteningly austere room furnished with black horsehair chairs and sofa and a highly polished mahogany table. There was a sideboard and a few empty vases. Pictures of the Pope and Ignatius Rice (the founder of the Order), the Blessed Virgin and the Sacred Heart were the only decorations. I did not know what to expect and was surprised when Bang started to explain how wrong I was to be pro-German. He spoke to me as if I was grown up and after a while I found it not only easy but a pleasure to talk back at him. It was the first time anyone tried to convince me that perhaps I was mistaken, instead of just telling me I was wrong. I am very sorry that I was not exposed in my adolescence to more of that kind of reasoned argument. I am equally sorry that I was not old enough then to appreciate that Brother Crane was a man of great learning and breadth of mind.

He had worked in Newfoundland and was appointed a Government Inspector for Schools. He was a considerable scientist and deeply versed in astronomy and was also a Biblical scholar. He was secretary of the Order's Education Committee and it was quite likely that he was in and out of the Castle on the business of the Order. He stayed in Synge Street only a year or two and I lost touch with him. After our encounter in the parlour, he always stopped in passing to exchange a few words with me or ask what I was reading. On one such occasion I happened to be carrying an illustrated edition of *The Three Musketeers*. The page at which it opened showed d'Artagnan hopping out of the bed of an outraged Milady. Bang asked me if I saw nothing wrong with the picture and handed me back the book with an indulgent smile. Of course Brother Crane was not typical of the Order, but there were many men throughout the Christian Brothers of a similarly high intellectual quality.

Contrary to an assertion often made, the Brothers did not deliberately indoctrinate their pupils with Irish nationalism or hostility to Britain. Their pupils developed nationalistic and anti-British attitudes as a by-product of the teachings of the Catholic Faith which it was the basic objective of the Brothers to inculcate. The persecution of the Catholics rather than the persecution of the Irish as such was the burden of the Brothers' history teaching. Most of the heroes held up for our edification were post-Reformation. But where their pupils were concerned the end result was the same; they became anti-British and nationalistic in outlook. However I never heard any criticism at school of contemporary Protestants nor was I ever told, as I have often heard asserted elsewhere, that nobody could hope for salvation outside the Catholic Church.

The Brothers created in their pupils an awareness of the distinc-

73

tion between the Irish and the English. Without the groundwork of the Christian Brothers' schooling it is improbable that there would ever have been a 1916 Rising and certain that the subsequent fight for independence would not have been successfully carried through. The leadership of the IRA came largely from those who got their education from the Brothers and got it free, or at very little cost. This was the first generation of the men of no property among whom secondary education was sufficiently diffused to provide an effective leadership for a revolution. For that the Nation has to be thankful to the Brothers. Yet it has to be said that it was in no sense the aim of the Christian Brothers to produce leaders for a Revolution. Rather was it their aim to produce Catholic Irishmen who would not be hewers of wood and drawers of water; this was the height of their secular ambition. Thousands of individual Irishmen have reason to thank their Christian Brothers' schooling for providing them with a satisfying way of life which, without the self-sacrifice of the Brothers, would have been beyond their hopes of realisation. The Brothers were good men.

Within their frugal, austere setting, they were not all cast in the same mould but all of them were men of character. When I first went to Synge Street, the headmaster was Brother Hayes, nicknamed 'Daddy'. Like most of the Brothers he came from rural Ireland. All I remember about him was that he seemed very gentle and often put on magic lantern shows dealing with Bible history. A year or so after I joined the school he was replaced as Principal by Brother Burgess, a Carlow man, soon known as 'Burgie'. He looked a very old man although he was in his mid-fifties. Burgie had spent most of his religious life setting up the Brothers' school in Gibraltar. An earlier attempt to establish a mission failed through lack of funds. The second attempt was more successful, but not without considerable local friction and at the expense of great physical hardship to the six Brothers engaged in the project.

By the time Burgie left the Rock, the school was well established and flourishing. In Synge Street he never taught class, but frequently gave religious instruction, which was largely taken up with reminiscences of his Gibraltar experiences and denunciation of Free-masonry and Socialism. He used to boast that in all his years in Gibraltar he had never been in the house of a Gibraltarian and he was fond of quoting the piece from St Paul about 'being all things to all men' which, because of the religious factions in Gibraltar, he seemed to have found a useful piece of advice. He was reputed to know all the boys in the school — several hundreds of them — and certainly he always had a joke or a friendly word for everyone as he met them in the yard or around the buildings. He had acquired a quite distinctly Spanish accent and we had fun imitating him. He had the reputation of being a Spanish scholar and had translated many text books from English into Spanish. He also had the reputation of being a very pious man as well as being short-tempered. I could well believe the piety to be genuine but I never saw any manifestation of the short temper and he never resorted to corporal punishment.

Before we moved into the post-primary system, we had Brother Fleming in charge. He was a Galwayman and Irish was his mother tongue. It was said that an elder brother of his had to leave the country because of his association with the Invincibles, the secret society responsible for the 'the Park murders'. He was known as 'The Golly' because he resembled a large animated Gollywog. He spoke slowly with a rather frightening deliberation; in appearance he certainly bore every evidence of the constraints of the vow of poverty. He was believed to insist on doing his own washing and mending. He gave the impression of being a rather amiable goon, but was not all that amiable in the pursuit of discipline and correct behaviour; he often resorted to the leather, though not excessively, nor did he ever strike the boys with his hand.

His great expression of disapproval was to call you 'a shabby fellow' or to enquire 'are you mouthing' when you were gossiping in class. At the beginning of the war a few boys in the class wore Union Jacks in their buttonholes and some of us wore tricolour buttons. Naturally there was much badge snatching with the result that The Golly forbade all badges. This produced a blast of protest from Arthur Griffith in *Nationality*. Poor Brother Fleming was very upset, doubtless thinking of his Invincible brother but of course he made no reply. He had the sympathy of all of us boys and we made sure that there was no more badge trouble in class. Anyway, there had been no really bad feeling between those who were pro-British and the Sinn Féin partisans. Brother Fleming's main teaching work was concerned with Christian Doctrine. When we left him we were well grounded in the Ten Commandments, the precepts of the Church and the mysteries of religion. We knew the Bible only as we knew the Arabian Nights, from selected and illustrated stories.

When we left the simple and pious Brother Fleming we moved into the secondary school, shedding members of the class who had to go and seek work. The total number left in the senior school was about sixty, divided into junior, middle and senior grades. It was possible to accommodate the entire school in one very large class-room.

The ratio of teachers to pupils in the senior school was very high. The Brother in charge was Brother Roche who taught English, History, Science and Latin. He was assisted by three laymen, Mr Harkin who taught English, Mr Hayes who taught French and Irish and Mr Crowley who taught mathematics.

Brother Roche was a man in his mid-thirties, of below average height and above average width. He had golden hair, wore gold rimmed glasses and bit his nails. His bright eyes, his mobile, good humoured face, his walk and all his movements, indicated exceptional physical and mental energy. He had taken a degree in Physics and Chemistry. He came from an urban background—his father was a middle grade civil servant—and his appearance and manner were more refined than his colleagues. He was less isolated than the other Brothers from the boys and paid more attention to their individual personalities than was customary. He was often exasperated but never angry. When I came under his care, I was going through a difficult period of my life and his understanding and sympathy were a great help to me in moving from adolescence to young manhood. I became quite attached to him and remained his friend long after I left school. Brother Roche was posted to Rome and became an important figure in the Vatican diplomatic service.

School life followed a regular pattern. Starting at 9 a.m. sharp with morning prayers, lessons until 12 noon, then the Angelus, followed by half an hour's religious instruction and half an hour for lunch, lessons until 3 p.m. and then home. The atmosphere in the senior school was quite different from that in the junior schools. Discipline in the matter of punctuality and order in the classrooms was strict, but there was no problem in enforcing it. The boys were there because they wanted to learn, and relations with the teachers were friendly. Generally speaking, there was also a good relationship between the boys themselves. The fact that all the classes were held in the same room and began and finished at the same time meant that, over the years, boys of different school generations made friends with one another.

There was no recreational space except for the school yard, which was no better than a medium sized courtyard, so we streamed out into Synge Street or down to Grantham Street to take our lunch. In the first years this still consisted of bread and jam sandwiches and anyone with a penny to spend bought sweets in Morris' shop in Grantham Street. Recreation consisted of pushing and shoving and cap snatching or playing ball with the ever present shammier along the streets and back lanes.

From time to time there were serious quarrels between boys. Then a formal fight was staged after school in one of the back lanes between the parties concerned. The rules could hardly have been simpler. The contestants took off their coats and the other boys formed a ring and saw to it that there was fair play and that only fists were used. The spectators also acted as referee taking care to prevent too much violence. Usually a black eye was the worst damage inflicted. The fight ended with handshakes. The black eyes were explained to the Brother in charge and to the parents as having resulted from bumping into the railings of St Kevin's Chapel.

As we grew older, we stopped bringing our lunches to school and cut out horseplay and football during recreation. Instead we bought coffee and a few cakes in a café in Camden Street and strolled round the Camden Street/Harcourt Street block on our way back to school. At that time the Municipal Gallery had its temporary home in Harcourt Street and very often on our lunch hour strolls we called in to look at the pictures.

At that time all the Lane pictures were in the Municipal, but we had not even heard of Hugh Lane or the Impressionists or indeed of any other school of painting. The only paintings we had ever previously been familiar with were the reproductions of the Madonnas and the Crucifixions and Adorations of the Magi with which our school was liberally decorated. Some aesthetic value was probably gained from our visits to the Gallery because, in my case, two of the paintings greatly attracted me. One was a portrait of a biretted and very aristocratic Monsignor in scarlet — Monsignor Merry del Val by Philip de Lazlo — and the other was a painting by Nathaniel Hone of cattle in a field at Malahide. It seems a great pity that with the Gallery and its superb collection so near at hand no effort was made to make us aware of their importance, but I suppose as art appreciation was not on the curriculum, the time could not be spared. The Brothers were no more backward in this respect than any of the other secondary schools in the city.

In the matter of sex education the Brothers were of no great help. The half hour of religious instruction ran through the Commandments and the Precepts of the Church. The instruction on the sixth commandment produced extreme embarrassment to Brother Roche and giggles from the boys in the senior classes. Even at that, he never got further than vague references to 'immodest thoughts'. In those days boys had to cope with adolescence without guidance or information from anyone. They knew nothing about their bodily development. My verbal erudition in eroticism acquired in Terenure was of no value as a guide to sexual behaviour. Much of one's psychic energy was dissipated in keeping one's mind away from 'bad or immodest thoughts' and, being thoroughly unsuccessful in this regard, still more energy was spent on feeling guilty. Confession, to which frequent resort was made, provided no solution at all because the priest only succeeded in aggravating one's sense of guilt.

I got some superficial measure of sex education from the soldiers in Terenure, back on leave from the front. Some of these returned soldiers were neighbours with whom I had spent my early childhood. I regarded them as my contemporaries, even if they were a few years older than I. I was curious to hear what the war in France was like and spent hours listening to descriptions of barrages, shellholes, barbed wire, ghastly corpes and villages destroyed.

Some of these young soldiers were more mature than others and with great secrecy produced condoms and 'filthee pictures'. The use of the first I did not understand and I was thoroughly ashamed of having fearfully and fleetingly glanced at the pictures. But like all these boyish experiences, they were remembered. Some of these lads who volunteered for the British army never came back. There was a boy named Reilly, the only child of a widow, who lived a few doors from us. He was a big red-headed boy, always friendly and soft natured. He never got a steady job and his mother had to go out to work as a charwoman to keep them both alive. After about six months in France he came home on a short leave, most of which he spent sitting, in his uniform, on the wall outside his house gossiping with the neighbours. I spent a lot of my time talking to him about the war. Within a week of the end of his leave his mother got a telegram to say that he had been killed in action. Tom Reilly was to me a symbol of the 50,000 Irish men who lost their lives in the British Army in the Great War. He went to war with another 250,000 Irishmen at the behest of the leaders of the nation. I could never feel that they were less patriotic than we who took part later in the Volunteer Movement. It was, I think, a mistake on the part of the post-1916 leaders of the Volunteers to have repudiated the Irish survivors of the war; they should have publicly sought to recruit them into the Volunteer Organisation.

At the time of the 1916 fiftieth anniversary celebrations in 1966, Harry Mundow, the Chairman of the Office of Public Works, suggested to me that, as a symbolic gesture of recognition that these ex-British soldiers were part of the historic tradition of the Irish nation, a bridge should be built across the Liffey linking the Phoenix Park with the very beautiful War Memorial Park designed by Lutyens on the other side of the river. I thought it was a highly imaginative and generous idea. I broached it to Seán Lemass. He was not prepared to go along with it, feeling it was too late to do anything. I regretted that Dev was no longer Taoiseach. It might have appealed to his expressed desire for a union of hearts. Dev believed with Pascal that the heart has its reasons of which reason knows nothing.

My school days were happy days. I am more than grateful to the Brothers. I feel they educated me adequately, if not liberally, to do the State some service both before and after independence.

* * * * *

In the summer I visited my cousins in the sleepy country towns of Wicklow and Tullow. To me these were occasions of great happiness. My memories of them are what all memories of happy boyhood holidays should be — long, pleasant, adventurous summer days in fairyland. There were picnics to Tullow Hill, Aghade and along the banks of the Slaney. We always went by pony and trap and it was a great joy to me to hold the reins and drive the pony along the empty, dusty, leafy country roads. There were no young people for me to play with in Tullow but in Wicklow a cousin, Joe Byrne, who was a little older than I, had a boat in which he used to take myself and his sisters sailing on the shallow waters of the Murrow.

Joe was very skilful in his use of the boat, often to the point of deliberately nearly capsizing it; in fact he once succeeded in doing so, pitching his sisters and myself into the water. It was very shallow and we had no difficulty in scrambling back on board but the experience made me very nervous of boats. I got it into my head that I would end my life by drowning. Good swimmer as I was, I never ventured far from land and I hated boating of any kind.

In Wicklow, too, we drove out in a pony and trap to picnic in the Devil's Glen and the Silver Strand. I thought the Devil's Glen with its river and rills and ferns and almost tropical trees was the loveliest place I ever would see. In my imagination I had no difficulty in peopling it with Indians, parrots, monkeys and pumas. I don't know why I chose pumas rather than lions or tigers but I suppose it reminded me of something I read about the Amazonian forest.

Both the Byrnes of Wicklow and the Murphys of Tullow were comfortably off but not by any means wealthy. Mrs Byrne was the

79

sister of my Aunt Lily and Uncle Patrick of Tullow. They were rather distant cousins but I always called them uncle and aunt and in fact I was very close to Lily who was my godmother. My mother had been very ill after my birth and Lily came to live in Summerhill to nurse me for the first year of my life. She was a gay-spirited, practical woman. She lived to a great age and I was very fond of her till the end. Her sisters, except Mrs Byrne, having become nuns, she, as so often happened, stayed at home to care for her parents and, after they died, her brother Patrick. Despite, as she told me, several 'offers' she never married.

The Wicklow household was dominated by Mrs Byrne with a fanatical puritanism and a horror of sex that made me wonder how she ever produced children. I am sure the children, when they grew up, had the same thought. In both houses the family rosary was said every night, the lenten regulations were observed rigidly and evening devotions were regularly attended. In Tullow two Masses were attended on Sunday and holydays. To the joyful, sorrowful and glorious mysteries of the rosary were added what my father, who sometimes cycled down to stay there for the weekend, called 'the trimmings': mortuary prayers for the individual members of the family, prayers for the Pope's intentions and endless 'Glory be to the Fathers'.

It was curious how the memory of the 1798 rebellion persisted in this part of the country. In Wexford, Wicklow and Carlow, inspired by Wolfe Tone and the United Irishmen, the rebellion had been more widespread, more intense and more savagely suppressed than anywhere else in the country. Both families were steeped in its traditions. Hardly a day passed that some reference was not made to the heroes and villains of the period. I heard of Bagenal Harvey and Michael Dwyer and the dreadful 'Hunter' Gowan, of Hugo of Glendalough and the atrocities of Newtownmountkennedy: The great local heroes are Billy Byrne of Ballymanus and Father Murphy who was hanged in Tullow for his part in the rebellion and whose statue was just outside the Murphy house. Father Murphy had become the symbol of faith and fatherland. The fact that he was a rare, almost unique, example of clerical participation in the rebellion was never referred to; the general opposition of the Church to the rebellion was forgotten.

The first thing I had to do when I came back from Wicklow or Tullow was to write my 'bread and butter' letter with my mother standing over me and making me rewrite it if there were too many blots on the paper.

At home, my parents continued to be very generous to me and I got whatever money I wanted, but that of course was not much. None of us in the class at school smoked. My father was a heavy pipe smoker and a spittoon was a most necessary part of the furniture at home, much to my mother's disgust, but he didn't countenance cigarettes. Of course neither I nor any of the boys in my class drank. From my earliest days, a horror of public houses was drilled into me. I never got over my distaste of pubs and when over the years circumstances brought me into them, I never felt quite at ease. Betting or card playing or playing pitch and toss, which was a common Sunday morning pastime in Terenure, were also deplored by my parents and their dislike for gambling has stuck with me all my life. Without cigarettes, drink or gambling my money wants were very small. Sixpence a day was enough for my tram fare to school, inclusive of coffee and a cake for lunch. A shilling covered my tram fare and the 6d entrance ticket to the back of the pit at the Abbey Theatre. An occasional sixpence or shilling was enough to buy a secondhand book or lemonade and biscuits as a special treat.

The years before and during the war, until the Rebellion of 1916, have nothing but pleasant memories for me. Life was uncomplicated for a boy in his teens. I wanted for nothing and at home I enjoyed my hobbies of reading, fretwork and photography. I got pleasure from the company of my school companions. When the war broke out I lived for a while in dread that my father would have to join the army and it took him some time to reassure me that he had no intention of doing so. He did not believe in war. He agreed with the attitude of Larkinites in Liberty Hall, over which was displayed a huge banner reading 'We serve neither King nor Kaiser but Ireland'.

From the beginning of the war my sympathies were pro-German, influenced by what I had heard from Ewart Wilson as well as what I read in the 'mosquito press', as the Sinn Féin periodicals were known. The ostentatious displays of loyalty by all the Protestants and Castle Catholics around Terenure enraged me and increased my longing for a German victory. The display of Union Jacks multiplied. Flag days for all sorts of war purposes were a source of annoyance to me. A most astonishing example of how British we had become was when the Dublin Corporation expunged the name of the Celtic scholar, Kuno Meyer, from the list of freemen of the city for no other reason than that he was a German. As Yeats wrote about them in another, no less despicable connection:

What need you, being come to sense,
But fumble in a greasy till
And add the halfpence to the pence

And prayer to shivering prayer, until
You have dried the marrow from the bone?

I became absorbed in the anti-war campaign and read every scrap of anti-war and anti-British propaganda I could lay my hands on. I used to call at a shop in Stephen's Street every week after school on Friday to buy *The Irish Volunteer, The Spark* and the other underground periodicals which came and went as they were suppressed by the British and reappeared under another name. Sometimes I bought *The Eye Opener,* a scandal sheet which was non-political but directed at exposing the sex life of British officers. They got their revenge. McIntyre, the editor, was murdered at the same time as they murdered Sheehy Skeffington during the 1916 rebellion. Sometimes I bought *The Free Thinker* out of curiosity but I was nervous about reading it lest it should endanger my faith.

Occasionally I picked up *The Irish Worker* which, after it was suppressed, was re-issued as *The Worker* and after that *The Workers' Republic.* James Connolly edited all these papers but except for his anti-British sentiments I had not much interest in them, particularly as he often attacked Eoin MacNeill, the editor of my favourite — *The Irish Volunteer* — because MacNeill was not extreme enough politically. My father often brought home *Nationality* — which was Griffith's paper — until it was suppressed and transformed into *Scissors and Paste. Scissors and Paste* was great fun to read because it published extracts from British and pro-British Irish papers, often deliberately taken out of context, which highlighted British hypocrisy and self-righteousness.

I had large war maps pasted on boards hung up in my room and every day I read the war bulletins and moved my little coloured pins as the armies advanced and retreated. I had no views or feelings one way or another on the merits of the Germans or the Russians or the French or the Serbians or the Greeks, but I was against allies of the British. As the war went on, I became progressively anti-British and ever more hostile, almost to the point of hatred, to the Irish politicians who supported the war and particularly to John E. Redmond, the leader of the Irish Party, because of his speech offering to place the National Volunteers at the disposal of the British forces.

This speech was a major weapon in the hands of Sinn Féin although in fact at the time it caused no major upset in Irish public opinion. Indeed thousands of the National Volunteers joined the British Army and these were the best of the fighting men. The majority of the people, especially in Dublin, accepted the situation that Ireland was involved in the war; there was general sympathy for 'little Belgium' and nearly everyone believed that the Angels of Mons intervened to save the retreating British army. The stories of the Huns bayonetting Belgian babies and deliberately burning all the books in Louvain University did not surprise them. The anti-German propaganda — a word which was only coming into general use — was very effective. There was no general protest at the postponement by the British Government of the introduction of Home Rule until the end of the war.

The Irish Volunteers (as the section of the National Volunteers who broke away because of Redmond's collaboration with the British was known) found it very hard to make progress in the face of the prevailing mood of the country and the continued trust of the people in Redmond's policies although, with so many of the Redmondite Volunteers joining the British Army, enthusiasm for soldiering amongst those who stayed at home declined to vanishing point. There was a Company of the Sinn Féin Volunteers (as the breakaway section now became popularly called) very active in Terenure. It was known as the 'A' Company. I had a friend and neighbour, 'Bones' Rogers, who was an enthusiastic member. He always told me when they were going on route marches and I accompanied them on these outings. I was allowed to hold their rifles when they were walking at ease and was shown how they worked. The Company was the best equipped in Dublin. It had Lee Enfield rifles and some of the 'Howth' rifles, but at the the age of fourteen these were too heavy for me to handle.

In August 1915 the Irish Republican Brotherhood, the secret militant society which believed that only force would get the British out of Ireland, intervened actively in the situation. They decided to bring home from the United States the dead body of the Fenian hero, O'Donovan Rossa, and give him a national funeral. The divergence between the Redmondites and the Sinn Féin Volunteers now became apparent. The Irish Republican Brotherhood manipulated the occasion so that the Sinn Féiners took charge of the funeral procession, supplied the guard of honour and fired the volleys over the dead Fenian in Glasnevin. The National Volunteers took part in the demonstration but only half heartedly. Colonel Maurice Moore, their leader, was bitterly disappointed by their turnout and said so publicly. But more important, P. H. Pearse availed himself of the occasion to make an oration which was a masterpiece of patriotic rhetoric. It stirred passions, with results that Pearse may have wished for but could not have foreseen. I filed past Rossa's coffin where it lay in the City Hall and was up early to get a good view of the start of the

83

procession, enthralled and proud to see the smartly uniformed and armed Volunteers, some of whom I knew, mount the guard of honour at the removal of the remains. The O'Donovan Rossa funeral was a major propaganda coup for the IRB, the existence of which was virtually unknown in Ireland at that time. It is said that even Connolly did not know of it.

The next great demonstration organised by the Volunteers was in the autumn of 1915 when the whole Dublin brigade — there must have been over a thousand men — mostly well armed, marched into the Dublin mountains on manouevres. For me they were a wonderful sight. I was sure that they were going to set Ireland free and avenge the Croppies of '98 and I was reminded that one of the few successes of the '67 Fenian Rising was at Stepaside and Glencullen where the manoeuvres were taking place. I lay in a field under the Three Rock Mountain gazing over the beautiful countryside and imagining British battleships steaming into the bay and being blown to bits by guns which, in my imagination, I placed at strategic points around the hills.

On Sundays I used go to Aeriochts (open-air concerts) in St Enda's and in Larkfield which was owned by Count Plunkett, one of whose sons was executed in 1916. Eamonn Ceannt, also executed then, always played his bagpipes and Pearse often made a speech on these occasions. Having read and learnt by heart Pearse's oration over the grave of O'Donovan Rossa, I went to any meeting around South County Dublin where he was billed to speak. I loved listening to him and his constant plea of Ireland for the Irish. At the Aeriochts, competitions were often held for the best drilled and best equipped Company in the Battalion and I was thrilled when 'my' Company, 'A' Company of the Fourth Battalion, took first place. I thought that, when the war against the British came, 'A' Company would be in the van of the Irish Army. The kind of war visualised in my imagination was that which was going on in France, but I thought of it as something which would take place only in the distant future.

But my most thrilling experience as a camp follower of the Volunteers came on St Patrick's Day, 1916, when Eoin MacNeill, as Commander in Chief, reviewed the Volunteers in College Green. In our school books after the picture of Patrick Sarsfield lamenting as he died on the field of Landen 'Oh that this was for Ireland' was a reproduction of a painting of the Dublin Volunteers parading in College Green in 1779. The original, by Wheatley, which is in our National Gallery, shows the Volunteers — horse, foot and artillery — massed in College Green with Trinity College and the houses of Parliament in the background, and the equestrian statue of a garlanded King Billy in the foreground, and surrounding the statue on the left a regiment of what look like dragoons. In fact they were the Dublin Regiment of Light Horse led by Viscount Mountjoy. In the centre of the picture was the Duke of Leinster, described as Colonel of the First Regiment of the Dublin Volunteers. There were other members of the aristocracy like La Touche and Fitzgibbon but also amongst the officers in the painting were coachbuilders, booksellers, goldsmiths and the ironmonger, Napper Tandy, who became a leader of the United Irishmen and who to this day is remembered with affection by all true Dubliners, chiefly, it must be said, because of the song 'The Wearing of the Green' which is better known to Irishmen all over the world than 'The Soldier's Song'.

I met with Napper Tandy and he took me by the hand
Saying how is old Ireland and how does she stand?

The sentiments of the Volunteers of 1779, as depicted in Wheatley's picture, were certainly not the republican sentiments of the United Irishmen but I was not very clear on that. To me they were heroes ready to die to liberate Ireland.

Here in 1916 with Eoin MacNeill, bearded, smartly uniformed and wise-looking at their head, was the reincarnation of the glamorous army of 1779. What with hero worship for MacNeill and P. H. Pearse, the thrill of seeing the Volunteers march past the saluting base, remembering the picture of their predecessors of 1779 and recalling all the stories I heard in Wicklow of the rebellion of 1798 my boyish imagination was in a state of excitement that kept me for days planning deeds of derring-do for Ireland.

I hoped the war would come soon, echoing quite unconsciously Mitchel's prayer 'Send war in our time, O Lord'. When a few weeks later an RIC sergeant was wounded in a raid on the Volunteer Hall in Tullamore, I was sure the fighting would soon begin. I had intended to go with 'A' Company on manoeuvres on Easter Sunday, but the *Sunday Independent* newspaper had a notice from MacNeill calling off the parade. I went up to see my friend, Bones Rogers, but he had gone away for Easter and I thought no more about the matter. I went to the Zoo instead.

Ever since I was a small boy I was literally fascinated by the wild animals in the Zoo. When we lived in Summerhill, my parents often took me to the Zoo on Sundays but it was not so easy to get there from Terenure. Most things I liked to do in the company of others, but not visiting the Zoo. By myself I could stay as long as I liked looking at whatever animals attracted my attention and let my imagination run loose on the wild places they came from. I could see the lions roaming the African plains and bringing down their prey while hyenas and vultures waited round them for their share of the kill. I knew the difference between the African elephant, which was untameable and destructive, and an Indian elephant which pulled teak logs in Burmah or carried a howdah with a mahout in it bearing the Rajah, and of course the Sahib, on tiger hunts. There was a picture in an early school book of ours showing a white ivory-hunter aiming his rifle at a charging elephant, identified as an African elephant by his huge ears, and underneath the picture was a quotation from the story it illustrated 'I aimed between the eye and ear and slowly pressed the trigger'. I read too some description of the natives killing an elephant for meat, of the feast which followed and how the most prized part of the elephant was its foot; when baked, it was scooped out by hand. Whatever impression this story left on me, to this day I never eat ox tongue without thinking of the texture of the meat as being identical with the texture of elephant's foot.

In the Zoo there was a polar bear which was reputed to have eaten a child who fell into his pit, the crocodile which never moved, the felines which never stopped moving and the parakeets and the famous parrot which became a Dublin institution. He, or she, spoke only one phrase: 'Any water?' but generations of Dublin children knew it. At that time the Zoo had no hippos or rhinos, orang-utans or gorillas. I had a particular wish to see a gorilla because I had read a book about Dr Chailliu, the French explorer, who had discovered pygmies and the gorilla in Gabon in equatorial Africa. For years no one believed his account of the gorillas.

I think I was fortunate to have grown up in a city with a wide range of public amenities. The one from which I got the greatest continuous pleasure was the Zoo. Since those days, more than sixty years ago, many animals have been added to the collection and their accommodation has been improved. Still, as a menagerie, the Dublin Zoo cannot compare with the great zoos in London, Paris, Antwerp, Berlin, New York or Moscow, all of which I have visited over the years. But as a public garden none of them can compare with ours in Dublin and I do not think this claim is just born of local pride.

My adolescent interest in wild animals had the secondary effect of stimulating my interest in travel and exploration, particularly in Africa. I read about Mungo Park, Stanley, Livingstone, of the savage atrocities of Lobenguela and of Chaka the Zulu king. But while I continued to read any books I could get dealing with animals in the wild and on Africa, this turned out to be my last visit to the Zoo for a long time. I spent the rest of the day working on my war map and reading *The Count of Monte Cristo* which I thought was the best book I had ever read. My father was always laughing at this attempt at literary criticism; according to him the last book I read was always 'the best'.

On Sundays and holidays my mother brought me breakfast in bed so that on Easter Monday having nothing special to do I lay on late, enthralled by *Monte Cristo*. When I finally got up, my father asked me to go up to the village to get him tobacco. When I arrived at the tram stop, which was the focal point of the village, I noticed something unusual. The trams had halted and some of them were pulling into the stables. The tobacconist had heard that there was some trouble in town but was not very interested in the matter and certainly showed no excitement. I questioned the tram men, most of whom I knew, and was told that Sinn Féin Volunteers had taken over the General Post Office and Stephen's Green. They did not know why, or what exactly was happening but had been told to stable the trams. Being a holiday and dinner hour there was scarcely anyone on the streets; the odd person passing did not seem even curious to know what was going on.

The driver of the next incoming tram was a man named Cranley whom I knew well. He had been one of the most active of the 1913 strikers and had been lucky to have been taken back into the tram company's employment. He was very excited and delighted at what was reported to be happening in the city. According to him a rebellion (and this was the first time I had heard the word) had taken place and the Volunteers had occupied the Castle, all the railway stations, the Four Courts and the Shelbourne Hotel and were in command of the docks. A regiment of the British Cavalry had been slaughtered in O'Connell Street. A Republic was proclaimed and Patrick Pearse was in charge. The Volunteers had risen in Cork, Galway and Wexford and the Germans had landed in Kerry.

Believing, as I wanted to believe, all this, my first act was to dash into the nearest church and say three 'Our Fathers', three 'Hail Marys' and three 'Glory be to the Fathers' for the success of the rebellion. Having gathered all the information I could I rushed home to tell my parents, asking the few people I met if they had heard the news of the rebellion and crying 'up the rebels' as I passed. My parents were not aware of anything amiss but I was told to stay indoors for the rest of the day. My father went over to Ewart Wilson to see if he could throw any light on the situation and they walked back to our house, picking up more rumours on the way, but nothing was known for certain.

Next day I was forbidden to leave Terenure; even if I wanted to I would not have known where to go. At the crossroads people were gathering in small groups discussing the situation or rather swapping rumours. A neighbour whom I knew well, Arthur Nolan, was a baker in Boland's Mill and it was from him that I got first hand news, as distinct from rumours, of the events in the city. He had gone to his place of work at the Mill to find it occupied but had entered the building and had spoken to the Volunteers. He was very sympathetic to the rebels, which is a lot more than could be said for most of the loungers around the crossroads and the tram stop. In the two days that followed he became the centre of a small group who had similar sympathies. As he went in to Bolands every day, he was better informed than most. He told us of the British troops landing at Dun Laoghaire (Kingstown) and the success which the rebels had in defeating them on reaching Mount Street Bridge. On Thursday we heard a rumour that the Wicklow Volunteers were advancing on Dublin from Tallaght. A friend and I set out to meet them. We got as far as Templeogue, meeting not a soul on the road. As nothing had been seen or heard of the Wicklow men in Templeogue we came home via the Green Lanes, stopping to carve our initials and the date on a beech tree to commemorate the rebellion which we thought was only beginning when, in fact, it was nearly over. Even as boys of fourteen and fifteen years of age, we were fully aware that something of great moment was happening in the history of the country.

Arthur Nolan brought us news of the surrender as he had seen the rebels evacuating Boland's Mill. He must have seen De Valera who commanded this post but, if he did, Dev made no special impression on him. A few days after the surrender patrols of British troops began to appear in the suburbs. Some people welcomed and consorted with them offering them cups of tea — hospitality well remembered and mentally recorded by the rebel sympathisers. At the same time the sympathisers kept their sympathy to themselves. My parents were terrified that I would say or do something to provoke reaction from the military because there was real fear of wholesale arrests in Dublin as was happening throughout the country. My father destroyed all the copies of *The Volunteer* and dozens of pamphlets which had accumulated in the house. The newspapers were back on the streets. In them we read condemnation upon condemnation of the madness or treachery of the insurgents. The executions began and the *Irish Independent* distinguished itself by calling for the execution of James Connolly who had been the bitter opponent of its proprietor, William

Martin Murphy, in the 1913 strike. Connolly was duly executed but, as a result of the *Independent's* attitude, many families swore that they would never let the paper into their houses again. Many have kept that promise until this day. The following is an extract:

> Certain of the leaders remain undealt with, and the part they played was worse than that of some of those who had paid the extreme penalty. Are they, because of indiscriminate demand for clemency, to get off lightly, while others, who were no more prominent have been executed?

The executions, which followed the defeat of the Volunteers, horrified the nation. The way in which they were spaced out compounded the barbarity. On 3 May, there were three; on the 4th there were four; on the 5th one. There was a pause until the 8th when there were four; on the 9th there was one, this time in Cork; another pause until the 12th, when the last two, Connolly and MacDermott went. It was not until 3 August they hanged Roger Casement in London.

When we went back to school after the Easter holidays, Brother Roche lined us up and lectured us in most circumspect terms about 'the time that we were in' and 'how very difficult it was for everyone' and 'how people had to be careful of what they said' and that 'some people did what they thought was right' and so forth and so on. But he got the message over to us which was to keep our mouths shut about the activities of the carefully unmentioned Mr Hayes, who taught us French and Irish. He of course knew that we knew and we knew he knew that we knew: Mr Hayes had been 'out' in the rebellion. He had escaped at the surrender. One of the boys in the class was his next door neighbour and the families were friends. For a month or two we all behaved as if nothing had happened but after that oblique references were made to the rebellion and after a little while we began to accept openly that he was one of its heroes. He did not deny the role. A couple of the boys in the class had British sympathies but they were far too decent to think of informing on him. Mr Hayes was subsequently the first Ceann Comhairle of the post-treaty Dáil Éireann, professor of Irish at University College, Dublin, a Senator, and in time he became the principal apologist for the Anglo-Irish Treaty.

The first open manifestation of the deep public feeling aroused by the executions was at the Month's Mind for the dead leaders. A Month's Mind is the Mass celebrated for the soul of a relative or friend a month after his death. It was the first opportunity that sympathisers of the rebels had to come out in the open. I went with my father to the first of the Month's Minds, which was for the brothers Pearse, at Rathfarnham. We arrived well in time for Mass but could not get into the church and the forecourt was packed right out to the road. I was surprised to see so many well-dressed and obviously well-to-do people present. The Volunteers I knew were shop assistants, small clerks, labourers or tradesmen. I did not realise that there was, quite apart from the effect of the rebellion and the executions on public opinion, a sizeable section of Irish nationalists, disillusioned with Redmond and the Irish Parliamentary party, who were anxious to find an alternative outlet for their beliefs. In the subconscious of every nationalist, there was a sympathetic response to rebellion.

I went to the other Month's Minds without my father — to Merchant's Quay, John's Lane and other city churches. For us young people these Masses were occasions for quite spontaneous demonstrations, shouting insults at the Dublin Metropolitan Policemen who were always around but, having learned their lesson during the 1913 strike, were anxious to avoid trouble. We jeered at the 'separation women' with their Union Jacks. The separation women were the wives of the soldiers in the British Army who lived on their separation allowances. They were very poor and were fanatically loyal to Britain. The allowance really did do something to relieve their poverty and the war was not at all that unpopular with them. They presented us youngsters (although we did not feel all that young at fourteen years of age) with a target at which to wave the tricolour and flaunt our rebel badges. These little badges displaying the green, white and orange flag became very commonly worn over the city as the months went by and evoked mutual recognition and sympathy among a large section of the people. We used to sing the 'Soldier's Song' and it was around this time that it first became popular as the signature tune of the Volunteers.

At that time, Rathmines people represented for nearly all Dubliners the ultra respectable section of the city with social aspirations disproportionate to their means. The Rathmines accent was a stamp of affectation and parodying it was a common form of amusement. 'The mutting is rotting in Britting Street' (the mutton is rotten in Britain Street) was a favourite example. There were many West Britons in Rathmines; the women in particular served on every kind of war charity committee which would bring them into contact with the garrison or the Castle establishment. In the ordinary way when coming home from school we always rode on the top of the trams but whenever we saw these women coming in numbers from some meeting or other decorated with red, white and blue favours, we made it our business to invade the lower deck of the tram wearing our tricolour badges as conspicuously as possible, talking loudly of any and every British setback in the war. The Battle of Jutland, especially the first accounts of it, was a great satisfaction to us and we exploited it fully. We were delighted when Kitchener was drowned, though not any more pleased than his colleagues in the British Cabinet, as it subsequently transpired. We talked loudly, to the evident disgust of the other tram passengers, of the great German victories and the possibility of a German invasion and what in that event we would do with General Maxwell who had been the executioner-in-chief of the rebels. It was not good-mannered conduct, but we were very embittered. No doubt we were branded as 'proper brats'.

These few months following the rebellion had an effect on me and many of my contemporaries which determined our future way of life. The executions imprinted on my young mind an abiding hatred of British domination in Ireland. Ireland and its destiny became an obsession which was to remain with me for the rest of my life. I made a resolution, in conformity with the stated aims of Wolfe Tone, to do my utmost 'to subvert the tyranny of our execrable Government, to break the connection with England, the never-failing source of all our political evils, and to assert the independence of my country — these are my objects'. I hope I have kept my resolution.

We read everything that was published about the rebellion and about its leaders. The 'mosquito press' had been suppressed and the only sympathetic publication was the *Catholic Bulletin,* with its thumbnail biographies of the leaders. A favourable comment from anyone of prominence, like the Bishop of Limerick, was music to our ears.

Little as we cared about the British Parliament we were deeply touched by the speech which John Dillon, the leader of the Irish party, made in the House of Commons: 'I say I am proud of their [the rebels] courage and if you were not so dense and stupid as some of you English people are you would have these men fighting for you ... It is not murderers who are being executed; it is insurgents who have fought a clean fight however misguided, and it would have been a damn good thing for you if your soldiers were able to put up as good a fight as these men did in Dublin'. I have never forgotten this powerful protest for his memory. We heard with joy about the protests made by the Irish organisations in America and the evident embarrassment these were causing to the British Government.

We attended British Army recruiting meetings at cross roads and interrupted the speakers. At the start of the war many leaders and hangers-on of the Irish Party appeared on the recruiting platforms. After 1916 only ex-officers of the British Army took part in these proceedings and recruiting dropped to insignificant proportions. We helped to collect parcels for the prisoners transported to English jails and internment camps and to raise money for the National Aid and Prisoners' Dependants' Fund. Mrs Kerrigan, a neighbour of ours, organised on her own initiative the collection of the food parcels and took them over in person to Knutsford, where most of our local Volunteers were prisoners. She was a working class woman, a mother of a large family, and had indomitable spirit and patriotism. She was typical of the rising spirit of the nation.

One of the rallying points for Sinn Féin sympathisers was a series of concerts given in the Mansion House for the prisoners' dependants. Patriotic songs and recitations worked the packed audience into a frenzy, the most popular item being a recitation given by a very beautiful young woman resplendent in the highly romanticised kilt and cloak of the 'Inghine na hÉireann' (Daughters of Ireland). It began:

> God's curse be on you England!
> God strike you London town!

We went to Gaelic League classes and when the prisoners were released from the English internment camps at Christmas, 1916, we went to meet them at Westland Row Station and cheered them all over the city.

School became a secondary part of my life. We read Irish history no longer as a school subject but as something we wanted to know and understand. We went very often to the Abbey Theatre where we were enthralled by *John Bull's Other Island* and emotionally exhausted by *The Rising of the Moon*. This is, I think, the only Abbey play which, if he had written it, might have justified Yeats' lines:

> Did that play of mine send out
> Certain men the English shot?

Yeats certainly flattered himself in thinking that anything he ever wrote or did might have sent anyone out to die. In my opinion the Boucicault plays in the Queen's Theatre had much more influence in that direction than ever Yeats or the Abbey had. But the Kiltartan plays of Lady Gregory did give us, native Dubliners, a new slant on Irish life because we were nearly all totally ignorant of rural Ireland.

In the summer of 1916 I was sent down to Longford to keep company with my grand aunt, Kate Wilson, and her husband. The only son remaining at home in Longford — Hubert Wilson — had been arrested and deported to Knutsford in Cheshire, England. I think the real reason was that my parents thought I was making myself too politically boisterous in the neighbourhood and might get into trouble with the police.

That was my first real contact with rural Ireland and it was a strange world to me. A peculiar and very pleasant smell permeated the town of Longford and it took me a little time to realise that it came from turf smoke, turf being the universal fuel used locally. I saw a bog for the first time but only in the distance. I saw a fair for the first time: the bargaining, the hand-slapping, the luck penny, the shouting and the ballad singers, the donkey cars and the turf creels, the three card trick men, the pedlars and crowded noisy pubs, the bundles of pound notes. It was all wonderful to me.

I also saw an Assizes for the first and only time, with the Judge sitting in a carriage in full-bottomed wig and scarlet robes, escorted by cavalry with drawn swords and guards giving salute, and the silent crowds looking on. There were plenty of Union Jacks around, despite the fact that a few months later Longford was to elect a Sinn Féin M.P. in what was one of the critical elections in Irish history. I met some of the boys of the town and we went swimming in the shallow, sluggish, muddy-bottomed Camlin river, a great contrast to my tumbling gravel-bottomed Dodder.

We went for picnics on bicycles to Castleforbes with its glorious woods and I marvelled at the width of the line of reeds along the river Shannon. My grand aunt Kate and my uncle Joe were politically very conscious as well as very religious. My aunt had been an active anti-Parnellite. She was reputed to have turned up at one of the Parnell meetings with a hatchet under her cloak and had been dissuaded from throwing it at the platform by her very gentle husband. The Parnellite period was as vividly real to Aunt Kate in 1916 as the Civil War is to my generation or to such of us as have survived it.

Aunt Kate was a formidable woman. She was almost the exact opposite of her sister, my gentle grandmother. She spoke with very precise diction and had an air of authority and decision. She fully approved of the rebellion, having lost faith in the Irish Party. Once my uncle remarked to me in his mild voice and kindly manner that, despite everything, Parnell was a good man. In her most level tone, putting the matter beyond dispute or futher discussion, Aunt Kate said 'Sir, Parnell was not a good man, he was a thoroughly bad man'. I was frozen by the intensity of her feeling and had no difficulty in resisting the temptation to ask about the truth of the hatchet story.

This incident gave me a better insight into the deep animosities of that period than any history book could have done. It was easy for me, later on, to understand perfectly the Christmas party scene in James Joyce's *Portrait of the Artist as a Young Man*. I could see my Aunt Kate as the hysterically angry anti-Parnellite Dante crying 'God and Religion before the world' at Mr Casey and his defiant reply: 'Very well then (he shouted hoarsely) if it comes to that, no God for Ireland'. I doubt if any Mr Casey ever faced Aunt Kate's frightening stare.

It was said, possibly apocryphally, that Ewart Wilson (Aunt Kate's son and my mentor) who was born when Parnell was the uncrowned King of Ireland, was to have been christened Patrick Stewart, with Stewart as his common name. When Parnell fell out of favour, the first two letters were removed from his name and he was called Ewart, after Gladstone. It was by this name he was always known.

When we returned to school in the autumn of 1916 to start on the last stage of our preparation for a career, I was nearly fifteen years of age. I had grown quickly like a weed and was as thin as a bean pole. On account of my height I was the butt of endless teasing: 'Eh Mister is it cold up there' and 'Hand me down a star' and 'lampost'. In addition to being abnormally tall and thin, I was inflicted with unusually prominent buck teeth and a long nose. Outside my own environment I became self conscious, shy and aggressive. My brother, whose existence I had virtually disregarded, was now ten and he came with me to Synge Street. On account of the difference in age between my brother and myself, we were each brought up as an only child. Although there were only four of us in the household, the only meal at which we sat down together was Sunday dinner. My brother and I slept in separate rooms, we had our breakfast in bed, our mid-day dinner at different times, our companions were different.

It was not until my brother came to school in Synge Street that I had any real contact with him. Even then it was minimal. I was expected to 'keep an eye on him' but that presented no problem because he was fortunate in arriving at Synge Street at a time when the Brothers were beginning to organise games and theatricals. He did not require any assistance from me at school. He turned out to be a natural athlete, bringing honour to the school by winning the schoolboy all-round athletic championship of Ireland. He was equally successful as a hurler, a Gaelic footballer and when he grew up, a soccer player. He became a full international soccer player and captain of Bohemians. He loved music and theatricals; in his later years he became president of the famous Bohemians Musical Society (nothing to do with the football team). With the warm support of our mother, he developed a loathing of politics of any brand which persisted through his life.

* * * * *

In March, 1917, I joined the Rathfarnham Company of the Volunteers. I was fifteen. For the moment I ceased to regard my schooling as a stepping stone to earning a living. I devoted almost my entire energy to preparing myself physically and psychologically for the next stage of the rebellion: The Volunteers, both before and after 1916, were organised on the model of the British Army with brigades, battalions, companies, right half companies, left half companies, sections and squads. At Company level, there was an O.C. or Captain, First and Second Lieutenant, Adjutant and Quarter Master. The Company organisation also provided for an Intelligence Officer. There was a Company Council consisting of a Captain, Lieutenant, Adjutant and Quarter Master. The training, such as it was, followed the British system as laid down in the army training manual which was freely to be bought in Eason's bookshop.

The Rathfarnham Company, designated 'E', was part of the Fourth Battalion, Dublin Brigade, and, unlike the rest of the Brigade, the Company area, apart from Terenure, was mainly rural and extended from the Dodder River to the mountains and from Templeogue and Firhouse on the west as far as Milltown on the east. The area was policed by the Royal Irish Constabulary and not by the Dublin Metropolitan Police.

St Enda's School was situated nearly in the middle of the Company area and 37 men from 'E' Company had left Rathfarnham with Pearse on Easter Monday, 1916. When I joined in March, 1917, I was one of the few members of the Company that had not been with Pearse in the General Post Office. I was recruited by a friend and neighbour of mine, who thought it would be better to belong to a Company outside our own parish as we would be less under the eye of the police. It was not too easy to join the Volunteers then. You had to have a proposer and seconder. This was not a mere formality. Enquiries were made into a candidate's background. You also had to pay a subscription of 3d per week. I arrived wearing a 'skull basher' as a school cap was called. I was told to wear something more appropriate at my next parade.

My first parade was in Butterfield Lane on a Sunday morning in March, 1917. I felt very nervous and very much the odd man out among the heroes of the GPO. We went on a short route march and dispersed in time for dinner. Afterwards we met once a week in the granary of the old mill at Willbrook in which we installed a vaulting horse, parallel bars and a medicine ball to give it the appearance of a gymnasium rather than a drill hall. I am sure the local RIC were not in the least deceived as to the purpose of the gymnasium but the sergeant was on the point of retirement, one of the constables was courting the sister of one of the Volunteers and the others, except for one who was a very bad type, wanted to avoid trouble. The exception finally joined the 'murder gang' which was organised from a squad of RIC men drawn from all over the country who roamed the city in civilian clothes and were a trigger happy band of thugs. It was this character who recognised me one morning in 1921 as I walked into the murder gang in Summerhill only to be arrested and marched to the Castle.

Gradually many of the older men dropped out of the Company and new men came in, especially from Terenure, so I renewed contact with several of the lads with whom I used to play in Shaw's Wood and with whom I swam in the Dodder when we were mere children. After a while, we had sufficient Terenure men to form a half Company. The duty of the different ranks had to be duplicated. Having plenty of time on my hands and being most anxious to undertake any responsibility, I carried out, as occasion required, the duties of Adjutant, Assistant Quarter Master, Section Commander and Squad Commander.

Whilst our headquarters were at the old mill in Willbrook, we did not meet there regularly. Each week we were notified where to meet and whether to bring sticks or not; the sticks served us in lieu of rifles. I used to notify the Terenure men and the mobilisation note was most peremptory and very formal: 'You will parade in Stockton Lane on Wednesday 7 June at 7.30 p.m. Bring sticks' and signed with an undecipherable signature. We drilled once a week: 'Move to the right in fours; form fours'.

There were NCO classes for the battalion in a hall in Camden Street or in the old St Enda's in Oakley Road. Sometimes we used the library in Ballyboden for first aid classes and on Saturdays some of us went to a house in Thomas Street where we cast concrete grenades, shaped like Mills bombs, filled them with gelignite and fitted them with detonators. Of all the activities that I engaged in this was

96

the one I liked least. All the time I handled the gelignite, I was afraid it was going to explode in my hand. As well as this, the handling of the material was reputed to produce some form of skin disease. It was also a futile exercise because when we tested the grenades at Tymon Castle, near Tallaght, they exploded in a cloud of dust instead of in fragments as a Mills bomb would have done. We had a few real Mills bombs in the Company and later on we claimed that we were the first of the Dublin Volunteers to have used them against the British.

The regular attendance at our weekly parade hardly ever exceeded twenty men and these were the hard core of the Company. There were possibly another twenty who were excused parade for one reason or another but were expected to be available, if called on, to do intelligence work, steward meetings, do dispatch riding and attend public funeral parades. The members of 'E' Company were drawn entirely from the lower middle and working class. They were labourers, printers, grocers' assistants, van drivers, junior civil servants, engine drivers, mechanics, painters, milkmen, stone cutters, blacksmiths, university students, plumbers, carpenters and gardeners. They are nearly all dead now. I knew them well and, with a couple of exceptions, the 'revolution' did not in any way alter their economic circumstances except that a few of the labourers got jobs as messengers and gate keepers in Government Buildings or preventive officers in Customs and Excise at Dun Laoghaire or the North Wall. Without them and their like throughout the country, there would have been no Irish Ambassadors in the Holy See or in the Court of St James. Our historians might remember this:

> Parnell came down the road, he said to the cheering man;
> Ireland shall get her freedom and you still break stone.

The Company meetings, whether in the old mill at Willbrook or in some remote centre round Ballyboden or Templeogue, always began with roll call and the collection of the weekly 3d. subscription. The Quartermaster was Paddy Donnelly who was a very fine gentle character. He seemed to us an old man but he was only in his late forties. He had been with Pearse in the GPO. By occupation ne was a greenkeeper in the Grange Golf Club. In 1917 his official duties were not very onerous. The Company's armament consisted of one .22 rifle, a shot gun and two .22 revolvers and he looked after them. There was a meeting of all the Company Quartermasters of the Battalion once a month. Phil Cosgrave was Battalion Quartermaster and the meetings were held in his house at James' Street where he lived with his brother, William T. Cosgrave, who much later succeeded Arthur Griffith as President of the Free State. Phil was later Governor of Mountjoy Prison; the Civil War literally broke his heart. Like so many of the Volunteers of the time, soldiering was alien to his nature. He was a Volunteer only as a matter of belief in the Fenian tradition — according to P. H. Pearse.

The regular attenders at our 'E' Company parade were mainly men in their late teens or early twenties; the older ones who had fought in 1916 attended fewer and fewer meetings. I think most of the later recruits felt that we had been very unfortunate not to have been 'out' in 1916. Though we were in any case too young to have taken part in the Rebellion, we felt a sense of guilt for not having been actively involved. To the extent that any of us thought about the future of the Volunteers, or what we were training for, it was to start another, and perhaps a bigger 1916 insurrection, but in fact I don't think we gave any thought at all to the future military objectives of the Volunteers. We had not even heard of Seán O'Casey or of his claim to have been the proponent of guerilla tactics. Guerilla tactics were never mentioned.

In the meantime some of us enjoyed the drilling and marching and the very rare occasion when we had what was rather grandiloquently known as musketry practice with our .22 rifle, for which we never had enough ammunition to give any individual more than three shots at the target. We were young and there was a lot of the boy scout spirit amongst us. We also had the universally satisfying feeling that comes from belonging to an exclusive club or to any group of conspirators. We were enthusiasts in the sense in which Father Ronald Knox describes the nature of 'enthusiasm' in relation to the Church: 'There is, I would say, a recurrent situation in Church history — using the word "Church" in the widest sense — where an excess of charity threatens unity. You have a clique, an *elite* of Christian men and (more importantly) women who are trying to live a less worldly life than their neighbours; to be more attentive to the guidance (directly felt they will tell you) of the Holy Spirit. More and more by a kind of fatality you see them draw apart from their co-religionists, a hive ready to swarm . . .' If we substitute the Irish nation for the Church, a belief in physical force for charity and the dead generations of separatists for the Holy Spirit, it seems to me a perfect description of the standpoint of the deeply committed Irish Volunteer who was active from 1916 until 1924.

At that time, we who were in the 'Movement' had created for ourselves what was in effect a mystical view of Ireland. In the matter of religion we lived our lives in the age of Faith, much as had any

98

thirteenth century schoolboy. We subscribed to an association known as 'The Holy Childhood'. We had a subscription card on which we punched holes for every penny subscribed. On the front of the card was an oleograph showing nuns with fly-away headresses pulling Chinese female babies out of a river into which they were thrown by their parents because they were regarded as economically useless. Each of our pennies bought a baby and prevented it being thrown into the river, a soul being saved as well as a body. Thinking of this barbarity, I enquired from Brother Roche why it was that Divine Revelation was made only to the Western world while there were millions and millions of Chinese and Indians and Africans left in pagan darkness. Poor Roche was so taken aback that I think it must have been the first time in his whole life that he had heard anyone question our religious beliefs. He muttered something about the inscrutability of God's design and the matter was dropped. But not in my mind.

With our profound Catholic faith it would have been quite impossible for us to imagine ourselves breaking the First Commandment 'I am the Lord thy God. Thou shalt not have strange Gods before me'. Even if we wanted to we could not have found a little yellow idol to light joss sticks to, but we created a god from our own minds. Eoin MacNeill once pointed out, and well before the Rebellion, that there was no such person as 'Caitlín Ní Uallacháin' nor 'Róisín Dubh' nor the 'Sean Bhean Bhocht', who was calling on us to serve her, nor was our country a political abstraction. James Connolly made the same point when he declared that Ireland, apart from its people, had no meaning for him. Well, it had for us and so too had 'Caitlín Ní Uallacháin', 'Róisín Dubh' and the 'Sean Bhean Bhocht'.

Our Ireland was an Ireland which had nothing to do with economics, property, or with how people lived or loved or prayed. It had in fact become a political abstraction, and from Caitlín Ní Uallacháin, Roisín Dubh and the Sean Bhean Bhocht proceeded the Republic. The fact that we had never seen any of these mythical personalities did not dismay us. We had been taught to believe profoundly in God and the Holy Spirit, neither of whom we had ever seen; our whole upbringing had been based on mysteries, glorious, sorrowful and joyful.

The Sinn Féin Clubs, of which hundreds sprang up around the country towards the end of 1917, began to attract more and more members. The Volunteers encouraged the formation of these clubs and we arranged to form one in Rathfarnham. Our club met in one of the old class rooms of St Enda's which had remained closed since the

Rising. The membership included some very old men, usually trades-men and labourers, as well as women of various ages and conditions of life. There were girls who served in shops or worked in laundries and some secretaries. Other of the women members were housewives with very strong feelings on the subject of women's rights. Although they never had any clear notion of what these rights should be they had a feeling that something was wrong with the status of women in the community. In the beginning they wanted the vote, which they got in 1918 (but only on reaching thirty years of age). This was a sufficient grievance on which to hang many a debate. The men in the club were astonishingly conservative not merely on that issue but on all sorts of social questions. It might be expected that men who were prepared to support a rebellion against the political status quo would have shown some liberality of view but they had no sympathy for any campaign to rectify the disabilities suffered by women. It was sur-prising even to me, who at that time had no fixed ideas on the subject, how bitter a debate could become on the matter of women's rights. The suffragettes were not popular in the 'Brothers Pearse' Sinn Féin Cumann. Social questions such as housing, land division, public health, education, were seldom discussed and generally the subjects for debate were of the 'England's difficulty, Ireland's opportunity' variety, or 'Is it true that the women are worse than the men', the latter being a quotation from a popular ballad.

Most members of the club and indeed of the Volunteer Company had some knowledge of Irish history even if only its high spots. They knew about Dermot McMurrough who had brought the English into Ireland. They knew about Kinsale and about the O'Neills and the O'Donnells and their flight to Europe but they would have been a bit vague as to the cause. They knew about Cromwell and the Drogheda and Wexford massacres. They knew nothing of the Battle of the Boyne except that King Billy won it and that he was to be seen in the fanlights of Protestant homes in statuette form, riding a white horse, or on his statue in College Green. They knew he was the hero of the Orangemen. The Penal Laws were known about and it was accepted that Daniel O'Connell was a coward because he called off the Clon-tarf meeting and, what was worse in the eyes of the Sinn Féin club members of 1917-21, he was a politician.

The club members would have known of Robert Emmet and Wolfe Tone but Emmet was their darling. I doubt if any of them passed the spot in Thomas Street, where he was executed, without saying a prayer. They knew about the Famine, the Manchester Martyrs, Parnell and the Boer War and finally, they knew with deep bitterness about what was regarded as Redmond's national betrayal when he offered England the service of the Volunteers in 1914. For the members of the club, Redmond was the epitome of politicians in general and all politicians were regarded as low, dirty and treacherous. This was the attitude of the Volunteers as well as of the members of the Sinn Féin clubs.

On the other hand, T.D.s, i.e. the members of the Dáil, were not regarded as politicians. At the level of a Sinn Féin Club or of a Volunteer Company the method of selecting T.D.s was unknown, although it was assumed that anyone becoming a T.D. was actively involved in and dedicated to the Movement. There was no particular advantage in being a T.D.; in those days they did not get a salary. One thing was certain, a T.D. had to be acceptable to the Volunteers; in effect that meant to Collins and the IRB. From 1916 to 1921 there were no political processes as we now know them, except of course in the North East where the Nationalist majority did not come over en masse to Sinn Féin.

The Company did not take the deliberations of the Sinn Féin Club seriously but recognised its utility as a means of collecting money for the arms fund and for the prisoners' dependants and as a cover for the Volunteer activities. With the help of the club members, céilidhte (Irish dancing only — the High Caul Cap and the Walls of Limerick, being the easiest, were the favourites) and concerts were run in the library at Ballyboden. A dramatic society was formed which put on plays also for the arms fund or the prisoners' dependants. At these functions I confined my participation to collecting money at the entrance.

It was surprising how often it became possible, if the money was available, to get a revolver, usually from some British soldier. A very mean-minded neighbour, a publican in Terenure, sent word that he wanted to see me and when I called on him I was brought into a snug where, after a lot of talk, he offered me a .38 revolver for £5. I thought he should have given the gun to us for nothing (anyway it was not worth £5) but, before handing it back to him, I fired a shot through the floor of the snug. In the confined space the noise of the explosion was disproportionately loud and the publican was thoroughly frightened. He decided to give me the gun for nothing provided I took it away at once, which of course I did.

Whenever there was a big political meeting I tried to be there and I was in the crowd outside Liberty Hall when Inspector Mills was killed by a blow of a hurley while the police were trying to arrest Cathal Brugha and Count Plunkett. We regarded the Irish Convention, set

101

up by Lloyd George to draw up proposals for the government of Ireland, as a fraud, as indeed it was. When, as a gesture of 'goodwill' to the Convention, the 1916 prisoners who had been given long-term sentences were released from English jails we went to greet them in our thousands. We were lifted to a high emotional plane by this event. There was also the excitement of Tom Ashe's death on hunger strike and his wonderful funeral when the whole Dublin Brigade marched openly in military formation. It was a heady wine for a youngster to be walking through College Green as a soldier of Ireland.

I felt proud to be selected by my Company to help steward the Sinn Féin Ard Fheis of 1917. I had two problems: one was to get off school and the other was the shame of being seen in my father's hat (which I had to wear instead of my school cap) by friends of my parents or my own school companions. As for getting off school, I told Brother Roche that my parents wanted me to stay at home for a few days. It would never have occurred to me to 'mitch' as I had never had any reason for not wanting to go to school. I was disappointed that my stewarding assignment was outside the Mansion House and not inside. All the same, I saw De Valera and Cathal Brugha but not Michael Collins although at that time Collins would not have meant very much to me. As a boy of sixteen it was a stimulus to my imagination to see the great ones of the nation at close quarters. They were all great, none of them had feet of clay. 'Bliss was it in that dawn to be alive, but to be young was very heaven!'

There was always something happening to occupy one's time or interest. One afternoon my mother sent me into town to get her some message and I saw a small crowd standing round the front gate of Trinity College, where the Lloyd George Convention was sitting, waiting to see the members coming out. One of the first to emerge was John Redmond, the Irish Party leader, always referred to by us, derisively, as Johnny Redmond. He was easily recognisable and someone in the crowd began to boo. The booing was taken up by the rest of us and as the crowd grew larger and larger the boos grew louder and louder while Redmond walked along Westmoreland Street. By the time he reached *The Irish Times* office, the crowd was transformed into a threatening mob. Some passers-by with a sense of responsibility threw a cocoon round Redmond taking him into the office of *The Irish Times*; the crowd then dispersed. One of the passers-by who stepped in to rescue Redmond was, I learned afterwards, R. C. Barton, who was to be a signatory of the Treaty in 1921. I am quite sure that if any of the mob had offered physical violence to Redmond I would have joined in.

Heckling and interrupting recruiting meetings for the British Army, which became fewer and fewer as conscription was threatened, provided amusement and activity for us. One afternoon I met Earle as I left school and, having nothing much to do, we went to a recruiting meeting in the Mansion House, positioning ourselves in the gallery. The fairly big audience was made up largely of well-dressed women and oldish men. The speakers on the platform were all in uniform. They were nearly all officers speaking with either what was known as the Rathmines accent or an upper class English accent. After every sentence from the platform Earle and I shouted a derisive 'Heah, heah'. To our delight a few people on the opposite side of the gallery took up the cry and soon other voices chimed in, so that a regular chant of 'heah, heah' made it impossible for the speakers to continue and the meeting dispersed. It was a minor triumph for us.

The anti-conscription campaign gave us plenty to do, organising protest meetings and gathering signatures for the anti-conscription pledge and money for the anti-conscription fund. At the same time, we had many offers to join the Company, but being selective in those we were prepared to accept, many who wanted to join we directed to the Sinn Féin Clubs instead.

Early in 1918 we got a new Company Captain. He was what we regarded as an oldish man, from West Cork, named F. X. Coughlan. At that time Coughlan was in his late thirties, married with two children. He was a man of medium height who spoke quietly in a soft Cork accent. To us he seemed very mature. He was an attractive personality. We felt he was a man we could trust. He had a very striking face dominated by a spiky nose. On a visit to Venice many years later I saw Verrochio's famous equestrian statue of the Condottiere Colleoni. Colleoni's face might have been modelled from Coughlan's although it would be difficult to imagine anyone with less of the characteristics of a Condottiere than Coughlan. He had no ambitions for glory, possessions or power, and he was quite unwarlike. As I thought of the incongruity of Coughlan, helmeted and in armour, sitting on a charger I remembered that we Irish also had our heroes. Unfortunately we have no Verrochios; when we erect statues to our heroes we employ local stone masons so that posterity, looking at these statues, will have every reason to think that the Volunteers of the Army of Independence were mini-men, or that we had invented a new art form — a kind of bonsai sculpture — to perpetuate their memory.

Coughlan had been 'out' in 1916, as a result of which he lost his job in the Civil Service where he had been a junior member of the staff of the Land Commission. When he returned from internment in Frongoch he got a small job in the National Aid organisation and when the New Ireland Assurance Company was formed by the internees he became an agent, which meant that he collected money weekly from door to door from his clients. It was a poor enough living, but it had the advantage when he had to go 'on the run' that he did not have to give up his job. He was a rare bird to find in the Volunteers. He had mildly socialist views — the only one amongst my friends and acquaintances who had, with the exception of my father. My father did not know he was a socialist though he would have agreed with Flaubert, had he ever heard the phrase, that 'the beginning of wisdom is hatred of the bourgeois'. However, my father's dislike of the Dublin bourgeoisie could hardly be called socialism.

I don't think Coughlan had any very clear idea of what category of socialism he subscribed to. Like everyone else in the Movement he welcomed the Russian Revolution but most of us approved of it because it was a blow to the Allies and helped the Germans; not because we were concerned about the peasants or the workers of Russia. Coughlan was very conscious that there was no social content in the rebellion, despite the part played in it by James Connolly. Indeed, he was contemptuous of the Citizen Army; he thought they were useless and blamed them for ineptitude in failing to occupy the Castle in 1916. He regarded that incident and Austin Stack's botching of the great chance he had to rescue Casement from the RIC as two of the major blunders of 1916. He could never understand why Stack was brought back into the counsels of the nation, much less allowed to become a leader.

Coughlan became a father to the Company and to me in particular. All my life I seem to have been attracted to and influenced by much older men. Apart from my father, there was my cousin Ewart in my earlier boyhood, then Coughlan and later on R. C. Barton and, for much of my later life, De Valera. When Coughlan came to us, we assumed he was a member of the IRB, since we knew he was intimate with the leaders. In fact, he distrusted the IRB. Far from being a member, he would not allow any of us to join it on the grounds that as Volunteers we should not owe allegiance to any other organisation. On the other hand, Coughlan had a passion for secrecy which he instilled into the Company to such an extent that we never discussed the affairs of the Volunteers outside parades or ever sought to find out who were the senior officers beyond the Battalion level; these we met from time to time at NCO classes or manoeuvres, route marches, and funeral parades. Although I was very close to him, I never heard or saw any of the top men except for brief meetings with Clancy and McKee. McKee was the Brigadier of the Dublin Brigade who, with Clancy, was murdered by the British in Dublin in 1921.

One of the great strengths of the Volunteers and the IRA of our time was the secrecy which characterised the organisation. The British enemy was kept always guessing. No individual knew very much beyond his immediate concerns. The leaders gave no press conferences, made no threats and did not interview newsmen. Had there been television, they most certainly would not have appeared on it. There was no craving in the Volunteers of 1917 to 1921 for personal publicity. The very effective publicity and propaganda of the Movement was left to Sinn Féin.

Coughlan was not the most active of officers in organising military operations. He was inclined to restrain the younger members who wanted action, particularly against the RIC barracks in Rathfarnham, which seemed to many of the Company and particularly to the First Lieutenant, James Kenny, to be a standing rebuke to us. A view with which I agreed. Coughlan, probably inspired by GHQ, was convinced that if we attacked the RIC in Rathfarnham, St Enda's would be burned as a reprisal. But when the chips were down, Coughlan was no shirker.

Our First Lieutenant was James Kenny and he was in charge of the right half Company, the members of which lived in Terenure. He came from a family of four boys and two girls and, being the eldest, he was taken from school at the age of fourteen and apprenticed to the provision business. Kenny was typical of many of the Volunteers of 1916. He was a man of rather below middle height, fair haired and very serious in manner. The Volunteers was his only activity outside his work. He had some interest in golf but the only way he could get a game was to get up early in the morning and play a few holes on the links at Rathfarnham or the Grange. This was done surreptitiously but, with the connivance of the greenkeepers, before the possible arrival of members who, at that time, would have regarded Kenny and his like as 'gutties'.

Kenny had a 'Protestant drop' in him. His mother was a Protestant blacksmith's daughter from Shillelagh in Co. Wicklow and his father a small Catholic farmer's son. His parents eloped to Dublin and, after many vicissitudes in varying degrees of poverty, started their small dairy. Perhaps it was this 'Protestant drop' that produced in Kenny an extreme puritanism. He did not swear himself nor would he tolerate it in others. He did not smoke. Drink was anathema to him. Anyone in the Company who took the odd pint was un-acceptable as far as Kenny was concerned; they were not to be trusted. Very few of the Company did take pints, if for no other reason than that they could not afford it. Kenny's attitude to drink was not untypical of the Volunteers. 'It was the drink that got us down' was part of the folk wisdom of the Movement; the disasters of the Wexford men in 1798 were commonly believed to have been due to drunkenness.

It was characteristic of Kenny's seriousness that having fallen in love with a neighbour's daughter — an exceptionally beautiful golden-haired 'flapper' of the twenties — he never let his eye wander and after a steady courtship of several years he married her. He regarded philandering as scarcely less objectionable than drink and he regarded philanderers, of whom there were several in the Company, as nearly as unreliable as drunkards, but in this prejudice he was in a minority.

Kenny adored the memory of Pearse but felt that the 1916 rising should have been less of a blood sacrifice and more of a country wide rebellion. He believed it would have been but for the opposition of Eoin MacNeill. Like Coughlan in regard to Stack, he believed, as indeed did many of the Volunteers, that it was a mistake to let MacNeill play any further part in the Movement. Kenny was a most enthusiastic Volunteer and never missed a parade or an officer's class and devoted himself to preparing for the day when a successful rebellion would redeem the failure of 1916. When the shooting began, the fear of St Enda's being burned did not inhibit the activities of his half Company.

The Second Lieutenant in the Company was Frank Burke. Frank had been at St Enda's as a school boy and was one of Pearse's favourite pupils. He never left St Enda's, taking his degree in UCD from there, and he stayed on as a teacher. He went 'out' with Pearse in 1916 and was interned in Frongoch. When he was released the British soldiers were in occupation of St Enda's and the school was restarted in Oakley Road where Frank resumed teaching but, more than this, he became a kind of surrogate son of Mrs Pearse. He devoted his life to the interests of the Pearse family, Mrs Pearse and her daughters, Margaret and Mary Bridget. It was an important responsibility and his duties in St Enda's, even when the school returned to the Hermitage in Rathfarnham, were regarded as taking priority over his obligations to his half Company so that Coughlan undertook most of the Second Lieutenant's duties. It was not a very satisfactory arrangement and Frank Burke was, I thought, a great loss to the Company. He had been a famous All-Ireland footballer and hurler for his native county of Kildare. While it is true that proficiency as a hurler or Gaelic footballer was less important on the national scene than it later became, Frank, with his close connection with Pearse and his conduct in the GPO, where he had shown conspicuous bravery and leadership, could have been a political power in the land. He had the advantage of being better educated than the average member of the Company as well as having an exceptionally pleasant and modest personality.

We had only a few married men in the Company. Two of them were neighbours of mine in Terenure and I was very friendly with them. One was Arthur Nolan, the baker in Boland's who had kept us in touch with the progress of the insurrection. It was he who caused me to join 'E' Company. He was a frail red-headed man and his complexion was such that his face always seemed to be covered with flour. He worked on shifts, which made it difficult to attend regularly for parade; it also made it hard for him to have much free time with his family and, of course, the family never had a holiday. Like most of the men in the Movement, he loathed drink. Life was hard for him but whatever time he had was given unsparingly to the Movement. Just as Paddy Donnelly knew what went on in Rathfarnham, Nolan knew everything that was happening in Terenure — who was with us and who against. Local knowledge of this kind was part of the strength of the Volunteers.

My other neighbour in the Volunteers was Johnny Tully. He was a box maker in Jacob's biscuit factory and had a wife and two small children. He lived in rather less than frugal comfort in one room in a small house in Terenure. He was something of a health fanatic, his particular hobby being long distance running. Once a week, winter and summer, he togged out and ran about five miles along the road from Terenure around Whitehall and Templeogue. Once he induced me to accompany him but by the time we finished the course I was exhausted. I realised that marathon running was not for me. Tully, if he could have afforded it, would have been something of a dandy. He always changed into his best clothes for parade and emulated the discipline of the British soldier. Talking to Coughlan on parade, he insisted on standing to attention and calling him 'Sir'. He thoroughly enjoyed parades and route marches. If he had been born into different circumstances he could have done well as a scout master.

From time to time in a long life, I have met a few men who had all the qualities that I regarded as most admirable. Kevin O'Carroll was only sixteen when he went 'out' with Pearse in 1916. He was beside

The O'Rahilly when the latter was killed in Moore Street; Kevin himself was badly wounded in the stomach. He was the son of a printer who was also a superb gardener and a herbalist. Old O'Carroll had the immense pride in his calling that was so commonly found amongst the Dublin tradesmen of his day. He was a grumpy, crotchety old man who absolutely tyrannised his family of two boys and two girls. He carried on a life-long feud with the nuns in Loreto Convent in Rathfarnham, who were his landlords, finally getting the better of them when a special Act of Parliament was passed by a sympathetic Government to meet his case. He was a very hospitable man, his house being open to any of the 1916 men who were out of work.

Whether he liked it or not Kevin was sent into the printing business, a closed shop reserved for sons of the Printers' Union. Kevin, being dutiful, became a printer and was very happy. If he had been a street cleaner or a civil servant he would have been happy too, because he had the qualities of goodness and generosity of mind. Arland Ussher, in his very perceptive book *The Face and Mind of Ireland,* points out that there are two words in Irish for a good man viz. *dea-dhuine* and *duine maith*. Roughly speaking as I interpret it, the *dea-dhuine* is the decent man, the man with the warm heart, who may not be too particular about paying his debts and who might borrow from one person to lend to another. He would lend you his spade or his scythe but might not be too scrupulous about his religious duties. The *duine maith* (or 'good person') is above all very punctilious about his religious practices and takes to heart the advice of Polonius about being neither a borrower nor a lender. Kevin O'Carroll had none of the defects and all the good qualities of both these types. He was always even tempered, patient and kind in deed and word. He never spoke badly of anyone, not even the British, who had treated him very well when he was wounded. He was, as far as the country went, a complete idealist, no work being too humble or difficult if of some service to the national interest. In his old age he spent day after day helping physically in the restoration of Kilmainham Jail. He never complained of the tyranny which compelled him to spend so much of his little spare time working in his father's garden and, when he became a father himself, he was adored by his children. He had no ambitions to have anything more than could be gained from the hard work of his trade or to be anything except a good Irish citizen.

It would be wrong to give the impression that all the men in our Company were saints. We were the successors of the legendary army of the Fianna and, no less than they, we had our Conán Maol, our Bricriu and our Diarmuid. Conán Maol was an elderly horse coper, who gave the impression that he was a native Irish speaker by larding his talk with stage-Irish expressions such as *Acushla, Avick, Monom on jowl*. His approach was sufficiently effective to be able to collect good money for the Company funds. Cyril Connolly describes in *Enemies of Promise* a visit to a friend in Rathfarnham during which he was taken on a horse ride over the Dublin hills by a groom who was believed by his hosts to be in charge of the local battalion of the IRA. Our Conán Maol is easily identifiable as Connolly's guide; one can readily imagine the impression he made on Connolly.

It is said that the original Bricriu could raise blisters on those who were the subject of his satire. Our Bricriu was a handsome curly-haired bachelor mechanic from the country who professed no personal regard for anyone in the Company or the Sinn Féin Club. He particularly liked baiting the horse coper by talking Irish to him and teasing the more religious members of the Sinn Féin Club by reminding them of what the Bishop of Kerry said about the Fenians and how the priests denounced the rebels in 1798. Once, out of devilment, he nearly created a riot at the club by suggesting that Connolly was a greater man than Pearse and that Connolly was an atheist.

Our Diarmuid had a particularly large love spot, despite being a low barrel of a man. He knew and loved many of the servant maids living in the big houses round the Company area and thus we were kept informed of the movements of the owners and their guests and whether or not arms were kept in their mansions. Unlike alcohol, sex was not regarded as a security risk.

Without exception, the men in the Company were men of no property, except for what little furniture the few married men had accumulated. Their houses or apartments were rented. But they were all in regular employment and even if their jobs were menial, very badly paid and rarely secure, none of them were destitute. They had a minimum of food, shelter and clothing. Being members of the Volunteers gave all of us, whatever our circumstances, a purposefulness and sense of comradeship we would not otherwise have enjoyed. The amusements and distractions open to the young men of the lower middle and working classes of that time were very limited indeed. Very occasional visits to the cinema, playing or watching Gaelic or soccer football — hurling was seldom played or watched and rugby was neither played, watched nor even read about — country walks or, if there was a bicycle available, cycling trips, an annual visit to the Queen's Theatre were the usual recreational outlets. The parish missions, given annually by the Redemptorist Fathers, were also regularly attended. These missions were an important event in the life of the County Dublin parishes because not merely did they give the young people an occasion to repent the sins they probably did not know they had committed but also gave an excuse to boys and girls to stay out late without questions being asked. It was well known in our parish of Terenure and Crumlin that after the evening mission ceremonies were over it was difficult for a courting couple to find a niche in the local lovers' rendezvous, the Green Lanes on the Kimmage Road. The Green Lanes provided a coarse form of amusement for younger boys — 'clodding the mots' — a game which consisted in finding a pair of lovers stretched in embrace and interrupting their passion by throwing sods of grass and earth on top of them. The Green Lanes are now built up and called by the ridiculous name of Greenlea Road, just as the historic and once beautifully named Butterfield Lane, also in our Company area, has become Butterfield Avenue.

In February, 1918, the Dublin Companies were asked for volunteers to help in the South Armagh election and, of course, although it was in the school term I volunteered to go. However, I ran into the most unexpected difficulties. I asked my mother for my fare to Armagh but she not merely turned down my request for the money but refused outright to let me go. I could hardly believe that she was serious so little difficulty had I, as a rule, in getting my own way. I knew it was not a question of the expense which was little enough. I was so surprised at this opposition that I became very angry, shouted at my mother, accused her of being a West Briton and told her that I would get the money from my father and furthermore I was not going to live with her any more. My mother, letting me rave on, turned on me her coldest light-blue eyes — they seemed to me like the eyes of a fish — and her Mona Lisa smile. She made no comment beyond asking if I understood that I was not to go to Armagh. I repeated that I would leave the house for good and that I would get the money from my father. Leave the house I did, having taken sixpence from the till (I had always permission to take money from the shop till but was expected to mention the fact) to pay my tramfare to my father's office in Capel Street.

My father, who had just sold what was known as a rummage sale, welcomed me heartily and took me into his office wondering what was the reason for the visit. I told him of my mother's unreasonable behaviour and asked him for the money to go to Armagh and I pressed him to rent me a room in town as I was not prepared to live with my mother any more. My father listened with an expressionless face; he made no mention of Armagh but said: 'No, I won't set you up in a room on your own, but I tell you what — I'll send your mother out of the house in Terenure. Would that suit you?' I was so flattened and flabbergasted by this retort that I muttered something, declined his offer of my tram fare and went back home to my evening meal of rasher and eggs. My mother said nothing, nor did I. I was contrite and speechless for about a week and in addition I had the humiliation of telling my Company Captain that my mother would not let me take part in the Armagh campaign because I should be attending school.

At the prompting of Michael Hayes, our teacher of Irish, who was a supporter and habitué of Ring Irish College, I asked my mother to let me go to Ring for the 1918 summer holiday course. She most willingly agreed, partly, I imagine, as compensation for refusing to allow me to volunteer for Armagh, or perhaps she thought I'd be out of political trouble for a while. She certainly did not care whether or not I learned Irish. Going so far away from home by myself was an adventure. I had never been out of Dublin except to Longford, Tullow or Wicklow where I always stayed with relatives. My father came to Kingsbridge station to see me off which was lucky for me because the money for my return ticket to Dungarvan was in my outside pocket and, while buying newspapers for the journey at the bookstall, my pocket was picked. My father had to come to the rescue with the price of a second ticket. The only other experience I had of pickpockets was many, many years later in Johannesburg when £800 (fortunately in travellers' cheques) was taken from me.

Ring in 1918 was a microcosm of resurgent Ireland. The people I met were of all ages from children to greybeards, boys and girls, men and women from all over the south-east of the country — Kilkenny, Wexford, South Tipperary, Wicklow and Waterford. There were only two families from Dublin apart from two (to me) elderly women national teachers whom I had met on the train on the way down to Dungarvan. The Dublin families with children ranging from eight to seventeen were those of a journalist and a civil servant. The rest of those attending the course were the sons and daughters of doctors, comfortable shopkeepers, 'warm' farmers, secondary and national teachers, one or two priests and two university professors. It was a representative sample of the essentially bourgeois classes, lower and middle, of which the Gaelic League was made up — the classes of the Language Movement which provoked so much flaccid derision from Seán O'Casey.

There was a feeling of common purpose throughout the College. In all its aspects the place was dominated by 'An Fear Mór'. He was, literally, the most conspicuous character in the language side of the Independence Movement. Six foot six inches in height, he had a very well built frame carrying a magnificent head which would have flattered the most noble of the Romans, or he might have been a descendant of the Fomorians or of their King Balor, minus the evil eye. He *was* the College. He organised the language classes, the music and dances, supervised the abundant if simple meals, kept his eye on the health and hygiene of the young people. He was omnipresent as well as being omniscient of everything that was happening in or about the College.

His great insistence was that everyone should speak Irish to whatever extent they knew it. It was surprising how easy it became in this environment to make an effort to speak Irish. None of the younger people in the College had such deep thoughts to communicate that they could not get by in Irish. If we broke into English we were almost bound to hear An Fear Mór's voice booming 'Béarla, béarla!' The camaraderie of the Movement made everyone of whatever age friendly, if not friends. There were endless activities over and above the classes; swimming and boating in Dungarvan Bay which was so shallow that it was possible to walk a mile from the shore without getting out of your depth. On the other hand, swimming at a place called Faill na Staicín beside Helvick Head, provided great breakers where it was a joy to dive in and be carried back on the swell to the sandy inlets. Football was played in a field running down to the cliffs on which the College was built. The fishermen from the adjacent village of Baile na nGall came up in the evening to play with us. They were big, very black-haired men, known locally as 'na Turcs'. It was said that they were the descendants of Barbary pirates who were wrecked on the coast around Helvick Head. I got very friendly with them. They had a Gaelic football team in which I was invited to play against a team from Kilrossanty. The game was played one Sunday evening in Dungarvan Park. Every time I got the ball two of the Kilrossanty players converged on me. I was the ham in the sandwich. I was tripped from the front or tripped from behind so that I never succeeded in kicking the ball. I was glad to get back to Ring with no bones broken. Many years later I read in the sports columns of the press that Kilrossanty Club had been permanently suspended from the GAA. I suppose standards had changed.

To me the Ring of 1918 was a fragment of the Ireland Pearse dreamed about and wrote about in *An Claidheamh Soluis*. Everyone appeared to be gay, good humoured, light-hearted, companionable — all inspired by the vision of a Gaelic Ireland. All appeared to me 'Kindly Irish of the Irish, neither Saxon nor Italian'. I came home enchanted.

Sinn Féin lost the election in Armagh. The Irish Party was still a force in the North and indeed I think it is fair to say that the Nationalists of what has since become the Six Counties never threw their full weight behind the campaign for establishing a Republic and complete separation. Even the IRA in Ulster do not appear to have had a very deep separatist conviction. When the Free State army was established in 1922, Northern IRA officers joined eagerly in great numbers and played a significant part in suppressing the second Dáil and in crushing the Republicans in the Civil War.

In pursuit of principle — I think it was the first time I understood the word which was to take on such a significance during the Treaty debates — I abandoned Dalymount Park and soccer football and joined the local GAA team, Terenure Sarsfields. I was young enough to play for the junior side and good enough to play for the senior side and I played for both. I was so very enthusiastic that one Sunday I cycled from Terenure to Crumlin to play a senior match against Crumlin Independents and afterwards cycled to the Phoenix Park to play a junior match against Clondalkin Round Towers and then cycled home for my dinner. My enthusiasm did not last. As a soccer player I had a poor opinion of Gaelic football. In my view three skills only were required for playing Gaelic football: a capacity to field a ball, ability to kick it high and hard in the direction of goal, and at least elementary boxing skills. Ball play, positioning, passing did not exist; the only tactics employed were to kick, rush, push and pull your opponent's jersey. I had neither the strength nor the temperament for that form of entertainment and in a game in the Phoenix Park, having endured many buffetings, I got into a fight with an opponent and both of us were rightly sent off by the referee. In due course I was summoned by the local GAA council to show cause why I should not be suspended but I had neither the time nor the inclination to put in an appearance in my defence. I was glad to sever my short association with the GAA although I did play Gaelic again later on in an internment camp, where no other game was permitted. I think Gaelic football is technically a bad game; to me it is a spectator sport to be avoided.

In any case I did not really approve of the GAA itself. I thought they were not making a real effort to propagate the Irish language and on the other hand I thought that their ban on foreign games and dances was just absurd. Finally, they were as much dominated by the priests as the Orange Order was by the parsons. They seemed to me to be as much a sodality as a sports organisation. These were the views commonly held by the Dublin 'Jackeens' of the time. What I did not appreciate was that but for the GAA, and their ban on foreign games and dances, rural Ireland would have been just as anglicised as was Dublin.

Every day as the revolt escalated, and a revolt it was indeed, there was some new reason for excitement: the election of De Valera for East Clare, the death of Tom Ashe and the defiant display of arms at his funeral, the appeals for help to America and the endless arrests and hunger strikes. The wild rage at the announcement by Lloyd George that the British intended to apply conscription to Ireland encouraged us in the Movement and assured us of the support of the people. The anti-conscription pledge—'denying the right of the British Government to enforce compulsory service in this country, we pledge ourselves solemnly one to another to resist conscription by the most effective means at our disposal' — was enthusiastically taken up by the people.

To us the pledge meant resistance in arms and we intensified our drilling and organisation but even at this stage it was not at all clear what form military action was to take. *An tÓglach,* the official organ of the Executive of the Volunteers, which began publication in August 1918, at that time gave no indication of a guerilla campaign being contemplated. On the contrary the second issue of *An tÓglach* in September 1918, visualised the organisation of the Volunteers in barracks and laid down in considerable detail the requirements for a Company of eighty. They included boilers for potatoes, suitable stoves for cooking, two cooks and two kitchen orderlies as well as mugs, knives, forks, spoons, ladles and large knives.

But the fourth issue of *An tÓglach* introduced a very different note, protesting against any thought of passive resistance and advocating a course of action which was in fact put into effect later on: 'We must', it said, 'recognise that anyone, civilian or soldier who assists directly or by connivance in this crime against us, merits no more consideration and should be killed without mercy or hesitation as opportunity offers. Thus, the man who serves on an exemption tribunal, the doctor who treats soldiers or examines them, the man who voluntarily surrenders when called for, the man who in any way, shape or form applies for exemption, the man who drives a police car or assists in the transport of army supplies, all these, having assisted the enemy, must be shot or otherwise destroyed with the least pos-

114

sible delay . . . If we fight with utter ruthlessness and ferocity and fling the full strength of our people everywhere against the enemy it is not impossible that he will recoil and seek a return to the status quo.'

This was a comprehensive blueprint for the 'terror' but the Volunteers of 1918 who may have read it would not have taken it as anything but rhetoric. At that time they were certainly not psychologically attuned to killing any individual except in pitched battle. When a few months later and after the danger of conscription was past, Dan Breen and his three companions, Robinson, Treacy and Hogan, acted on the letter of the *An tÓglach* decree and shot two policemen dead at Solohead in Tipperary, they got very little approval from either the Volunteers or the Movement generally. But the British soon changed that by declaring Tipperary a military area, harrassing the lives of the people. Breen always claimed that the Solohead shooting was a deliberately considered act, taken on his own initiative, to get the guerilla campaign started but I doubt that very much. I think it was an operation that just went wrong. Elsewhere many RIC had been disarmed without being killed. Nevertheless it did for the first time bring home to the Volunteers that the shooting war had started and quite a few of them decided, on grounds of conscience, that they could not continue.

Our Company had as yet no active contact with the military or police beyond a silly episode at a Victory parade and review in College Green of the British troops by Lord French, the Viceroy. The city was en fete with Union Jacks flying from every business premises and public building and thousands had congregated to watch the march past of the troops, armoured cars, tanks and artillery. It was an impressive display of force and of loyalty (or curiosity) on the part of the onlookers. The Dublin Brigade, such of us as could be armed, were mobilised and stationed at different points along the route of the procession from Cork Hill to Westmoreland Street. Earle and myself, each armed with a .22 revolver, were stationed at the corner of George's Street and Dame Street and were told to await orders to open fire on the troops. The absurdity of any such action was so patent that no order was given. A little boy lost in the crowd attached himself to Earle who passed his pearl-handled .22 to me and took the child to Brunswick Street Police Station which he reached with difficulty. If we had not justified ourselves as Volunteers, at least we had acted as good boy scouts.

An unexpected move by the British Army nearly succeeded in rounding up the whole Company while we were drilling in the fields around Firhouse, but we scattered and all of us got safely away. The soldiers must have had orders not to fire because they saw us quite clearly. Otherwise we drilled and manoeuvred and continued our limited rifle practice without interference.

In the autumn of 1919 we took the Oath of Allegiance to Dáil Éireann. Coughlan, our Company Captain, administered it in an atmosphere of solemnity in the Ballyboden Library. It was anything but an ordinary parade of the Company. Coughlan warned us that we were undertaking a serious obligation. He suggested that anyone who had doubts should 'fall out'. Nobody did. But before that there had been much discussion as to the implications of the Oath. Some were worried that they were joining a secret society condemned by the Church, some that they might be required to shoot policemen. In fact it was made clear to any enquirer that the shooting of policemen was something which might have to be undertaken. On that ground three members of our Company decided to resign. Their decision was not held against them.

For myself, I was sorry we took the oath to Dáil Éireann. I thought, or rather felt, that no outside organisation should have any say in the activities of the Volunteers. In 1919 parliamentary democracy was a word not so often heard used and abused. The only democracy we knew of was British democracy and that had less than nothing to recommend it to us. Lloyd George, who was a ripe fruit of that democracy, had a poor view of Irish republicans. According to his son: 'Father was sick of the Irish republicans. He was quite willing to let them have what they seemed determined to become, an impoverished semi-peasant community with their peat fires and undrained bogs and dreams of glory seen in a fine mist of alcohol.' It hadn't occurred to the writer that the British were responsible for the condition of our country, whatever it might be.

I did not, of course, foresee the devastating consequences that the IRA would suffer from the oath: the Treaty split, Civil War and permanent partition. Nor did I like the change of name from the Irish Volunteers to Irish Republican Army. The word 'army' seemed to have overtones of professionalism which conflicted with the idealism of the Movement.

It was a couple of months afterwards that 'E' Company undertook its first positive action in law breaking. We raided Sir Frederick Shaw's 'Big House' at Bushy Park in search of arms. In the light of subsequent events, such a raid seems a trivial action. At the time it did not appear trivial to us. We had not accustomed ourselves to forcing our way into private houses. We felt squeamish about the idea. Within a few months we were going into every house in the

Company area that we thought might have arms of any kind. At that stage we went in twos and threes, knocking at the doors and politely enquiring if we might look round for arms and were never refused. But the raid on Shaw's was different. It was most carefully planned and executed. If it had been a military post we could not have been more soldierly.

The house and surrounding buildings were, of course, large but to take about thirty men on such a raid was ludicrous. Coughlan took four men into the house to search it. They walked past the butler into a sitting room where they found Sir Frederick who became apoplectic at their intrusion. He ordered them to take off their hats when coming into a gentleman's house. Some of the squad were about to obey until Coughlan reminded Sir Frederick that British soldiers did not take off their hats when they raided our houses. The etiquette of the situation having been made clear, Coughlan ordered the indignant Sir Frederick to accompany him and his squad round the house which they searched thoroughly. They did not find as much as a horse pistol.

With two others, I was on guard at the front door with orders to let no one in or out. As luck would have it, at this juncture one of the young women of the house arrived. When I told her there was a raid in progress and that she could not go in, she let loose a torrent of abuse. Blackguards, robbers, criminals, ruffians and goodness knows what else she called us in a hysterically rising voice. This we could endure, but when she tried to force her way into the house we did not know how to react. My inclination was to gag her, as she was making too much noise, but neither I nor my companions could overcome the taboos which forbade us to 'lay a hand on a woman' so we just stood there in front of the door and let her push and scream her head off. But when the raid was over I did not feel too good about it.

Early Manhood

Volunteers to Truce

I finished school in June 1919 as the end product of a Christian Brothers' education. I believe I got from my schooling as much as I was capable of absorbing. Even the Brothers cannot draw blood from a turnip. I had neither the intellectual equipment nor the temperament to avail myself fully of all the teaching offered me.

I had not the capacity to grasp the logical processes necessary to cope with mathematics. I envied my classmates who had no difficulty with differential calculus, co-ordinate geometry or the significance of sine, co-sine and tangents; to me they meant nothing. My real interests in the curriculum were English literature and history. I loved poetry and knew all the poems in the school text books by heart. I had Palgrave as a bedside book. In the milieu in which I moved it would have been regarded as an affectation to admit that I got great sensuous pleasure from reading a few lines of poetry such as:

> Not poppy, nor mandragora,
> Nor all the drowsy syrups of the world,
> Shall ever medicine thee to that sweet sleep
> Which thou ow'dst yesterday.

Nor could I admit that Tennyson's *Ulysses* and *Tithonus* excited my imagination and stimulated my curiosity about the Greeks and their world.

I am sure that some other boys in the class reacted to poetry as I did but we behaved as if such an indulgence was a secret vice. To me this was a major defect in the Brothers' teaching. Poetry and literature were regarded as examination subjects and not as an end in themselves. History was taught rather in the same spirit except in so far as it affected the Catholic Church, when it assumed an importance over and above its purely academic value.

On leaving school I had a broad, if superficial, knowledge of the history of English literature and had at least sampled some of the classics, Fielding, Smollett, Defoe, Dickens, Scott and Thackeray. I had read most of Macaulay's essays. My father picked up a beautiful bijou edition of Gibbon's *Decline and Fall of the Roman Empire* and with some temerity and fear for my faith I read his famous chapters fifteen and sixteen on the progress of Christianity. It became clear to me why the Church had thought it necessary to put Gibbon on the Index. My sense of irony was titillated but my faith remained unshaken. Nevertheless, when I wanted to be amused and entertained I often returned to Gibbon.

I knew both Irish and English history reasonably well and had a fair knowledge of the history of Europe, particularly of the Wars of Religion and the French Revolution.

I am a poor linguist, having a blunt ear and apparently deficient vocal chords. I find it impossible to reproduce even the simplest tune. Nevertheless, through extremely good teaching I was able to get by conversationally in Irish and in French. I was also deeply interested in 'La vie française' and read extensively (in English of course) Hugo, Balzac, Dumas and Anatole France. The apparent blasphemies of Anatole France's *The Revolt of the Angels* and *Penguin Island* so amused me that I thought it necessary to mention the matter in confession. The priest, probably erroneously, told me that Anatole France was on the Index and, before I got absolution, I would have to undertake not to read him anymore. He spoke so offensively that I refused to give the required undertaking. I left the confession box in mortal sin. In future visits to the confessional I never bothered to mention what I read.

Latin was badly taught except for Latin grammar which was drilled into us largely with the aid of mnemonics. I acquired the rudiments of Latin through the medium of Caesar, Cicero and Virgil, thus being introduced to something of the manners, customs and political organisation of the Roman world. I knew just enough of the language to enable me to understand Latin tags.

We had a well-equipped chemistry laboratory. Chemistry was taught seriously. Even I, who was not particularly interested, learned enough to remember something about atoms and molecules, elements and compounds and the difference between organic and inorganic substances. That was not bad for a schoolboy in 1919.

There were all sorts of gaps in our education. Darwin we knew about rather as a joke connected with the 'missing link'. Marx was never mentioned. Of Lenin's role in contemporary events we had only a vague idea. We knew nothing of economics. Freud had not appeared on the Irish horizon.

119

Oddly enough religion was indifferently taught. The practice of religion was perfect at least so far as the formalities were concerned. Morning and evening prayers, the Litany of the Blessed Virgin Mary, the Confiteor, the Creed and the Rosary were said regularly. We would not dream of missing Mass on Sundays or Holydays of Obligation; we went to confession and communion once a month and we knew the catechism (halfpenny and penny) off by heart. But we had a very imperfect understanding of the liturgy of the Mass and, except for awesome reverence at the consecration, attendance at Mass was very much a mechanical process.

At school we got religious instruction for half an hour every day. In the course of time we got from these lectures a familiarity with the highlights of the Gospel. But the Gospel texts were never read through in their entirety. We did not have any clear idea of the difference between Matthew, Mark, Luke and John nor did we know of the history or the provenance of the Gospels. We never heard the word 'synoptic'. We were even more uninformed about the Epistles which were read at Mass in Latin. We knew little about St Paul beyond what happened on the road to Damascus. We did not know where Ephesus was nor why Paul should be writing to the Corinthians.

As for the Old Testament, our information was derived from a book called *Bible History*. Unlike our other school books we were not expected to own it. Copies were distributed to the class at not very frequent intervals, one copy between two or more boys. In that way we became familiar with the stories of Adam and Eve, of Mount Sinai, of Jonah in the belly of the whale, of Moses in the burning bush and the crossing of the Red Sea. We read the Scripture stories as we had, as children, read *Grimm's Fairy Tales* or *Gulliver's Travels*. We were not given the feeling that we were expected to believe them. Of the Bible itself we had no first-hand knowledge. Even the names of the Biblical books would be totally unfamiliar to us, except by accident. We knew Ruth from Keats, Job from his patience and Daniel from the lions' den; but Exodus, Deuteronomy, Esther, Ecclesiastes or Isaias would never have been heard of. In truth, we regarded the Bible as a Protestant document having no bearing on our faith.

The aim of the Christian Brothers was to provide their pupils with a religious formation which would enable them to lead their lives in a way which would ensure salvation and eternal happiness in the next life. The Ten Commandments and the Precepts of the Church were the basis of their instruction. So well had we absorbed their message that we developed an acute awareness of what was to be regarded as right and what was to be regarded as wrong and sinful. Truthfulness, discipline, punctuality and respect for authority were insisted on. We were inclined to feel that all pleasure, even legitimate pleasure, was, if not sinful, at least undesirable. When through human weakness, we did commit sin or indulge in some frivolity which gave pleasure or satisfaction, the value we got was discounted in direct proportion by a sense of guilt. Our formation did not assume the possibility of a carefree, joyous life on this earth. Without ever having heard of them, we had become a variety of Jansenists.

In any event the circumstances of the time in Ireland of 1919 afforded a Christian Brothers boy very limited opportunities to commit any of the seven deadly sins, be it pride, covetousness, lust, envy, gluttony, anger or sloth. Effectively to indulge any of these vices, except lust, requires either money or power or both. As we had neither we had few temptations to resist.

Even though on leaving school I had no academic distinctions I had made up my mind to go to the University. Brother Roche encouraged me on the assumption that I would get a County Council scholarship. To his annoyance I failed to do so. Notwithstanding this he came to see my mother and urged her to send me to the University to study law and become a barrister. He insisted on interviewing my mother at the hall door, refusing to come in for a cup of tea; apparently to visit a house was against the rules of the Order. I thought that it was an absurdity for a small-time Catholic to think of the bar as a career. To me the bar seemed part and parcel of the British administration.

There were several reasons why I wanted to go to the University. Principally it would give me considerable freedom to pursue my activities in the Movement. Some of my older friends were already there and the majority of my classmates were going, mostly on scholarships. It would provide me with a chance to play plenty of football because the College sports grounds were beside my home in Terenure. It did not occur to me that my parents might reasonably expect me to earn my living; in fact they did not press the point nor, indeed, mention it.

My father made some comment that my mother in sending me to the University wanted to make me a gentleman. To my father a gentleman meant someone who was pretentious, pompous and with a poor sense of compassion and an even poorer sense of integrity where money was involved. My mother had made up her mind that at whatever sacrifice I would go to the University because she, in fact, wanted me to be a gentleman, defined — in a totally different way from my father's concept — as a person who had a secure income and a good social status in the community. That is the wish of most mothers for their sons and when they settle down most men wish it for themselves and their families.

But in 1919 I gave no thought to earning my living. I assumed my parents would support me as long as I found it necessary. My assumption was right as, in fact, I never brought any money into the house. I earned scarcely a penny until 1926 and by then I was spending what money I earned in courting my future wife or saving to get married. The cost to my parents of this self-indulgent attitude of mine was no holidays, few theatres, no entertaining, no visiting, although curiously enough both my parents spent generously on clothes for themselves.

Having decided that I was going to university my parents gave me the money to pay for a second summer in Ring. This second visit was not at all as agreeable as the first. The gay, carefree atmosphere which dominated Ring in the previous year was overshadowed by the sombre events which were now happening with increasing frequency throughout the country. Raids by the British forces created a certain tension in the college; some of the students were 'wanted men'. Among the students who were at Ring at that time was Seán MacBride. He had a little difficulty in settling down in the Gaelic-speaking environment. However his stay was cut short by an urgent summons from the Lord Mayor of Cork, Terence MacSwiney, who wished to consult him on some important national business.

I went to the university in the Michaelmas term of 1919, being then just turned eighteen years of age. Because all the boys from my class and Earle, who had started a year earlier, were doing chemistry, I decided to do likewise. Unlike Trinity or the English universities where courses were 'read', in University College, Dublin, and the National University of Ireland generally, we 'did' our courses. I had only a peripheral interest in chemistry at school. Practical experiments had amused me — turning blue litmus red, making lemonade from citric acid, playing with mercury and phosphorus and making multi-colour solutions in test tubes — but I could have had just as much amusement from a good chemical set bought in a toy shop. I would have preferred to do Engineering but that was out of the question with my mathematical ineptitude although even for chemistry one had to take some maths.

I had no idea of what university life would be like. I had not deluded myself into the belief that I was going to see dreaming spires, centuries-old lawns or great dining halls with high tables, all contributing to the ambiance of urbane living. But I had not expected to encounter the barrack-like atmosphere of the central hall of Earlsfort Terrace, where the College was then located, and the long, bare and none too clean corridors.

The new first year students were milling round the main hall, waiting to be registered in the College office. Having registered, our next duty was to present ourselves individually to the President, Dr Denis Coffey. Dr Coffey was President by grace of the Irish Party and the Church. Most of the professors occupied their chairs by virtue of the same patronage. Dr Coffey had the reputation of being a polymath. He probably derived this reputation from his ability to divert discussion from any subject on which he did not want to take a decision into the highways and byways of literature, geography, comparative religion or features of the Kerry landscape.

Dr Coffey was a low sized, extremely dapper, white haired man. His alertness and the way he constantly moved his head reminded me of a sparrow. He was much criticised by the Movement for compromising with the Castle. The criticism was unjustified. His primary obligation was to keep the College open and in this he had a difficult job, considering the state of the country. He was said to know the name and face of every one of the three thousand students in the College. He certainly knew me and never failed to bid me, by name, a friendly time of day.

The most conspicuous figure that a first year student noticed in the main hall was the head porter. He was a tall, lanky individual with heavily greased black hair and a thin black moustache. Dressed in a uniform of vivid green he was, we soon learned, known as the 'Emerald Gem'. I was only a few days in College when he approached me and asked if I was Mr Andrews. I was unused to being called Mister and was even more surprised when he enquired if I was the son of Christy Andrews, the auctioneer. It seemed that a female cousin of the 'Emerald Gem' (Mick Ryan was his real name) was one of the dealers who bought at my father's auction. Apparently my father had been boasting to his clients that he had a son at university. The cousin told the 'Emerald Gem' to look out for me and to 'keep an eye on young Christy Andrews'. Thus I made in the beginning an exceptionally useful contact in the College.

The head porter was a source of all the College information. He knew where lecture rooms were, when lectures were to be given and, more important, when they really would begin. Many of the lecturers were habitually unpunctual. Mick Ryan gave me a base in the porter's lodge. I could leave my coat and hat there, I could leave and receive messages from friends, I could use the telephone. I was also kept up to date on gossip about both students and professors. Mick Ryan helped me greatly in settling into the College life.

Boys who were lucky enough to get to the university from the Christian Brothers' Schools had clearly in mind the dual objective of getting a degree and finding a job. That was not so in my case. I had so much confidence and reliance in my parents' capacity and willingness to support me indefinitely that I did not feel the necessity to look as far forward as earning my living. This was something like presumption in the theological sense. It was certainly 'a foolish expectation of salvation without using the necessary means to obtain it'. Basically, I felt that with the country in such turmoil — with ambushes, assassinations, military law, newspapers suppressed, and widespread arrests the order of the day — the moment of truth in the form of an examination day would never arrive. I think that this was the general feeling of the young people who were really committed members of the IRA.

The Irish 'went out to battle and they always fell'. It seemed to us that inevitably what life had in store for us was imprisonment or even worse. In these circumstances careers did not seem important and anyway in the mood which prevailed at that time among IRA men it would be regarded as indecent to associate material gain with the Movement.

My frame of mind at university, however irresponsible and selfish, had the advantage of giving me a sense of independence and of liberty of action to pursue my own interests which continued to be games, literature and history, the Abbey Theatre and the Movement. Surprisingly, in spite of my interest in books and my familiarity with some of its leading personalities, derived from frequent visits to the Abbey, I had no consciousness of living in the midst of a great literary renaissance. I knew nothing about Lady Gregory except that she was a successful playwright and Yeats, moving in his stately fashion among the half-empty stalls, seemed nothing more than an elderly poseur every bit as ridiculous in appearance as he was depicted in Max Beerbohm's famous cartoon, now in the Municipal Gallery, introducing George Moore to the Queen of the Fairies. At that time I had never even heard of George Moore. I frequently saw AE going into town on the top of a Terenure tram — he was always known to us irreverently as the 'Hairy Fairy'. I learnt from my father, who used to read the *Irish Homestead*, that AE had taken the workers' side in the 1913 strike but that was the extent of my knowledge of him. James Joyce's name meant nothing to me but, of course, *Ulysses* had not yet been published.

In this respect the university did not help me in any way. Had I joined some of the Arts Faculty Societies I might have become aware of the Irish Literary Renaissance, although since the death of the 1916 insurgents, Pearse, McDonagh and Plunkett, no literature had come out of University College, Dublin. I did think of joining the Literary and Historical Society and looked in at a few of their meetings on Saturday evenings. What I saw I did not like. The L & H was run mainly by sons of Castle Catholics and the detritus of the Irish Party. The whole proceedings seemed to me to lack seriousness (as it was of course intended to do) and to be downright frivolous in character. What I did not understand was that the L & H was a training ground for lawyers and careerists who were poised in waiting for the coming of Home Rule and who, in the event, reaped the benefit of the IRA struggle and embraced joyfully the advent of the Free State as providing for their talents something even more advantageous than Home Rule. The fact that they regarded the IRA as gun bullies and even murderers did not prevent them from accepting and cultivating the like of Collins and his 'squad of gunmen'.

Professor George O'Brien, who might fairly be described as the finest flower of the Literary and Historical Society and a figure of whom the Society is extremely proud, expressed the thinking of himself and his kind when he wrote in the *History of the Literary and Historical Society:* 'Our professors, without knowing it, were forming the minds of a new governing class' and again 'We all took it for granted that, if Home Rule was achieved, we should be among the politicians of the New Ireland' and again 'So certain were we of the approach of Home Rule that some of the students neglected to prepare for a profession, believing that they would get a good job when self government came'. They certainly got the good jobs but few enough of them gave much help to us when we were on the run, in jail or fighting the British.

Looking over the list of contributors to the *History of the Literary and Historical Society*, it will be seen that the contributions they made to the country were fully matched by the advancement of their own careers, which is much more than can be said for the rank and file of the IRA. I can vouch on behalf of my comrades in 'E' Company of the Fourth Battalion, Dublin Brigade, that with a handful of exceptions, none of them were better off, socially or economically, as a result of the revolution.

One thing I was determined about: I would not emigrate. I had seen my friend and neighbour, Jack Maguire, after a particularly distinguished academic career in Engineering, being forced to make that

125

decision and was aware of the distress it caused his mother and himself. Jack Maguire is now a very senior citizen in Montevideo del Uruquay. Over the years he has been home on holidays several times and we write to one another often. He has never lost the yearning for his youthful haunts: Terenure, Bushy Park and Blackrock Baths. But he has been too long abroad and the country has changed too much to make it possible for him to settle down here, even though he has many nieces and nephews and cousins in Dublin. I think I was lucky in my resolve never to emigrate.

My mother was determined to ensure my embourgeoisement. Quite sensibly, I suppose, she thought that I should learn ballroom dancing. She realised that the lack of a sister or of any association with young women was a great social disadvantage to me and persuaded me to take dancing lessons. I joined a dancing class at the very well known Morosini's Dancing Academy in Harcourt Street. I was intensely shy and even more intensely self-conscious about my gawky, tall, ungainly appearance. I felt it absurd to two-step round a room with a girl whom I did not know, and to whom I had nothing to say, to the tune of 'The wild, wild women are making a wild man of me'. I had not 'a heart too soon made glad'. I abandoned the effort after two of the scheduled twelve lessons. I have never got over my sense of the absurdity of dancing except with the girl with whom I fell in love and whom I married.

The only club or society that I joined in the university was the Soccer Club. It was one of the smallest in the College and was predominantly composed of students from the Northern counties, particularly those who had been at school at St Columb's, Derry. Earle joined with me and that year there was an influx from the Christian Brothers school in North Richmond Street where the boys had been reared under the shadow of Dalymount Park, the home ground of Bohemians. Most of the members of the UCD Soccer Club were medical students. It was a most friendly body and being very small and not very highly thought of by the big Gaelic and rugby clubs, the members tended to become introverted and on the playing pitches, which were located in Terenure, we kept ourselves to ourselves. This kind of conduct, if not in keeping with the spirit of the university, bound the members of the club very closely together and resulted happily in the formation of many permanent friendships.

Shortly after my joining, the first team visited Belfast to play in the Collingwood Cup and I was taken along as a sub. It was my first visit to Belfast but at that time Belfast was much less foreign to us than Cork, Galway or Limerick would have been. We knew all about the

Belfast soccer clubs — Glentoran, Linfield, Celtic — we kept track of their form and their players were familiar names to us. We did not regard Belfast as any less Irish than Dublin. At one time I used to go out late on Saturday evenings to buy the Belfast sporting paper, *Ireland's Saturday Night,* which contained long and detailed descriptions of the Irish League matches.

My principal concern as a soccer fan at the time was for the progress of the Bohemians. Even now I remember the names of the Bohemians team at the height of my interest in the club: Heir, McConnell, and Irons; Laverty, Brennan and Magwood; Seymour, Hannon, McDonnell; West and Willets. After a while, I got a regular place on the College first team as right half. We played in the Leinster Senior League and it has to be said that we won very few matches but enjoyed ourselves greatly.

The first-year medicals, engineers and chemists took their chemistry lectures together so that the big lecture theatre was packed for first year chemistry. On one famous occasion when Hugh Ryan, the professor, was in the middle of his lecture on the 'Ketones' the door of the lecture room was pushed open and an excited voice shouted 'Up National — Trinity are here'. Almost the entire student body, bored with the lecture and delighted at the chance of some excitement, rose and dashed out into the corridor leaving behind the girl students, a few clerics and the professor. Sure enough out in Earlsfort Terrace a big mob of Trinity students had gathered singing 'Rule Brittania' and 'God Save the King' and waving Union Jacks. They were celebrating the first anniversary of the Armistice. The porters had closed the gates of the College but we forced them open and made a wild rush at the Trinity students punching and kicking and screaming 'Up Dev' and 'Up the Republic'.

The Trinity boys managed to reform their ranks and retreated along the Green towards Grafton Street, still singing and waving their flags while we harrassed them from the rear. Every messenger boy seemed to have collected from miles around, armed with stones to fling at the retreating Trinity students who succeeded in keeping their ranks intact till reaching Grafton Street where they broke up completely under the weight of our attack. It was nearly *de rigeur* for students in those days to carry a cane and absolutely *de rigeur* to wear a hat. Many of our opponents were dispossessed of their canes and hats, several were pushed through shop windows and chased right up to the gates of Trinity College in College Green. Fortunately, they managed to shut the gates in time because at that point the riot had ceased to be a student prank; a mob with its own personality had taken

127

control. Our contingent was also swelled by citizens anxious to 'have a go' at the Trinity students and serious damage might have been done if the mob gained entry. After a while calm was restored. We reformed our ranks and returned to Earlsfort Terrace to celebrate our victory by making a bonfire in front of the College of the many canes, hats and a few overcoats we had collected as trophies.

I, being so very tall, was especially conspicuous in the riot. I gained some notoriety and was invited to contest the Students Representative Council election on behalf of the Faculties of Engineering and Chemistry which were combined for the purpose of representation on the SRC. The invitation came from a group headed by the most colourful of our first-year men named James Dillon. He was prompted less by a predilection for me than by a wish to keep out my opponent, a first-year chemist named Percy Hurley who had become involved against Dillon in the politics of the Literary and Historical Society. Dillon, knowing nothing whatever about me, undertook to be my election agent and between his efforts and the help I got from the eight or nine Synge Street boys in the College I was elected by, as Dillon boasted, more votes in the ballot box than there were on the register.

James Dillon was the son of the leader of the Irish Party and in time he himself became a very important figure in Irish politics. As a first-year student he appeared to us a sort of Stupor Mundi in his self assurance, his conversation and his apparent breadth of knowledge. In his dress he was equally egregious; his wide black hat, an expensive walking stick rather than a cane, rimless glasses and very well cut clothes, gave him a dandified appearance quite different from the rest of us. Unlike the rest of us, too, he had a poor opinion of games, except Bridge, and unlike most of us he was a pacifist and an advocate of law and order. While we were devising a way of prolonging the excitement of the Trinity riot and had decided to demonstrate in the Theatre Royal that same evening, he issued a solemn warning — everything he said was either solemn or portentous — about the dangers of clashing with the police and finding ourselves in jail. He certainly did not lack moral courage as one might expect from his family tradition. In politics he suffered from arrested development due, I think, to a laudably filial attempt to justify the policies of his father and the Irish Party. His oratory commanded the admiration one gives to an accomplished actor. As a man he was friendly and decent.

The proposed Theatre Royal demonstration was duly carried out. We rushed the attendants and occupied seats all over the theatre. The principal artistes on the bill were Shaun Glenville and Dorothy Ward singing 'If you're Irish come into the parlour'. We listened quietly to the show until the band played 'God Save the King' at the end of the performance. As the opening notes were played a hail of sticks, bottles, cushions and any detachable object to hand, even the bones from the College anatomy theatre, landed on top of the orchestra. That was the last time 'God Save the King' was played ritually in a Dublin theatre.

The whole episode had more the character of a student prank than a political demonstration and the most active participants were the students on British Government scholarships back from the war. They were all much more mature than we who had come straight to the university from school. I made friends with many of them and loved to talk to them about their war experiences. Some were very serious students intent on a degree and a career. Some were there because there was nothing better to do. Whether they were serious or not, politics was not for them. One of them, Frank Algar, I had known at school. He was a couple of years older than I and had quit school at sixteen, passed himself off as eighteen and joined the Army. He left school because he could not stand the rigour of Brother Gilsenan's regime. From 1915 to the end of the war he was in the trenches, and took part in the great battles of France, including Passchendale and the Somme, without getting a scratch. An older brother, who had joined for patriotic reasons in response to John Redmond's call, was killed almost as soon as he arrived in France early in 1915.

Frank Algar was a very slightly built man of average height and no great physique. Even as a boy he never played games. His descriptions of the mud, the lice, the wounds, the noise of the barrages and the fear of 'going over the top', of lobbing bombs into German dugouts, fascinated me. I suppose no experience in human history tested mankind's capacity to endure almost limitless physical and mental hardship and to survive, as did the artillery barrages of the First World War. I tried to recruit Frank Algar into the IRA, but he had only three fixed objects in life, namely to get his Engineering degree, find a job and get married; all of which he did.

Before being allowed to sit for the examination a minimum number of lectures had to be taken in each subject. I attended the minimum and spent much of the day very agreeably gossiping in the main hall or in the engineering laboratory where we sometimes helped the laboratory assistant to test concrete blocks for Professor Purcell who carried on his private practice from the College. The Engineers regarded themselves as a tough lot and could be relied upon to make

129

a great deal of noise at concerts and the like with their rally-song, the refrain of which was 'The Engineering faculty is the terror of the land'. In fact they were the most disciplined and hard working faculty in the College. As for myself, I was too deeply involved in other activities to be bothered with College society or indeed with chemistry studies.

I learned to play Bridge, which I found boring, and Slippery Sam and Pontoon played extensively in the College basement, where a couple of large deal tables and a few forms were the sole amenities in what passed for students' recreation rooms. The wins and losses at these card games could be reckoned in pence, because no one had any more to spend. The Adelphi billiard room in South Anne Street was another mid-morning attraction. I spent a fair amount of lunch money trying very unsuccessfully to excel at billiards and snooker. I got half a crown a day from my mother for my tram fare and lunch but it also covered the cost of the snooker and card games as I had no other expenses, being a non-smoker and a non-drinker.

We always had our lunch in Roberts' Café, initially in Suffolk Street, but when they opened a branch in Grafton Street we changed to that. Lunch was invariably the same: two rolls, a butter and a bun or baked beans on toast. Roberts' became a sort of club for us and we got to know the waitresses very well. Some of them became life-long friends of mine. Later on, my wife and I used to dump the children there to be looked after by the staff while we went shopping in Grafton Street. This sort of arrangement illustrates the advantages of living in your native city and in a stable society.

There was a teacher from Synge Street named Patrick Caffrey who came to settle in Terenure and with whom I got very friendly. Caffrey, an only child and unmarried, lived in a small terrace house with his mother. They came from the Liberties where they had lived in very humble circumstances. Paddy left the National School at fourteen to be apprenticed in cabinet making. Like so many Dublin tradesmen he hankered after learning and read and read and read. He spent all his spare money on books and built up a very good collection, mainly English classics and historical works, from second-hand book stalls. He acquired a very wide knowledge of English literature and of history in general. He taught himself Latin well and acquired a fair working knowledge of both Irish and French. He switched from woodworking to teaching and by some unknown process he was engaged to teach a pass class in the Intermediate grade in Synge Street where he worked under the severe Brother Gilsenan.

This, in itself, meant that he was not allowed much initiative and was not very highly esteemed by the boys who associated him with the Gilsenan barbarities. Apart from this, he suffered the disadvantage of being short in stature and having a prune-like face, which made him a figure of fun. His accent, which was pure Coombe and the Liberties in origin, incongruously contrasted with the breadth of his vocabulary and fluency of expression. Meeting him outside the school and on more or less equal terms had a profound influence on me.￫At last I found someone who was interested in poetry and history, who talked with great facility, especially about Shakespeare, and encouraged me to read plays other than those which had been on our course at school He also persuaded me to go along with him to the Shakespearian Society which was flourishing under the guidance of Professor Magennis, a magnificent figure of a man with a wonderfully mellifluous voice who never stopped talking except to recite, beautifully, passages from Shakespeare. The Shakespearian Society was a new and delightful experience for me and soon I had read *Othello, Richard III, The Taming of the Shrew* and *Julius Caesar* and heard them discussed and evaluated by people like Caffrey deeply steeped in Shakespearian scholarship.

Caffrey was rather crude in his manner of life and after the death of his mother, shortly after they moved to Terenure, he lived alone and did his own housekeeping and cooking. He had no interest in his appearance or in what he wore or in what he ate or drank. He had considered 'The Lilies of the Field'. He lived basically on bread, eggs and tea. He had skin like a pachyderm and shaved with a cut-throat razor using neither hot water nor soap. He hated fresh air and never allowed a window to be opened. His passion in life was learning and teaching and his regret was that, being without a university degree, he was not quite accepted by the teaching profession. He reacted to this feeling of deprivation by lacing his conversation with quotations from Shakespeare, Latin tags and historical references. Later on he developed a taste for wine, under the inspiration of Horace. Often on Sunday afternoons he used to heat up the kitchen stove to the highest possible temperature, settle himself in a chair with a bottle of what became for him Falernian wine and read Horace until the wine was finished and he fell asleep.

Caffrey was a strong Republican and he provided a dump for arms and a meeting place for the IRA. He became an active member of the Sinn Féin Club in Terenure where he was a popular speaker. All his speeches began 'I am no orator like Brutus here'. He was a courageous man. In his early forties he took his B.A. degree, set up a tutorial correspondence college and developed a very successful business. He married late and reared two sons who became distinguished in the academic world. While he was regarded generally, however affectionately, as a 'bit of a cod' by his teacher colleagues, I got great benefit from his company, his conversation and his books. He was the only one with whom I could discuss literature except Earle, although the latter's reading interest diverged more and more towards the sentimental novel. Of course there were in the College many first-year students who were better informed and with as wide a range of interests as I but I did not have much contact with them. Except for my Synge Street schoolmates I had no friends outside the Soccer Club and the Engineering School.

I met very few students who came from the Jesuit schools. They neither played soccer nor did engineering. Some of them who lodged in University Hall — their hostel in Hatch Street — played cards with us; I met a few in this way but a card school is not the best place to discover a man's real qualities. At that level what distinguished the Jesuit boys from us who came from the Christian Brothers or from students of schools like Rockwell and the Diocesan Colleges, was their conversational confidence and their indifference to money — I am talking about shillings — lost or won. Even by standards of Synge Street I found the boys from the Diocesan Colleges exceptionally gauche and ill at ease in the free and easy atmosphere of University College.

The clerical students from Clonliffe Seminary formed a totally separate group in the College. They arrived every morning, like the animals in the ark, two by two and took their places immediately behind the few nun students in the front rows of the class. They never spoke to any of the other students. They moved like a flock of starlings, in unison. For the rest of the students they did not exist as individuals. Most of them would later become curates and parish priests in the diocese of Dublin and considering the extent of their isolation as students from the world at large it was not surprising that the Church was so remote from the problems of the day to day life of the people of the city. The world was not with them, either late or soon.

All my absorption in the Movement had not prevented me from observing with intense interest the current events in Europe. It was like looking at a very great drama on a very great stage with constantly changing scenery and a constantly changing cast. I did not realise it, of course, but what I had witnessed was not a drama but a cataclysm. I was witnessing the destruction of the social order.

For me the personification of the barbarity of modern war had been Field Marshal Haig. The English erected a monument in London to this insensitive fool of a general who allowed his troops to be massacred at Passchendale and the Somme with as little care for their fate or feelings as if they were grouse on his Scottish moors. In his vocabulary pheasants and peasants had the same meaning. A better way to commemorate Haig might have been to follow the example of the people of Pisa who decided to kill a successful but intractable condottiere and honour him by making him their patron saint. The French generals had been equally indifferent to the fate of their men and in the pursuit of La Gloire through battle after battle at Verdun had driven them eventually to mutiny.

From the Russian Revolution a new galaxy of names appeared in the newspapers. Kerensky, Kamineff, Lenin, Trotsky, Kolchak, Wrangel — Stalin was as yet unheard of. The first victims of the deluge sweeping over Europe were the aristocrats and the bourgeoisie of Russia.

The Germans had made their last great effort in March 1918 and, as they advanced on Paris, I had moved the pins on my war map with great pleasure. I had nothing against Paris or the French; I hoped the Germans would win the war being naive enough to believe that we, being their 'gallant allies', would achieve independence through a German victory. The German offensive failed and they were only too willing to accept Wilson's Fourteen Points to enable the ruling classes to save what they could from the national wreckage which they had themselves created. But it was too late and the Kaiser had to go. The German Empire was disintegrating.

For us in the Movement the proclamation of Wilson's Fourteen Points raised real hope of securing the recognition of the Republic. We were political innocents. We deceived ourselves about the influence of the Irish vote in America and were totally misled by the newspaper reports of the enthusiastic reception extended to De Valera during his American tour and its effect on public opinion. We should have realised that, so far as Irish independence was concerned, there was nothing to be gained from the Peace Conference or from the Fourteen Points. Wilson had already told the delegates of the Irish Race Convention whom he received in Paris that no small nation might appear before the victorious nations to plead its cause unless with the unanimous approval of the Four Great Powers. Ireland's case would not be heard because England would not agree. Wilson himself was as naive in his relations with the French, Italians and British as we were in our reliance on the Americans. He might have been on his guard when he heard Clemenceau's cynical

133

comment on his Fourteen Points — 'God has only ten'.

Ours were not the only hopes raised by Wilson's intervention in Europe. He raised the hopes of the common man everywhere. In Rome, Paris and London he was received as if he were the Messiah and it is said that if he had appealed directly to the people over the heads of the politicians any form of World Government, no matter how Utopian, which he might seek to establish would have received popular sanction. Despite the fact that one of his Fourteen Points provided for open covenants openly arrived at he made the fatal mistake of agreeing to have the Peace Conference held in secret.

From that moment his cause was lost. For the second time in a century liberty shrieked. The major western powers were quite determined that what had happened to Russia was not going to happen to the ruling classes in France, Italy and England. Instead of peace and justice, Wilson found himself involved in a carve up of national territories and the creation of spheres of influence. It was not long before the capitalist press of Europe turned on Wilson for what was described as his impractical idealism. He did succeed in founding the League of Nations but on his return to America it was repudiated by Congress and the League, without American participation, was quite ineffective.

Wilson — after all he was a white Anglo-Saxon Protestant — regarded 'the Irish question' as the exclusive problem of Great Britain. We had no hope there. The effect that the whole Versailles and League episode had on me was to convince me that if Ireland was ever to achieve independence it would have to be through our own efforts. I came, too, to the belief that any energy, any emotion, any money an Irishman had to expend should be devoted to the advancement of Irish interests rather than the interest of any other nation. I was determined that I would never join a 'hyphenated Irish' organisation whether it was French, American, Spanish or Soviet. I came to the conclusion that in quarrels between nations or in civil wars which disrupt other countries it is no business of an Irishman to meddle. Nor was it the business of Irishmen to get themselves involved in helping the victims of floods, earthquakes or typhoons. There are enough opportunies in Ireland for money well spent to fulfil the aspirations of the most public-spirited idealists.

*　　*　　*　　*　　*

Between raids on private houses and through 'marks' in contact with British soldiers the Company was gradually building up a collection of weapons. We had three Lee Enfield rifles, half a dozen shotguns and about a dozen small arms varying from .22 single-shot pistols to .45 Webleys, Smith and Wessons and one Parabellum. We had also acquired half a dozen Mills bombs. These were all carefully stored in a dump, cleverly made by the Company carpenter, Patsy Toole. The dump was situated near Toole's house in Green Lanes and was damp proof and raid proof. All over the country these miniature arsenals were being constructed and their contents were gradually added to from one source or another.

At the beginning of April 1920 a few of us got the word from Coughlan to be ready to mobilise on Easter Saturday night bringing 'dogs' ('dog' was the word we always used for a revolver) but on Easter Saturday afternoon the order was called off. Not before I had taken the opportunity to go to confession. We always made sure to be in a state of grace if there was dangerous work to be done. In fact the job we were designated to carry out involved little danger. The Dublin Brigade raided the houses of income tax collectors and inspectors all over the city and destroyed their records. It was an effective, if minor blow, at Government administration. Our particular part of the operation was called off because Coughlan was taken suddenly ill. I left my gun back in the dump and went home as usual having no reason to expect anything untoward happening. I was wakened about midnight, not by any midnight knock but by noises on the stairs and landings. I was not too surprised when my mother appeared at my bedroom door carrying a candle, closely followed by a young British officer who told me to get up and dress as I was being arrested. When I got into my clothes I went out to the landing to find my father almost fully dressed and looking very worried. My mother, on the other hand, gave no sign of emotion. When the officer said he had instructions to search the house she said she would show him around. She behaved to him as she would have behaved to a new customer buying a loaf of bread in the shop. The officer was a very young lieutenant who was conventionally polite to my mother, clearly not liking the work he was doing. With him were about a dozen soldiers, also very young, who scattered about the house to search it. The search was merely a visual inspection of each room. Nothing was touched or disturbed in any way. My brother was not even asked to get out of bed. The whole operation took less than an hour. There was scarcely any conversation except on the part of my father who asked why I was being arrested, where I was being taken and when I would be back. The lieutenant was sorry he could not answer any questions but suggested that I take with me a change of underwear, some sweets and cigarettes. My father very promptly told him I didn't smoke. My mother packed a small case with a night shirt, toothbrush, toothpaste, several pairs of socks, handkerchiefs, a muffler, a pair of boots. She packed a large bag of sweets, took two pound notes out of the till and gave them to me. My father was so worried that he could hardly say goodbye but my mother came to the halldoor waiting to see me safely installed in the lorry. The lieutenant formally saluted my father saying 'Goodnight' before taking his seat beside the driver.

I was neither surprised nor dismayed by my arrest nor was I in any way apprehensive. For months I had been conditioning my mind to the probability of some such thing happening. I had no reason to fear anything worse than a spell in jail. A year later if I had been arrested in the same circumstances I would have been terrified but at this time the Black and Tans had only just arrived in Ireland and their atrocities had not yet begun. As the reign of terror developed the physical safety of arrested IRA men was increasingly at risk. Two of my friends in the Company who were captured in this way were taken from Rathfarnham to Rathmines where they were told to run for it and were riddled with bullets as they did so. One of them died at once; the other survived with eight bullets in him, although a cripple for life. Instead of being nervous or apprehensive I was mildly elated as well as being curious as to my destination. I felt that I had at last put my toe in the stream of national effort in which Tone, Emmet, the men of '47, the Fenians and Pearse had drowned. One of the soldiers in the lorry said cheerfully 'Keep your heart up, Paddy'. That was the only remark addressed to me though they talked a lot amongst themselves. They spoke in some North of England dialect and the only word I could understand clearly was 'buckshee' which constantly cropped up in their conversation. As we passed the Town Hall in Rathmines the tower clock struck the half-hour, 1.30 a.m. Soon we turned into Portobello barracks. I had once before been in the precincts of the barracks when, as a small boy, I climbed over the wall to see an Army Soccer Cup Final. One of the teams represented the Buff's Regiment; I don't remember the name of the other. I do recall that it was a very rough game and that the spectators, almost exclusively soldiers in uniform, were noisily partisan.

When we got off the lorry I was escorted by a couple of soldiers to a large room empty of anything or anybody except a few chairs, a table and two made-up beds. There was a blazing fire in the grate. I was wondering whether or not there was a guard outside or whether I might just walk out to investigate the possibility of escape when the door opened and a young fellow was pushed into the room. The newcomer, a lad slightly younger than I, apparently had been protesting to his guard about his civil rights — hence the rough treatment. He continued to complain to me vociferously about the indignity inflicted on him by his arrest. He was a bespectacled, delicate youth who spoke in an accent and used a vocabulary not usually found among the IRA. He never stopped talking; he required no response from me. In no time I had found out that he lived with his mother who was a widow of a colonel in the British army. His mother wrote poetry, was sympathetic to the Movement and moved in a circle I should have known about (but didn't) which was at the heart of the Irish literary renaissance. He himself was writing a book as well as studying painting. To me he was a rare bird. He was Cecil Salkeld, aged seventeen, who later became a writer, poet, critic and painter. The Chinese say that a genius is an immortal banished from Heaven. I think Salkeld was a genius who was banished from Heaven for giving too many backanswers to the gods. He spent his life dissipating the superabundance of his talents.

I listened, fascinated, to an hour of Salkeld's autobiography. We were disturbed by a lieutenant, different from the first one I had met, who told us to get ready to move. Cecil demanded to know where we were going. The lieutenant just said 'Hurry up'. We got into another lorry with another squad of soldiers. After about twenty minutes we arrived at a building which turned out to be the Bridewell. Here we were handed over to the civil arm, the police. A weary old DMP man wrote our particulars into a ledger, searched us but took nothing except the two pounds which my mother had given me. They left me the sweets. We were put into a cell-like room which was filthy, gloomy and smelly and barely lighted by a twenty-watt bulb. There were a couple of plank beds. It was now nearly 4 a.m. The excitement of arrest was wearing off and Salkeld's interminable talk began to weary me. At that age it is easy to sleep anywhere and even the filth of the place couldn't keep me awake. I stretched out and fell asleep immediately.

I was wakened after a few hours by the DMP man bringing in breakfast consisting of bread, margarine and a mug of the foulest tasting liquid I have ever had before or since. It was called shell cocoa. I got into conversation with the policeman who told me I would probably be taken to Mountjoy jail during the day and sure enough, late in the afternoon, Salkeld and I got orders to move. We were

137

offered no food, as apparently in the Bridewell the cooks did not work on Sunday. I shared my sweets with Salkeld and sustained by Mackintosh's toffees we were put in yet another lorry with its escort of soldiers. This time we were taken to Mountjoy jail only a few minutes' drive from the gloomy, obnoxious Bridewell. A couple of warders received us and went through the same booking routine that we had experienced at the Bridewell. Salkeld made numerous protests culminating in a demand to see the Governor. The warders wearily explained that he could repeat his request tomorrow but they pointed out that, tomorrow being Easter Monday, the Governor was likely to be at the races at Fairyhouse. I said nothing because I felt it would be undignified, if not disloyal, for a member of the IRA to protest against his arrest. Being arrested was a trial which it was our duty to endure. Leaving the reception centre we were taken into the main part of the jail which looked a very frightening place with wings and tiers of cells extending out from a centre circle. Everything seemed designed to depress the prisoners. For the first time since my arrest my heart began to sink. A warder opened a cell door, told me to enter, banging the door behind me. The bang of the door put all thoughts of the Sean Bhean Bhocht, Caitlín Ní Uallacháin or Róisín Dubh out of my mind. A great cloud of loneliness came over me and I wanted more than anything in the world to be back at home with my parents in Terenure.

I had never been in such a predicament before. For all the eighteen years of my life I had always had someone to turn to for support when in difficulty but now I was alone with no one to talk to. I even wished they had allowed Salkeld to share my cell for a few weeks. I would have acquired the beginnings of a liberal education though it was not until many years later that I realised Salkeld's unique qualities. I lay on the bed indulging my depression and homesickness though it never occurred to me to think of how worried and upset my parents were. Neither of them were anxious to have a son among 'the felons of our land'. In fact I learned afterwards that my father was literally ill with concern about my fate. My mother was made of tougher material; no problems of living ever made her ill. Just as it was getting dark my self-pitying reveries were interrupted by the light going on in the gas jet placed in a glassed-in recess in the wall of the cell. It was only then that I took note of the furniture which consisted of a bed and blankets, a wooden chair, a small table, a night bucket, a water jug, an enamelled plate and mug, and a knife, fork and spoon made of bone. Everything was tidily arranged and clean. I looked around to see if there was anything to read, hoping perhaps that there might be a Bible, as I had heard that all prison cells were furnished with Bibles, but there was nothing. To be alone without something to read, even old newspapers, was a new and odd situation for me. It added to my unhappiness. I heard with relief the clatter of the cell door being opened; a warder appeared and glanced around the cell but said nothing. I asked him if I could get anything to read or some note-paper and envelopes. He replied civilly enough that I could get a book in the morning from the prison library and that I would then have permission to write a letter.

Having nothing else to do I got into bed and slept till I was wakened by the cell being opened and breakfast brought round. It consisted of porridge soaked in milk, a hunk of bread topped with a hunk of margarine and a mug of heavily sweetened tea. It was a great relief not to have to face again the smell of the shell cocoa. I learned the truth of the saying that hunger is the best sauce because I had scarcely eaten anything except sweets since tea-time on Saturday and it was now Monday morning. I felt like asking for more porridge, more bread and margarine and more tea but realised that they didn't serve second helpings in Mountjoy. After breakfast all the cells in the prison wing were opened and the prisoners — thirty or forty of us in all — were herded into the exercise ring. Except Cecil Salkeld there was not a single person whom I knew by sight. Before I could make any contacts with my fellow prisoners, one man called out to us to fall in. We formed up in two ranks and the leader, who had apparently been appointed by the prisoners, addressed us. He said that as volunteers we were prisoners of war and that we had a right to be treated as such. He had on behalf of the prisoners conveyed that demand to the Governor who had ignored it and insisted on treating us as prisoners on remand for criminal offences, despite the fact that no charge had even been made against us. In these circumstances it had been decided that, as a protest, we should go on hunger strike until we were recognised as prisoners of war or released. He was careful to explain that anyone undertaking the hunger strike must do so only after full consideration of the possible consequences to himself and his family. Anyone deciding not to participate was assured that such a decision would not be held against him now or in the future. He proposed that those who decided to participate should pledge themselves to eat or drink nothing but water until our demand was granted. Anyone undertaking the pledge would be expected to keep it. The man who addressed us was named Peadar Clancy. Simultaneously a similar scene was being enacted in the exercise rings of the two other wings of the jail where political prisoners were housed.

As and IRA man I would probably have lacked the courage to stand aside and refuse to take part in the hunger strike but any reluctance I might have had would certainly have been overcome by the extraordinary impact Clancy's personality had on me. I had never heard or seen Clancy before nor, indeed, did I ever see him again but he left on me an indelible impression of the superman, a man whose commands I at least would have had a compulsion to obey as if I had been hypnotised. Only once again in my life did I meet anyone whose personality had that overwhelmingly mesmeric effect on me. Many years later Gunnar Myrdal, the Swedish economist, Nobel Prize winner and author of that wonderful book *An American Dilemma* made the same impact on me as had Clancy. My meeting with Mydral was nearly as brief as the encounter with Clancy. In the presence of both of them I felt a mere puppet on a string.

As I afterwards learned, Peadar Clancy was in fact vice-O.C. of the Dublin Brigade, in the topmost council of our Headquarters staff where he was regarded as a man of unusual determination and resource. Within months after the hunger strike he was taken prisoner again, having been betrayed by a 'tout'. The British murdered him and two companions in Dublin Castle. Over all these years the impression of his powerful personality has remained vividly in my mind.

Before we were ordered back to our cells, a fellow prisoner with a fatherly manner came and asked me my age. When I told him I was eighteen he said that one as young as that would not be expected to go on hunger strike. It is true that in 1920 a boy of eighteen would be regarded as a much less mature individual than one of that age today. Nevertheless I did not regard myself as all that young and I told him that I had been a Volunteer since I was fifteen years of age and thought it was my duty to strike with the others.

On returning to our cells the first meal which we had to refuse was brought in; it consisted of a mug of soup and some potatoes and meat on a plate. It looked a miserable meal but had I not been on hunger strike I would have been glad to eat it. I reminded the warder that he promised to get me a book to read and some writing materials. Later on he brought me several books to choose from and writing paper and an envelope. The book I selected, mainly because it looked a long one, turned out to be about travels in China written by a Protestant missionary. I wrote to my mother explaining where I was, warning her not to send any parcels and telling her she might be allowed to visit me.

The next meal to be refused was evening tea, after which we were locked up for the night with nothing but our own long thoughts and, in my case, the book on China to occupy us. I began to feel hungry but not excessively so. I drank plenty of water. At that time we had not heard of the virtues of 'hunger strike soup' which consists of water, pepper and salt; with a little stretch of the imagination it could taste like beef tea. Sleep was my great resource. I had the capacity all my life to turn sleep on at will. Through all the vicissitudes I encountered I have never lost a night's sleep. So in the morning when the slop buckets were collected by the common criminal prisoners and breakfast was again brought around and refused, I was fully refreshed after a good night's sleep and ready to face the day.

That day we were not let out of our cells as usual. We had to await the visit of a doctor who eventually arrived with his entourage of warders. He was a horsey-looking man, with a beery face and bulging eyes. Without bothering to examine me he declared that I was too young to be on hunger strike and a few days without food at my age would impair my health for ever. Having failed to persuade me he went on to say that on account of my youth I would be removed at once to the prison hospital and in fact that was what happened. I was told to pack up and was conducted to a room in the prison hospital. The room was rather bigger than my prison cell and much better lighted. It seemed to have less furniture but had a regular bed into which I was put. I spent the remainder of my jail term in that bed. For the first few days I felt hungry and thought often of food. The food visualised in my imagination was not my mother's steak and mashed potatoes and rice puddings but the two rolls, a butter and a bun and baked beans on toast so often eaten in Roberts' Café. As the days went on the pangs of hunger did not seem to be getting any worse nor did I seem to be any weaker. The doctor called in every day with the same prescription, although after a week he used a stethoscope and took my pulse and temperature. At this stage I began to get nervous, feeling that I should be nearly at the end of my tether since Tom Ashe had died after only six days on hunger strike. I was not comparing like with like. Tom Ashe died from forcible feeding, not from hunger.

We got no newspapers but an air of excitement began to permeate the jail. Every now and then some of the prisoners would break into patriotic songs: 'The West's Awake', 'The Felons of our Land', 'A Nation Once Again'. The warders were very sympathetic to us. They told us about the thousands gathered in demonstrations outside the prison, protesting and saying the rosary for our welfare. They told us that a nationwide general strike had been declared and rumours were going around that we were about to be released. Then it was announced that we were going to be allowed visitors. The door of the hospital cell was left open continuously. Newspapers were passed to us by the warders and we were greatly elated by pictures of the crowds assembled outside. I was embarrassed to see a photo of my father, obviously depressed, talking to Maud Gonne and another one showing him being consoled by the Lord Mayor, Larry O'Neill. I was more than surprised to read headlines telling of the anxiety that was felt for my life because, being so young, I was assumed to be in a critical condition. In bold type on the sixth day of the strike the *Evening Telegraph* reported that 'Christopher Andrews, a boy of eighteen, one of the worst cases on account of his youth and delicate health had collapsed a couple of days ago and was this morning in a state of delirium. His father visited the prison today but did not see the prisoner'. I was finding it hard to convince myself that I was dying after six days without food because I did not feel any weaker. At no time had my health been delicate. I could not read my book on China because my mind was largely occupied in trying to reconcile how well I felt with how badly I should feel. I had a visit from the prison chaplain. I thought he was going to sympathise with my dangerous plight and offer me the Last Sacraments. Instead he warned me that I was wilfully endangering my life which was an immoral act totally forbidden by the Commandments. He did not use the word 'suicide' but that was what was meant. He was a miserably unpleasant personality. Thin lipped, thin faced, he was as narrow in mind as in looks. He spoke with a strangulated accent so often found amongst Castle Catholics of which he was one; otherwise he would not have been a chaplain in Mountjoy. I was sorry that he did not ask me if I wanted to go to confession; being in the state of grace since the previous Saturday I could have had great pleasure in refusing his ministrations. However I assured him that I was not going to take food and that he was not helping by pressing me to change my mind. I never saw him again.

My father was allowed to visit me on the eighth day. He was greatly upset and very pessimistic about the chances of our release, although there were rumours of our being let out conditionally. The 'cat and mouse act' of the suffragette days was going to be applied to us; this, from our point of view, was unacceptable. In his depressed state I found it almost impossible to convince my father that my health, as far as I could judge, was as good now as when I arrived in jail. I told him that the newspaper reports of our condition were totally exaggerated and that being confined to bed so long would probably do me more harm than the absence of food. I suggested to my father that he call on some of the other prisoners along the hospital corridor and talk to them. By this time the jail was so disorganised and the staff, including the governor, the doctor and the warders were in such a state of confusion that it would nearly have been possible for the prisoners, or some of them, to slip out unnoticed but that would have depreciated the value of the propaganda since theoretically we were too weak to escape. The chaplain was the only one of the prison staff who kept his nerve and did his duty although in our estimation 'doing his duty' was merely doing the dirty work required by his British employers. He continued to demoralise the prisoners by hints of eternal damnation if they died of hunger. But by this time we knew the nation was supporting us. It was unlikely that if any one of us died we would be considered damned and in our minds the verdict of the nation was more important than the opinion of the prison chaplain.

I was anxious for news of 'E' Company. I asked my father to get Earle to visit me in the guise of my brother. I had no difficulty in convincing Earle that my condition was not as low as the press reports indicated. He brought me newspapers and magazines to read and took out letters for my mother and Ewart Wilson. Earle rightly regarded the General Strike, the Mass, the Rosary, the demonstrations as a marvellous exercise in the pressurization of the British. Dublin Castle was in disarray and tried to compromise with the prisoners even to the extent of offering political treatment. This is where Peadar Clancy showed his mettle. He realised that the British Government's nerve had gone. He refused to accept political prisoner status, informing the British that the hunger strike would only be called off if we were released. His determination won the day and we were all released after ten days. So my first sojourn in jail could hardly have been shorter nor my experience of jail less injurious. I was in bed for nine of the ten days. I had met scarcely any of my fellow prisoners. It transpired that Cecil Salkeld was released after a couple of days' detention.

I was taken out of the prison in an ambulance with another man who had been hospitalized during the strike. We were driven through a cheering crowd, hysterical with joy, en route for the Mater Hospital. Outside the prison gates two priests and another man, to whom everyone seemed to defer, climbed into the ambulance to provide an escort for my companion who, it transpired, was a leader of the strike and was obviously a person of importance. I was astonished by my fellow prisoner's appearance. He seemed evidently in a weak state as he answered in a low melodious, pronouncedly Northern accent the solicitous enquiries of his friends. He had a magnificent head of titian-red hair. His beard, of the same colour, was beautifully trimmed despite the rigour of the ordeal he had just undergone. His large brown liquid eyes expressed fortitude, compassion and sadnesss. He could well have been a model for a statue of the Sacred Heart so commonly seen in repositories and homes in Ireland although I feared I might be guilty of blasphemy in imagining the resemblance. I was very flattered to find on arrival at the Mater Hospital that I was given the bed next to him. The hospital personnel were as much excited as the crowds outside. Nurses, nuns, doctors and medical students showered us with greetings. The ward was decorated with flowers. We had a specially prepared meal of porridge and milk with fruit. Visitors, mainly clerics, crowded into the ward to shake our hands. There was even a bishop amongst the visitors. For the first time I kissed an episcopal ring. Considering the attitude of the bishops as a whole this was a rare enough experience for an IRA man. I had no chance to talk to my companion of the ambulance. Although he was obviously weak and slightly sad in manner his bed was surrounded with admirers until the ward was cleared of strangers and the lights were put out for the night. I turned over to sleep in a mood of high patriotic exaltation.

I must have been asleep for a couple of hours when I was wakened by some noises coming from the bed next to me. Alas, it was a sad awakening. My Christ-like companion of the ambulance, a leader of the hunger strike, had succeeded against, it must be said, mere token resistance in pulling one of the nurses on to his bed.

After a couple of days in bed we had all recovered from any ill effects we may have had from the hunger strike. Personally I had none. I doubt if anyone else had any either. We stayed in the Mater for another few days, receiving visitors and exchanging views and experiences. It was the first chance I had to meet my quondam jail companions. They were young men from all over the country, all active Volunteers and all anxious to get back to their units to take part in the growing tempo of the fight against the British. Of course, they were not adverse to the hero's welcome they were sure to receive on reaching home. I met many of them again later on in internment camps, jails or in their own localities and the contacts made in the course of our shared experience of Mountjoy were a great advantage to me in subsequent years.

The hunger strike had been the first mass hunger strike to take place in Ireland, or indeed anywhere. Over a hundred men participated in it. In the light of subsequent experience, ten days is a relatively short time to be without food but other factors operate to condition men's minds besides mere hunger. Family worries, uncertainty, and a pervasive fear of unwanted death, as well as religious scruples, all have different effects on different temperaments. In the case of the IRA it is an error to think that hunger strikers participated voluntarily. The moral pressure deriving from the wish and the need to show solidarity with one's comrades is so powerful as to amount to an order. It would be an exceptional character who would refuse to join in a hunger strike to which all his comrades were committed except those specifically excused because of some infirmity. It is also a total misjudgement of human nature to think that a hundred men taken at random will sustain a hunger strike to the point of death. Only unusual individuals can sustain a prolonged hunger strike to its ultimate conclusion. A hunger and thirst strike is an absurd form of protest even for individuals; it cannot last for more than a few days. In our case, if the hunger strke had gone on for a few days longer almost certainly someone's resistance would have broken. With each succeeding day a few more men would have taken food. Possibly half a dozen rare spirits would have carried on until the bitter end. Even if only two or three men broke down, say, after fourteen days, the Government's will would have been sufficiently strengthened to refuse our demand. As events turned out, the hunger strike gave the Movement an enormous boost of morale at very little cost. The British will to govern was weakened. It is also doubtful if the industrial strike which had been organised in our support could have been carried on much longer. A majority of the labour leaders had little enthusiasm for it from the beginning and the workers were beginning to feel insupportable hardship.

I got no welcome in Terenure on my return except from my parents and my friends in 'E' Company. The local population could not be said to be enthusiastic Republicans. When I got home I reported back to the Company which was about to burn the old police barracks at Rockbrook near Glen Dhu. Coughlan would not let me take part in the job, reckoning I was not yet fit. I found it impossible to convince him and many other people, including particularly my parents, that the hunger strike had not had even the slightest adverse effect on my health or fitness. More to prove my point than for any other reason, I accepted an invitation from a football club to play for them in the Leinster Junior Cup Final in Shelbourne Park. I was technically eligible to play in an under-eighteen competition. We lost the match but I gained a runner-up medal. It was the only one I ever won in my life despite my participation in so many sporting activities: soccer, Gaelic football, cricket, swimming, handball, rowing, hockey, golf, tennis. I treasured that medal greatly.

*   *   *   *   *

When the dust settled after the excitement of the hunger strike I was presented with the problem of how to organise my daily life. I was instructed by Coughlan not to sleep at home. At that time the British had not devised any method of picking IRA activists up off the streets; they had no police force, the DMP having been neutralised. They did not usually raid houses except after dark so that, apart from sleeping away from home, it was possible even for a known IRA man to lead a normal life.

In principle I should have gone back to College, taken my lectures and sat for my examination in June. The belief that something of major consequence would happen in the Movement at any moment made examinations seem unimportant. I had not the disposition to study. Nevertheless, I went into College in the mornings mainly to discuss the political situation with my friends there. We had plenty to discuss: the dockers refusing to unload munitions in transit from England and the railwaymen refusing to carry troops or munitions on the trains, although when they sought the co-operation of their brother trade unionists in Britain they got a dusty answer.

A news item in the English press predicted that hundreds of block houses were to be established throughout the country garrisoned by troops. Remembering what the British had done to the Boers with the aid of block houses, it was a worrying prospect especially as at the same time the British Army were forming para-military units drawn from the unemployed who became known as the Black and Tans. An elite section formed from ex-officers were known as Auxiliaries. These were the temporary 'gentlemen' of the Great War, now without visible means of support.

All that summer and autumn the RIC and the British troops came constantly under attack and a concerted effort was made to uncover and eliminate touts and political detectives. A raid on the military guard at the Kings' Inns netted rifles, ammunition and machine guns, the weapons we most lacked. Arms were seized and army stores destroyed at Kingsbridge. The Chairman of the Dublin South Eastern Railways, Mr Frank Brook, who was serving on an advisory committee to Lord French, the Lord Lieutenant, was shot dead in Westland Row station. After the shooting of Alan Bell for somewhat similar undercover activities, it might have been expected that Brook would have learned some sense.

We followed the news of De Valera's campaign in the USA for the recognition of the Republic. We heard of the great meetings he had addressed, the resolutions that had been passed in favour of Irish independence. They all amounted to words. Words which don't resolve themselves in action are useless. We got some money that by our standards seemed substantial but by American standards was derisory. The US government did nothing to help. On the contrary they made sure we got no arms from sympathisers in the States.

In the afternoons I went frequently to the cinema though the pictures, except for the Pathe Gazette, were often so heavily censored as to be unintelligible. Two or three afternoons in the week I went to the university sportsground in Terenure for practice matches and on Saturdays I played for the College in a league match under a false name, C. Coll. In the evenings I was never at a loss for something to do. I went to Rathfarnham where there was always some activity to be undertaken in connection with the Movement, like parades, sometimes patrolling the area looking for touts and one tout in particular. On two occasions I was sent into town with my 'dog' to report to Dick McKee, the O/C of the Dublin Brigade. On both occasions I was kept waiting with some men I did not know for nearly two hours and dismissed without being offered an explanation.

McKee's office was in Gardiner Street so that, instead of recrossing the city, I went up to my grandmother's house in Summerhill nearby. Abortive missions of this kind when nothing happened and we got no explanations were a frequent occurrence. When the College broke up for the summer holidays I spent most of my days with Earle visiting the public library, swimming in Blackrock Baths or simply walking and talking. On our walks he carried his tuning fork and as he walked sang his way through Gilbert and Sullivan. At night I slept in Ewart Wilson's house or occasionally at my grandmother's in Summerhill.

Our first contact with the Black and Tans was in December, 1920. One Sunday morning we held a Company council meeting in St Enda's. It was over early and with Coughlan I went to play handball in

147

the wooden alley which Pearse had built. Coughlan was a very good handballer, having been junior champion of Ireland. I always had an ambition to beat him even if only once. I thought my chance had arrived as I was leading him by a few aces when we heard first one, then another and still another volley of rifle shots. They sounded quite near us. We ducked into the woods and waited for further developments but since nothing happened we decided it was safe to come out on to the road and walk home. Sauntering along, we heard the noise of lorries. Soon two lorries manned by the infamous Black and Tans and literally crammed with prisoners drove by. We had no difficulty in recognising the prisoners as members of the newly formed Fifth Engineering Battalion of the Dublin Brigade. We knew several of the prisoners personally; one of them, Danny Mulhall, was an intimate friend of mine since school days. It did not take us long to find out what had happened. The local people brought the news to Coughlan as soon as the Tans were out of sight.

The Fifth Battalion had been on unarmed manoeuvres in the mountainy country around Ticknock when the Tans appeared and opened fire. One of the Battalion was killed in the first volley and about twenty were captured, the others escaping across the hill. We were told that a number of the Fifth Battalion Volunteers had cycled out from the city and parked their bicycles near St Columba's College. Coughlan collected all the 'E' Company men at hand to rescue the bikes before the Tans returned. Obviously someone had given the IRA men away but we thought it curious that none of the local police had taken part in the raid. It was to be expected that they would act as guides to the Tans who presumably were English and strangers to the locality. We suspected, almost certainly wrongly, that the Tans received their information from St Columba's College — a bastion of the ascendancy. This episode was the first blood the Tans drew in Dublin. Our manoeuvring on the mountains was effectively ended.

Shortly after this incident Kevin Barry, an eighteen-year-old medical student, was captured in an ambush in the city. I knew him in College but not very well since he was a rugby player and a Jesuit boy. I knew he was one of 'us' although this fact in no way helped to foster our acquaintance. In the College there were a number of students who were known to be IRA men but, unless they were in the same Company or Battalion, they never spoke or associated with one another on the basis of their common allegiance to the IRA and if they were friendly it was for altogether different reasons.

One of my close friends in the College was a medical student named Andy Cooney from Tipperary. I knew him to be an IRA man and, of course, everyone in the College knew of my IRA connections because of the hunger strike publicity. I played cards with Cooney and saw a lot of him in the sports ground in Terenure but we never mentioned our membership of the IRA. This attitude was indicative of the extreme secrecy which was the strength of the IRA and which distinguished it from all previous separatist movements in Ireland.

An intense national and international campaign to save Kevin Barry's life helped more than any single incident since 1916 to stoke the fires of hatred of the British. Not since they hanged Casement in August of 1916 had anyone been executed. I doubt whether even Terence MacSwiney's death, which occurred a few weeks before, aroused such bitter anti-British feelings. MacSwiney, who had been Lord Mayor of Cork, had died after 73 days on hunger strike in Wormwood Scrubs Prison. As rank and file IRA men we could not visualise ourselves cast in the same heroic mould as the Lord Mayor of Cork. But it was easy to imagine ourselves sharing the plight of Kevin Barry. Indeed a fellow student and friend of mine, Frank Flood, was taken prisoner and executed within a few months of Kevin Barry's death. But as Kevin Barry passed into the nation's mythology, Frank Flood's name is scarcely remembered.

There was relatively little activity by the IRA in Dublin until late in 1920 apart from the General Strike and a day of national mourning for Terence MacSwiney. Life in the city was normal except for the curfew which lasted from midnight until sometimes 5 a.m., sometimes 3 a.m. The citizens suffered little inconvenience in going about their business or amusements. The theatres and picture houses were open. Football matches were played before big crowds at the weekends in Dalymount, Jones's Road and Lansdowne Road and, of course, there was racing. I doubt if the horsey people were aware that there had been a 1916 Rebellion; they may have associated it with Fairyhouse Easter Meeting which took place on the same day.

Conditions in the provinces were much more disturbed than in Dublin at least until the closing months of the year. The Black and Tans and the Auxiliaries had burned, looted and wrecked towns like Tuam, Balbriggan, Mallow, Lahinch, and Ennistymon. The pogram had begun in Belfast when County Inspector Swanzy, the policeman who had murdered Thomas MacCurtain, Lord Mayor of Cork, was shot in Lisburn. The mayhem caused by the Black and Tans and the Auxiliaries created the illusion in the mind of Lloyd George that he had 'murder by the throat'. For myself, apart from not sleeping at home and avoiding the centre of the city, where the Black and Tans and Auxiliaries now began to appear on foot, there was little change

149

in my way of life.

With the deep emotion generated amongst us by Kevin Barry's death, the question of some gesture of retaliation arose in the Company. Kenny, the first lieutenant, again urged an attack on Rathfarnham RIC barracks, the existence of which seemed a constant reproach to us. I spent hours drawing up plans for such an attack using the whole Fourth Battalion and, if necessary, the Third. I am afraid my plans were based on pipe dreams; an open uprising would be required to carry them out. Anyway, Coughlan was firm in his refusal to let us fire even a few shots at the barracks if only to show cause.

This was my frame of mind and that of a group of us in the Company when one afternoon in the middle of November Coughlan called at my house. He got no warm welcome from my mother; to her he was a purveyor of trouble and mischief and she didn't like him. He asked me to come outside as he had something important to say. We strolled around the corner and he started to talk about the atrocity that had just been committed by the British in murdering Kevin Barry. He pointed out that Barry's death was an example of British terror tactics — tactics that had been used too often, and successfully, against us. These tactics had to be stopped.

For the first time I heard of the network of British agents which had been established under various guises throughout the city. Coughlan went on to talk of Leonard MacNally and Thomas Reynolds, of Pierce Nagle and Lecaron, the informers on the United Irishmen and the Fenians and, of course, Carey who informed on the Invincibles. I was beginning to wonder what all the circumlocution was about when at last he came to the point and it became clear that he was screwing my courage to the sticking place in advance. Headquarters, with the approval of the Minister for Defence, Cathal Brugha, had decided to kill all the known British agents at 9 a.m. on Sunday 21 November. The Companies of the Dublin Brigade had been selected to carry out the executions. Our Company had been ordered to deal with a man who was regarded as a key man in the British network. He lived with his wife, or some woman, at a house in Ranelagh and went under the nom de guerre of Captain Nobel.

Coughlan had decided that he, Earle and I would go into the house and execute Nobel. A picked squad from the Company would cover our retreat in case anything went wrong. He told me to see Earle, tell him in outline what had been conveyed to me and bring him along to Ballyboden Library that evening at eight o'clock. I got very strict instructions not to mention the matter to anyone except Earle, not even to Kenny. He said that he would himself talk to Kenny later.

After leaving Coughlan, I took the tram to the College in Earlsfort Terrace interrupting Earle in his work and suggesting that he should come home with me for tea and arrange to sleep at home that night instead of going back to Blackrock Castle, where he was obliged to reside by the terms of his university scholarship. He protested at the interruption but the grumbling ceased when, as we walked along Hatch Street, I told him of Coughlan's conversation with me, leaving out the bits about British terrorism and the historical references to informers.

We were very excited by the assignment but the prospect of killing a man in cold blood was alien to our ideas of how war should be conducted. We neither of us relished the idea. We were apprehensive, too, because it could be a very dangerous operation. We were already being affected psychologically by the terror of the Tans. On the other hand it was an article of my national faith that separatism had always been wrecked on a reef erected by informers and spies. I believed that it was justifiable to kill informers, spies, touts, traitors and active collaborators with the occupational forces. This policy combined with insistence on extreme secrecy at all levels of the organisation had so far enabled the IRA to survive. Further strength was added to the Movement by the penetration of the British administration in Dublin Castle by agents of the IRA. For the first time in the history of separatism we Irish had a better intelligence service than the British. In my opinion this was Michael Collins's great achievement and it is one for which every Irishman should honour his memory. We never saw his like before.

Believing this, I saw no objection in principle to shooting Nobel much as I disliked the harsh reality. Earle and I reported to Coughlan at Ballyboden and he repeated what he had already told me, including the references to terror and counter-terror and to British secret agents of other times e.g. MacNally and Reynolds and Lecaron and Nagle and Carey, adding Corydon — he knew them all. He also told us that about twenty British agents were to be executed by simultaneous strikes on Sunday 21 November.

In the meantime Earle and I were to spend half an hour a day each watching the house in Ranelagh in the hope of identifying Nobel. Our reconnoitering was unsuccessful. Earle and I were now faced with a dilemma. We were both due to play in a league match for the UCD soccer team on Saturday 20th. It might not look well if we both cried off although this is what we would like to have done rather than run the risk of injury. It would have been thought a disgrace to have missed for any reason so important a mission. We tossed for the privilege of not playing. I lost, played the game and in the last quarter of an hour of the match the inevitable happened. An opponent's head collided with mine, resulting in bad concussion. I lost my sight temporarily but nearly lost my mind with the worry of being unable to perform my allotted role the following morning. I felt that, short of actual death, I would be unable to persuade my comrades in the Company or in the Battalion that I had not faked an accident to avoid the mission. This, of course, was nonsense but I felt that I could not live with myself if I failed for any reason to turn up.

Fortunately, after a bout of vomiting my vision returned leaving me very groggy but sufficiently recovered to walk to Ewart Wilson's house where I had parked my 'dog', a .45 long Webley, and where I intended to spend the night. I lay down for an hour but was well enough to go to a meeting at 7.30 p.m. in a house in Rathmines where the final arrangements for the morrow were to be made. In addition to Coughlan, Earle and myself as principal actors, there was Kenny who was to take charge of the group of men outside the house, protecting our getaway and making sure that Nobel did not escape through the back door. Coughlan, using a piece of paper and pencil, set out the exact position to be taken by every man with added instructions of what was to be done in case we were surprised. Before we left he ostentatiously burned the paper. He told us that when the job was completed we were to hand our 'dogs' to a taxi-driver who would take them to the dump. When the 'dogs' were disposed of we were to disperse separately to our houses.

On leaving the meeting we were told, as a precaution, to go home singly. Some of the men went to Confession in Rathgar or Rathmines Churches. I had gone to Confession that morning at Mount Argus where a Passionist Father was always available. In 1920 our morale required that we should be in a state of grace, at least sporadically. I returned to Ewart Wilson's house, went to bed early and read a few pages of Dreiser's *Jenny Gerhardt* which Earle had recommended. I found it difficult to concentrate on the book but soon I slept easily and dreamlessly.

I was up and ready to go to our rendezvous at 8 a.m. It was only then that I felt genuinely uneasy and doubtful about the job. I had increasing fears that we might be surprised by the Tans. If that happened and we were captured, we would have been shot or hanged. It is not an agreeable prospect for a nineteen-year-old psychologically unattuned to assassination. These were my preoccupations on this calm, fine, grey winter's day as I walked, feeling rather desolate, the mile from Brighton Square to the canal at Charlemont Street Bridge where I met Coughlan, Earle and Kenny at five minutes to nine. Punctually at 9 a.m. Coughlan, who was carrying a stick, knocked at the door of the house. It was opened by a girl of about fifteen years. Coughlan pushed the stick into the hall to prevent the door being slammed, walked rapidly up the stairs to the front room, which we knew to be Nobel's, followed by Earle and myself. We had our 'dogs' cocked as we opened the door of the bedroom expecting to see Nobel. Our orders were to shoot him on sight as he was certain to be armed. We found the room empty except for a half-naked woman who sat up in bed looking terror stricken. She did not scream or say a word. I was very excited but, even so, I felt a sense of shame and embarrassment for the woman's sake. I was glad to get out quickly and moved to the next room where there was a man shaving. He was literally petrified with fear. His safety razor froze in mid-air. Thinking he was Nobel I was going to pull the trigger of my .45 when Coughlan shouted 'He's all right'. He was a lodger in the house and was apparently one of our intelligence sources.

We went downstairs and looked through the other rooms. Kenny and two other members of the Company were in the hall as had been arranged. To my surprise there were also two armed strangers who greeted Coughlan familiarily. They were from Collins's squad and their object was to get hold of Nobel's papers, but in fact none were found. There were only women and children in the rest of the house but that did not prevent the pair from the squad behaving like Black and Tans. In their search for papers they overturned furniture, pushing the occupants of the house around, and either through carelessness or malice set fire to a room in which there were children. Coughlan was furious at their conduct. Having seen the children to safety he directed Kenny to bring two more members of the Company into the house so that we could form a bucket chain from the tap in the basement (the only tap in the house) to the first floor where the fire was becoming serious. Nearly half an hour was wasted putting out the fire before we were able to get out of the house, dump our 'dogs' in the waiting taxi (oddly enough the taxi-driver was not a member of the IRA) and disperse singly on foot.

As I went back to Terenure through quiet suburban roads and lanes well known to me, I wondered whether I was glad or sorry that Nobel had not been at home. I would certainly have felt no remorse at having shot him but I found it hard to get the memory of the terrified woman and indeed, the equally terrified lodger, from my mind. We all arrived home safely and a few of us appeared prominently among the congregation leaving the 11 o'clock Mass in Terenure.

In those days exceptional news reached the suburbs by *Stop Press*. The newsboys ran all the way from town with bundles of papers specially printed to carry exceptional news. Strangely enough, there were no *Stop Presses* that day. The excitement of the morning had not penetrated to the suburbs. At home the dinner table conversation was as desultory as always. Coming from Mass my parents had heard that there had been some row and shooting in the city. My brother was thinking of going to Croke Park to see the big match between Tipperary and Dublin but I frightened him off by telling him that I had heard that a couple of Tans had been killed in town. If this had occurred there were bound to be raids on Croke Park but I did not, of course, anticipate the mini-massacre which took place there that afternoon.

After dinner I took myself up to the College grounds at Terenure just to keep out of the way. I met only one student I knew — Andy Cooney who was a member of the Third Battalion. Instinctively I knew that he had participated in the events of the morning. Equally well Cooney guessed that I had been involved but we both carefully feigned ignorance of the whole business. I invited him home to tea and he gladly accepted; as in the case of all students it was a relief to get away from his digs. After tea my father went out to see a neighbour while Cooney and I chatted about the political situation, which was the only subject of interest between us. We wondered what truth there was in the rumours of peace which were circulating freely amongst the Companies. We suspected that the rumours were being spread by the British to lower our morale; no one wants to risk death or imprisonment if peace is in sight. We talked about the possibility of some intervention by the League of Nations but had little hope that anything would come of it or indeed that any real help could be expected from any other country.

My father returned with a garbled and exaggerated account of the events of the day. Rumour had it that hundreds of people had been killed in Croke Park; the Black and Tans were rampaging through the city shooting indiscriminately and martial law had been declared. His information was not quite accurate but accurate enough to persuade myself and Cooney to get to our lodgings without cutting curfew too close. That evening with Cooney formed the basis of a long and, as it happened, significant friendship between us.

Our Company had been instructed to keep away from Croke Park that afternoon and I assumed that all the units who were involved in the morning's operation were similarly warned. Cooney, who was a Tipperary man and a GAA enthusiast, would certainly have been at the match in the ordinary way. It is most unlikely that many of the IRA men who were 'out' that morning were in Croke Park in the afternoon. Nevertheless, because of the indiscriminate killing of twelve people in the crowd who were watching the match, it was the GAA that appropriated 'Bloody Sunday', which the day has ever since been called, as part of their contribution to the Movement. The men who carried out the IRA operation got no credit for what in fact entailed considerable physical and — even harder to endure — great psychological and moral strain.

I have heard one historian in a Thomas Davis lecture on Radio Éireann say that IRA men were brought from the country brigades to help in the 'Bloody Sunday' attack on the intelligence officers. This is not correct. Only the members of the Dublin Brigade and of the Collins squad were employed. Another error of omission appears among the historians of the event: the fact is that the majority of the raids made by the IRA were abortive because, as in our case, the man sought was not at home or in several cases the Companies concerned bungled the job. In our Fourth Battalion there were at least four abortive raids. In one case, a British intelligence man — an Irishman — bluffed his way out of his precarious situation by pretending to be someone else while his companion was identified and shot. Nevertheless the success of the operation, followed as it was a few weeks later by the success of Tom Barry in wiping out a unit of the 'invincible' Auxiliaries at Kilmichael, convinced the British that they could not win at a cost they could afford to pay. Tom Barry, who had fought with the British army in the 1918 war, had organised the most spectacularly successful flying column. His exploits became legendary. He became a folk hero in his lifetime.

It was a pleasure for me to read the English papers of Monday 22 November 1920. They sucked Roget's *Thesaurus* dry to find words to denounce us. We were gunmen, terrorists, extremists, murderers, assassins, butchers, thugs. They were particularly vocal about the sense of horror that swept their nation. No race commands such an inexhaustible supply of horror as do the British when their interests are adversely affected. I also bought *The Irish Times* to see what it had to say. I was not disappointed. The leading article was headed 'The Dublin Murders'. Here are some chosen extracts from it: 'Every good Irishman will read with shame and horror the story of wholesale murder which we print this morning. Yesterday was Dublin's most dreadful day since Easter week of 1916' and 'Nearly all the murdered officers had been engaged in the administration of justice; some had collected evidence, others had prosecuted at court martials. It may be that the assassins hoped, by these desperate deeds of blood, to impede the law and to terrorise its servants. If that was their hope it was, of course, futile. These murders will confirm the Government in its resolve to crush the campaign of crime. They will result, not in less and milder, but in greater and sterner, activity by the troops and the police. Of necessity, they will multiply the number of raids and searches and will aggravate existing restrictions on the liberty of the citizen. Moreover, they will harden the temper of the English nation — Englishmen and Scotsmen were murdered yesterday in Dublin — and in the House of Commons will strengthen the Irish Government's case for the need of repressive measures' and 'A country whose capital can be the scene of fourteen callous and cowardly murders, on one Sunday morning, has reached the nadir of moral, and political degradation'. The leading article reflected the views of the Ascendancy but it also showed a complete lack of comprehension of the public frame of mind as well as a complete alienation from it. Having read the article, I felt sorry we had missed Nobel.

On Monday an air of tension pervaded the city. Reprisals in one form or another were expected. Except for the intensification of raids on the houses of known or suspected IRA men nothing happened. Apparently the Croke Park shootings and the murder of McKee, Clancy and Clune abated, at least temporarily, the fury of the Crown forces. McKee, the O/C of the Dublin Brigade, and Clancy, who was our leader in the Mountjoy hunger strike, were picked up on the information supplied by a tout on the evening before Bloody Sunday. The killing of the intelligence officers spread terror among the numerous touts, informers and spies as well as those professional agents who escaped death through absence from their lodgings or otherwise. Frank Gallagher in his book *The Four Glorious Years* describes the scene at Dublin Castle as follows: 'In the next few days Dublin saw one of the strangest sights that the old city had ever witnessed. From all corners of the capital there began a trek of minor spies and spotters and touts into the Castle which was the size of a small town. They brought their families and their personal belongings. They crowded in behind those high walls in full admission that their day was done. Apparently the "G" division of the DMP had been driven in; then the heads of the RIC and now a motley gathering of undesirables of all kinds and sorts who had looked for blood money and in this day of doom wanted nothing so much as protection'. One tout who had not the wit to seek that protection was the informer who betrayed McKee and Clancy. He was a British ex-soldier, well known in the neighbourhood of Gloucester Street as a ne'er-do-well and a drunken 'bousy'. It was a few weeks before Collins's squad caught up with him. They eventually found him in a pub near the Five Lamps — a well-known Dublin landmark — enjoying a morning pint and reading the *Independent* newspaper. They shot him there and then.

I felt I could no longer take the risk of moving around openly during the day time and living at home except at night. I got some money from my father for the pictures and left the house intending to call back some time in the evening to collect a second outfit of clothes, shoes and underwear. I went down to Rathmines to see Earle only to find to my dismay that he had been 'lifted' (the word we always used for arrested) in the early hours of that morning. At a loss to know what to do I took what was for me a courageous and revolutionary step. I asked Earle's sister, Eva, to come to the pictures and she accepted. It was the first time I had ever been out alone with a girl. This was not due to misogyny; on the contrary I spent most of my idle time indulging in fantasies about girls and making unsuccessful efforts to avoid immodest thoughts. Avoidance of immodest thoughts was not easy for a young man in the twenties as women's skirts shortened and their neck-lines deepened. The fact was that I never met any girls except in 'coveys' at the Sinn Féin Club or at Gaelic League functions or at Morosini's dancing school. Any of these girls I liked particularly always seemed to have their mothers around. Mothers were not deliberately installed as chaperons; it happened that way. Even if I wanted to detach a girl from her mother, and in one case I would have liked to, my self-confidence was inadequate to cope with this problem.

Eva Earle was a tall blonde girl, a year older than her brother, Bert. In retrospect I realised that she could have been a very beautiful woman if she had not preferred the role of blue-stocking. We had no difficulty in sustaining conversation as we walked the few hundred yards from her house to the cinema, the 'Princess' in Rathmines. The details of Bert's arrest by the British military was a sufficient topic. During the showing of a Charlie Chaplin comedy followed by advertisements and the Pathe Gazette, we sat in passive silence. Eva enjoyed the music supplied by a violinist and a pianist. Neither of us thought highly of Charlie Chaplin and we left before the end of the show. Being unable to take the chance of going back to her home for tea in case the house was watched, she invited me to a nearby café. For the first time I learned something about her. She was not much interested in men, loved music and went to many concerts but her principal interest was reading fiction. We were on common ground there. She had just finished a new book by H. de Vere Stackpoole, a piece of information which immediately drew *The Blue Lagoon* into the conversation. *The Blue Lagoon* was regarded at that time as almost compulsory surreptitious reading for post-adolescents who read at all. It seemed as daringly explicit in the early twenties as *Lady Chatterley's Lover* was a decade later. I was surprised that Eva had not only read the book but had seen nothing immoral in it. Neither did I but I thought a respectably genteel girl should be shocked by it. From the beginning, quite without knowing it, I had accepted the doctrine of double standards for men and women. Brief as our encounter was, Eva and I established a rapport which lasted over the years even though we never went out together again.

Having left Eva I took a tram home to Terenure. It was dark as I walked down from the tram terminus to my home. Although I passed several of the 'locals' none of them spoke to me. This did not surprise me as in my relations with the people of the neighbourhood I worked on the scriptural principle of 'he that is not with me is against me'. I only spoke to or passed the time of day with people whom I knew to be sympathetic to the Movement. Nearing the house I saw what appeared at first to be a crowd outside it. On closer inspection they turned out to be an Army detachment. I arrived just in time to see my father being helped into a lorry by the soldiers. The thought that my father might be arrested instead of me had never occurred to me. I reckoned without the meticulous attention to orders required in the British Army. They were sent to arrest Christopher Andrews. My father's name was Christopher. As far as the Army was concerned one Christopher was as good as another; their instructions did not provide for a birth certificate. I was very upset to see my father being taken away. Not because I thought the soldiers would harm him but because I feared his health would not stand up to imprisonment. I regarded him as an old man although in fact he was only forty-nine years. I was also worried as to what I should do next. It was clear that I was now really on the run. I was reluctant to go to Wilson's, where I usually slept, fearing I might have overused it as a safe house. With Earle already lifted and in the generally tense atmosphere of the time I got the jitters. I decided to go to the house of one of the members of the Company who was unlikely to be known to the British as an IRA man. Unfortunately one of the leaders acting on the same assumption had been staying there for some time. When I arrived, the sound of the strange voice in the hall led him to think that the house was being raided. I had seen nothing since the incident in the Mater Hospital to diminish my deep respect and belief in the leaders. To me at that time anyone who made a public speech, or even appeared on a Sinn Féin platform, was a leader to be looked up to. The one I now met was well known to me by sight even before 1916. When I entered the room I found him trembling and panic-stricken. On realising the true circumstances he behaved like a mother who barely succeeds in preventing her child from running under a motor car and gives it a walloping out of sheer relief. I was roundly abused for having brought suspicion on the house and, of course, endangering his safety. He left me in no doubt of his importance to the Movement as compared with my insignificance. Even from leaders I was not prepared to put up with that sort of per-formance and made my feelings clear to him in not too polite a way. I left, much to the distress of my host. I learned two lessons from this incident. It is never wise to catch a man with his trousers down for he will never forgive either you or himself for his humiliation. I also learned to be a little more careful in accepting leaders uncritically.

I was badly in need of some refuge where I could come and go with reasonable security. I was also anxious to find out what had happened at home and what the position was there now. Further I had to get in touch with Coughlan or Kenny to report the most recent developments. I had the good luck to think of my old friend, Paddy Caffrey. His house was fairly safe. He gave me a warm welcome metaphorically and literally. His book-lined kitchen was heated to a temperature well into the 80s. He insisted on my having tea and a boiled egg. His cheerfulness and homespun philosophy soon restored my composure. Caffrey, decent man that he was, said that the first thing to be done was to find out how my mother was faring and where my father had been detained. He undertook to look after my mother and see what could be done to get my father released. In the meantime I had better make arrangements about sleeping accom-modation. In this he could not help. His spare bed had become a dis-orderly bookshelf.

It was now getting late in the evening. I had had a long stand-ing invitation from a school friend named Morewood who lived alone with his widowed mother in a house in Rathmines (which betokened considerable affluence) but had never been sure whether to take his invitation seriously or not. Now I was rather desperate. I would just have time to try Morewood's and, if that refuge failed, to return to Wilson's or even Caffrey's if only for a night. In fact More-wood didn't fail me. I got a kind welcome from old Mrs Morewood who turned out to be an ardent supporter of Sinn Féin. She was glad to be able to help in putting me up. It was here I slept for the next few weeks and many nights on and off afterwards. Mrs Morewood was a gay, light-hearted woman in her late fifties or early sixties. She lived on her means and in considerable comfort. My friend, Dick, was the only son. Her four daughters, who were very typical modern women of the twenties, were all married comfortably. Neither the daughters nor their husbands shared their mother's view of the Movement. As they often dropped in and out of the house it was necessary for me to keep out of their way. Not because they were likely to betray me to the British but they would object to their mother taking the risk of harbouring me. This meant that I had to leave the house before 11 o'clock each morning so as to keep clear of family intrusions.

On the Tuesday after my first night in Morewoods I went to see Kenny who worked in a grocer's shop in Rathmines. I learnt from him that Coughlan's house had been raided simultaneously with mine on the previous day. I then called on Paddy Caffrey who had quit teaching in Synge Street and was running a correspondence college for schools from his home. He had seen my mother who, through the good offices of a DMP man who was a neighbour, learned that my father had been lodged in the Bridewell. Remembering my brief experience of the Bridewell I felt very worried about how my father would survive the filthy conditions and even filthier food but it turned out that my fears were groundless. The neighbourly DMP man happened to be on duty in the Bridewell on the night my father arrived. He realised that a mistake had been made by the Army and saw to it that my father got a bed and a small room to himself. He told my mother that she would be allowed to visit my father and bring him parcels. Paddy Caffrey arranged for himself and my mother to see the Lord Mayor to seek his intervention with Dublin Castle on my father's behalf. The Lord Mayor's efforts were successful. After four days my father was released. He was quite undamaged by the experience; rather enjoyed it in fact. He was very proud of having been arrested but it was thought better that he didn't sleep at home thenceforward. He got lodgings with a neighbour and slept away from home from the end of November 1920 until the Truce in July 1921. My brother, who was now fourteen, and very big for his age was also sent to another neighbour's house to sleep. The life of the family was completely disrupted but it was a very wise decision because from then until the Truce the house was constantly raided by the Army and several times by the Auxiliaries. My mother carried the burden of all these raids phlegmatically and uncomplainingly.

My problem now had become one of putting in the time since I could no longer risk attending College or going to Terenure to play football. I heard that the Brigade was forming an active service unit of wholetime IRA men. They were paid only enough to maintain themselves. I asked Coughlan if he could arrange for me to join. He refused, telling me I was not suited for that kind of organisation. He didn't explain why he thought I was unsuitable. I think the real reason may be that he didn't want to lose my companionship. He was a lonely man without many friends; I supplied him with some mental pabulum. We often talked about the progress of the Russian Revolution, particularly about the apparent failure of the Bolsheviks to deal successfully with the peasants and agriculture. Coughlan was very interested in all questions affecting the land. He thought, like Davitt, that it was a mistake to have created peasant proprietorship in Ireland. He was the only person I knew who seriously considered what economic policies we would pursue when independence was achieved. The fact is that very few of us expected that we would ever bring the struggle to a successful conclusion. While we talked of getting rid of the British, in our hearts we thought of our revolt as only one more chapter in the history of national resistance and likely to prove as ineffective as all those that went before. I was rather relieved at Coughlan's decision as I was still in that mood of high idealism which considered that it was somehow wrong for an IRA man to take even maintenance money when fighting for the Movement. I felt, as had always been my belief, that this was an inevitable manifestation of the difference between the Volunteers and the IRA. It was, of course, easy for me to feel that way as I could rely on my parents to support me. Many young men in the organisation were jobless and had no such parental advantage. The flying columns in the rural areas managed differently from the Dublin active service unit. They could safely rely on the kindness and hospitality of the people of the countryside to maintain them.

It was my grandmother who solved my problem. She knew Peter Kennedy, the head of the biggest bakery business in the city, and arranged for me to be taken on as a temporary clerk. The bakery and its offices were only down the road in Britain Street from 42 Summerhill where I had spent the early part of my life. I installed myself as a permanent lodger with my grandmother, occupying the room in which I was born, and I spent most of my evenings either in Terenure or in Rathfarnham on Company duties. Even though getting into the village of Rathfarnham presented no difficulty, it was necessary to pass the RIC Barracks. However, the RIC seldom appeared during the day and never after dark. They were immobilised for all practical purposes. Indeed except for one small group of a sergeant and five men, none of them were particularly hostile. I sometimes could not get across the city to Summerhill before curfew. In that case I stayed overnight in Mrs Morewood's or sometimes in Wilson's house. The job in Peter Kennedy's lasted until February when I felt I could not stand clerking any longer. I told Mr Kennedy that I was very grateful to him for having helped me out of a difficulty but I was going to risk resuming my College studies. My fellow clerks in Kennedy's were old hands who for years had spent from 9 a.m. to 6 p.m. adding up columns of figures and making entries in ledgers. They were very kind to me. Often I found it impossible to concentrate on the long tots and made arithmetical errors which caused inconvenience all round. They would frequently take sheets of figures from me and, to my amazement, run their pens down long money columns doing the calculation in one operation whereas I would have laboriously to add first the pence, then the shillings and then the pounds. My colleagues were as quick at this operation as the modern adding machine but for me it meant miserable boredom and were it not for the kindness of my fellow workers I would have left the job much earlier.

My friend Paddy Caffrey then came to my rescue. He suggested I should come into his office and help to correct the model Intermediate examination papers he set in English literature and history for his correspondence students. There wasn't much money attached to the job but it was exactly the kind of work which suited me. I had plenty of time to browse through Caffrey's large book collection and was particularly attracted to H. G. Wells' *History of the World* which he had bought as it was issued in fortnightly instalments. The book had given offence to theologians but the points at issue were too subtle for me to understand or care about. I was fascinated by Wells' theories of the origins of the universe and his description of the age of reptiles and mammals, the pre-glacial period and the beginnings of civilisation. What most impressed itself on my mind was the insignificance of the Earth in the universe. Although I had long since discarded the idea of creation having occurred precisely four thousand years ago the historical speculations of H. G. Wells were a revelation to me and added considerably to the rag-bag of my mind. Working in Caffrey's I had the additional advantage of being able to slip in by the back way to my own house and see my parents briefly, usually to get money. Having now acquired the habit of smoking, my lifestyle became more costly particularly as I had developed a taste for the more expensive brands of cigarettes. My father thought that if

I must smoke I should smoke a pipe. He presented me with a pipe and a pouch filled with his favourite Maltan tobacco. I tried to meet his wishes at least sporadically but the convenience of the cigarette prevailed.

Ever since the raid on the house when my father had been arrested he had been in a state of anxiety and depression about me. He was afraid to open a newspaper lest he should read that I had been arrested or shot. My mother complained to me about causing my father so much anxiety but she never gave expression to her own worries beyond enquiring rhetorically what I wanted to belong to that lot for? — 'that lot' being the IRA. I had plenty of anxieties of my own. The fear of being arrested was always present in my mind. The British Army were constantly cordoning off large areas of the city, conducting searches of houses and people in daylight. At night, both before and after curfew, lorry loads of soldiers drove noisily through the city and suburbs. Being on the run became an increasing strain on my nerves. I felt under constant tension even when my mind was absorbed in reading the chapters in Wells, 'On the Introduction of Agriculture' or 'Of the First Priests and Kings'.

Towards the end of January 1921 the Fourth Battalion organised a system of armed patrols. Each Company in the battalion, armed with what small arms they had available, patrolled the Company area with the instructions to 'hit up' any armed British forces we encountered. We walked around the area in files of two hoping to meet a lorry load of soldiers. Coming down Rathgar Avenue on patrol duty one evening I and my companion, Larry Kane, were first to arrive at the main Harolds' Cross Road where we halted to get instructions from Coughlan as to what direction we were to take. The rest of the Company were strung out behind except for two who, armed with Mills bombs, had taken up a position at the corner of Kenilworth Square. Kane and I had only been standing at the junction for a few minutes when we heard a lorry approaching from the direction of Terenure. We pulled our 'dogs' (we each had .45 Webleys) just as the lorry drew level. It was packed with soldiers. They were singing the popular song of the time 'I'm forever blowing bubbles, pretty bubbles in the air'. We immediately opened fire with Kane shouting in his excitement 'We'll give you f——ing bubbles'. The soldiers returned our fire and the lorry accelerated just as Kenny and his companion, Tully, from the opposite corner threw their bombs at it. The bombs hit the side of the lorry and two British soldiers were wounded either by the bombs or by our gunfire. I think this was the first time that bombs were used in attacking army lorries. A couple of weeks afterwards 'C' Company had better luck in a similar action. They lobbed a bomb into the middle of a lorry killing two and wounding five soldiers.

When Kane and I exhausted our meagre ammunition, consisting of six rounds each, we retreated, or rather ran, towards Rathgar Avenue. We passed a civilian who had been hit by the indiscriminate fire of the British soldiers. As we turned into Rathgar Avenue a man tried to stop us. He actually caught hold of my arm. I shook him off but not before Kane hit him in the face with the butt of his 'dog'. He must have been a very brave man and very loyal to the British to have attempted to apprehend us. Had we any ammunition left we would have shot him in the belief that he was an enemy agent. We got away finally and regrouped with the rest of the Company at Brighton Square. Our guns were collected by a couple of the Terenure men to be returned to our dump in the Green Lanes. Coughlan decided that he and I should get totally out of the neighbourhood that night. We walked to a quiet tram stop on the Rathgar Road and took a tram across the city to my grandmother's house in Summerhill.

The ambush at Kenilworth produced in me a state bordering on ecstasy. I had achieved my burning ambition to fire a shot for Ireland. I felt that I could now justifiably claim a place in the ranks of those who through successive generations had fought for Irish freedom. In terms of war or fighting the incident was trivial. Nevertheless we had risked our lives — the risk being exaggerated by our own stupidity and ignorance of what has since become known as urban guerilla warfare. We had never been trained for any such operation and acted purely on the impulse of the moment without even attempting to take cover. If it were not for the fact that the soldiers singing 'I'm forever blowing bubbles' were as ill-trained as we were, we would most certainly have been killed. As it was, our nightly patrols of the area continued without interruption.

During January and February of 1921 I slept in different houses, sometimes in Morewood's, sometimes in Wilson's, sometimes at my grandmother's. Up to February it was safe enough to move around the city and suburbs on foot or by bike or tram but, from time to time, the British cordoned off large blocks of the city and started to search pedestrians. These were, from their point of view, largely futile exercises. The intelligence service had been shattered on Bloody Sunday so that there were no touts or detectives to help the troops to identify wanted men. Despite the fact that there was little chance of being picked up while getting around the city I was in a constant state of apprehension. In particular I missed the stability and security of my home. An occasional dash-in through the backyard to see my mother only accentuated my feeling of deprivation. I was worried by the fact that my mother had to endure frequent house raids. I found the days tedious notwithstanding the kindness of Paddy Caffrey. The activities of the Company were not enough to satisfy my youthful energy or my wish to become more involved in the national struggle. In fact there was very little real fighting going on in the city. What action there was was mainly directed at individual British personnel. I approached Coughlan again on the subject of joining the active service unit. He repeated the view that I would not be suitable adding, lamely I thought, that I was too conspicuous a figure. I told him frankly that my present situation was getting on my nerves. A few days later he came to tell me that GHQ had initiated a scheme to send students from the Dublin Brigade into the country for the purpose of organising Flying Columns in areas which were inactive. If I were interested he thought he could arrange for me to be sent on one of these missions. I was delighted at the suggestion. The achievements of Tom Barry's Column in Cork had inspired everyone in the IRA to want to join a Flying Column. The mere word had a romantic ring. Apart from Barry it revived memories of DeWet and his commandos of the Boer War. But before anything could be arranged my fears of being picked up by the British were realised.

To remedy the defective intelligence system, at least partially, the British devised a clever scheme. They formed a group of RIC men drawn from different parts of the country. This group, known to us as the IGO gang or the murder gang, moved unobtrusively around the city in squads of twelve to fourteen men. They were dressed in reach-me-down civilian clothes. They walked the streets in files of two with each pair following the next at about ten paces. Any IRA man visiting Dublin from any part of the country was at risk. They had an awe-inspiring reputation for murder and torture of prisoners. I don't know of what murders they were guilty and I know only of one man, a fellow student named Farrell, who was injured while in their hands. In an attempt to escape he was shot but not killed. The movements of the IGO gang — named after their leader — were unpredictable and elusive. The IRA active service unit and the Collins squad, despite sustained efforts, never made contact with them. I unfortunately did. I left my grandmother's house one morning in early March at ten o'clock intending to go to Paddy Caffrey's to visit my mother. In the manner of the students of the time, many of whom cultivated a positive dandyism, I was most respectably dressed. That is to say, I wore a collar and tie and well-creased trousers. One put one's trousers under the mattress when going to bed at night to keep them creased. I wore kid gloves and carried a cane. I walked down Summerhill intending to cut across Gardiner Street (now Parnell Street). I passed two tall men of whom I took no particular notice but when I passed two more and then another pair I began to feel uneasy. My uneasiness was justified when I passed still another pair and recognised among them an RIC man from Rathfarnham named Killeen. The fourth pair of the group halted, produced revolvers and told me not to attempt to run. They asked me my name and address. I gave it as Christopher Moran of 42 Summerhill and produced letters to prove it. They told me they were taking me to Dublin Castle. The whole squad turned in their tracks and marched me right across the city, through O'Connell Street, College Green, Dame Street into the Lower Castle Yard. I realised I had fallen into the hands of the IGO gang and waited for the beating and torture to begin, saying many fervent prayers for my preservation. I was very frightened. The gang broke up into groups when they arrived in the Castle Yard and only two men stayed with me. They again demanded my name and address and occupation. I continued to protest that my name was Moran, that I was a university student and was missing lectures due to my arrest. They seemed a bit doubtful about my identity and one of them left apparently to again consult Killeen. Returning after a while he brought me into an office where there were a few military clerks and delivered me into their custody under the name of Andrews of Terenure. One of the clerks took down the particulars as supplied by the IGO man. After a short delay two soldiers arrived with rifles and fixed bayonets and with one on either side I was marched a little distance to what turned out to be a room in the City Hall.

There was another man in the room but he did not speak or show any interest when I told him my tale of injured innocence. No explanation was offered of his presence and I came to the conclusion that he was some kind of tout. That feeling was based on an obsessive suspicion of anyone unknown to you in the Movement which was prevalent at that time. I was greatly relieved when later on in the day another prisoner arrived. He was an enormous, good-humoured Tipperary man who had been arrested when getting off the train at Kingsbridge Station in much the same circumstances as I. According to his account he had come to Dublin from South Tipperary to buy farm machinery. He didn't know why he had been arrested. It seemed to me a most improbable story. He was dressed without collar and tie, like a farmer who has just left the plough to talk to a passing neighbour. I was fairly certain that, unlike the other morose member of the trio, he was connected with the Movement and immediately we established a rapport. This enabled us to speculate on what was going to happen to us at the hands of the British while not, of course, admitting to one another our true identity. We felt fairly safe from beatings as long as we were in the custody of the military though it was shown later that this was a misconception. The soldiers belonged to the East Lancashire Regiment. They often came into the room to chat. They were very sympathetic to me because I was supposedly missing my studies. They got me a pencil, paper and envelopes and undertook to post a letter to my mother, a promise which was duly kept. In return, at his request, I wrote to my mother asking her to send a bunch of shamrock to Private Ross, one of my jailers at the Castle. The note reads as follows:

> 10503 Private Thomas Ross
> 9 Platoon, C Company
> 1st Battalion
> The Lancashire Fusiliers
> Ship Street Barracks
> Dublin

Dear Mother

Please send some shamrock to the above address as quickly as possible. I'm all right and wrote to you this morning. Send the shamrock as Private Ross has been very kind to me.

Goodbye,

> Your son,
> Christy.

P.S. This place is O.K. but I expect to be shifted soon.
P.P.S. Just send him the shamrock and box, nothing else.

If Private Ross is still alive and ever sees this he must know that at least one old IRA man remembered him kindly. For a couple of days nothing happened. Our silent colleague disappeared. The Tipperary man, whose name was Dan O'Keeffe, and I had the room to ourselves. There were no, what the soldiers called, 'ablutions' in the room or its vicinity. Every morning, and at other times when we wanted to go to the toilet, we were escorted by a soldier with fixed bayonet around the front of the City Hall to a toilet built in Castle Street. The view down Parliament Street and Capel Street was cut off by a canvas sheeting but I was tall enough to see over it. Every time I looked down Capel Street where my father had his office, I felt a pang of regret for the worry my detention must be causing him and my mother.

After the second day the monotony was varied by being marched to Ship Street, nominally for exercise. In fact these trips were identification parades. It was quite easy for us to see the outline of women obviously observing us from the windows overlooking the exercise yard. I was in a state of terror that I might be picked out as being concerned in the Bloody Sunday affair. After a few days of this I was called out of the room and marched across the Castle yard to what are now the State Apartments. I was taken into a large well-furnished office where there were three well-dressed civilians and one man in the uniform of an Auxiliary. The other feature of the room that etched itself on my memory was a large vase of daffodils on a side table. The soldiers who brought me over from the City Hall withdrew. I was sure that the inquistion and the beatings were about to begin. I was told to take a chair facing one of the civilians at the desk. The other two civilians sat around the desk but the Auxiliary stood aside looking on. Except for the Auxiliary in the background and the daffodils, the scene might well have been an interview board for a post in the public service — a scene with which I was to become familiar in later life. Only the civilian in the centre seat at the desk spoke. He had a marked upper class English accent. He was quite polite in his interrogation which went something like this:

'Your name is Andrews?'

'Yes.'

'Why did you give a false name when you were arrested?'

'Because I had been arrested before and sent to Mountjoy Jail for no reason. I didn't want it to happen again. My career was seriously set back.'

'You live on the south side of the city? What were you doing on the north side so early on the day you were arrested?'

'I was visiting my grandmother and stayed the night with her. I should tell you that she is the widow of an inspector in the DMP.'

I didn't add that my grandfather had died forty years before.

'What brigade are you in in the IRA?'

'I am not in any brigade in the IRA. I am not a member of the IRA.'

'We know you are in the IRA.'

'I am not. I am a member of Sinn Féin but that is very different from the IRA.'

'Don't you know that the 3d per week subscribed to Sinn

Féin goes to buy arms for the IRA which are used to murder British soldiers?'

'I don't know any such thing. I have no sympathy with the murder of British soldiers.'

'Where do you hold your meetings of Sinn Féin?'

'We don't hold any meetings now because we are afraid of being arrested.'

'Where did you hold your meetings?'

'In University College.'

'Who else was in Sinn Féin with you?'

'Nearly every student in the College.'

To my surprise he seemed satisfied with my answers to his questions and the interrogation concluded with a homily on the iniquities of the IRA and advice against associating with Sinn Féin. The two soldiers of my escort were called in and I was taken back to the room in the City Hall where Dan O'Keeffe was anxiously waiting to hear my story and his own turn for interrogation which, however, never materialised.

I often pondered on the ease with which the British interrogators accepted my story. I came to the conclusion that all four men in the room were Englishmen. They had, thanks to their own propaganda, formed in their mind an archetype of the IRA man wearing leggings and trenchcoat and cap with neither collar nor tie who was also, by definition, illiterate. I did not conform to that image. I was respectably dressed, spoke coherently and grammatically and whereas an Irish interrogator would have placed my class origins from my accent to the Englishmen my accent was only another version of the brogue. The fact that I was a university student added to their conception of respectability. Respectability was the last quality they would attribute to the IRA. On the other hand the fact that Kevin Barry and Frank Flood were students didn't stop the British from hanging them. I was surprised to find myself experiencing a perverse, rather masochistic, sense of disappointment at not having been beaten up or at least subjected to harsher methods of interrogation. The unflattering thought crossed my mind that the British and even the IGO gang regarded me as a harmless enthusiast. Any resentment I may have felt about not being beaten up was soon dissipated. The evening after my interrogation we were joined by another prisoner. He was only with us for half an hour or so when he was taken out and returned a couple of hours later beaten to ribbons. His eyes were closed, his lips were split open and he could barely drag himself from the door to the bed. His name was Traynor. We asked no questions about his background but it soon transpired that he had been caught in an ambush in Brunswick Street (now Pearse Street) where a soldier had been killed. He was tried for murder by court-martial and hanged. So it seemed that our military guard were less of a protection from beating and torture than we gave them credit for. A couple of days after this episode O'Keeffe and I were removed to Arbour Hill Jail. I was delighted to get out of the Castle.

Arbour Hill was used as a detention centre. Prisoners were collected there before being sent to internment camps or in some cases held for trial or even released. I was greeted by two old friends from my school days. They were also members of the Fourth Battalion, Myles Ford and Jack Knowthe. Myles was working in the family dairy business and Jack was a clerk in some city firm. Both of them had been arrested at home and had been in Arbour Hill for a fortnight before my arrival. They arranged for me to have a bed in their cell and initiated me into the routine of the jail. Dan O'Keeffe met some friends from Tipperary among the prisoners, quickly establishing his credentials as an IRA man. We were able to exchange freely the true account of our arrest. Indeed we began then and continued over several months the stories of our lives. He became and remained for many years a close friend of mine.

There was virtually no discipline in the jail enforced by either the prisoners themselves or by the military authorities. The population was unstable, prisoners being removed and replaced by others at frequent intervals. It was impossible for the inmates to set up a regular Camp Council and a more or less permanent O/C. Essentially Arbour Hill was an Army prison and it housed military as well as political prisoners. So far as the military authorities were concerned the political prisoners were free to do what they liked so long as they did not escape. They regarded their responsibilities as at an end when they counted the prisoners each evening. The food was totally uneatable. The prisoners lived on the generous supply of parcels received from relatives and friends. For most of the day we were free to use the exercise yard. We played football in a way which must have approximated to the game as originally played between parishes. There were no fixed sides and no rules. The object was to get the ball and kick it anywhere. Nevertheless it was great fun as well as providing a satisfactory outlet for all the youthful energy bottled up in a jail. We played cards ('twenty-five') for matches and indulged in rough-housing such as raiding some cell and upsetting the bedding — another outlet for physical energy.

We were relatively happy in Arbour Hill and there was always the chance of being released. One morning when I had been there for about two weeks a Sergeant came along, called my name out and told me to pack up. I was so sure I was being released that I didn't even bother to ask where I was going. Forde and Knowthe helped me to get my odds and ends together. I undertook to contact their families and went off with the Sergeant. To my horror and bitter disappointment, instead of going home I was conducted to the basement cells of the jail and placed in solitary confinement. The only other prisoners in this part of the jail were soldiers undergoing punishment for offences committed against military law. They were treated savagely. They were never allowed to stand still. When they were stationary they had to mark time and when they moved they moved at the double, that is they ran. Their food, which I shared, was even worse than what we had been given in the political wing of the jail. The only thing that was clean about the place was the floors. Cleaning the floors was the only occupation available to the military prisoners. They were not allowed any association nor were they allowed to speak to one another. I would rather be 'an ass to a tinker' than a military prisoner.

After my first night in the basement I demanded to see the Governor. Apparently such a request was within my rights because he sent for me the next day. I pointed out that I was an untried and uncharged political prisoner and that I had a right to associate with my fellows. The Governor, who I think was a major, briefly glanced at his files. He then told me gruffly that I was about to be tried for murder and would have to stay where I was until arrangements were made for my trial. I was marched back to my cell. When I was locked up my spirits reached a nadir which they have never touched before or since. I was thoroughly frightened. Pessimistic by nature I could already visualise the death chamber and feel the hangman bind my hands. I saw my father and mother saying goodbye to me. The only recourse I had was to prayer. I knelt down and prayed to God to spare me the ordeal of a trial and death by hanging. I am sure I prayed for a long time. Afterwards I felt more composed in spirit and less panic stricken, more ready to face what the future would bring. Once, through the door, I caught the glimpse of another civilian going into a cell opposite mine. I questioned the guards about his identity but they were unable or unwilling to give any information except that he was an important prisoner with a special guard to himself. The mystery surrounding him and the secrecy maintained by the guards was reminiscent of *The Man in the Iron Mask*. Long afterwards I learned that the prisoner was Eamonn Broy, one of Collins's inside men in the Castle. He was lucky to escape with his life. In 1934 he was appointed Commissioner of Police. The special police force which he formed was mainly responsible for enforcing the law against the Blue Shirts and was known as the 'Broy Harriers'.

* * * * *

I was altogether about five days in the basement of Arbour Hill when I was again ordered to move and this time I thought my destination would be Mountjoy. Happily I was wrong. I was returned to the general body of political prisoners rejoining Myles Ford and Jack Knowthe in their cell. A few days later about fifty of us were told to get ready to move. This time we were left completely in the dark about what was going to happen us.

For me an infuriating aspect of prison life was the sense of helplessness. If some Glasgow guttersnipe in uniform told you to go or come, you went or came. You were told to pack up but no reason was given. You were told to get into a lorry but you never knew where you were going. Worst of all when you were untried and unsentenced you never knew how long you would be held in detention. You were automatically deprived of a future. My special friends Ford, Knowthe and O'Keeffe were among those ordered to pack up. Having done so we were left in our cells for over an hour without being given even a faint indication as to what was in store for us. We asked some of the soldiers what was going on and were told that they did not know. They were telling the truth. They were treated with as little consideration as we were. Finally we were summoned from our cells and marched with our luggage — mainly cardboard boxes — into the courtyard of the prison where there was another long delay. We passed the time speculating on our destination. The general opinion was that we were going to be deported to England. At last we were marched outside the prison gates and loaded into a convoy of covered lorries but there was a hold-up for more than an hour before the convoy moved off. By this time we were physically limp from standing around and mentally limp from uncertainty. Finally the convoy with a mixed cargo of soldiers and prisoners and several car loads of officers got under way.

We had no idea of what direction we were taking through the city but after travelling for about an hour we realised we were not being sent to England. Stops were made a couple of times en route for about five minutes, presumably for the convenience of the officers. It apparently was assumed that neither the prisoners, nor the common soldiers who were guards, had bladders. After about three hours we came to what was apparently our destination because we heard the sounds of more soldiers and the shouting of military orders. Nearly another half hour elapsed before we were ordered out of the lorries and at last discovered that we had been brought to the Curragh for internment. It was another hour before we were finally processed into our billets.

We found we were in the Rath Internment Camp which, as prisoner number 1569, hut 32, became my address for the next five months. There were already nearly one thousand prisoners in the Rath Camp. We got a great welcome from our fellow internees who helped us to settle in and got us tea and sandwiches. They showed us how to make up our beds which consisted of a bed board and hard cushions, called 'biscuits', a pillow and blankets. We had no sheets. It took us only a few days to settle into the routine of camp life.

To build the camp the British had enclosed about ten acres of the Curragh plain in a rectangle of barbed wire entanglements. There were two wire fences ten feet high and separated by a passage twenty feet wide which, after dark, was lit up by searchlights. At each corner of the rectangle was a watchtower manned day and night by sentries armed with rifles and machine guns. Beyond the main barrier, the camp was surrounded by another fence consisting of five single strands of barbed wire about four feet high. This fence was designed, not to keep the prisoners in, but rather to prevent animals approaching the main barbed enclosure. Nevertheless, it was a further obstacle to the possibility of escape. To add to the difficulties of intending escapees, a giant searchlight was mounted on the watchtower of the main military camp. During the hours of darkness the beam from the searchlight lit up the entire Curragh plain.

Inside the enclosure there were some fifty wooden huts which served as sleeping quarters, canteen, cook-house, chapel and library. There was a sports ground large enough to provide a football pitch. The Curragh Racecourse could be seen in the distance and on race days it was possible to see the horses at the start of the long distance races. However much turmoil gripped the country the horsey men carried on business as usual. We resented their activities and anyway gambling was against the spirit of the Movement. The Turf was the preserve of the Garrison and the Anglo-Irish community and we did not see why, while we were in jail and our comrades outside were fighting, they should enjoy themselves as if normality prevailed.

Our hut, number 32, was occupied exclusively by Dubliners and our O/C was a man named Liam Murphy. We had no say in his selection; he was appointed by the O/C of the camp, a man from GHQ called Peadar McMahon. Murphy was in his middle twenties and was a Lieutenant from the Third Battalion of the Dublin Brigade. He had a quality of leadership that made the discipline of the hut, while strict, relatively painless. I was sorry that I never got to know him well and lost touch with him completely after leaving the camp. He was a paradigm of the ordinary man who made up the Dublin Brigade. Most of what has been written about the Black and Tan war has been concerned with the Flying Columns of Cork and Tipperary or the Active Service Unit in Dublin. Not much recognition has been given to the Liam Murphys. These were the men, some of whom never fired a shot, who were the infrastructure on which the Columns and the Active Service Unit and General Headquarters itself rested. It was no small thing after a day's work with pick or pen to turn out in the evening to do minor routine jobs or even to attend parades.

Life in the camp was, in a physical sense, far from unpleasant. Indeed for the first few weeks I found it agreeably exciting meeting new people including some national personalities, exploring the library which was surprisingly good, playing football, learning the procedure for receipt of letters and parcels and examining the canteen. I had during these first few weeks the additional pleasure of receiving my internment order. The internment order was a fairly certain guarantee that the British had nothing against you for which you could be tried by court martial. For me this was a great relief.

The prisoners came from all parts of the country including a few from the North although Northern prisoners were usually sent to Ballykinlar for internment.

The routine of the camp was dictated by two disciplinary systems. On the one hand the British regulations set the times when we were locked up and let out, the number of letters we might write and the food we got. We had our own disciplinary system which dealt with the 'fatigues' allotted to the prisoners. These fatigues were mainly devoted to keeping the huts clean, hygienic and orderly. From time to time rows or disputes between prisoners had also to be settled though these were rare as a great sense of camaraderie prevailed and morale was very high. The main function of our O/C was to deal with the British O/C concerning our constant grievances about the quality of the food. Theoretically, according to the British regulations, we were supposed to rise at 6.30 a.m. to be ready at 7 a.m. and standing by our beds to be counted. We were counted twice a day by a Sergeant accompanied by a couple of soldiers with fixed bayonets. The second count took place a half an hour before sun-down when we were locked up for the night.

After we were locked up a few of the prisoners with good voices usually started a sing-song. The songs were heavily patriotic, the most popular being 'Down by the glenside'. 'All round my hat I wear a tri-coloured ribbon-o', 'The grand old dame Brittania'. 'The Soldier's Song' was often sung but it had no special significance and never rated as the National Anthem. Last thing in the evening before going to sleep the whole hut joined in saying the Rosary aloud. Not one decade but five decades. There was always someone who knew what five mysteries were appropriate to any given day. The Rosary was much more than a prayer. It came to be a secular slogan interwoven into the fabric of the Movement.

In fact the morning count never took place until 8 a.m. when we were let out for breakfast. We had complete freedom until we were locked up in the evening. After breakfast we did whatever fatigue we were assigned to, for cleaning up the hut. Once per week it was washed out thoroughly with Jeyes Fluid. The latrine fatigue was the least popular. Not much less popular was the washing up of the plates, mugs and knives and forks. It had to be done in cold water. The food, although it was the same food as the soldiers got, was, except for the tea and bread, abominable. It was assumed, rightly, that everyone liked extremely strong tea with plenty of sugar in it. The bread was good, freshly baked every day. The margarine stank and was quite uneatable. The meat might have been good before it was cooked but the cooking ruined it. The potatoes were rotten and the cabbage, which was the only other vegetable supplied, was invariably worm eaten. We would certainly have been hungry except for the generous parcels received from home.

In the huts we formed 'messes' of three or four prisoners, who shared their parcels in common. There was always a shortage of cigarettes because not every 'mess' got them from home and even if you had money they were not sold in the camp canteen. The canteen, which was run by the British (payment being made in camp chits) had a limited but very useful stock. Buttons, needles, thread, darning wool, matches, shaving soap, razor blades were the main items. We got quite useful at darning socks, sewing on buttons and mending tears in our clothes.

We had very little contact with our guards. Periodically they would patrol the camp at night. Sometimes, if they had read of some successful attack by the IRA, they would bang on our huts with their rifle butts, wakening us and swearing at us. Sometimes they would conduct exhaustive searches of the huts during the day. They belonged to a Scottish Regiment — I am not sure if it was the King's Own Scottish Borderers or the King's Own Scottish Light Infantry — but their attitude to us was very hostile. In the course of the searches they never passed without calling you a bastard or threatening you with their bayonets. They were all young conscripts who seemed to loathe us and they treated us very differently from the Lancashire Fusiliers whom I had encountered in Dublin. They were particularly offensive when they succeeded in finding an escape tunnel of which there was always at least one being dug by one or other of the Companies into which the internees were organised. When a tunnel was found the whole camp was punished by the stoppage of parcels and the closure of the canteen. Once we had a fine of five shillings per man imposed because bed boards were missing; they had been used either for fuel in the stove with which each hut was furnished or as pit props for the tunnels. As not everyone got money from home, those who did refused to accept any in protest. The British replied by closing the canteen and stopping the newspapers. We got the Irish newspapers fairly regularly and I had the *Sunday Observer* sent to me weekly directly from O'Kennedy's, the newsagents in Terenure. It arrived most weeks, as did a sports paper called *All Sports*.

I had no difficulty in putting in the day in the camp. I worked out a satisfactory way of life for myself getting gradually on friendly terms with different internees. I often went to the library, spending my time looking through the books and talking to the assistant librarian, a man named Cotter who was also the champion chess player in the camp. I regret that I never learned to play chess. The nominal head of the library was Desmond Fitzgerald, the most important prisoner in the camp, a well-known national figure. Before his arrest he was the highly successful Director of Publicity for the Republic and was responsible for the production of *The Irish Bulletin*. The *Bulletin* was one of the most important weapons of the Republican Movement. It was worth several Flying Columns. The British had censored the daily Press. They had suppressed completely all the Republican weeklies. Had it not been for the exposures of the *Bulletin* the British campaign of terror could have been conducted relatively quietly and the measure of resistance of the IRA would never be known to the outside world. Desmond Fitzgerald, with the aid of two very able journalists, Bob Brennan and Frank Gallagher, had made a major contribution to the Movement. Thus when I saw him in the library I

176

looked on him with some awe. This awe was increased when I overheard him discuss French literature, particularly Balzac, with Professor Liam Ó Briain of Galway. I was surprised by Fitzgerald's drawling English accent, which was in such contrast to the rapid, decisive mode of speech and pronounced Dublin accent of Ó Briain. I never dared to speak to Fitzgerald as I quickly gathered that he was in the category of people satirised by the epigram:

-My name is George Nathaniel Curzon
I am a most superior person.

There was one person to whom he spoke daily: Captain Keating, whom the British had appointed as liaison officer to the prisoners. As it happened, Keating was the eldest of a family which I knew very well and who were neighbours of mine in Terenure. I had spent many days with the two younger boys swimming in the Dodder, exploring Shaw's Wood and playing round their house in Brighton Square. While the younger boys, Ned and Tom, and myself swapped the *Magnet* and the *Gem,* Willie, the older by several years, read the sporting papers. I don't think he read anything else. He was destined to go sheep-farming in Patagonia but when the First World War broke out Willie got a commission in the Army.

With my activities in the Movement, I lost touch with the Keatings although I knew that Willie had survived the war. I was more than amused to see the supercilious Desmond Fitzgerald walking around the compound in deep conversation with him every day. I wondered what they could be talking about. It certainly was not Balzac, nor yet was it Irish nationalism because Keating would not have heard of Davis, Mitchel or Tone. Robert Emmet and Daniel O'Connell perhaps. I could only conclude that Fitzgerald regarded Keating as an acceptable audience for a monologue.

Amongst the internees was an old friend of mine, Phil Cosgrave, the Quartermaster of our Battalion. He was also a T.D. His brother was Minister for Local Government in the Dáil. He was a much older man than I but was always very kind to me. Phil introduced me to a card school where he and I and Jim Crowley, a T.D. from Kerry, and a well-known Dubliner called the 'the Boer' Byrne played solo every forenoon between finishing our fatigues and dinner time.

'The Boer' Byrne was so called because he had fought with Major McBride in the South African war although we could never get him to tell of his adventures there. We played for camp chits but the stakes were small: half a crown would be a major win. Usually we won or lost 6d in a morning. We talked as much as we played. We were constantly arguing about the League of Nations. We were particularly interested in the American refusal to join the League. Jim Crowley and Phil Cosgrave regretted it while 'the Boer' was indifferent. I did not believe in the efficacy of the League and I did not think that any nation, except Russia, was likely even to express sympathy with us much less extend any material help. Jim was a very intelligent and well informed man with an unusual knowledge of Irish history. He was always good humoured, entertaining us with anecdotes about his native Kerry.

In May rumours of peace negotiations with the British began to sweep through the camp. Naturally, it was the main topic of conversation not merely at our solo school but among all internees. The general feeling was that nothing would come of them. We were much more interested in the course of the fighting. We were always on the look out for news of activities which took place in our own particular areas. It was a shock to me when the murder of Christy Reynolds and the maiming of Barney Nolan by the Black and Tans were reported. They were members of my Company. But I rejoiced when I read of British lorries being 'hit up' along the Templeogue Road. I knew Kenny and 'E' Company were being active. At the same time I felt depressed at the thought that when we got out I would have to listen to tales of action which I had missed. I felt rather like a deserter.

We were all thrilled by the burning of the Custom House in May, regarding it as a great triumph. It affected us internees in as much as the British stopped our parcels as a reprisal. My mother was very indignant that parcels were stopped. She wrote me a letter 'crying a plague on both your houses'. I replied that she should write to the generalissimos of both armies, not to me. I had not burned the Custom House.

We played a lot of football — Gaelic, of course, since foreign games were forbidden. I was regarded as something of an oddity because I was interested in cricket. There were test matches being played that year which I followed daily in the newspapers. I was specially interested in the exploits of Hobbs and Hayward who were the opening batsmen for England. We organised a football league competition between the Companies. I was good enough to be picked on the 'D' Company team. The league matches were of a high standard as the teams were studded with All-Ireland players from different counties. The games were very tough. I was introduced to what must be the most infuriating foul in any code of football. When you are about to jump, with arms extended to take a ball out of the air, you find your feet are stuck to the ground. Someone has hung on to the tail of your jersey. An almost murderous feeling of exasperation overwhelmed me when that happened. I could not resist lashing out with my fists; hence I developed a reputation for being a very rough player.

World affairs made little impact on us. We scarcely noticed the rise of Fascism in Italy although through reading *The Observer* I took some interest in the war between the Greeks and the Turks. We paid no attention to the opening of the Northern Parliament in June by King George V. I don't think a man in the camp read his speech although it had a major significance for British politicians. To it is attributed Lloyd George's initiative in opening the truce negotiations. We were much more interested in the fate of the King's escort who were, on their way back to barracks from the ceremony, successfully ambushed by the South Armagh IRA. We were even more interested to read that De Valera had been arrested and released.

Apart from Phil Cosgrave, Desmond Fitzgerald and Jim Crowley, we had several other T.D.s: Alec McCabe from Sligo, Joseph McBride a brother of Major McBride from Mayo, Dr Brian Cusack from Co. Dublin and Tom Derrig from Mayo. Brian Cusack, the most popular man in the camp, looked after our cuts, bruises, colds and fevers. He had a small hospital hut and dispensary. There were always a few patients in the hospital. Only once during my internment did we have an influenza epidemic. Rumours filtered out from the camp about it. By the time they reached my mother via the newspapers she was convinced that we were on the point of death and wrote a suitably alarmed letter to me.

At this time T.D.s were not 'politicians' in the sense that they were shortly to become. They were either active members of the IRA or nominees of the IRA. I regarded the Dáil as merely an adjunct of the IRA, a weapon to help make government impossible, a source of propaganda aimed at embarrassing the British abroad. I had no interest in the mode of government of the country. The Departments of the Dáil — Local Government, Home Affairs, Labour, Industries, Agriculture or even Defence — were to me mere ancillaries to the militant core of the Movement. My only aim was to break the connection with England. To do that I believed deeply that force was the only way.

Alec McCabe was one of the few men in the camp who shared my interest in soccer football and we often gossiped about it. Alec was also interested in Irish. He taught one of the dozen Irish classes in the camp. Nearly everyone tried to learn to speak at least a few words of Irish, even if it was only 'Lá Breá'! Professor Liam Ó Briain, as well

179

as teaching Irish, conducted a French class. Half a dozen of us attended regularly and profitably; he was a first-class teacher. Apart from teaching the French language he lectured us on French history and literature.

But one of our prize prisoners (if that is the appropriate word) was a priest named Father Smith from Co. Meath. To us in the IRA the Catholic religion meant as much emotionally as did the Movement. We were disappointed that, except for some individual priests and one or two bishops, we had not got the support of the Church. De Valera tried, without success, to get the Hierarchy to issue a statement recognising the Government appointed by Dáil Éireann as the legitimate government of the Irish people. The presence of a priest in the camp was a consolation to us; he helped to sustain our morale. We had, I think, a subconscious fear that we might be denounced by the Church as the Fenians were. Somehow Father Smith as a fellow prisoner, sharing our common lot, gave us an assurance that this would not happen. To be deprived of the sacraments would have created a conflict of loyalties for us. We did not want to have to choose.

Most of the prisoners were in their twenties or early thirties. Anyone over thirty was to me an old man but, as it happened, there were two men in their sixties with whom I became very friendly. One, John Farrell, worked as a time-keeper in the Dublin Gas Company. In appearance and manner he was like Pickwick, out of Dickens, except that he did not wear glasses. In his habits he emulated the reputation Matt Talbot acquired for saintliness. He acted as sacristan to the Chapel hut which he tended lovingly and beautifully. On the long summer days he installed himself in a chair outside the chapel, exchanging a cheery word with all passers-by. He was an expert draughts player, by far the best in the camp. He did not always find it easy to get someone to play but I liked him very well and was always willing to oblige. I was a very weak opponent. He always won. When he swept all my pieces off the board at one move, I used to shock him by letting out a big swear word. 'Oh, Christy, Christy! You shouldn't say that', but day after day the same scene was repeated. He was strongly nationalistic and had known some of the Easter Week men intimately. We used to talk about them and about the Dublin docklands with which I was familiar. But always he would come back to religion, trying to get me to go to daily Mass and weekly Communion. I teased him by telling of the Frenchman who, when he was rebuked for not going to Mass on Sunday, replied 'I am a Catholic but not a fanatic'. 'Oh Christy, Christy'. In the camp I was sometimes called

180

'Todd' and sometimes 'Christy'.

John Farrell, like at least half the men in the camp, was an avid collector of autographs. His album was always open. Collecting autographs seemed to me to be a childish occupation. I thought it was even more childish to fill them with patriotic doggerel. Many years later one of these autograph albums came into my possession in an odd way. A friend of Liam Tobin — Collins's right-hand man — was given it as a token of appreciation of his 'record' at some Irish function in San Francisco. He sent it as a present to Liam who, seeing my signature in it, gave it to me. Some of the doggerel, naive though it is, reflects the feeling and the sentiment of the time:

> May the god above send down a dove
> With wings as sharp as razors
> To cut the throats of English rogues
> Who killed our rebel leaders.

A poem to Kevin Barry goes:

> We knelt at Mass with sobbing hearts
> Cold in the dawn of day
> The dawn for us, for him the night
> Who was so young and gay.
> Then from the altar spoke the priest
> His voice rang thin with pain
> Bidding us pray, a boy must die
> At England's hands again.
> The cruel English tortured him
> He never shrank or cried
> Sublime his faith the gallows tree
> He faced that day with pride.

Another entry:

> The grass is green as green can be
> The daisies silver white
> The buttercups of yellow gold
> All make a pretty sight
> Now green white and yellow
> The colours of the true
> And God who loves the grass and flowers
> Must love the rebels too.

The book is spattered with poems in Irish from many sources and aphorisms from Mitchel and Pearse. Only once in the album a

181

woman is mentioned. There is a drawing of a young woman entitled 'A Cumann na mBan girl' and the comment: 'If Ireland's fight for independence is lost, Seaghan, it won't be through the fault of her woman soldiers'. It was remarkable that anyone even mentioned a woman. In the camp sex was never discussed. Considering the age group, it would be difficult to persuade a foreigner that this was so.

Fintan Murphy was the other older man with whom I became very friendly. He was a London-Irish schoolmaster in his sixties and had been deported from England illegally. He was a friend of the Fenians, knew John O'Leary well and corresponded with Devoy in America. He had sent his sons to be educated in St Enda's by Pearse. The older of the two, Fintan, went out with Pearse in 1916. Subsequently he became Q.M.G. of the Volunteers. The younger, Desmond, was about my age. He was the only boy with whom I had made friends in St Enda's and we remained so for life.

I met Fintan Murphy in the library. I told him I had known his sons. Despite the discrepancy in our ages we became friendly. The library was well stocked, not merely with thrillers but with classics. Fintan Murphy spent a long time with me going through the books and suggesting what I should read. Sometimes his recommendations were beyond me. He was an enthusiastic admirer of the Russians, persuading me to read Dostoievsky's *The Brothers Karamazov*. I started the book with the belief that I was going to get as much pleasure from it as I had earlier in life from Tolstoy's *Anna Karenina*. I did not. Respect for Fintan Murphy kept me going as far as the *Grand Inquisitor*. The gloom emanating from the dark recesses of the human soul proved too much for me. On the other hand, amongst the books he pressed on me was the *Cloister and the Hearth*. The rich pattern of fifteenth century life amongst the Dutch painters fascinated me. It was the first time I had heard (with something of a shock) clerical celibacy questioned. The human woes of Margaret and Gerard touched my heart. It is a book I have always remembered with great pleasure. Fintan Murphy was not long with us. His detention and deportation was challenged in the courts and he was released. I missed him very much.

No matter what diversions we had from time to time, I became afflicted with fits of depression resenting bitterly being cooped up in a cage. At such times I walked dozens of times along the perimeter of the compound trying to will myself out of it. I missed my friends in University College. I missed my comrades in 'E' Company and I missed my home. My mother wrote to me every week and sent me a parcel. I wrote to her weekly and demanded a particular kind of parcel. The demand for cigarettes was incessant; we were always short of them. Theoretically, we shared our parcels in our own small messes in the huts. In practice we shared them all round. In the matter of possessions the hut was a commune. That system applied to all huts and indeed to the camp generally. The only commodity that was in superabundance was home-made soda bread. Every mother apparently assumed that, like American apple pie, her bread was what her son wanted. The result was extreme waste of good food.

My mother's parcels must have been quite expensive, a fact which never occurred to me at the time. She kept most of the letters I wrote to her and they certainly make me sound like a spoiled brat. The letters, written in the style of schoolboy irony, are not as impertinent as they read. They were written in that fashion to amuse my mother. I could see her showing them with mock indignation to her cousins and intimate friends with the fond comment 'Isn't he a right pup?' As my letters had to pass through the censors they could not communicate much of interest but here are two of them:

C. S. Andrews. 1569.
Hut 32. D. Coy
Rath Internment Camp.
The Curragh,
Wednesday 8th/6.

My dearest Mother,

I received today a letter from you written on Sunday. I wrote to you on Saturday last and doubtless by this time you have received mine. I also had a letter from you the other day dated 29th/5 in which you mention five parcels. I only received three of them. One contained jam sandwich, biscuits and fags; number two contained the handkerchiefs etc.; number three contained plain cakes, fags and something else. Anyway, three parcels arrived intact but of the other two I hear nothing. Inquire about them at the P.O. as I suppose they were registered. By the way, that letter reminded me of some of the gems which appeared in the *Morning Post* during the last War and really it wasn't my fault that the parcels and letters were stopped for ten days or so and I did not burn the Custom House! You obviously have a grievance against both parties and you ought to vent it on the generalissimos of the respective armies. Please spare me! Well, mother, the exams concluded this week which means another year wasted. It's a pity but as you say it cannot go on for ever. The advisory committee was down here last week but as I did not bother to appeal I was not called before it. As was said of a more famous prisoner than I 'Hope springs eternal in the human breast' and I have not abandoned hope by any means so cheer up! From the purely material and physical point of view this place is quite all right or nearly so, but it entails a constant strain on the mind and nerves that sometimes becomes intense. The only consolation and variation of the monotony is letters and I don't get half enough: a few fellows from the college who all say the same thing, when they say anything, and those I get from you and Paddy. How is Larry? I want you to tell Paddy his letter is overdue and tell him also that the maximum length of a letter is not necessarily two pages. I'll hardly write to him next week as I want to write to the college and sympathise with the lads on their defeat by Trinity and with individuals on the results of exams. I suppose my father was at the Sports. Frank O'Dea and Jimmie Flah didn't shine much. Frank must have been dead off form! I will probably hear the inner history of the fiasco from Flah! It was a bit of a fiasco though Cussen must have been wonderful. Pat, you say, is fed up. Is his little exam troubling him and will he get honours? If he doesn't, let him look out for squalls from me. Lest I forget I want you to send me my shoes and please see that they are in good repair not like the boots you sent me. The soles and uppers were seeking a divorce when they arrived and a decree was granted after about a week. I've very little else to say except to advise you to follow Nellie's example and take a holiday yourself. I'd suggest the 'Isle of Man' or somewhere 'far from the madding crowd's ignoble strife' and you won't get that desirable state in Ireland at present to judge from the newspapers which we get very nearly regularly here. By the bye, I wrote to Mr O'Kennedy for some sporting papers about six weeks ago. I wonder did he ever get the letter? I didn't get the papers anyway! I might remark in conclusion that I am very badly off for cigs. and matches. Send no more Turkish cigarettes but a few Russian would be acceptable and send the Grand Parade in tins. The packages are most inconvenient while the tins are much more desirable. Anyway, you taste them. The last biscuits too, you sent were delightful. Hoping this finds everything as it should be at home, I remain, yours affectionately,

Christy.

Please remember me to Bro. Roche. Is he leaving School this year?

P.P.S. I also want stamps. Send a book.

Monday, 20th June, '21.

My dearest Mother,

I received today a parcel, which you posted on Friday, containing stamps, a cake, tinned fruit, shoes and 50 cigarettes. I also had a parcel on Wednesday last containing 30 cigarettes amongst other things. The total value of cigarettes in both parcels is 4/-. Now, my dear mother, if you cannot afford to send more than 4/- worth of cigarettes per week I would respectfully suggest that you would leave out from my parcels biscuits, cakes, fruit, butter, jam, rashers and everything else and convert their value into fags. If this does not ease the financial situation, which must have changed greatly since I have been home, you have perfect liberty to sell my bicycle, watch, cameras and cricket bats and buy me some cigarettes because you have no idea how much they are needed here or how scarce they are. My attitude on the question is the attitude of all. Let cigarettes be the principal thing because they offer the greatest consolation. And please don't say you were surprised to hear I wanted more of them because since I've come here this has been my principal need.

I wrote to the College last week and Doyle will call on you. I asked for certain books, breeches, leggings etc. Since then I met with a couple of accidents which ruined what was left of my trousers so you will please send my flannel trousers immediately. Since I wrote the above early this morning I've got over my disgust at the 50 fags so you needn't mind what I said but I have not the energy to rewrite my address on the top. I hope all at home are quite well. Remember me to J. J. Maguire and I will probably acknowledge his letter of some time ago next week. Also remember me to Paddy and Anto. I had a letter from Paddy and I'll write to him in due course. I'm all right and the place is as usual which is really what is wrong with it. Let me have all the news from home omitting things like K's bankruptcy. That fact hasn't even a remote interest for me. Please send my parcels on Thursdays and Mondays instead of Fridays and Tuesdays and include a few Russian fags in them as well as matches. I want you to send every week only one plain cake with jam, butter and rashers alternately for the hut mess.

I'll conclude now as my surroundings lack the power to

inspire and the barbed wire is beginning to get on my nerves. Indeed so much of it do I see that I fear if I'm not released soon I'll get B.W.P. (barbed wire phobia).

Goodbye and wish Pat good luck in his exam and congratulations to him as an athlete.

Yours affectionately,
Christy.

When the Truce came in July my mother assumed that we would be released immediately, writing to inquire if I would wire to let her know what time she should send a car to pick me up. We felt no such certainty of a final settlement and release. A certain way to get out would be to dig, successfully, a tunnel. A Leitrim miner named Jim Brady had started a tunnel almost as soon as he arrived in camp. He had not got very far when the soldiers found it. That was in April, shortly after my internment began. In the meantime, several other tunnels were started from time to time in other parts of the camp but all of them were detected.

Just as the Truce was declared Liam Murphy, the O/C of our hut, decided to organise another tunnel excavation. He took the precaution of failing to tell our camp O/C Peadar McMahon or any of the camp council about the matter because if the project was successful we of the Poor Bloody Infantry (P.B.I.) would have had to give precedence in an escape to our seniors. Since the T.D.s had been released in August by the terms of the Truce there was less danger of this happening. Their departure put an end to our solo school and I particularly missed the companionship of Phil and Jim. My bouts of depression became more frequent and more acute. On leaving, Phil Cosgrave took with him an uncensored letter to my mother. It was not much more informative than if it had gone through the censor. It still contained requests for parcels but it reflected my low spirits. However, the propects of the tunnel escape gave a boost to my morale.

Jim Brady, helped by a man named Jim Galvin, actually dug the tunnel. The site was under the hut next to our number 32. The clay from the excavations was sneaked away in jacket pockets or paper bags to be spread under the other huts when the opportunity offered. My contribution to the enterprise was minimal. I kept 'nix'. Only a very expert miner and a brave and strong man could have dug that tunnel. Brady was all of these. Galvin was also brave and strong and determined. The only tools they had were a metal bar and knives and spoons from the cook-house. The tunnel was propped at intervals by pieces of bed boards. At the beginning of September Brady reported to Liam Murphy that the job was completed and except for the outer barbed wire barrier we were ready to go. For that fence he had secured a wire cutter. No one asked questions as to how he came by it.

From the time in the forenoon when the decision was taken to go until we were actually outside the camp boundaries, I was in a state of tension that increased hourly. Myles Ford and I talked all day about what direction we would take if we succeeded in getting away. We had no maps. We agreed we would make for Dublin but the only compass point we had indicating the direction of Dublin was the stand of the racecourse. We decided to head for that. We didn't even know what towns or villages or landmarks lay between the Curragh and Dublin. This was a measure of the ignorance of Dubliners of our time about rural Ireland or indeed of the geography of Ireland in general.

At midnight the breakout began. Murphy arranged that we should leave in groups of two or three at three-minute intervals. He allocated us our groups and our place in the queue. Myles Ford, Jack Knowthe and myself were to go together in the sixth group. As we heard no sign of commotion from the groups that had preceded us we knew that they had got away safely. We got no directions from Murphy as to what route to take once clear of the tunnel. That was left to ourselves. Our only instructions were that we should not get off our bellies until we judged we had got out of the possible view of the sentries in the watch towers of the camp.

After three months internment a prisoner was entitled to 'procure' a new suit of clothes from the British. I had claimed mine. The suit was of the type issued to soldiers on demobilisation. It was known variously as a 'Martin-Henry' after the manufacturers (who were reputed to have made millions on the supply) or a 'Hamar' (after the Chief Secretary) or a 'bum-freezer' (because the coat had no vent at the back and was very short). It was made of the shoddiest material dyed a blue colour which would run in a shower of rain. I had intended to keep it to be worn on my release. I decided to wear it for the escape.

We were not allowed to wear boots in the tunnel but there was no objection to taking them strung around your neck. I very wisely did this. Myles Ford and Knowthe unfortunately did not. The tensions of the day mounted to their peak as I slipped out of the hut and under hut 31 to the mouth of the tunnel. After the first few yards I was seized by a fit of terror. I had no idea that the passage was so small. It was about three feet wide and rather less than two feet high. As I

187

wriggled along, my shoulders touched the sides. Occasionally, if I failed to keep absolutely flat, I touched the roof. I was afraid that at any minute the roof would collapse, suffocating me. My body was pouring sweat. Once a boot got caught under my armpit, requiring me momentarily to stop wriggling to dislodge it. The pause of a second or two felt like hours. At last when, after a quarter of an hour or so, I reached the end of the tunnel and got into the open air and on to the green grass my whole instinct was to get up and run. With a great effort I resisted the temptation, continuing to wriggle to the fence, the bottom wire of which Brady had cut. I could hear the sentry in the watch tower call out his routine report 'No. 1 post and all is well'. By this time I was calmer and, thanks to the wet grass and a light ground mist, cooler. Here I found Myles Ford and Jack Knowthe waiting for me as we had arranged. We still had to wriggle several hundred yards, crossing the dirt tracks before we reached the main Curragh Road.

Myles, who was by far the calmest of us, took the lead until we at last reached the racecourse. Here we were able to crawl rather than wriggle. After a few hundred yards we felt justified in getting to our feet. We ran to the racecourse stand where we paused for breath and to take counsel. I put on my boots. Neither Myles nor Jack had ever been even as far as Bodenstown for the Wolfe Tone Memorial celebrations but I had. I knew that Bodenstown was near Sallins and since in getting there we had never crossed the Curragh I reckoned that Sallins must be north of the Curragh. But we did not know that Newbridge and Naas lay between us and Sallins. The obvious route for us to take seemed to be along the railway line, but we felt that progress would be dangerously slow, stepping from sleeper to sleeper while the stone ballast between the sleepers would make walking impossible for Myles and Jack in their stocking-feet.

We decided to use the side roads keeping as near to the railway as possible. We considered knocking up some household, throwing ourselves on their mercy and asking for help, but rejected the idea because it was fairly certain that anyone living in the vicinity of the Curragh would be in some way connected with the military or, what was the same in our estimation, the gentlemen of the Turf. It was now between 1 and 2 a.m. The night was calm and soundless and the ground mist had gone. We had walked four or five miles when we heard a motor car or lorry coming towards us. We jumped into a ditch, landing in a bed of nettles. The nettle stings were a substantial addition to our growing discomfort. Myles' and Jack's feet began to give them trouble but we pushed on. After walking for a couple of hours we found ourselves in the middle of what seemed a large town. There was neither a soul nor a light to be seen. We did not know where we were but we hurried through it as quickly as possible. In fact it was Newbridge, a large military centre. As Newbridge is only three miles from the Curragh, we must have been walking around in in circles before we blundered into it. We met nobody.

When we got through the town we abandoned the main road, continuing to walk blindly in the direction, we hoped but were not sure, of Dublin. My companions' feet began to give out completely when we found ourselves on what was obviously the outskirts of another town. This town was Naas, but we did not know that. We decided that Myles and Jack would rest while I went into the town to explore the possibility of getting help. I found the place, like Newbridge, deserted. There was no light showing in any house, nor of course were there any street lamps in those days.

I knew we could not go on much further. I thought there must be a priest somewhere at hand who, even if he was not sympathetic, would neither give us away nor turn us away. He might even put us in touch with the local IRA. I saw the church. There was a small house near it. I knocked. After a long pause, a window opened. A voice asked gruffly and nervously what I wanted. I told him that there had been an accident and I was looking for a priest. With reluctance the voice directed me to a house which was easy to find as it was situated at the junction of the street we were standing in and the main road. I approached and knocked at the door. A window in the upper story opened after some delay. A man appeared to enquire what was the matter. I repeated the story about wanting a priest to tend to some people involved in an accident. He told me he was the priest. After being interrogated as to who I was, what I was doing out at that hour of night, what accident had happened and so on, I began to realise that my efforts at persuasion were wasted. With the state of my nerves and bodily exhaustation I was not prepared to conduct any further conversation at the top of my voice with this unhelpful priest. I got very angry with him, told him in four letter words what he could do with himself and went off to rejoin the others. When I calmed down, I was very conscience stricken about having spoken to a priest in that way.

As it happened the priest — Father Flavin I think was his name — was most sympathetic to the Movement. Had he known we were escaped prisoners, he would have taken us into his house and looked after us. But unfortunately I did not know that at the time.

There was nothing for us to do but trudge on although by this time

Myles' and Jack's feet were in ribbons. They were finding it so difficult to get along that we felt we had no choice but to waken some household and look for help. We were considering this when after walking a couple of miles we came to another village. Here we saw a light and made straight for it. It turned out to be Sallins Railway Station and the light came from the office of the night porter. We pushed open the door to find the porter reading a newspaper before a bright fire. To us it was a most comforting scene. I told the porter that we were three IRA men who had escaped from the Curragh and wanted to be put in touch with the local IRA. His face lit up. 'Bejaysus', said he, 'I'm the local quartermaster'. We were safe! He sat us down and gave us strong tea and some bread and butter while we told him of our adventures and our need to get to Dublin. He assured us that there would be no difficulty in fixing that. A goods train to Dublin would be coming through in a couple of hours and it would drop us off anywhere we wanted along the line.

We were a dismal sight. Dusty, wet, sore footed, nettle stung. While having tea we were given a basin of hot water to bathe the battered feet of Myles and Jack. When daylight came we went outside to collect dock leaves, of which there was an abundance, to treat our nettle stings which were still painful.

Before getting on the train the porter gave us half a crown each. The money, he explained, was from the funds of the local IRA Company. When the train arrived he signalled it to a halt, explained our problem to the guard and driver. It was decided that they would drop us off just beyond Clondalkin at Bluebell. From there we cut across the fields to a garage on the main road where Myles Ford knew that a taxi could be obtained. With the seven and sixpence we got from the porter at Sallins we hired a taxi to take us to the house of Ford's relatives at Templeogue.

My first action, when I arrived, was to send my mother this letter by one of the Ford girls:

My dearest Mother,

I do not want you to express any surprise or amazement that you should hear from me from the above address so soon. The fact is I was one of a number to make a somewhat sensational escape from the Curragh last night at about 12.30. By dint of crawling, walking, riding on a train, begging, and a motorcar I arrived safely here at 12.45 this morning feeling dead tired and absolutely filthy dirty but safe and sound. So dirty and wet am I that the clothes (Hamar's by the way) are no longer of any use and you must send me a complete rig-out from boots to hat as soon as possible. I do not think you have boots so don't bother with them. Send the rest, collar, socks, stud and all. Miss Ford, who will deliver this will take them on her way home. I want you in no circumstances to try to see me for the present the reason why being apparent. I must see in what postion I stand with reference to the truce first. I may make a descent on you very soon, if possible this evening, but don't you attempt to see me at all yet. Would you please send me a little money to keep going with. I need hardly remark that my hurried departure prevented me from taking anything but a suit with me — not even a hat, but everything will be in safe hands.

Another thing, nobody whatever except father must know what has happened, not even Pat or Paddy Kerrigan. *Nobody* remember? I think that's all and I'll say goodbye and I hope to see you very soon.

With very best love from
Christy.

I notice my cautious mother cut off the address and the date, which was 9 September 1921. Several members of the Company lived in Templeogue. I got them to inform Coughlan and Kenny of my escape. Back at the Rath Camp the breakout continued until dawn when, of course, it had to stop. Curiously enough, the British did not become aware of the situation until roll call at 8 a.m. Over forty prisoners were missing. By the time the British were able to organise search parties to scour the neighbourhood, they had no chance of recapturing any of the escapees and after one day the hunt was abandoned. The usual punishment was inflicted on the remaining prisoners. No parcels, no letters, no money, no newspapers and the usual bullying from the Scotch gutties in uniform who formed the camp guard.

Coughlan came along to see us. He said we could safely go home after dark but advised us not to go out for a few days until the dust settled. I sent word to my mother to expect me and late in the evening a taxi collected Myles, Jack and myself and dropped us at our respective homes. My parents greeted me affectionately; my mother by saying 'You're a nice fellow, giving us all that worry'. My father had already begun to accumulate newspapers to read about the escape. My mother assumed I was starving and apparently had spent the day from the time she heard of my escape cooking a variety of jam sandwiches, jam rolls and apple tarts to round off a meal consisting of a pound of sirloin steak, a plateful of potatoes and a bowl of cabbage. I did my best to please her but I really only wanted to have a bath and go to bed. It was not to be.

Paddy Caffrey and Ewart Wilson came in. After hearing the story of my escape, they got into a discussion as to whether Dev would succeed in getting Lloyd George to agree to a peace conference on terms acceptable to the Republican Government. Although I was very tired I listened to the spate of speculation from which I gathered that the feeling among the people at large was that there would be a conference and there would be a settlement. Everyone seemed to think that the resumption of hostilities between the British and the IRA was out of the question. I was very surprised at this view because I did not think the British would give anything we could not forcibly take. I assumed that the IRA were availing themselves of the Truce to reorganise and procure arms for the resumption of the war.

It was after 1 a.m. when Ewart and Paddy left and at long last I staggered into a bath and from that into the deep, deep comfort of a feather bed. A feather bed is superior to any chaise longue and certainly to 'biscuits' and bed boards even without the hurly-burly. I did not wake until midday to find myself surrounded by the three Dublin morning papers (even *The Irish Times* was bought that morning) together with several English papers and the *New Statesman*. In case I had not enough to read, Paddy Caffrey had left me in two volumes of Mommsen's *History of Rome* and Prescott's *Conquest of Mexico*. These were my bedside books from then until the start of the Civil War. Indeed during that period they were almost the only books I read, or rather dipped into. They made an abiding impression on me. When I think of the defects of our people, I recall Mommsen's quotation from the historian Thierry describing the Celts as a people who lacked perseverance, had an aversion to discipline and order and who were addicted to ostentatious and perpetual discord — the result of boundless vanity. To this Mommsen adds the observation that 'such qualities — those of good soldiers but bad citizens — explain the historical fact that the Celts have shaken all states and have founded none'. It was several years before I had the leisure to read fully Prescott's *Conquest of Mexico*. I know of no book which contains within its covers such a kaleidoscope of human villainy, greed, treachery, human sacrifice, brutality, ritualism, cannibalism and superstition coupled with physical endurance and bravery — the commonest and most over-esteemed of human qualities.

The I.R.A. Split

Historical happenings in Rome and Mexico were very far removed from my problems in early September 1921. While I waited at home for instructions from the Company as to my next assignment I read the daily speculations of the newspapers on the probable outcome of the sparring match going on between Lloyd George and De Valera on the possibility of a Peace Conference. I also observed from the newspapers that not all Dublin was as preoccupied with the Truce, its duration and outcome as I was, and that the many visitors I had during my seclusion from the Company and College life in the days immediately following my escape had other divisions.

While I was in Rath Camp the sight of the race-goers carrying on their usual sporting activities annoyed me, but racing people were exceptionally low in my scale of values. I was surprised to find the life of the city proceeding with total indifference to what were to me the great issues of peace or war. From the newspapers I had got the impression that the country generally was in turmoil with normal life suspended. I read of reprisals and counter reprisals, transport workers refusing to move British military stores, raids by both sides on private houses, establishment of Sinn Féin Courts, resignation of magistrates, destruction of village halls, arrests and internments and executions. A measure of my immaturity was my difficulty in understanding how, in the grave circumstances confronting the nation, 'Paddy the Next Best Thing', played of course by a second-rate English company, could be packing the Gaiety Theatre, and the picture houses, the Pillar, the Corinthian, the Scala and the Princess, were carrying on as usual. Charlie Chaplin was invited to Dublin by the Irish Cinema and Amusement Guild. Race meetings were held at Baldoyle, Mullingar, Sligo and Dundalk. Except for West Cork, where the fighting had been more intense and tension still continued, life in the country was equally normal. I began to wonder did it really matter to the man in the street whether the British stayed or got out.

I had visits from my neighbour and friend, Paddy Kerrigan, who had just got a job as a clerk in the Dublin and Blessington Steam Tram Company. He was paid 15/- per week and regarded himself as the luckiest man in Terenure. Paddy was quite certain that the Truce would end in some form of settlement acceptable to the nation. He had joined the IRA only after a great struggle with his conscience. He was a man of moral and physical courage who, as he was in a continuous state of grace, did not fear death. He was sure of his eternal reward. His abiding terror was that at some time he might be asked to kill someone. The sense of relief engendered by the Truce made it impossible for him to imagine that the war would be resumed.

Kenny, our Company Lieutenant, called with news of a couple of ambushes the Company carried out during my internment on the Templeogue Road. He told me that there had recently been a great rush of recruits into the Company and accordingly it had been decided to divide it into two separate units, 'E' and 'K', that he was taking over 'K' as Captain and that Coughlan had decided to keep me in 'E' as his Lieutenant. The new recruits to the IRA were very welcome at the time but when the split came a very vicious campaign was carried on against those who took the anti-Treaty side. Kenny did not think the Truce would last. He was obsessed with preparing his new Company for a continuation of the War. He had heard that a cargo of the newly-invented Thompson machine guns had been imported. With these in the hands of the IRA it would have been impossible for the British — either Army or Black and Tans — freely to move around the city or country in anything but large units. As it happened, his information was wrong. A half dozen Thompsons had been smuggled in but the major cargo had been stopped and confiscated by the American Secret Service. White Anglo-Saxon Protestants of the American State Department had no intention of helping the Irish — lace curtain or not — if it meant offending their opposite numbers in Britain with whom they had, by tradition, a special relationship.

I had other visitors from the Company as well as school friends. Among the latter was Frank Kerlin who was the best all round student in our Senior Grade class. Whether in maths, literature, languages or science, Kerlin led the class. In each grade he was an exhibitioner. He won a scholarship to the university, where he elected to take a degree in chemistry. Before the Truce, despite his difficult family circumstances, he had joined the IRA. His parents came from Derry to Dublin where they started a painting and decorating business as well as a shop selling retail paints and wallpaper. His mother died while Frank was quite young and just before he left school his father died leaving him with the responsibility of supporting a family of two sisters and two brothers. The older sister, who was only a year younger than Frank, decided to carry on the retail part of the business. It was a heavy burden for a boy of eighteen and a girl of seventeen to carry but Frank Kerlin was not merely exceptionally intelligent but also unusually determined.

His sister Bridie was no less determined. Between them they kept the business going at a sufficiently profitable level to educate the two younger boys and the younger sister — a girl of great beauty who, as she grew older, wanted to be a ballet dancer. To launch her on a career as a ballet dancer which involved training in London was beyond their resources although Frank and Bridie indulged the younger children more than would the most doting of parents. Frank did not think the Truce would last and he was already deeply involved in preparing for the resumption of the war. I listened to his opinion with great attention because I always thought that he had a clearer as well as a more mature mind than any of my contemporaries. Frank Kerlin during the Civil War became the deputy head of the Republican Intelligence — his signature 'K' became famous. The Staters never caught up with him.

Seán Lemass admired him greatly, persuaded him to go into politics and had him elected as his running mate in the 1929 election. Had he lived, I think he would have been a major force in Irish politics. Kerlin died from T.B. before Fianna Fáil came to power. The traditional political cliche of being 'a great loss to the nation' was rarely more appropriate.

At this stage as discussions about the possibility of a peace conference still dragged on, it occurred to me for the first time in my life that speculation about future events in the absence of any real information of the forces which were shaping them was no less futile than speculating on historical might-have-beens. I certainly had no inside information but I was still in a frame of mind which believed that our national leaders could do no wrong. At the same time I began to reflect on what I would do in the event of there being a settlement with the British.

I would have to take some steps to earn my living. It never occurred to me to think of having a career rather than just earning a living. Having regard to my brief experience of clerical work in Kennedy's Bakery, I eliminated the possibility of a career in clerking. More as a gesture to show my parents that I was conscious of living on their bounty, I suggested that I might take over my mother's shop or, alternatively, join my father in the auctioneering business. I was not surprised when they made it clear that neither course was acceptable and, moreover, that they regarded these suggestions as merely a piece of play-acting on my part. In this they were, of course, right. I really had made up my mind to go back to the university but I had no wish to continue chemistry. At that time Guinness's Brewery and Jacob's Biscuit Factory were the only industries where chemists were employed but in Guinness's and Jacob's the only jobs open to

Catholics were those of clerks and labourers. It would be wrong to say that I gave any profound thought to the job problem; it was not a matter of any urgency since my parents seemed to be content to subsidise me indefinitely.

My immediate problem was solved by my Company O/C Coughlan who sent a note telling me to call to see him in Rathfarnham, adding that he thought it was safe enough for me to appear on the streets as there was no likelihood of being re-arrested. After five days' confinement at home I was glad enough to get out. I noticed that the people in the village of Terenure seemed much more friendly than they had been before my internment.

Coughlan confirmed that the Company was being divided but as to myself he said that at long last he had been successful in having me appointed to the staff of G.H.Q. I was to be assigned to the training staff, reporting to Commandant Emmett Dalton, the Director of Training, for instructions.

I saw Commandant Dalton by arrangement in the Plaza Hotel. He was alone in a miserable, gloomy room. I had of course heard of Emmett Dalton but when I met him I was surprised at his youthful appearance. There was no mistaking the sense of authority he emanated despite his quiet and pleasant manner. As a mere boy, he had won great distinction fighting with the British Army in France and it was he who led the attempt to rescue Seán MacEoin from Mountjoy. This episode was the most spectacularly daring event in the Tan War.

Dalton told me that it had been decided that I was to take charge of a training camp for senior officers of the Donegal Brigade to be organised in Dungloe. I had never heard of Dungloe nor had I anything but the vaguest idea of what Donegal or Donegal people were like. The Brigade had been fairly active in the pre-Truce fighting. They had carried out ambushes and attacks on barracks. A particularly successful operation was the derailment of a train causing substantial British casualties. The people had suffered considerably from British reprisals, a number of men being shot 'while trying to escape', and the British also burned down premises in Donegal town and Mount Charles. The Donegal columns had the exceptional handicap of maintaining themselves in a mixed Catholic and Protestant population.

While I was delighted at being given so much increased responsibility, which I always wanted, I felt it right to tell Emmett Dalton that I had no experience of training beyond Company level. He said I would have the assistance of a highly trained ex-British Army sergeant who would act as my adjutant. Details of the course to be covered were set out in the official curriculum and with the guidance of this and of the adjutant, I should not have any difficulty. He arranged for me to call back next day to meet my adjutant and receive the curriculum with instructions on whom to report to in Donegal.

I suppose that every individual reacts, at first sight, to those with whom they are likely to be closely associated. In my case the chemistry of attraction and repulsion is particularly strong. I am very much aware that my own particular personality has the same effect on other people. People have auras which are particularly incompatible. One look, plus five minutes conversation, produced in my mind what was metaphorically speaking a bad smell from my adjutant. I don't think my immediate impression misled me. When a couple of days later we set out from Amiens Street Station, I found that he was as remote as could be from my conception of how an IRA man should think, feel and behave. He had only contempt for the amateur military qualities of the IRA which *he* was going to put, right. He had not even a vague idea of what Sinn Féin or the Movement was about. He was unaware of the existence of the Gaelic League or of the Irish language. From the beginning he showed an excessive capacity to drink pints of porter which was not regarded by me as a permissible quality in an IRA man. He seemed to me no better than a corner boy. We had nothing in common but a Dublin accent but his fractured English did nothing to compensate for that.

After a long and tedious train journey we ultimately arrived at the tiny Dungloe Road Station where we were met by Commandant Joseph Sweeney. It turned out that Joe Sweeney remembered having seen me at St Enda's where he spent all his school days — a tenuous connection but clearly we had something in common. The adjutant and I were billeted in Sweeney's Hotel where the adjutant immediately proceeded to the bar. Commandant Sweeney was a young man, not much older than myself, who had distinguished himself at Pearse's side in the GPO in 1916. He had just been appointed Commandant-General of the First Northern Division, the division being made up of the four Donegal Brigades. He was a fine, fairhaired man. His manner was pleasant, displaying a diffidence which was unexpected in so senior an officer. While the training course was in progress he attended every parade or lecture, never saying much nor interfering in any way. He was convinced that the Truce would not end until an agreement was reached with the British. I met the Donegal Commandants — there were about fifteen of them billeted in houses around Dungloe — in a small village hall. Having all the Dubliner's ignorant misconceptions of countrymen as being characteristically slow witted, not to say inarticulate (a view not consistent with my admiration for the Flying Columns of the rural IRA or of my experience of the men I met in the Rath internment camp who were mainly from the midland counties) I wondered when I first saw my students how I would get any of them to participate in the discussions which according to the curriculum were to follow my lectures. The lectures dealt with subjects such as 'advancing under fire', 'organisation of intelligence units', 'the use and care of small arms'. The curriculum also provided for outdoor activities such as drilling, the use of cover and marching at night. Training in these outdoor activities was the function of the adjutant.

I read my first lecture, dealing with the organisation of Companies and with communications, with a feeling of trepidation. It was the first time I had ever addressed a group of strangers. When finished I looked around wondering if any of the group could be induced to open a discussion. My eye lit on one man who seemed rather older than the rest and I asked if he would care to comment on the subject matter of the lecture. He stood up immediately, pouring out a stream of words arranged in fluent, well balanced sentences full of striking imagery and laced with quotations from James Connolly. I was almost stupefied with surprise and completely unnerved by this response. I fleetingly thought that if the rest of the group showed similar qualities of fluency and assurance I would not have the face to finish my two-week course. The speaker was sensitive enough to discern my predicament. Although he was of lower rank than Commandant Joe Sweeney, he in effect took over the direction of the meeting. As it turned out I had no need to feel inadequate because the speaker was Peadar O'Donnell who was to become one of the most remarkable men of our generation.

At this time Peadar was only twenty-eight years of age. While there is at that stage of one's life a considerable maturity gap between twenty-eight and just under twenty, which was my age at the time, we began a life-long friendship. Peadar has been described as 'the greatest agitator of his generation' and despite the age gap it was also my generation. Peadar recognised that I was a stranger in a strange land with the problems of confidence which that situation presents. He also recognised that my adjutant was no help to me nor to the success of the training course nor to the impression (the word 'image' had not been invented) of Dublin and G.H.Q. that he was leaving in Dungloe. He suggested I talk to Sweeney about the situation. I proposed that I should send the adjutant home forthwith and Sweeney agreed with my decision. When I told the adjutant that he would have to go back to Dublin, to my surprise he made no protest. He was apparently as glad to get back to the pavement as I was to be rid of him. I sent a note to G.H.Q. explaining that I found him unsuitable. I never heard of him again.

After our first meeting, Peadar O'Donnell with his great kindness and comprehension took me in hand smoothing over any difficulties I encountered. We finished the course quite successfully. I acquired some minor réclame because I was a very good rifle shot as well as being quite expert in stripping and assembling automatic pistols: the Peter the Painter, the Colt .45 automatic and the Parabellum. Small arms was the only mechanical device I ever had any capacity to cope with. I spent most of my evenings talking, or rather listening to Peadar as he described the way of life of the people of the Rosses, of which Dungloe is the principal town. He told me of the annual migration of the 'tatie-hokers' to Scotland, of the hardships they had to endure and of his own efforts to improve their lot. When the course was finished, he took me home to meet his mother. It was easy to see where Peadar got his intelligence and his warmth. She gave me a great welcome showing a good deal more interest in me and my family than in the problems of the locality or of the nation. I was not used to being treated in so flattering or even so adult a fashion. She appeared to me to be a woman of very fine quality, shrewd and full of common sense, who was content with life despite what must have been a hard struggle to rear her children.

Before returning home Peadar arranged that I should spend a while seeing something of Donegal. Somewhere he acquired a car in which he took me on a tour of the Rosses visiting Gweedore, circling Errigal, finally depositing me at Letterkenny Station to begin my homeward journey. The trip with Peadar revealed a new world to me. I thought the Rosses with their tiny fields heavily cultivated amid miles and miles of stone walls an astonishing place for people to live in. We stopped at several houses where Peadar had particular friends. We were invited into the tiny kitchens for the ritual cup of tea with home-made bread. The people were obviously very poor but it was a different kind of poverty from what I was so familiar with in Dublin. However small and sparsely furnished the kitchens, which also served as living rooms, they were clean and tidy. There was no tinge of slummery about them nor any crippling air of destitution, although I am sure the people were often reduced to very meagre rations. But what struck me most forcefully was the atmosphere of independent self-reliance which contrasted so noticeably with the feeling of help-lessness prevailing in the poor areas of Dublin.

If this journey around North West Donegal was my introduction to peasant Ireland, no less was conversation with Peadar O'Donnell my introduction to the theory of Socialism in an Irish context. I felt nothing less than bewilderment at his references to the 'uprising of the masses' or 'the gathering together (with appropriate gestures) of the workers, small farmers and peasants' or 'the expropriation of the landlords and the taking over of the means of production'.

The 'class war' about which Peadar spoke so convincingly would have been unknown — even as a phrase — to almost everyone in the Movement. In our estimation there were only two classes. There were the British with their dependants and hangers-on, of whom the most objectionable group was the Castle Catholics, and there were the Irish. There was no Marxian slide rule appropriate to Irish social conditions. The difference between a publican living over his shop and a publican living in a detached house in the suburbs was one of the main class distinctions in Ireland, a difference unlikely to provoke any kind of war.

I think even at that time I knew rather more about the Russian Revolution than Peadar but I never mentally associated the mechanics of Socialism with Ireland nor, while I was familiar with the great Dublin strikes of 1913 and the origin of the Citizen Army, did I think they had any lasting significance for the country. So much for the influence of Connolly on the thinking and motivation of the IRA! What I heard from Peadar depicted in my mind at least an alternative future for Ireland which someone might want to create. While it lasted and while Peadar's spell was on me, I was fascinated by these new ideas. Alas! When I said goodbye to Peadar at Letterkenny the vision he had evoked for me vanished. I reverted to the 'Aisling' which Pearse had created for the nation.

While in Donegal I read in the papers that an agreement had finally been reached between De Valera and Lloyd George to hold a full scale conference in London to explore the possibility of a settlement. I got home just after the delegates left for London to find my mother waiting for me with a present of a pair of gloves which she had got for my twentieth birthday. With all the excitement of the visit to Donegal, I had forgotten about it. It was now the middle of October and my birthday had been on the seventh.

I sent a report on the training camp in Donegal to G.H.Q. via Coughlan who was still my superior. I took on the duties of Lieutenant in 'E' Company which had been swollen in numbers to over one hundred men despite the fact that its right half had been hived off to a newly formed 'K' Company under Kenny. From the time the delegates went to London in October morale in the IRA had clearly deteriorated. The general belief was that a satisfactory agreement would be reached in London so that there would be no more fighting. Such training as was done in the Companies seemed to be directed to victory celebrations rather than to resuming military operations. A worse feature of the situation was that men who had played an active part in the fighting began to strut about taking their bows as local heroes which too often meant accepting alcoholic hospitality. These old hands were also inclined to belittle the recruits who had joined since the Truce. The word 'Trucer' was coined even at this early stage and it was to have a devastating significance later on. The population at large had no doubt that the fighting was finished for good; they were not too worried as to what kind of a settlement was made so long as hostilities ceased.

The Delegation began their deliberations in mid-October and the agreement, miscalled a Treaty, was signed on the 6 December. The course of the negotiations was accompanied by endless speculation in the newspapers. It was characteristic of the IRA, and of the Movement generally, that personal publicity was avoided. In the absence of 'leaks' from the Delegation about the progress of the talks journalists were unable to form sound political judgements. *The Observer* whose editor, J. L. Garvin, would have access to many political news sources had no better information than the *Irish Independent* which was generally regarded by Republicans then as low in the scale of political acumen.

We, that is the ordinary IRA men, had no notion of the personal animosities within G.H.Q. and the Dáil Cabinet that preceded the appointment of the Delegation to London. We did not know that Griffith loathed Childers or that Brugha loathed Collins. Nor that Collins despised Stack. Nor that De Valera regarded Cosgrave as a 'ninny'. I was in thrall to Pearse; to the standards of Cúchulainn and Fionn. I thought all the leaders of the Movement were equally in thrall to these standards identifying them in character and outlook to Pearse's ideal of a teacher: 'He must in the first place be a man of fine character and lofty ideals. He must in the next be warmly Irish in sympathy. This does not mean that he must of necessity be a rampant politician. It means only that he must love Ireland with an intimate and discerning love; that he must regard himself as a worker for Ireland; that he must realise the awfulness and the responsibility of his position as one into whose hands it is given to mould for good or ill the character of future Irish citizens'. To me the Movement encapsulated in the Cabinet was an irrefrangible monolith. Every member of it had feet of iron. I could not have thought of them as having feet of clay.

I was not specially unintelligent nor was I, for my age, specially uninformed. But when I look back over the years I find it difficult to understand how I, and hundreds like me, had such a simple trust in our leaders. We who were Christian Brothers' boys were fully conscious of Original Sin. But we did not attribute it to our leaders. I certainly thought in my stupid simplicity that they were *all* cast in the mould of Pearse and the men of '16. Between October when they went and December when they returned, we remained under the illusion that nothing but good could result from the Delegation's deliberations in London.

In the meantime we carried on the parades and training of the Companies in the Battalion. We organised Céilithe, Feiseanna, Concerts, Aeríochtaí and whist drives in aid of the arms fund. We even organised donkey races and 'flapper' meetings i.e. race meetings outside the jurisdiction of the Turf Club.

On the whole it was for me a pleasant and carefree interlude. In the mornings I went into University College, making gestures at attending second-year lectures in chemistry. We who were active IRA members were given credit for our first year examination as had the students who joined the British Army in the European war. In fact, I spent most of my morning gossiping about the political situation in the centre hall of the College, drinking coffee in Roberts' Café, strolling in Grafton Street or playing snooker in the Adelphi billiard-room. I resumed my acquaintance with Andy Cooney with whom I had spent the afternoon of Bloody Sunday in Terenure. Cooney, a medical student, had been sent by G.H.Q. to organise the IRA in Kerry and had been very successful there. We were to become very closely associated in the IRA a little later on.

At this time too I became very friendly with John Dowling, the O/C of our Fourth Battalion, and his brother Frank, who was a Lieutenant in 'C' Company of the Battalion. Pearse had described Frank as the ideal of an Irish boy: a re-incarnation of Cúchulainn. The Dowlings were the boys who had bullied me in the days when I travelled with them in a brake from Terenure to St Enda's during my short time as a day-boarder there. In time John Dowling was to become one of my closest friends, exercising an important influence on my intellectual development.

Sometimes I filled in the afternoons at the cinema but rarely sat through a programme without falling asleep. I went to the Abbey often. There were no new playwrights and very few new plays. Lady Gregory, Lennox Robinson, T. C. Murray, George Shiels, were put on week after week but the actors, Barry Fitzgerald, F. J. McCormick, Eileen Crowe, Michael Dolan, were in their heyday and the plays were wonderfully produced by Robinson or Dolan. At that time the theatre was ill patronised; often the actors had to play to pitifully small audiences. Yeats and Lady Gregory with Dublin's theatrical chronicler, Joseph Holloway, seemed often to be the only occupants of the stalls. If O'Casey had not emerged on the theatrical scene it is doubtful if the Abbey could have survived.

I spent several evenings a week and part of most weekends training the new men in the Company or attending meetings of the officers of the Battalion as a result of which I enlarged my circle of IRA acquaintances. At this time I acquired the habit of awakening every morning at 6 a.m. It is a habit that has remained with me all my life. I applied the early hours to reading. Thanks to this habit I did not have to await my retirement, like many others in the public service, to satisfy my appetite for books. I was fortunate in having no personal worries nor any anxiety about the future. Politically I had complete confidence in the leadership. I was an innocent. But the age of innocence was coming to a close. My Aisling world of Cathleen, the daughter of Houlihan, was about to be dissipated.

The Treaty was signed in the early hours of the morning of Tuesday 6 December 1921. The first I learned of some of its principal terms was when my friend Paddy Kerrigan brought me a copy of an evening paper on the evening of the 7th. I was in bed recovering from an attack of quinsy. The news had obviously been hurriedly put together for inclusion in the 'Stop Press' column. But there was one clause, the purport of which there was no mistaking, beside which the remaining terms could be of no importance to me. It provided for an Oath of Allegiance to His Majesty King George V, his heirs and successors. I was shocked and hopefully incredulous. I thought something must be wrong with the newspaper report. Collins could not have agreed to this. It was hard to believe that any of the other Irish representatives could have agreed to it either. Next morning I waited for the papers to come. The whole terrible truth was confirmed. As I read the clauses allowing the British to retain the ports, paying pensions to the hated RIC, leaving the defence of our coasts to the Imperial power, substituting the title of Governor-General for Lord Lieutenant, I literally got a recurrence of my illness through rage and disappointment.

Griffith issued a statement asserting that the proposals gave Ireland control of her own destiny. The newspapers reporting the contents of the Treaty latched on to this view, representing the agreement as a great victory. The daily papers — not for the first time — did everything to stampede the nation into the Empire. The Treaty meant just that to me. I refused to allow myself to believe that the agreement should be taken at face value. Surely, I thought, Collins must have had some reservations or provided some safeguard not yet made public. When, almost immediately, De Valera refused to accept the agreement or recommend its acceptance to the Dáil, my fears of betrayal were greatly relieved because, innocent that I was (as were most of the rank and file of the IRA) I could not think that the leaders of the Movement were capable of fundamental differences on matters of national policy. I certainly thought of all these men as Knights of the Round Table. We knew nothing of the dissensions that had developed in the Irish Delegation in London leading to Barton, Gavan Duffy and Childers quitting their official headquarters in Hans Place. Nor could we have imagined that Griffith was having meetings with Lloyd George without the knowledge of his colleagues. Nor were we aware of the lionisation to which Collins was subjected by London socialites. Nor did we know that there was heavy drinking at Hans Place. Nor did we know of the role of the IRB. It took a little time for all this information to percolate down to my level. In the meantime I hoped, indeed believed, that some miracle would prevent the shattering of the monolithic unity of *The Four Glorious Years* to which Frank Gallagher's book owes its title.

Such a unity might have been achieved if it had not been for the violent (sometimes vile) propaganda of the newspapers. The Bishops fully supported the Treaty, thus adding to the difficulties of re-establishing unity either in the Movement or the country generally. Every conservative force — landlords, business men, gombeen men, large farmers, all the traditional opponents of separatism—came out to shriek their approval. With the notable exception of the Professor of Chemistry, Hugh Ryan, and the Professor of Law, Arthur Clery, virtually the entire staff of University College were strongly, indeed violently, in favour of the Treaty. The products of the Literary and Historical Society saw the dawning of the day when George O'Brien's vision of power and position was about to be realised. The handful of students who had been active in the IRA resented the fact that those who had remained doggo during the struggle should now emerge in search of spoils. Some of the more truculent and belatedly pugnacious members of the staff organised a weekly soirée at one of their houses where the evenings were spent denigrating De Valera. It was at this hate-fest that De Valera's 'vanity' was discovered.Here it was revealed that he had once read (or at least had a copy of) Machiavelli's *The Prince*. According to this intellectual coven it was De Valera's vanity and the teaching of Machiavelli that motivated him to oppose the Treaty. The hatred that spread from this source was a major factor in the embitterment which marked the early stages of the Treaty discussion in the country. The Labour movement, such as it was (and that was not very much) cast itself in the role of 'Fear na headarghabhála' — the go-between — but in effect it supported and, very fully, the Treaty. At the time I regarded the Labour leaders, Thomas Johnson with his side-kicks, Cathal O'Shannon and William O'Brien, as a contemptible lot.

On a country-wide basis the IRA were in the main anti-Treaty. They began to remember that they were Volunteers with an Executive which was their governing body; they owed allegiance to the Dáil only as the Government of the Republic. There was an alternative course of action to be resorted to if the Dáil failed them. The first person to call my attention to this situation was Andy Cooney, who was most strongly opposed to the Treaty. He thought that Griffith, Collins and the other signatories should have been arrested at Dun Laoghaire on their return from London. I gathered that his proposal had some support from the South Tipperary Brigade but neither Dublin nor Cork would countenance any such course. The arrest of Mick Collins, however badly they felt about the Treaty, would be like Tibetan monks arresting the Dalai Lama. There was a widespread belief in the IRA that, whatever the outward appearances might be, Collins had something up his sleeve which would effectively allay their misgivings.

The Dáil met to debate the Treaty on 14 December 1921 in the Council Chamber of University College, Earlsfort Terrace. After a discussion where signs of the coming acrimony already began to appear, the Dáil went into private session to consider what we learned afterwards (and not long afterwards) was De Valera's Document number 2. As it happened, Document number 2 turned out to be a deadly weapon in the hands of the pro-Treaty propagandists. It was represented as compromising the demand for full national autonomy.

The Dáil met again on 19 December in public session. Within hours it became clear that the breach between the pro and anti-Treaty viewpoint was irreparable. At the public sessions the Press was, of course, fully represented but there was not enough space to admit the public — even if the public in any numbers wanted to attend.

By this time the common assumption was that the Treaty would be accepted and worked. A manifestation of this was the total absence of crowds, even of the usual rubbernecks, outside Earlsfort Terrace. By using my influence with the porters in the main hall of UCD, I was able to sidle up to the Council Chamber where, by remaining quietly inconspicuous leaning against the jamb of a door, I was able to hear most of the debates which, adjourning for Christmas, resumed on 3 January 1922 and continued until 7 January when the final vote was taken.

It was my ill-luck that the first speaker I heard was a Deputy named Seán Milroy who was a representative of Tyrone. He appeared to me to have all the characteristics of the Northern politicians of the variety of Joe Devlin of the Irish Party — voluble windbags. Milroy had the distinction of having been with De Valera when he escaped from Lincoln Jail which, in my eyes, only added to the distasteful-ness of his performance.

The fact that Milroy was speaking for the Treaty had nothing to do with the impression he made on me. He was a middle-aged man with hunched shoulders, the face of a boozer with the voice of a corncrake. Apart from what he had to say, the manner of his saying it was insult-ing as well as portentous. He kept repeating that he was going to 'take the gloves off'. This meant that he was going to breach the con-fidence of the private session of the Dáil by revealing the contents of Document number 2. His abrasive truculence brought him no plaudits even from his own side. Milroy and his like were tributaries to the sea of bitterness in which all the decencies and comradeship of the Movement finally drowned.

I knew some of the deputies of old — Phil Cosgrave, Michael Hayes, Jim Crowley, Brian Cusack, Alex McCabe — I had merely a nodding acquaintance with Desmond Fitzgerald. As it happened all of them, with the exception of Brian Cusack, voted in favour of the Treaty; at this stage my relations with them were unchanged. I was consciously aware of seeing Collins for the first time in my life. He did not resemble the picture I had built up of him as a beau sabreur; he looked serious minded, intense, but very confident. Griffith, whom I had seen often in 6, Harcourt Street, the Headquarters of Sinn Féin, seemed to me to have aged disproportionately. He gave an impression of irascibility. He assumed a proprietary interest in the Treaty and seemed to regard arguments put forward against it as personal attacks on him.

The best that could be said for the speeches, for and against, was that they were highly articulate. By necessity, the points made were repetitive. The main burden of the pro-Treaty argument was to play on the fears of a renewal of the war; the anti-Treatyites invoked the memory of the dead. Both sides employed the history of Ireland since the Norman invasion to prove their case. The atmosphere of the debate was sombre, gloomy, not to say sad, as harder and harder words were exchanged. The nature of the occasion did not permit either humour or wit. I happened to be there when Brugha made his infamous attack on Collins. I think every Deputy — De Valera not least amongst them — was shocked or embarrassed by it. The attack diminished Brugha's stature while evoking sympathy for Collins. Only deep personal antipathy could have perverted Brugha's judgement just as later on after the Treaty had been accepted Griffith, animated by similar personal antipathy to Erskine Childers, called him 'a damned Englishman'; a remark from which terrible consequences for Childers followed.

On 7 January the vote was taken. The Treaty was accepted by sixty-four votes to fifty-seven. I saw the mixture of triumph, grief and worry with which deputies received the result. I saw the desolation of De Valera; as if he foresaw more clearly than the others the catastrophe which was to follow that vote, he broke down in tears.

I was shattered less by the vote than by what I had seen and heard and read of the debate. For years I had lived on a plane of emotional idealism, believing that we were being led by great men into a new Ireland. Now I had seen these 'great men' in action to find that they were mostly very average in stature, some below average, some malevolent and vicious. The only one that retained any residue of my absurdly high esteem was De Valera. Throughout the debate he had displayed dignity, compassion, a desire for compromise no less than an understanding of his opponents.

De Valera's attitude and reasoning convinced me that the Treaty could not but be disadvantageous to the nation. I was too inexperienced to understand the complexity of motives which persuaded the Delegates to sign the document or why they did not refer it back to Dublin for consideration. I did not even dream that the IRB could have had any covert part to play in its acceptance by the Dáil. I was rapidly learning. Never again, in my life, did I accept unquestioningly any man's claim to leadership, not even De Valera's.

Amongst the IRA at my level (i.e. Company and Battalion level) there were different views for and against the Treaty. For example, Coughlan who was not a member of the IRB was in favour of it. Kenny who was a member of the IRB was against it. At the

207

beginning of the debate, there was one fixed determination among the IRA. The comradeship of the years of the Black and Tan campaign must be unbroken. We discussed the Treaty endlessly — sometimes standing at one another's doorsteps into the small hours of the morning. Gradually fissures appeared in the facade of unity. Everyone agreed that it was unthinkable to take an oath of allegiance to the King. But soon it was discovered that 'what was good enough for Mick Collins was good enough for me'. Local discussions, as the debate in the Dáil wore on with increasing bitterness, descended into personalities and personal abuse. Everyone, whether for or against the Treaty, protested that they would not be guilty of 'letting down the Republic' which was regarded as the ultimate limit of culpability. But the best men in the IRA were for the Treaty or the best men were against it. 'Look at Thornton and Tobin' or 'look at Tom Barry and Seán Moylan'. Personal antipathies suppressed for 'the cause' broke out in sores and festered with surprising rapidity. A special vocabulary of abuse in word and phrase was created: 'windy louser', 'trucer', 'he swallowed the anchor', 'he put his monniker to the gadget', 'he had a lousy record'. The criterion of a man's record was the number of notches he had on his gun. The tough man, the 'hard chaw' was highly esteemed.

Since the days of the Irish Party and John E. Redmond, the word 'politician' was never applied to a member of the Movement. It was a word of ill-repute. Now nearly all the members of the Dáil overnight became in my eyes 'politicians'; a distinction was rapidly being drawn between 'the politicians' and the Army. In the critical situation now developing my hopes were pinned on the unity of the IRA being maintained and on the IRA effectively taking control of the institutions of Government. I fully sympathised with De Valera when he remarked 'I have only seen politics within the last three weeks or month. It is the first time I have seen them and I am sick to the heart of them'. I was even more in sympathy with him when earlier he pointed out that the control of the Army was not affected by the political situation. I was a reasonably well-informed member of the IRA but the dichotomy between the old Dáil, the new Provisional Government and new Parliament with, at the back of it all, the Sinn Féin organisation and its coming Ard Fheis, left me in such a state of confusion that I decided that the only clear authoritative element in the situation was the Army.

I was cheered when during the debate Deputy Seamus Robinson, O/C of the South Tipperary Brigade, pointed out that the Army had not been consulted about whether the Treaty be accepted or not. He drew attention to the fact that the Army Executive was the controlling body of the Army. He demanded that an Army Convention should be called to decide the issue of the Treaty. This totally expressed my feeling; I had never been happy with the Oath of Allegiance to Dáil Éireann. Having seen Dáil Éireann in action, I was convinced that the only hope of realising the national objectives was through the intervention of the Army. I would support any effort to maintain Army unity. Towards the end of February, a demand from senior Army Officers to hold a convention was agreed to by Mulcahy, the Minister for Defence, and sanctioned by the Cabinet. The date of the Convention was fixed for 26 March.

I was confident that such a Convention would restore the tottering morale of the nation. I also made up my mind that, much as I believed the Treaty to be a very bad political bargain, I would nevertheless accept the decision of such a Convention. In the meantime, I still had faith in the integrity of Collins and Mulcahy. Mulcahy had assured the Dáil that the Army would remain the Army of the Republic. Even Griffith pledged that until there was an election the Republic would be kept in being. I tried very hard not to become estranged from my pro-Treaty friends, at least in the Movement. This was not easy. In Ireland a great falsity is contained in the saying 'Sticks and stones may break my bones but names will never hurt me'. The vindictive abuse by the newspapers of the anti-Treatyites, particularly of De Valera, made it very difficult for us to refrain from replying in kind. Nothing was too low to be used to besmirch De Valera. He was a Spanish bastard, he suffered from overweening vanity while, crime of crimes! he had read Machiavelli. Since to most people Machiavelli sounded like some kind of nine-letter dirty word, this was damaging criticism. All the women deputies had voted against the Treaty; their virtue was called in question by whisper, by rumour, by innuendo and by dirty jokes.

As soon as the Treaty was ratified and the Provisional Government formed, the British began a withdrawal of their troops to Dublin, Cork and the Curragh. They arranged to hand over their barracks throughout the country to representatives of the Provisional Government which at this stage meant, in effect, mainly the IRA. General Headquarters had set up an evacuation staff under Commandant (now promoted General) Emmett Dalton. I was told by Coughlan that I was to become a member of the staff with the rank of Captain. I was instructed to report to General Emmett Dalton at the Gresham Hotel. When the Truce was proclaimed a liaison staff had been appointed by the IRA and the British to deal with the problems arising during the Truce. The liaison staff became the evacuation staff. The Gresham Hotel remained its base. Although I had been born within a stone's throw of the Gresham, the thought had never occurred to me that I would ever enter it. Only wealthy people from the country or abroad frequented such a luxurious establishment. My idea of its magnificence was fully realised when I presented myself to report to Dalton. Rich drapes, sumptuous arm chairs, deep carpets on this scale were outside my experience. It struck me as a highly improbable ambiance for an IRA Headquarters staff. As I was kept waiting for some time, I had an opportunity to observe the comings and goings of various people who seemed to have little or no connection with the IRA. Amongst them was a man who, when I was at school, had been a Christian Brother. He taught my class very briefly. We developed in the short time of our association a deep mutual dislike.

Dalton saw me briefly to tell me that I was to begin taking over a number of Military and RIC barracks from the British. I was to arrange with the local IRA units to occupy these posts when the British and RIC had left. He handed me over to a red-headed Captain named McManus for more detailed instructions. Being curious to know what my ex-Christian Brother acquaintance was doing among the other waiting characters, I asked McManus what they were all up to and was told that they were looking for jobs or other favours from the new State. He was very contemptuous of the whole business of political patronage. Such is the petty streak in nearly every man that I got considerable satisfaction at the plight of my ex-teacher. I insisted, as I passed by, on catching his eye to his considerable embarrassment.

McManus added scarcely anything by way of detail to the broad instructions of Dalton, except that the first barracks I was to take over was Mullingar. He gave me a paper signed by Dalton which constituted my credentials. The British O/C Mullingar had been told to expect me. Next day I departed for Mullingar and having found a room in the local hotel I got in touch with the local Brigade O/C of the IRA, whose name was Maguire, with instructions to be ready with a garrison to take over from the British when the occupation formalities had been completed.

I then called at the Barracks where I was received with chilly politeness by the officer in charge, a Major. We were to take over the complete contents of the barracks except arms. That meant tables, chairs, beds, cutlery, kitchen equipment, shovels, spades, picks, bed clothes. I was provided with a First Lieutenant, a Sergeant Major and two privates to escort me around. Each room had an inventory which was read out by the Sergeant Major and I was required to sign that for each location the list was correct. At the beginning, being an innocent but very conscientious official, I actually counted the number of items in each room. For two days we had a continuous repetition of 'two beds — Officers', 'one bed — Officer, married', 'ten beds—men, single', 'forks 100', 'knives 100' and so on till it dawned on me that such meticulous detail was quite unnecessary. Whether there were ten or twenty blankets in a room was not going to affect the future fortunes of either the Irish or the British nation. Even so, it took me a week working from 9 a.m. to 6 p.m. to get through the take over. I was surprised to discover the utter indifference of both officers and men to Army property. They left behind without any regret what I thought was a very fine hospital with a well-equipped operating theatre and a fully stocked pharmacy. I was able to get from the pharmacy a bottle of quinine with which I dosed myself continuously to get rid of a bad cold. I was so anxious not to let down the standards of the IRA that I offered to pay the Army Doctor, who was handing over the medical unit, for the quinine. I only made myself look ridiculous in his eyes. I realised for the first but not the last time that one can be too bloody righteous.

My job completed, the British left. So did the RIC who had been concentrated in Mullingar from various outlying stations prior to going to Dublin to be demobilised. But there was a marked difference between the departure of the British, who marched from the Barracks to a special train, and of the RIC who had to await transport. While waiting, they distributed themselves among various pubs around the town. The local IRA visited the pubs and held up the RIC men, taking possession of their rifles and revolvers. It was not a very high-minded effort. I certainly could not do anything to prevent it.

I had never been inside a military barracks before except as a prisoner in Portobello for a night. Unlike what little I remembered of Portobello, Mullingar Barracks was almost clinically clean. I suppose such a condition is a reflection of the character of the O/C. I was also struck by the relative luxury of the officers' quarters, including the mess which might well have been the dining room and bar of a high-class hotel. It was noticeable that their wines or other liquor were not included in the handover. I saw as little of the O/C of the barracks as he could manage. My relations with my escort were totally impersonal. Maguire, the local Brigade O/C, had some difficulty in mobilising enough men to garrison the barracks so that some had to be sent down from Dublin, including an officer to take charge.

My next job on the Evacuation staff was in Co. Cork. I took over Bandon, Bantry, Ballineen, as well as several police posts. But my biggest task was to take over Fort Charles in Kinsale. Seán McCarthy, who was afterwards a T.D. and Lord Mayor of Cork, was assigned to look after me, introducing me to the officers commanding the IRA in the different areas involved in the operation. Seán McCarthy was much older than I but he was kind and friendly. He was also typical of so many of the older men in the Movement. To him the Movement was a combination of the Gaelic League, the GAA, the IRA and the Catholic Church. He shared what was a commonly held opinion at the time that, unless you were a Catholic and a member of the GAA, you could not be a good Irishman. He was quite surprised when I confessed that my interest in football was confined to soccer. He was not far wrong in thinking that nearly all non-Catholics were opposed to independence; which is a belief not quite the same as that all good Irishmen must be Catholics. There were very few Protestants in the IRA; none that I knew of then.

At Bandon I had some difficulty. After my experience at Mullingar, I thought that if the British had a team to help them to hand over there was no reason why I should not be entitled to similar assistance. The British O/C was the infamous Major Percival. It was only after the evacuation was completed that I heard about his reputation of being tough with prisoners as well as with the civilian population. He objected to any of the local IRA being taken on to assist on the grounds that they were not covered by my credentials. I told him that unless the three men I had selected were allowed to assist me in checking the inventories I would refuse to take over the barracks. He realised I was prepared to create a scene, as a matter of principle, so after much hesitation and a prolonged conversation with his fellow officers my proposal was agreed to.

I met several members of the famous West Cork columns and at the same time I was broadening my experience of rural Ireland. All of the men I met, like Liam Deasy and Jim Hurley, were against the Treaty but like me they had confidence that the Convention would put things right. There was none of the abuse and recrimination that was already beginning to embitter relations in Dublin. Deasy and Hurley seemed to me particularly well informed men with a deep knowledge of Irish history. Physically they were distinguished looking men, exuding energy, Hurley especially so. They had the quality of leadership. They were the kind of men I wished to see at the head of affairs in Ireland.

The British made no objection to local IRA men being employed to help at Fort Charles in Kinsale. It was a very large barracks. It took me two weeks to get through the job even with assistance. The local O/C of the IRA was Commandant Seán Lehane with whom I established very close personal relations in the short time I was in Kinsale. He was later sent to Donegal just before the Civil War with a group of officers from Cork and Kerry to try, unsuccessfully as it happened, to stiffen the Republican resistance there. After the Civil War he came to see me whenever he was in Dublin staying sometimes in my parents' house. He died while still quite young. He was brave, good humoured and intelligent. Like Deasy and Hurley he had the quality of leadership. Even when we first met in Kinsale, he was quite certain that Civil War was inevitable. He was the only one, other than Andy Cooney, whom I heard advocating that we, who were anti-Treaty, should take the initiative in military terms by clearing the pro-Treatyites out of Beggar's Bush barracks in Dublin.

The Provisional Government had begun to establish what was a regular professional Army with its headquarters at Beggar's Bush,. the only barracks in Dublin as yet handed over by the British. Many IRA men, irrespective of their stand on the Treaty, had joined the new professional Army and Lehane was convinced that it was being built up in preparation for what amounted to a coup d'etat. I did not feel that way. Being very green in judgement I was confident that Collins, Mulcahy and De Valera would succeed in restoring to the Movement its unity, comradeship and determination to maintain the Republic even if it meant rejecting the objectionable clauses of the Treaty and risking a renewal of the war. I did not believe that in any circumstances the British would resume the war — a belief reinforced by my reading of *The Observer* and the *New Statesman*. Their Government was weak, to the point of dissolution. It was in a mess with its Middle-East policy. Their people were sick of war. British public opinion was not proud of the Black and Tans. Internationally British prestige was low. Their threat of 'immediate and terrible war' I regarded as mere bluff. It was about this time that Kemal Ataturk called the British bluff in Istanbul causing the fall of the Lloyd George Government.

To my horror Griffith, supported by the Cabinet, including Mulcahy on whose instructions it had been summoned, on 15 March proclaimed the Convention. The effect on me was to change my tolerant attitude to the Treatyites. I became convinced that they had no intention nor desire to keep the IRA together. I felt betrayed and disillusioned. For me it was 'never glad confident morning again'; I came to believe that Griffith in particular had determined to inflict the Treaty, with all its objectionable clauses, on the nation. I saw that Seán Lehane was right in thinking that Griffith, supported by all the conservative elements in the country, intended what was, from my point of view, a coup d'état. The professional Army which was being recruited was to be used to force the Treaty on a people fear-ridden by the virulent propaganda of the newspapers combined with the no less virulent propaganda of the Church. From nearly every altar every Sunday the priests denounced the anti-Treatyites although they had yet to achieve the crescendo of collective malignancy contained in the famous Bishops' Pastoral.

Despite the proclamation by Mulcahy and Griffith the acting Military Council of the IRA of which Rory O'Connor was Chairman decided to hold the Convention on 26 March. This Council had been formed in January by senior officers from Headquarters and the Divisions and it was they who had demanded a Convention initially. Its principal members were Rory O'Connor, Liam Mellowes, Seán Russell, Séamus O'Donovan from the Headquarters staff, with Liam Lynch from the South, Oscar Traynor from Dublin, Liam Pilkington and Michael Kilroy from the West.

When I came back to Dublin to report, it was suggested to me by McManus that I join the regular Army in Beggar's Bush. This I had no intention of doing. It was said that the ancient Chinese regarded professional soldiers as part of the lowest form of society. I felt equally badly about the profession. When I was about sixteen I read Creasey's *Fifteen Decisive Battles of the World*. I experienced from it some kind of an enlightenment. The utter stupidity and wastefulness of war, however decisive for either the victors or the vanquished, was revealed to me. Besides I had gathered from my reading a detailed knowledge of the Great War from which developed a passionate hatred of the criminal stupidity of the generals of all sides. While almost everyone subscribes to this view of war nevertheless the most esteemed men in every nation, those to whom great monuments are erected, are the victorious military commanders. I further realised that this country was too small to raise armies or to fight battles — as battles are reckoned by world standards. For that, if for no other reason, there was never a battle — even Aughrim or the Boyne — of any magnitude in Ireland. Nor did we produce any great commanders. Further, I think that the commonly held image of Irishmen as a 'fighting race' is largely a myth. There is very little evidence in our history of our fighting ability.

The military courage of the battlefield is merely a conditioned reflex induced by intense training supported by severe, sometimes savage discipline. We had in the Movement neither the facilities for training nor had we the inclination to discipline. I did not regard the IRA as an army in the accepted sense nor did I regard the struggle with the British Government as a war. It was terror and 'tyranny tempered by assassination'. Assassination correctly directed by Michael Collins was the real basis of our relative success. Having reflected on all these things I decided I did not want to be a regular soldier.

I returned home and resumed my links with Coughlan and 'E' Company of the Fourth Battalion, Dublin Brigade. At home my mother was glad to see me but kept urging me to give up 'all this political stuff'. My father's attitude was a bit different. He would like to have seen me settle down but he was so irritated by newspaper and clerical attacks on Republicans that he began to regard them as personal attacks on me. He made it clear that whatever I did I had his support. I surely had — and my mother's also. My brother was rapidly growing up and developing in the process a positive hatred for politics which he maintained, as he does a hatred of alcohol, into his old age.

By March 1922 there were over one hundred men in the Company. With four exceptions they were pro-Treaty. When the Convention was banned by the Provisional Government, it stated that any man attending would, ipso facto, cease to be a member of the IRA. None of my bitterness had extended to Coughlan even though at that time, I had walked out of houses after angry arguments about the Treaty with old friends.

I was far too junior an officer to be a delegate to the Convention but I told Coughlan that I did not intend to take any more orders from Beggar's Bush. I would do whatever the circumstances seemed to require. We argued, or rather discussed, the pros and cons of the Provisional Government, the Republican opposition and the oath to the Republic for hours. I was glad to be able to remind him that I had never wanted to take the oath. We parted on the most friendly terms, though I made it clear that he could no longer rely on my personal loyalty. He never suspected that I would do more than re-join Kenny's broken-off 'K' Company. Their opinion on the Treaty was more evenly divided with nearly half for and half against it, though in a much smaller Company.

The most senior IRA officer whom I knew well was John Dowling, the O/C of our Battalion. I turned to him for advice on what action the few anti-Treaty members in 'E' Company were to take. Being himself in a state of indecision he could not give me any clear direction. Dowling did not share my simple belief in our leaders; on the contrary, he had an irreverent, rather sceptical view of the Military Council as individuals and as a group. Except for Collins, his irreverence and scepticism extended to the members of the Provisional Government. Knowing him to be well acquainted with most of the members of both groups, I was taken aback by Dowling's open iconoclasm even though I had begun to develop similar reservations myself. This encounter with Dowling, although it was sterile in so far as the IRA issue was concerned, was to have important consequences for me. Having disposed of the business immediately at hand we went on to talk on general topics. Dowling seemed to have an extraordinary wide range of interests and I found his conversation fascinating. This meeting marked the growth of an intimate friendship which has lasted over the years. He introduced me to art appreciation and in particular to the Impressionists, to Browning, to George Moore, Joyce and to the so-called literary revival generally. But on the question of what to do about the Convention, I had to make up my own mind.

I spent days and night talking things over with Earle who was as undecided as Dowling whether or not actively to oppose the Treaty. Finally he agreed to a proposal I made. When the Convention met on 26 March Earle, Kevin O'Carroll, Jim Doyle, Nicholas Jackman and myself — the only anti-Treaty members of 'E' Company — hired a friendly taximan in Terenure and drove to St Enda's where the 'E' Company arms were held in a specially constructed dump. With the very reluctant aid of the late Patrick Pearse's gardener, Michael MacRuairi, we cleared out the dump, loading the arms into the taxi.

The weapons included a substantial number of shotguns and about a dozen small arms, varying from a .45 Colt automatic to a .22 revolver. There were several hundred rounds of assorted ammunition. We took them to a temporary dump which we had constructed in a dairyman's shed in Terenure. I went on to the Mansion House to report what we had done arriving as the Convention was breaking up and asked for an interview with some senior officer. I was introduced to a man who appeared to be registering the names of the delegates who had attended the Convention. I told him my story emphasising that the arms we had taken were being placed at the disposal of the Army Executive appointed by the Convention. The man I spoke to turned out to be Jack Plunkett, son of Count Plunkett and brother of Joseph Plunkett who, as a signatory of the Proclamation, had been executed in 1916. Jack Plunkett welcomed me, telling me to report the position to John Dowling who was a friend of his and who had finally decided to support the Convention.

Although by this time I was hostile to the Pro-Treatyites, I dreaded the thought of meeting Coughlan, knowing how deeply offended he would be by the seizure of the dump. I was very fond of Coughlan as I think he was of me. I decided I had better get the unpleasantness over quickly. I was on my way to seek him out when I encountered him on the street in Rathfarnham. Coughlan never raised his voice, never displayed anger nor was he by nature a resentful man. He did not now raise his voice but he left me in no doubt that he was resentful, angry, even bitter with me. He felt he had been betrayed, that the men in the Company had been robbed, that the Army Executive were a collection of disgruntled men aiming at a military dictatorship and that I should be ashamed of myself and my behaviour. He did not want anything more to do with me or with my companions in what he insistently called the robbery of the arms.

I made no apologies for what I had done but I felt sick at heart that so close a friendship should come to such a miserable end. I might not have been so downcast had I realised that very few friendships are life-long which are not based on a community of interests; when the interests cease to be commonly held, or conflict, friendships disintegrate or develop into enmities. The only way to preserve a life-long friendship is to maintain it through infrequent contacts. By this time, many friendships were being broken and many enmities created. Old friends and acquaintances began to pass one another in the streets. Our local newsagent, a neighbour from whom I had bought papers since I was a small boy, made some mildly disparaging remark about De Valera. I made some resentful reply, walked out of the shop and never went into it again for the rest of my life. I avoided anyone who favoured the Treaty, however passively.

The same situation was developing all over the country, exacerbated by the Press but particularly by the widely read *Freeman's Journal*. This paper published a thoroughly untrue report of the Convention. On this account the Army Executive had the machinery of the paper destroyed. At the time I felt that this was quite a proper thing to do, particularly as I was enraged by the villainous misinterpretation placed on a speech by De Valera in which he warned the country of a dangerous situation developing where men might have to wade through Irish blood. This was presented by the paper as an incitement to the IRA to wade through the blood of the Treatyites. It was the lowest level reached in Irish journalism since 1916 when the

217

Irish Independent called for the blood of James Connolly.

Not all Republicans took my view. The wrecking of the paper turned out to be a bad mistake in propaganda terms. It followed another bad mistake by Rory O'Connor who acted as spokesman for the Republican Army Executive. He called a press conference at which he spoke too much, particularly as he had no delegated authority, culminating in a bad political gaffe. Asked by a correspondent if the Republicans intended to set up a military dictatorship, he replied 'You can take it that way if you like'. In the spring of 1922 the idea of a military dictatorship in itself had not at all the frightening connotations it has now. Mussolini had not marched on Rome, the word 'Fascist' to the limited few who had ever heard of it had no untoward significance. Hitler had only begun the long haul to power, while Stalin had not yet undertaken the liquidation of the Kulaks or the show trials of the Old Bolsheviks. Equally, democracy had not been, as it since has been, elevated to the position of a goddess in the public mind. 'The democratic process' were words which would have fallen on uncomprehending ears in the Ireland of 1922. What the people understood by military dictatorship, as propounded by Rory O'Connor, was that they were liable to be pushed around at the whim of young IRA commanders. Discipline was rapidly deteriorating in the local units of the IRA. People began to feel unsafe in the enjoyment of their property and their freedom of movement.

I did not see anything wrong with an IRA military dictatorship but I resented the breakdown in discipline. I thought if the IRA took over the Government their first task would be to ensure discipline and order. But as the situation developed, it began to appear to me that the IRA leadership had not merely not envisaged setting up a military dictatorship but had not considered any alternative policy. This was made clear at the adjourned meeting of the March Convention which met in April and again in June. A new Executive was elected. A new Army Council was appointed with Liam Lynch as Chief of Staff. A proposal to set up a dictatorship was defeated. So was a proposal to prevent Senate elections being held.

From that moment we Republicans were beaten. In Dublin I met only one fairly senior officer who clearly realised the nature of the debacle. Andy Cooney, who had joined the professional Army at Beggar's Bush, had with many others left to give his allegiance to the Convention. He strongly favoured clearing out Beggar's Bush, an operation which at this stage would have presented no difficulty. Many of the Beggar's Bush garrison were in active sympathy with the IRA Executive. Many more would have had no positive objection to the IRA Executive taking over. None would have resisted to the extent of dying for the Provisional Government.

Cooney foretold exactly what, in fact, happened if we did not take resolute action. 'The Staters', as we now called them, would build up very quickly an army of professional soldiers to whom the Republic meant nothing. With the financial resources of the State plus the backing of the British, they would be much better armed than we were or could be. He held that if it came to civil war we would inevitably lose, as we did. Unfortunately Cooney had no influence. The Convention wound up with a number of futile resolutions. Among the Executive members there was no Lenin.

The Civil War

The Convention marked the physical 'split' in the IRA. Each side tried to pre-empt the other by taking over barracks and posts recently evacuated by the British. The Civil War had in effect begun although there was extreme reluctance to start shooting. We called the Beggar's Bush people 'Staters'; they called us 'mutineers' and later 'irregulars'. We both called ourselves the IRA.

Shortly after the April meeting of the Convention the IRA took over the Four Courts to serve as a General Headquarters and a few days later Andy Cooney brought me along there to meet Ernie O'Malley, who was Director of Organisation. He had as his assistant Seán McBride, subsequently Nobel Prize and Lenin Prize winner. I was installed in O'Malley's office as a clerk.

It was my function to read and file reports coming in from the country and to arrange for the duplication and distribution of general orders sent to the different units. It was not a very onerous job nor did it carry much responsibility. The communications coming in were few; they were also insignificant. The communications going out were just as few and just as insignificant.

By this time I had had my innocent beliefs in the inherent virtues of all the leaders of the Movement eroded. Nevertheless I was very pleased to work under O'Malley. O'Malley had taken part in more attacks on British soldiers, Black and Tans and R.I.C. than any other IRA man in Ireland. He had been wounded many times. Once he was captured and tortured by the Auxiliaries in Kilkenny and taken to

Dublin to be court-martialled for murder but he made a sensational escape. He was 'le plus brave des braves'. While he was generally admired he was not generally liked. He had the reputation of being a martinet, of being intolerant of anyone who did not come up to his almost impossibly high standards of valour or endurance. But worse, he was thought to be an intellectual. When men were gossiping around the fireside he held himself aloof reading, it was said, Epictetus or The Vedas. In my association with him I had no complaints against him on this score. I never knew of him reading a book nor did he embarrass me by discussing them. To the contrary, I was surprised at a certain element of frivolity he displayed. Almost every morning he and MacBride went up town to st ɔll in Grafton Street where they met some girls from College for coffee in Mitchels' or Roberts' cafes.

MacBride I knew as a fellow student in University College; also I had spent a couple of days with him in Ring. Apart from his very pronounced French accent, he was different from the general run of students. As well as the prestige attached to him as the son of Major MacBride, so vengefully executed in 1916, much of the glamour of his mother, Maud Gonne, had rubbed off on him. He was treated by everyone with a diffidence dissociated from his personal qualities, the principal one of which was charm. In the Four Courts he had the well-deserved reputation of having a good IRA record. I regarded him as playing the role of a boy on a man's errand. And indeed he was only a boy, being about eighteen years of age.

Being in the Director's office gave me the opportunity to become acquainted with members of the Executive, who often dropped into the office for discussions with O'Malley or merely to have a chat. I met them too in the Officers' mess. The mess consisted of a large room unpartitioned but divided in two. Part of it was reserved for officers; the other, larger part was reserved for sergeants and was known as the Sergeants' mess. As most of the sergeants knew most of the officers by their Christian names, there was little differentiation between the messes. The kitchen, with cook, was common to both, as was the food. The food, of the highest quality in materials, was ruined by the time it got to the table. Despite having forcibly requisitioned £50,000 from the Bank of Ireland, there was no money available to pay for food. The meat was requisitioned from the abattoir or from the shops of the larger butchers. The vegetables were taken from the markets. The unwilling suppliers were given chits in payment. These raiding operations created violent hostility to us Republicans. The same thing was happening all over the country where we occupied the local barracks. If a motor car was required for any purpose, there was no scruple in requisitioning at random the nearest one at hand. In general we treated the population with little consideration.

O'Malley got information that there was an armoury of police rifles in the Curragh. On his own initiative he took the one armoured car which we possessed together with three or four trucks and carried out a successful raid from which he returned with several hundred rifles, revolvers and ammunition. It was a personal buccaneering job undertaken on his own authority. It was the kind of stunt which O'Malley loved. If, on a similar impulse, at an earlier stage he had been inspired to raid Beggar's Bush as effectively as he raided the armoury at the Curragh, it might well have changed the course of history. O'Malley would have been exactly 'the man for the occasion' in organising such a coup. He was a man of action who acted on impulse. He never reflected. Nor do I think he had the capacity for reflection. But O'Malley was not at all characteristic of other members of the Executive whom I met at that time.

Liam Mellowes came into the office one morning when I was alone. Mellowes was a low-sized man with thinning sandy hair and merry blue lively eyes. His whole personality seemed to radiate kindness. He was a *dea-dhuine* (a decent man). In the course of a long chat he questioned me about my background and even asked my opinion about the political situation. I was flattered. It was the first time that a person of consequence had ever asked my opinion on any important matter. In reply I merely parroted Andy Cooney's and Seán Lehane's suggestion about clearing out Beggar's Bush. He did not comment, but seemed to me to be rather critical of Liam Lynch for placing too much trust in Collins' and Mulcahy's good intentions. Another morning Liam Lynch, the Chief of Staff, came into the office when I was alone but merely gave me a pleasant smile and departed.

A joint Army Council had been set up between Beggar's Bush and the Four Courts in an effort to preserve IRA unity. Lynch was the leader of the Four Courts occupation force while Mulcahy led the Beggar's Bush contingent. There were many meetings of the joint Council; a copy of the minutes came to our office for filing. They were almost entirely devoted to discussions as to which side the key posts in the Army would be allocated. The Council never succeeded in agreeing. For me the minutes made very interesting reading because even though merely records of fruitless discussion they gave me an insider's view of affairs. I enjoyed too the gossip of the place.

I met some of the other members of the Army Council and the

Executive in the mess from time to time but usually only to pass the time of day. Rory O'Connor, the Director of Engineering, seemed to me too forbidding a person to approach. He was saturnine in appearance, very dark skinned, always in deep thought, brooding and worried. He did not look a healthy man. Dick Barrett was a friendly, cheerful type. I was one of a group on a couple of occasions when he held the floor telling stories about his native West Cork. I met Joe McKelvey once; we had a long talk about soccer in Belfast. Mellowes, O'Connor, Barrett and McKelvey were dead before the year was out having been executed without trial, by way of reprisal, while prisoners of the Free State.

The Four Courts was garrisoned by the Dublin Brigade. The O/C was Paddy O'Brien, the Quartermaster was Seán Nolan, both from my own Battalion, whom I knew of old. The Adjutant was Seán Lemass, afterwards Taoiseach, whom I met for the first time. Lemass was notable for being extremely smartly dressed by any guerilla standards. He was reserved in manner, a characteristic which helped him to maintain strict discipline on Army barrack lines.

I knew that lorry loads of arms were coming in from Beggar's Bush to the Four Courts and that we were sending arms in return to Beggar's Bush but the purpose of the exchange was cloaked in rumour. It transpired that our arms were intended for an 'Army of the North' to be created by combined pro- and anti-Treaty forces with the object of mounting an attack on the recently formed Six County regime. The Army was to be commanded by Frank Aiken, O/C of the Fourth Northern Division, who at this stage had refused to give allegiance to either Beggar's Bush or the Four Courts. He clearly foresaw the coming disaster and probably no man made such disinterested efforts to prevent it. Collins and Lynch were the originators of the idea of an Army of the North. The exchange of arms was designed to prevent the identification of weapons which had been supplied by the British to the Provisional Government in the event of capture. Our arms, as well as some officers, were actually sent to Donegal while several hundred men from the North were brought to the Curragh to be trained. The latter never went back. Most of them joined the Free State army; with officers from the Northern units of the IRA who also flocked into the army they played a significant part in defeating us in the Civil War. None of the documents concerning the so-called Army of the North (if there were any) passed through my hands. Gossip was my only informant.

Andy Cooney had been appointed Commandant of the First Eastern Division in place of Seán Boylan who, with most of the men in the Division, had taken the pro-Treaty side. Cooney had installed himself in Millmount Barracks, Drogheda, which, on being evacuated by the British, had fallen into anti-Treaty hands. At Cooney's request I was sent there on loan for a while to help to reorganise the Division. Having visited several areas I discovered that, except for Leixlip and Mullingar, there was very little left to organise. In Leixlip there was a small group led by a very determined school master named Paddy Mulally. He had the fifteen or twenty men under him well trained and disciplined. Later he formed them into a column which fought well but were captured in an engagement. Several of them were executed. In the course of this tour I met Michael Hilliard in Navan. He was an exceptionally fine young man and the fact that he had little support in the area did not deter him from fighting. Many, many years afterwards he became Minister for Defence in the Fianna Fáil Government.

In Drogheda in addition to an Adjutant named Casey, whom he took with him from Kerry, Cooney had a supernumerary named Michael Price. He came from a well-known Republican family but his status in Millmount Barracks was indeterminate. He was a small man who, if he didn't bite his nails like Napoleon, had adopted Napoleon's stance carrying his right hand pushed breast-high into his jacket and all the time wore an expression whether of deep thought or depression I was never quite sure. His posturing amused me but it took a far from amusing turn when on his own initiative, without mentioning anything to Cooney or Casey, he organised an expedition to attack the Auxiliaries who had not yet evacuated the nearby camp at Gormanstown. The expedition failed, one of Price's men being killed. The body of the dead man was brought back to Millmount but nobody knew his home address. It took four days to find that he came from a remote village in Westmeath. As the weather was very warm the body began to decompose. Price kept walking continuously up and down the corridor outside the room where the corpse was laid out exactly as Napoleon must have paced the deck of the *Bellerophon*.

When we finally found out the dead man's native place we took him home to be buried. For the first time I experienced the repellent custom of funeral offerings in vogue in that part of the country. In this case a plate was laid on the top of the coffin which was placed in the nave of the chapel. The congregation filed past placing an honorarium for the officiating priest on the plate. I resentfully parted with one of the two half-crowns I had in the world.

Price's expedition had a tragic ending; Cooney organised an

operation which ended in farce. We got an intelligence report that the Auxiliaries in Gormanstown were about to dump their surplus arms in the sea. The proposal was that we should put to sea from the pier at Clogherhead in a motor boat which would pick us up at a pre-arranged time, intercept the vessel carrying the arms of the Auxiliaries, board it and take possession of the cargo. The exact hour of the expected departure of the enemy boat was notified to us. We arrived at Clogherhead but found no boat in readiness. After waiting an hour or so and fearing we would be late for our assignment, we turned our attention to the crafts in the harbour. There was only one sizeable boat — a very small coaster with steam up — which Cooney decided to commandeer. On board we found the captain, a middle-aged man, with two other sailors who comprised the crew. The captain resembled a comic character called 'Old Bill' who was featured in the wartime cartoons. His seaman's cap was tilted untidily on the back of his head. He was smoking a stubby pipe which he never took out of his mouth. He took our arrival quite imperturbably. Nor did he seem either surprised or overawed when we — there were eight of us, heavily armed — ordered him to set course for the coast off Gormanstown. It took longer than we calculated to arrive at our destination in the slow old tub. There was no sign of a boat in the vicinity. After sailing up and down several times off Gormanstown we were obliged to return empty handed to Clogherhead. But before we arrived at our home port we were all so thoroughly sea sick that 'Old Bill' and his crew had to help us to disembark. I could only laugh at the absurdity of the whole performance. My laughter did not appeal much to Cooney nor was he impressed with the Director of Intelligence in the Four Courts who had sent us on such a stupid expedition. No boat carrying arms and ammunition ever set out from Gormanstown. Even if any such plan was mooted by the British our ridiculous manoeuvres would have been easily spotted and a pair of binoculars would have revealed our intentions.

After the Clogherhead affair I spent a few more days in Millmount where I could not perceive that I had any useful function. Cooney came with me to the Four Courts partly to vent his annoyance on the Intelligence Department, partly to find out what was happening. Nothing seemed to be happening. The only real activity was the intensification of the Belfast Boycott but I had no involvement in this. It was an operation which aimed at preventing trade with the Six Counties in retaliation for the anti-Catholic pogroms. It had the effect of irritating the business people of Dublin and further alienating public opinion.

One Sunday O'Malley decided we would go for a drive into the country. O'Malley, MacBride and I started off in one of the garrison cars which had of course been commandeered from some harmless citizen. O'Malley's driving was erratic if not reckless and our route and destination were largely fortuitous. However, we finally arrived at the Rocky Valley about twenty miles from the city where we stopped to have some practice in pistol shooting. While so engaged a car pulled up and a passenger who had recognised O'Malley and MacBride got out and came over to talk to us. He was Eamonn De Valera. That was the first time I met him. Considering his eminence in public affairs he seemed to me extraordinarily friendly and informal. His capacity to charm affected me then, continuing to affect me all during his long life.

We got home safely that day despite O'Malley's driving but on another occasion we were not so lucky. Sean Nolan, the Barrack quartermaster, a lively spirited character who in civilian life earned his living as a carpenter and fiddle player, was with us. We had succeeded in getting as far as Lower Grafton Street when a British armoured car, followed by a heavy lorry full of troops, swung round the corner from Nassau Street. We escaped colliding with the armoured car but crashed head-on into the lorry. The bonnet of our car was crushed to the shape of a concertina, our windscreen smashed to smithereens, but for some odd reason none of the four of us had even a scratch from broken glass. MacBride dashed out of the car flourishing his pet .45 Colt at the soldiers but, when the armoured car swivelled its machine gun at us, we retreated into the gathering crowd of onlookers. The car was a write-off and we left it to be removed in due course by the Corporation without further thought of the consequences. It was not ours and we did not know or care who the owner was. Such was our frame of mind.

There was a rapidly increasing sense of frustration at all levels in the Four Courts. Among the rank and file it manifested itself in growing acts of irresponsibility towards the civilian population. In the Executive, when ultimately the talks with the Free Staters broke down, the feeling that 'something must be done' resulted in the summoning of another Convention and we were entrusted with the organising arrangements. In an effort to prevent strangers to us getting into the Four Courts — a rather futile precaution against spying — we issued the credentials to the delegates from the offices of a Trade Union in Parnell Square. I don't remember anyone who asked for them being refused credentials; there was nothing against which to check their bona fides. The Convention assembled in the

Mansion House on Sunday 18 June. Its purpose was to decide whether to attack the British in their remaining bases in Dublin, and by this means to re-unite the IRA. Commandant Tom Barry proposed the resolution to this effect. It was the daftest proposal yet conceived by a floundering Executive but to many of the youthful, immature delegates it did not seem so lunatic. It made no sense to Lynch who still had hopes of preserving IRA unity and the successful formation of the Army of the North. He, with most of the southern and many of the western representatives, opposed it successfully. When the proposal was defeated on a vote, Sean MacBride jumped up shouting in his queer French-accented voice, swinging over his head his .45 Colt automatic at the end of a lanyard, 'All who are in favour of the Republic follow me to the Four Courts'. His melodramatic gesture was unnecessary. He was merely voicing the intentions of Rory O'Connor, Tom Barry, the most famous guerilla leader of them all, O'Malley, Mellowes and several more of the Executive who were already leaving the meeting en route to the Four Courts.

In the few months since I listened to the Treaty debates in Earlsfort Terrace I had matured considerably. If I had not become quite cynical I began to appraise, by thought rather than by feeling, the qualities of the men whom I met or saw at fairly close quarters: their actions, their judgements, even their motivations. More important than any other revelation, I saw that the man with a record was not necessarily, nor indeed usually, a man with the qualities required to deal with the predicament in which we in the Four Courts found ourselves. I began to think that I was as capable of making a judgement as good as most of the men I met.

I did not follow MacBride to the Four Courts. I went home. The refusal of Rory O'Connor to accept the majority decision of the Convention, apart from the idiocy of the policy proposed, made me determined that I would take no further part in a process which led only to fragmentation of the IRA. I decided to retire to civilian life. Next day I went into the Four Courts to tell O'Malley of my intention. I found an extraordinary situation. Those who had followed MacBride to the Four Courts had locked out Liam Lynch, the Chief of Staff, with most of the senior officers of the Southern Division. This in fact meant that the Four Courts garrison had amputated their most powerful limb, effectively isolating themselves in the last bastion of the Republic. But it did not occur to them that the Provisional Government would avail of their isolation to attack them. I told O'Malley of my intention to go home. Like Liam Lynch, he too had still some vague hopes that an attack might be mounted against the North. He asked me to go up there on a special mission. I agreed to this suggestion but said I was not prepared to work in or for the Four Courts garrison in Dublin or anywhere else in the country. While awaiting further instructions I took part in what must have been, I believe, the saddest day among the many sad days of Irish Republicanism.

The Convention had met on Sunday the 18th. The anniversary of Wolfe Tone, the founder of separatism, fell on Tuesday 20 June. Normally the anniversary was commemorated at Tone's grave in Bodenstown on the Sunday following the 20th. Rory O'Connor, with the rump of the Executive, decided to hold the commemoration ceremony on Tuesday the 20th. A small convoy of three or four army tenders filled with senior officers and representatives of the Four Courts garrison drove to Bodenstown and I went with them. Mellowes made an oration filled with defiance of those who were trying to subvert the Republic. As we, a very small group, huddled together around Mellowes I felt, and I think nearly all the others felt, an atmosphere of approaching doom. The day was dark, overcast, muggy, a day just suited to suggest the pathetic fallacy to match our gloomy mood. Not, indeed, that anyone thought the Staters would attack us. That would have meant Civil War. No IRA man, whether in Beggar's Bush or the Four Courts, considered that a possibility; something would still be done to avoid that contingency.

On the way back to Dublin from Bodenstown I told Cooney of my conversation with O'Malley. I invited him home for tea, where we got a great welcome from my mother. All women, young or old, liked Cooney. We speculated at length on the future course of events but he had as few ideas as I. The proposed trip to the North provided an escape route for me because I did not like the idea of seeming to leave a sinking ship.

Cooney decided to go back to the Four Courts where he was acquiring, but too late, some influence. I also went in there to get instructions from O'Malley in preparation for my journey North the next day. I was to go to a place in Co. Cavan called Kilbride, situated a few miles from Bailieboro, very close to the newly formed border with the six separated counties. There I was to see the Commandant of the Cavan Brigade, Paddy Smith (afterwards a Minister in the Fianna Fáil Government) brief him about the intended attack on the North, discuss what part his brigade could play in it along the Fermanagh border, make an appreciation of the situation and report back to O'Malley.

Paddy Smith I found was a tall, fair-haired handsome young man, scarcely out of his teens, living with his parents in the comfortable circumstances of 'strong' farmers. He had been captured in a fight by the British and sentenced to death. The Truce saved his life. Smith was typical of so many of the sons of the better-off farmers who officered the IRA in the country. He reminded me of the men who so impressed me earlier in West Cork. He had arranged for me to stay with his family, which included a noticeably good looking teenage sister. The Smith family received me warmly with the slightly amused but kindly patronage which I so often noticed that country people extended to Dubliners. I could well have been a traveller from a distant land to whom they were anxious to show understanding and hospitality, at the same time impressing on him the superior advantages of country manners and customs. The whole family, father, mother, two sisters and Paddy were busy with the chores of midsummer. Mrs Smith was surprised at my apparent knowledge of butter making, a skill with which I was familiar because I had often helped my grandmother with her butter making in Summerhill. I garnered a little esteem from this. I also had helped my uncles drawing hay from some rented field in Raheny, so that hay making was not new to me. But I had never seen turf being cut, spread, footed, ricked or drawn. Paddy took me to see a bog being worked, explaining to me the different processes employed. Like all Dublin visitors to a bog for the first time, I was fascinated by what I saw and the experience helped to rid me of the concept of the bog as a symbol of rural poverty.

Several IRA officers came to Smiths' house to meet me, treating me rather as a curiosity. On Sunday we went to Mass where I half expected to hear from the altar a denunciation of the IRA in keeping with the kind of sermon commonly preached all over the country at Sunday Masses. This time the priest said nothing offensive. After Mass I ran into an old friend from the Rath Camp days, one Paddy Baxter, who had been an active IRA man but had joined the Farmers' Party and had been elected a T.D. at the Pact Election. He was very surprised to meet me but also slightly embarrassed to find me in the company of Paddy Smith with whom there was a coolness over the Treaty; the Farmers' Party had accepted the Treaty position. Baxter was deeply upset about the political situation. He told me he was going to Dublin that evening to see if he could do anything, however slight, to help to avoid the ever threatening confrontation. He did not question me about my presence in the area although no doubt he wondered as to the reason.

In a car which Smith mustered from somewhere we toured the area in which any possible attack on the Orangemen would be based. If the trip had no other advantages, it gave me a chance to see the unusual panorama of little lakes that makes the scenery there so attractive. As the journey proceeded, we discussed unendingly the possibilities of the attack on the Six Counties. Smith felt bitter about Partition; he had no faith in the good intentions of the Provisional Government in general and of the Boundary Commission in particular. He believed that the Orangemen were irreconcilable and that the British had no intention of removing their hold on the Six Counties; only by making the area ungovernable could they be persuaded to quit. He was confident that he could get together a strong flying column which would prevent the British writ from running in Fermanagh. I was preparing to go back with this hopeful news to O'Malley when early on Thursday 30th June, Baxter, in a very friendly gesture, came over to Smiths' house to tell us that the Four Courts had been isolated and had come under attack by the troops of the Provisional Government.

I was incredulous. I never thought it could happen that IRA men would try to kill fellow IRA men. I was too green and inexperienced to comprehend that there were forces in our society much more powerful than even an undivided IRA could resist. I failed to realise how embittered Arthur Griffith was as he saw his life's achievement — the government of Ireland by the King, Lords and Commons — tottering to destruction. Still less did I understand the virulence of the bourgeoisie as they perceived the threat to their hopes of power and position just at the moment of realisation. Nor was I aware of the lengths to which the Church would go to maintain its dominance of a peasant population steeped in superstition and an urban proletariat soused in Saint Joseph's medals, Saint Blaise's flannel and a dozen different variety of scapulars.

If I had my capacity to reflect developed sufficiently I might have had a better understanding of the forces aligned against us because I was well informed on and could see the analogy with the Paris Commune of 1871; even more contemporaneously, I had read in the newspapers of the fate of Bela Kun and his communists at the hands of the Hungarian bourgeoisie helped by the Church. Like the Parisian Communards of 1871, the Hungarian communists were massacred. While our situation and ideology (if we could be said to have had an ideology) were very different from Bela Kun's, they were not so different from those of the Paris Commune if for no other reason than that we were without a programme apart from opposition to the

Government. We also shared the tradition of Jacobinism. It was this Jacobin streak, always present in Irish Republicanism, that so frightened our bourgeoisie. A fearful bourgeois, of whatever nationality, is as savage as any wild animal. Had I adverted to these historical precedents, I might have forseen the Terror to which we were later to be subjected.

In our relatively classless society the bourgeoisie was small but it had a powerfully active element largely derived from, or actually based in, University College, Dublin. The weaker members and close associates of the Provisional Government, such as W. T. Cosgrave, whose ambition in life was to be accepted as respectable, were willingly guided or pressurised by the products of the Jesuits and the Literary and Historical Society of the College. After the Pact Election Ernie O'Malley, with a squad from the Four Courts, seized the ballot papers of the electorate of the National University of Ireland. Comparing the ballot papers with the register of electors he found that almost the entire faculty of University College, Dublin, had broken the Pact by voting for other than the approved Pact condidates. The Pact was an arrangement made by De Valera on the one hand and Michael Collins on the other to elect a parliament which would retain the same balance of pro- and anti-Treaty parties as had been in the Dail.

I did not think in these terms at that time, nor did I think that the fighting even in Dublin would extend beyond the Four Courts. Considering that the Southern Division, with the Chief of Staff and most of his senior officers, had been virtually expelled from the IRA Executive, I did not expect them to get involved in the fight. I had little confidence in the Dublin Brigade as a relieving force for the beleagured garrison because the best of the officers were either pro-Treaty or if they were anti-Treaty were already inside the Four Courts. The senior anti-Treaty officers of the Brigade who were left could hardly be said to be over endowed with qualities of leadership.

Motivated by the spirit of the boy scouts rather than by any patriotic fervour I felt, not very rationally, that my place was with my friends, particularly Cooney, in the Four Courts. O'Malley having given me the substantial sum of £10 when I was leaving Dublin, I had no difficulty in hiring a car with driver to take me back to the city which I reached after an unremarkable journey, unless the absence of road blocks or any kind of military activity could be considered remarkable in the circumstances.

At Phibsboro Church I left the car, paid the driver and started to walk into the city. The first sign of abnormality was the absence of trams. I had walked only a few yards when I encountered a friend of mine named Bobby Bondfield who had been a class mate at school. I knew he was a member of the Fourth Battalion and meeting him in this part of the city I rightly suspected that he was on some IRA business. All the members of his Company had been ordered to report to the Hammam Hotel in O'Connell Street. He was making his way there by a roundabout route because it was difficult to get through the Free State cordon on the south side of the city. He told me too that there had been a great explosion at the Four Courts and that there were rumours that the garrison had surrendered. I decided to go along with him and we made our way to the Hammam without incident. Bondfield was later picked up in Stephen's Green by Cosgrave's escort and murdered by them in Clondalkin.

I found John Dowling, the O/C of the Fourth Battalion, there. At that stage it was still uncertain whether the intention was to entrench ourselves in the block of buildings stretching from Britain Street (now Parnell Street) to Talbot Street and backwards to the Pro-Cathedral and Marlboro Street. I could not believe that we were going to indulge in such a foolishly futile military exercise. But so it turned out. I conveyed my view to Dowling but in a spirit of fatalistic resignation I got him to give me a rifle and a Thompson gun (of which I had the flimsiest knowledge) and assign me to a firing post to await events. I was installed in a top window of the old Tramway Company office which, being on a corner site, gave me a complete view of O'Connell Street as far as Westmoreland Street. Nelson's Pillar was towering over the post, only a few yards away. I found the other members of the garrison of the Tramway Office, between twenty and thirty in all, were members of the Fourth Battalion. I knew them all very well. In addition we had a squad, if that is the word, of pretty young Cumann na mBan girls to attend to our commissariat. It was unusual for me to find myself in the company of young women and I was surprised how agreeable I found this experience.

Our immediate task was to knock out the glass and barricade the windows of our firing post. The nearest material to hand were the tightly packed records of the Dublin United Tramway Company. Some of the records consisting of conductors' daily returns went back thirty years. My two immediate companions engaged in building up the barricades were bank clerks. Being experts on records, they were amused at the futility of keeping in storage for so long records of passenger journeys taken between Drumcondra and Nelson's Pillar thirty years before. Banking was an improbable occupation from which to recruit IRA men. But then my friends, Considine and Callanan, were not usual men.

We were supplied with some sandbags to reinforce the Tramway Company records. Our engineers had broken down walls between all the houses, shops and hotels in the block. It was possible to move freely from Liptons in Earl Street to the Gresham Hotel. This meant that we, the occupying troops, were supplied with the necessities — even luxuries — of life in abundance. We had deep mattresses, thick blankets, fresh fruit (for the first day), joints of lamb, boxes of chocolates, Turkish or Egyptian cigarettes at choice or any other brand we wanted.

All was quiet for the first evening and night of the occupation. The next morning we were subject to desultory fire, coming apparently from the Ballast Office. From our post the Ballast Office was an easy target for a Lee Enfield rifle. We had no difficulty in shooting out all the windows. We kept it under fairly steady fire all the morning. Our information was that the Free Staters who occupied this site suffered some casualties which caused them to evacuate it. It was strange to see, just opposite the Ballast Office at Purcell's Corner, a sizeable crowd of spectators watching the firing, indifferent to any danger from stray bullets. They behaved as if they were rubbernecking at a traffic accident. An even more curious phenomenon was the occasional pedestrian literally strolling down O'Connell Street, apparently unaware that fighting was actually taking place which might intensify into a real battle at any time. Bored with sitting more or less inactive at a firing post I passed the time putting rifle bullets, with which we were well supplied, into the back of the head of the statue of Nelson. Nelson was known to Dubliners as the 'one-armed adulterer'. I often wondered whether in shooting up Nelson's statue I was not ritually punishing him for moral turpitude, denounced by my Christian Brothers' training, every bit as much as I was indulging my nationalistic prejudices.

The first real attack came late in the evening when an armoured car pulled up at the corner of Henry Street, firing belt after belt of machine gun bullets into our positions. Our corner was unaffected except for one burst directed at us as the car was leaving and we suffered no casualties. For the first time I used a Thompson gun which, even if my fire did reach its target, did no damage to the armoured car.

The next day the shooting was more frequent but still spasmodic. The Free Staters had occupied the Metropole Hotel and this point commanded the particular post occupied by Considine, Callanan and myself. Thanks mainly to the presence of the girls, I suspect, we were not at all down hearted although recognising quite well that militarily we were in a hopeless position. When ultimately, at midnight, we came under a sustained barrage from at least two armoured cars plus several machine guns located in the Metropole and the re-occupied Ballast Office, I think we were all quite frightened by the mere noise. Bullets were raining through the building, sometimes penetrating the barricades of Tramway records with short bursts of flame.

Dowling, the Battalion Commandant, was in overall charge of the Tramway Office. His justifiable pessimism did not help our morale. Nor was it improved when some of the few priests who stayed with us inspired no less, it must be said, by patriotic than by religious motives began to say the Rosary. The responses were taken up by the entire garrison, most of us crouching under the window sills. The hum of communal prayer was like the sound outside a beehive, except that it seemed to presage doom. Communal prayer can be a wonderful solace in misfortune but in the circumstances it would be impossible to think of any exercise more capable of adding to our demoralisation than the drone of the Rosary muted as it was by the noise of the guns. I have to say that Considine, Callanan and I did not participate in this exposition of our faith; we, all three of us, were quite conscious of the unfortunate effect it was having on the spirits of the garrison.

The next morning was very quiet. I felt a wish to look around the other parts of the great block which we occupied. I first made my way down the Talbot Street side and into Earl Street where in Boyers' drapery store I picked up a fine green velour hat which I wore all through the rest of the Civil War. I went down to the Hammam Hotel (learning for the first time that the word 'Hammam' indicated Turkish Baths) and from there on to the Gresham. As I was walking across the hall of the Gresham I heard a frightening scream from a man standing nearby. He had been hit in the head by a sniper's bullet but, by a freak of good fortune, the bullet instead of blowing his brains out merely penetrated the skin. It turned out that the wounded man was named Coughlan, a first cousin of my lost leader, Frank Coughlan, and he recovered fully from his wound. I met Ernie O'Malley's brother, Charlie, in the building. A few minutes after we parted company he went out into the lane between the Gresham and the Pro-Cathedral where he was picked off and killed by a sniper firing presumably from Parnell Street.

In the Gresham I saw De Valera, Austin Stack, the Minister for Home Affairs, Oscar Traynor, the O/C of the Dublin Brigade, and the Minister for Defence, Cathal Brugha. Their presence did not in any way encourage me. Far less did they impress me. I had enough wit to realise that between them a mess had been made of the military situation in that we were hopelessly entrapped. Which of them in particular was responsible for this tactical blunder I did not know nor did I care. The four of them were standing around, apparently without purpose, in the big room otherwise bustling with armed men coming and going. They had been great names to me; now they seemed like wraiths. In fact, neither De Valera, Stack nor Brugha had any responsibility for our predicament even though they were the anti-Treaty members of the Cabinet. Oscar Traynor was in sole and complete charge of military operations.

That night we were again under attack, not quite so intensely as the previous night, but this time there was no Rosary. The following day all the girls, with some of the garrison, were ordered to evacuate the buildings. The troops concerned slipped away as best they could, but the girls left in a body walking up the centre of O'Connell Street quite unperturbed by the spasmodic rifle and machine gun fire. Before leaving they brought up two large containers of canned pears as well as a dozen cans of corned beef which they presented to us as an iron ration. With their departure I suffered a fit of despondency as if we were being abandoned to our fate. This was at least a new experience for me; for the first time in my life I had enjoyed and then missed female company. I think Callanan and Considine felt the absence of the girls even more deeply because they had begun to form personal attachments with some of them.

Later that afternoon a single armoured car approached, opening up this time almost exclusively on the Tramway Office. I was returning the fire rather futilely with my rifle when a hail of bullets caught my firing slit blasting sand from the barricades with great force into my forehead, right eye and cheek. A large bullet splinter penetrated my clothing, lodging in my forearm. I was stunned for a while. My face looked as if a pepper cannister had been shaken over it. I could not use my right eye which felt as if it were irreparably damaged. My arm was bleeding a good deal although there was no bone broken nor much pain. I was helped by Dowling to the first aid station in the Gresham where an elderly lady doctor bandaged my arm and almost certainly saved the sight of my eye, extracting the dozens of fragments of sand which had lodged in my eyeball by the unaesthetic method of licking them out. I was then removed by ambulance to the Mater Hospital where I found myself in a ward with several other casualties from the O'Connell Street fighting. All were much more badly wounded than I. Two had lost a leg, another an eye, another an arm. My injury amounted to what used to be known in the British Army as a 'blighty' wound. Mobility was unaffected except for the inconvenience of keeping my arm in a sling, an operation being necessary to have the bullet fragments removed.

I had streams of visitors during my stay in hospital. My family, even my grandmother, came as well as several friends from the UCD Soccer Club. One of them had qualified as a doctor and had joined the Free State Army. He had no inhibitions about coming to see me in uniform. I was dismayed to learn that Earle had been arrested while on his way to take part in some 'job'. He had been taken to Wellington Barracks from which he was paroled to visit me. This concession I attributed to the intervention of Coughlan. I was very upset about Earle. He had only been home for a few months, having spent over a year interned at Ballykinlar. I felt it was merely out of personal loyalty to me that he had taken any side in the split.

When Tom Brennan, the man without the arm, and Sean Brunswick, who had lost his eye, were sufficiently fit to move we were sent to convalesce at the house of the Resident Medical Superintendent in Portrane Mental Hospital, an elderly lady named Dr. Fleury. There we lived in considerable luxury and in beautiful surroundings until one morning the house was surrounded by a massive raiding party of Free State troops who arrived in three tenders. They were surprised at the paucity of their haul; apparently their information was that someone of importance was staying in the house. On finding out their mistake, they withdrew their sentries but none the less placed us under arrest. They treated us with consideration, helping us down the stairs from our bedrooms. At that stage bitterness had not developed between the fighting men. On reaching the hall I asked the officer who was helping me if I might go to the kitchen to say goodbye to the maids who had been kind to me. Without waiting for a reply I detached myself quickly, slipped into the kitchen, ran out through a back door and crashed my way through a surrounding hedge. My escape was so sudden that I doubt whether the officer ever quite knew what became of me. Having got through the hedge, I ran and ran till I reached an inlet of the sea where I was forced to halt and rest a while wondering what to do next. I saw a small house near the sea shore, so small that it seemed unlikely to be a human habitation. Occupied indeed it was by the most miserable looking family I had ever encountered consisting of a man, his wife, two teenage girls and a small boy. Even in the slums I had never seen such evidence of abject poverty. The house consisted of a kitchen and a bedroom. There was scarcely any furniture in it beyond a table and a couple of wooden chairs and a bench. There was presumably a bed in the bedroom but I did not penetrate that far.

I asked the man the name of the district and was told that it was Portrane although to me it seemed a long way from the Mental Hospital. There was no other house in sight and I was too tired to go any further just then. The man apparently lived by cockle picking, a poor livelihood at best, and he evidently suspected that I was on the run. I did not know how far he would have to go to reveal my whereabouts to the Staters but he certainly hinted that it would not be beyond him. I gave him a pound to ensure his silence. His wife provided me with a meal of stale bread, margarine and tea twice during the day. On each occasion I handed over a pound in payment.

When evening came I decided to move off even though I had no clear idea of my geographical position. I did know roughly the direction of Dublin. Keeping along the sea shore, I eventually reached the railway and started to walk, sleeper by sleeper, towards the city. As night fell I reached the first station on the line. There was sufficient light to read the name and to identify it as Donabate. There was no sign of life in the place but I knew I was, literally, on the right track. I trudged on through the night, through Malahide, Portmarnock, past Howth Junction. By this time I was quite exhausted. I got into a hayfield, lay under a haycock and, covering myself with hay, fell into a deep sleep.

It must have been several hours before I woke though I could not tell the time as my watch had stopped but I realised it was well into the morning because men were working in the fields. I felt very refreshed as I resumed my march along the sleepers continuing until I reached Clontarf Station where a number of people were waiting for a train. I thought it safer to go into the city by tram. I changed trams at the Pillar, arriving at the house of my cousin, Ewart Wilson, in Brighton Square, Rathgar, at about 10 a.m.

I had stayed with the Wilsons much of the time while on the run during the Black and Tan campaign. It never occurred to me that the family were taking considerable risks with their livelihood in providing me with a hideout. Ewart was a civil servant. If I had been arrested in his house he would have been dismissed and would have found it almost impossible to find another job. Lily, his wife, was a gentle, cultivated English-woman. She and Ewart had met while he was serving in London. At this time there were five young children, one of them an infant. Apart from the natural difficulties a woman of Lily's rather upper class English upbringing experienced in adapting to the Irish environment, the fears for the safety of her children had there been a raid, as well as for her husband's job, put a considerable nervous strain on her. By now I was rather less thoughtless than I had been, and more aware of the magnitude of the kindness I was receiving from her. I had nothing with which to repay her except my life-long affection and gratitude.

I spent three or four days with the Wilsons doing nothing but reading *Gulliver's Travels,* understanding it for what it is, a savagely profound satire on the absurdity of so much of human behaviour and pretensions. I have read it many times since finding it, even in my old age, a help in correcting my perspective of public men or public events. After nightfall, I called over to see my parents in Terenure getting the usual welcome as well as the usual plea from my mother to 'give up all this nonsense' which was duly ignored.

The time had come for me to report back to my Battalion. I learnt that the Dublin Brigade was engaged in planning an extensive operation designed to isolate Dublin by destroying the bridges carrying roads into the city. It was an ambitious exercise although what the follow-up was to be in the event of success was not clear. As it turned out the attempt resulted in complete failure with the most active elements in the Brigade being captured in the course of the operation. It transpired that an officer had been taken prisoner by the Staters, almost by accident, a couple of days before the action was due to begin. He had in his pocket a detailed plan of the proposed attack so that when our men arrived at the bridges armed only with picks, shovels and gelignite, they were readily rounded up. When the Civil War was long over and I had made my peace with Coughlan, he told me that it was he who arrested the officer with the plans of the bridge-blowing project having recognised him on a road near Ticknock. Coughlan was so proud of his exploit that he could not resist telling me about it. It was the only episode in the Civil War he ever referred to. He never mentioned that he had prevented some of the murder gang which became active a little later on from shooting Kenny, whom they had taken prisoner, out of hand. Nor did he mention that he had, on his own responsibility, released my brother from Collins Barracks where he was imprisoned after being taken off the field at Croke Park while playing in a hurling match. My home was never raided during the Civil War, an act of omission which I attributed to Coughlan's consideration for my parents.

After the failure of the bridge project another major operation was planned. With the collusion of some of the garrison it was proposed to seize Baldonnel Aerodrome and commandeer an aeroplane loaded with bombs which were to be dropped on Government Buildings. The aeroplane was to land on Merrion Strand when the raid was completed. Two expeditions to carry out the attack were organised. Originally Dowling was to take charge but in the middle of the preparations that decision was changed and Tom Derrig (afterwards Minister for Education) who had been brought from Mayo to the Headquarters staff in Dublin, was put in command. He postponed the plan for a week. When the second attempt took place, it was to be spearheaded by the Leixlip Column under the very determined Paddy Mulally. The full collusion expected from inside did not materialise, although a number of the Staters left to join Mulally's men and some of these were later captured and executed for desertion. Derrig called off the attack for the second time because of the failure of some of the attacking force to arrive. A historian of the period has attributed the leadership of the operation to me but this is nonsense. The role designed for me was, in retrospect, one of high farce — high is the correct word. I was to go up with John Dowling in the captured aeroplane to discharge the bombs on Government buildings.

The pilot selected to fly the plane was a man who, having reached the diaconate with the Columban Fathers at Dalgan Park, had left the Order to take part in the Civil War. 'The Deacon' as he was always referred to by us was, if his story was to be believed, something of a universal genius. I do not know who checked his credentials; it is quite possible that nobody did. He had, it was said, flown with a mixed British and French squadron in defence of Verdun. He had been decorated, it was said, with the Croix de Guerre by Marshal Petain. He had, it was said, the British Distinguished Flying Cross. When the war in Europe was over, he entered religion and his engineering skill, it was said, enabled him to sink wells and to construct a complete water system for the monastery at Dalgan Park.

When I was introduced to him as his bombadier, I found a cheerful, expansive, confident and friendly man. He did not impart to me the confidence he so obviously felt. I discussed plans with him: how high, how low we would have to fly over Government buildings, how did we aim our bombs, would we need any special clothing? For all the questions he had pat answers, but when I asked if he had checked whether the tide would be in or out when we came to land on Merrion Strand, he admitted that he had forgotten. My confidence unsurprisingly shrank. 'The Deacon' went to the scene of the action with Derrig. I joined a unit of about thirty men of the Fourth Battalion under John Dowling on the canal bank near Clondalkin from whence we were to link up with the main body of the attackers assembled outside Baldonnel.

We had scarcely arrived at the rendezvous when Dowling received a message from Derrig to the effect that the plans had been cancelled for the second time. We started back on the long trudge home in groups of two. I was accompanied by Larry O'Brien whose brother had commanded the Four Courts garrison. I confess that I felt very relieved because in my deep heart's core I did not believe that 'The Deacon' could fly a plane. O'Brien and I had not gone very far when a canal barge came abreast of us. We stepped on to the barge and got a friendly reception from the crew. They gave us tea and installed us in filthy bunks in the hold. Neither of us had ever been on a barge before. It was an experience we had reason to regret as the hold was alive with crawling insects and only considerations of safety kept us from abandoning ship until it reached Herberton Bridge near Dolphin's Barn where we got off. O'Brien knew a safe house nearby willing to take us in. Next day I made my way back to Brighton Square and stayed there for a few days, paying flying visits to my home in the evenings.

My spirits were at a low ebb. Physically I was tired and was glad of a rest. The heavily censored press continued its viciously low line in anti-Republican propaganda but, even though knowing that every success claimed by Staters was exaggerated, I could not deceive myself into believing that the progress of the military campaign was anything but disastrous for us. I got a despatch from O'Malley telling me to call to see him. I found him installed in an affluent household in Fitzwilliam Place. He told me he wanted me to go to Dundalk to see Frank Aiken on his behalf and find out his future intentions. The confidence implied in entrusting me with such an important assignment restored my morale. Amongst the Divisional Commandants Frank Aiken, himself a unique personality, had adopted a unique position. The project of the Army of the North, which he was to command, having failed, he had unsuccessfully pleaded with both Mulcahy and Lynch to desist from hostilities. He had not recognised the IRA Executive. He was determined that there was not going to be a Civil War, at least in his Division. To make sure that arms were not put to use he had them stored away in secret dumps. Though he continued to occupy Dundalk Military Barracks he refused to obey an order from Beggar's Bush to attack the anti-Treaty forces under Commandant McKenna which had considerable strength in the area.

The Provisional Government was gaining ground. Their attitude was one of no compromise. They sent a strong force into Dundalk, captured the barracks and interned Aiken and some three hundred of his men in the local prison. Even while in prison, although smarting from the humiliation which he endured, Aiken obtained parole to make another effort to persuade Mulcahy and Lynch to reach some compromise which would stop the fighting. He was unsuccessful. Lynch was as little inclined to compromise as was Mulcahy even though by this time he was clearly losing the war. But while the enthusiastic fervour which made men fight in the Black and Tan campaign had long since vanished it was rapidly being substituted by bitterness and hatred which can be just as potent, if much less admirable, motivational forces.

Aiken was not long in jail when, with the aid of McKenna's anti-Treaty forces, a breach was blown in the wall allowing all the prisoners to escape. Aiken still had not given any indication that he would take up arms on the Republican side. He made no contact with O'Malley or Lynch after his escape from jail and they did not know anything of his intentions; hence the purpose of my mission. O'Malley introduced me to a young woman who owned a car and had been detailed to drive me to Dundalk via Carrickmacross. She was Miss Kay Brady, a member of a wealthy Belfast linen family and a graduate of UCD. She knew everyone in the Movement to which she and two of her sisters had devoted their lives as well as their considerable means. Meeting her led me to a concatenation of minor surprises. I had never known anyone who owned a car except a taxi driver. A car owned and driven by a woman was a complete novelty. Miss Brady and O'Malley indulged in much mutual leg-pulling. I had never seen men and women in that relationship before and was impressed by the fact that her mental agility was much greater than his. My education in the qualities of women had begun and it continued as we drove to Carrickmacross. She was much better informed than I about past and present happenings in Republican circles and had an even lower opinion of the leadership of the IRA than I was coming to acquire. In thinking and behaviour she was rather violently feminist — a precursor of women's lib. I had never heard that sort of talk before and I found it very interesting. She was the second woman I had met who had read *The Blue*

Lagoon. We skated conversationally on the edge of sex; I for the first time with a woman. I found the journey to Carrickmacross all too short. My morale had quite recovered; intellectually I had passed the age of puberty.

Miss Brady and I stayed overnight in a 'safe' house in Carrickmacross, starting off very early in the morning for Dundalk. Our exit was well timed because the house was raided an hour after we left. In Dundalk I was deposited by Miss Brady in another safe house while my host arranged the meeting with Aiken. Apparently it was only after some persuasion that Aiken agreed to see me at all. After waiting all day it was well after nightfall when a courier arrived to guide me to the proposed rendezvous. We walked through the town and about half a mile along the Newry Road we stopped at a farm labourer's cottage where in one of the two bedrooms I met Aiken.

He was sitting on the bed and made no attempt to make me welcome. There was a chair in the room but I was not invited to sit down. He did not ask what I wanted. He looked at me in what he may have thought was a questioning manner but the muscles of his face did not appear to move. Finally a grunted 'Well?' indicated that discussion should get under way. I explained the purpose of my visit. He told me as laconically as possible to go back and tell O'Malley that he intended to attack and re-capture Dundalk. I asked feeling, but I hope not showing, some scepticism 'When?' 'In a few days' was the reply. The conversation was beginning to resemble a Red Indian pow-wow. I asked him if I might stay to take part in the operation. The reply was 'Ah, no. You'd better go back to O'Malley'. In a relatively lengthy speech, I shifted the tone of the conversation from a Red Indian to a Chinese dialogue, pointing out the loss of face I would endure if I missed the opportunity to participate in such a sensational achievement as the re-capture of Dundalk. In the situation in which we were, a military success on the scale he hoped would boost the morale of our people all over Ireland. As we were in the country of the Táin I was going to invoke the shades of Cúchulainn, but I thought that would be too corny and anyway I was not sure that he would understand the allusion. I was wrong. He would well have understood. However, he relented to the extent that I was allowed to stay but only in his own immediate company. He said I could sleep with him head to toe and to this I agreed.

The elderly woman of the house gave us tea with home made bread and butter before we turned in. Aiken never uttered a word. We rose very early next morning and got more tea and bread and butter with boiled eggs for breakfast. Still no word came from Aiken. After a while he took up a knapsack into which he had put his shaving kit, socks and change of shirt. He indicated by signs that we were about to leave and I was surprised to find a small Ford car with a red headed driver waiting outside the cottage door. The driver who was named Peter Boyle turned out to be a kind of Man Friday to Aiken. But beyond a monosyllabic direction to him, Aiken did not speak.

We drove for a few miles until we reached hilly country. Soon afterwards we abandoned the car, making our way across country on foot. Aiken's taciturnity had totally disconcerted me. I had seen men in all sorts of moods, behaving in all sorts of ways which were distasteful to me. I saw them angry, quarrelsome, drunk, boisterous, loudmouthed but never anything that discommoded me like this seemingly endless silence. I had lost track of our whereabouts when most unexpectedly Aiken pointed to some landmark saying 'That's the "Long Woman's Grave" '. I translated the place name into Irish as *Uaigh na mná móire*. Aiken showed some surprise, unreasonably I thought, asking me in Irish if I spoke Irish. I replied, still in Irish, that I did and we exchanged another few sentences together. It was clear to me that while my Irish was very inadequate, it was much more fluent than his and in this respect I had him at a disadvantage. From that point on his attitude to me changed. He became relatively talkative. He must have thought that, being a Dubliner, I could not have any sympathy with the Gaelic Ireland which, as I learned later, was for him a passionate dream.

Approaching a farm house we were challenged by a heavily armed sentry. Having satisfied him, we moved on into the farmyard where a large group of men were engaged in filling petrol tins with explosives and priming their caps with detonators. Aiken closely supervised the operation and then went on to discuss with the officers the plan for the attack on Dundalk. I was struck by Aiken's meticulous attention to detail, how he checked and rechecked every aspect of the operation making sure that each officer clearly understood what was expected of him in every possible contingency. There was an air of excitement about the place but it did not extend to Aiken who exuded calm confidence. After dark another heavily armed unit joined the group in the farmyard, making in all about sixty men. All were armed with rifles or Thompson guns and revolvers and about a dozen carried petrol tins and rolls of electric cable. The 'few days' of which Aiken had spoken as the probable interval before his attack on Dundalk had shrunken to to-night.

About midnight, Aiken assembled the party in order of march.

Although there was little likelihood of any interference from the Staters, he took textbook precautions to protect a body of troops on the march. We were only three or four miles as the crow flies from the military barracks which was our target and as the crow flies we marched, preceded by an advance guard and protected by flankers. Absolute silence was maintained until we reached the river on the opposite bank of which the barracks was situated. Boats were ready to take us across to a landing point just above the barracks. There we were joined by some of McKenna's men who were standing by in the town. The military barracks faced roughly north and south with large entrance gates at either end. When all the party had got across the river safely a group of ten men, five armed with Thompson guns and five carrying petrol tin mines, slipped around to the southern gate while a similarly assorted detachment approached the northern side. Each group was backed up by a party of riflemen.

A mine-layer from each group crept up to the gates, laid a mine and at a pre-arranged synchronised moment exploded it blasting the gates to smithereens. The machine gunners dashed through the entrances, putting the guards out of action, while the other mine-layers followed spreading out among the buildings, throwing their mines through the windows and exploding them. A few soldiers on duty offered resistance but were quickly dealt with by the Thompson gunners. Riflemen from the supporting parties overran the barrack blocks and firing soon ceased. It only remained to round up the prisoners and look after the wounded.

When dawn came the barracks presented a weird appearance. The frontage of the buildings seemed to have been sliced off. The upper floors, some containing beds with the troops still in them, were intact but could not be evacuated because the stairs had been blown away or blocked by rubble. At this stage a party of McKenna's men approached the local jail; the governor, learning what had happened, surrendered with his guards. Some two hundred Republicans from various parts of the country were released. They were replaced by the captured Free Staters to the number in all of about three hundred.

The very speed and suddenness of the attack limited the casualty list. Five Staters were killed and about ten were wounded. On our side only McKenna was killed and that by an accident. Aiken was a first class field commander. As a guerilla operation, his recapture of Dundalk was by far the most spectacularly efficient carried out by the IRA. Had it been directed against the British it would have had a larger place in the mythology of the period than even Barry's famous ambush at Kilmichael. In Civil War, alas, there is no glory; there are no monuments to victory or victors, only to the dead. With the captured rifles and machine guns together with the large quantity of arms already under his control Aiken could have easily put together a force of one thousand disciplined men. In the circumstances of the time a force of even that size, led by a man of the military competence and character of Aiken, might have marched on Dublin with some hope of success. Marching on Dublin was far from Aiken's mind. He was determined that he would not participate in the Civil War nor would he allow it to be carried on in his area. He armed those of the prisoners released from Dundalk jail who did not belong to his units, organised them into groups, supplied them with provisions and sent them back to their home bases which were mainly in the midlands. Nobody on either side liked having to take part in the Civil War, but I never met anyone who was so totally horrified or so saddened by it as Aiken.

I had completed my mission successfully, I thought. My problem now was to get back to Dublin to report to O'Malley. I hit on the idea of taking the boat which then ran from Greenore to Holyhead and returning on the Mail Boat to Dun Laoghaire. I found that two of the prisoners whom we had released from Dundalk had the same idea. One was Bobby Ivers, the medical student who had taken me to the hospital when I was wounded in O'Connell Street, the other was a brother of Bertie Smyllie of *The Irish Times*. We had a pleasant uneventful trip to Dun Laoghaire.

Equally uneventful was the journey by tram from Dun Laoghaire to Wilson's in Brighton Road whence, after a meal, I went to report to O'Malley. He had installed himself in Humphries' of Ailesbury Road which was to be his headquarters as Assistant Chief of Staff to Liam Lynch until he was captured in November. With the adrenalin still flowing I recounted the events in Dundalk but I could give no assurance that Aiken would throw in his lot with us. This news did not dismay O'Malley. He rightly grasped that the Free Staters would not acquiesce in Aiken's posture of neutrality. Within a few days a large body of pro-Treaty troops moved on Dundalk. Aiken realising that there was no hope of holding the town against an attack on this scale evacuated it and took to the hills. He was finally driven to taking sides.

O'Malley showed me a printed statement from Aiken from which it was clear that the earlier attack on Dundalk, resulting in Aiken's imprisonment, was undertaken, not on orders from Mulcahy or the Provisional Government, but on the personal initiative of General Dan Hogan, the O/C of the Fifth Northern Division which covered the area of Monaghan, East Cavan and South Fermanagh. General Hogan was one of the many northern officers who subsequently made careers in the Free State Army; he eventually became Chief of Staff but was forced to resign having, in the course of some disagreement, struck the Minister for Defence, Desmond Fitzgerald, it was said.

O'Malley wanted to retain me as an assistant in his HQ which had now been organised into a complete office. He had as secretary and typist Madge Clifford, a young Kerry woman who had worked for Liam Lynch in the Four Courts, had remained throughout the fighting there but was not arrested at the time of the surrender. Madge was a highly trained secretary who was as well-informed about every detail of the IRA as O'Malley himself. She was personally acquainted with all the members of the Army Council as well as with most of the members of the Provisional Government. Emotionally she was deeply involved in Irish Republicanism; one of the devoted band of women without whose help it would have been impossible to have carried on the Civil War for any length of time. These women of all ages and of different social strata acted as secretaries, nurses, housekeepers, but above all as couriers maintaining a wonderfully reliable system of communication until the end. Indeed the system of communications was the only really efficient part of the IRA operation during the Civil War. It never failed, thanks to the devotion of these women.

Watching Madge Clifford in action I realised for the first time that women had a role outside the home. Hitherto I had regarded women as appendages to men whose function it was to rear children, provide meals and clothes, keep the house clean and nurse men when they were sick. It never occurred to me that they could operate successfully as administrators or political advisers or that, other than in the case of very exceptional women like Maud Gonne MacBride or Mary MacSwiney, they could develop a consuming interest in politics which would dominate their lives. I had listened far too long to my mother's derisive comments on suffragettes though her attitude was not shared by my father.

In September O'Malley got a dispatch from Monaghan complaining about the inactivity of the senior officer there and I was sent up to investigate. Again Kay Brady was detailed to act as chauffeur but this time we avoided Carrickmacross, going directly to a place called Donamoyne where we met the local Commandant named Caraher. I spent a week or ten days with him going around the Battalion areas meeting the other unit Commandants. It was with some difficulty that I made contact with the O/C of the Division but having done so it did not take long to decide that a change in the command was necessary. I wrote to O'Malley suggesting that the whole area, including Cavan, should be placed under Frank Aiken and advised that he himself should come up to effect the necessary transfer.

He was very glad of the excuse to get out into the country; being deskbound did not suit him. It was agreed that Frank Aiken should come over to Donamoyne for a general discussion on the situation and to pledge his formal adherence to the Executive. The proposed changes in the local command structure were effected; not that it made much difference because the larger part of the Division had gone over to the Free State side. What was left was badly armed and poorly organised.

The Carahers were comfortable farmers but the house was not safe, having been raided several times. During the visit of Aiken and O'Malley we were billeted each night in different houses. One night the three of us — Aiken, O'Malley and myself — had to share a settle bed. None of us got much sleep on that occasion.

Going around the area on foot gave me a good opportunity to learn something of the hardship small farmers had to endure in a county so little endowed by nature as Monaghan; significantly it was only the small farmers (except for a few households like Caraher's) who had any welcome for us. It was in Caraher's that I spent my twenty-first birthday. By this time O'Malley had gone back to Dublin and Aiken to his HQ in the Carlingford area. Despite the kindness of the Carahers I felt lonely and very sorry for myself, thinking of the worry I was causing my parents and how much my mother would miss me on the birthday which marked my coming of age. I was very glad to get instructions from O'Malley to return to Dublin as soon as possible. With some difficulty Caraher arranged a car for me. I completed the journey without ever seeing a Free State soldier. Individual uniformed soldiers kept strictly to their barracks for fear of being shot as a reprisal for some unauthorised murder — the authorised murders were yet to come.

When I saw O'Malley he told me that it had been decided to appoint John Dowling, O/C of my old Fourth Battalion, as Director of Organisation and that I was to join his staff as an assistant. O'Malley was about to leave for an Executive meeting in the South and it was understood that in his absence I should attend at his office from time to time to give Madge Clifford any help she might require.

By the end of August Griffith and Collins were dead — the one by a heart attack, the other killed by our people in an ambush. The Free

State Government had virtually converted itself into a military dictatorship camouflaged as a democracy by the connivance of the Labour Party which assumed the fraudulent role of Parliamentary Opposition. In our opinion the only purpose they served in this role was to give moral support to what had, in effect, become a reign of terror. The first phase of the terror began with the setting up of a Criminal Investigation Department in Oriel House, a building previously occupied by the Dublin Metropolitan Police. The CID was staffed by ex-IRA men some of whom were genuinely embittered by the death of Collins, some of whom wanted to show how 'tough' they were, while a few were mere psychopaths. The terror took the form of torturing prisoners under interrogation which is to say they were beaten and battered sometimes into a state of unconsciousness. Some Republican activists, real or suspected, were picked up on the streets and never got as far as Oriel House. They were shot out of hand. These were the 'unauthorised murders' which belatedly upset the Bishops.

Terror is apparently an inevitable feature of all Civil Wars. The only effective response to it is counter-terror. Except in one or two places we were unable to mount a counter-terror campaign, partly because we lacked the means and partly because we lacked the necessary will and nerve. We also lacked an intelligence service which is an essential ingredient of both terror and counter-terror; on the other hand the Free Staters had a first class intelligence service. Our organisation was deeply penetrated by touts, spies and traitors. Our only successful penetration of the Free State inner councils had about it something of the elements of a farce. A rather silly Minister was charmed into taking a very beautiful and highly educated young woman into his office to continue a literary discussion on D. H. Lawrence. She succeeded in reading documents on the Minister's desk which indicated that there was a proposal before the Government to deport Republican prisoners to the Seychelles Islands. For one reason or another the proposal was never proceeded with, perhaps because we gave it publicity, though this was a shortsighted move because such publicity immediately shut out our source of information as it brought to an end the Minister's interest in the views of our Mata Hari on D. H. Lawrence.

Apart from the terror, the military situation went from bad to worse. As early as August De Valera realised that there was no possibility of winning the war. He wanted to call it off but Liam Lynch made it clear to him that any public action to this end would be repudiated by the Executive and the fighting would continue, as

247

indeed it would have. By now the bitterness and hatred Republicans felt towards the Free State regime had reached a point when nothing short of total defeat would have induced them to give up the struggle. It required an accentuation of the terror, which in turn heightened the motivating forces of bitterness and hostility, before this total defeat was accomplished.

I found that Dowling had established a Headquarters office for himself, a secretary named Maria Moloney, and me at a house in Rathgar belonging to a well-off IRA supporter, a middle aged lady named Miss Langan. While these arrangements were in train I received two psychological shocks which inflicted scars on my mind which never healed. The second phase of the terror had begun in the form of a combined effort by the Provisional Government and the Church — the Church threatening men's immortal souls by denying them the Sacrament of Penance which was their only hope of ensuring eternal salvation — while the Provisional Government threatened the lives of Republican soldiers caught in arms. The Government brought in a law ostensibly to obviate the necessity for the unauthorised murders by Free State agents which were becoming an increasingly frequent occurrence. It appeared to the Staters necessary not to stop these murders but to legalise them. The Labour Party opposed the Bill as it went through the Dail but their opposition was merely a futile gesture. If their objections to the provisions of the Bill were seriously intended they should have withdrawn from the Dail thereby proclaiming what, in truth, was the reality of the situation — that the Government was a military dictatorship. A proclamation was issued offering an amnesty if within a fortnight we handed in our arms; otherwise anyone found in possession of arms would be executed.

The effect of the proclamation on me was devastating. To have to face the certainty of execution if captured in some gun fight or even if I stumbled into a cordon of soldiers while carrying a gun was a terrifying prospect. Nevertheless it never even occurred to me to accept the terms of the amnesty and go home. I often recall my frame of mind at that time when the question of capital punishment for political offences as a deterrent comes up for discussion. The nett effect of the proclamation on me was merely to intensify my hatred of the enemy.

About the same time the Church issued a parallel proclamation entitled 'Pastoral Letter of His Eminence Cardinal Logue, the Archbishops and Bishops of Ireland, to the Priests and People of Ireland'. I always had an ambivalent feeling towards the clergy.

Growing up I had virtually no social contact with priests and neither in school nor at home did I learn to have any high regard for the local parochial clergy. On the other hand I had been gratified and pleased to see priests as well as a Bishop or two crowding into the Mater Hospital after the big hunger strike in Mountjoy to shake our hands or offer their rings to be kissed. The presence of a priest as a fellow prisoner in the Rath Internment Camp also seemed to have the effect of adding to our status.

My attitude to the Church as a power in the land was very different. As a separatist I had absorbed the received wisdom of the tradition emanating from Tone. I knew that Dr Troy, the Archbishop of Dublin, had issued a pastoral letter condemning the rebels of 1798. I knew that Cardinal Cullen had condemned the Fenians and I knew by heart the sermon of Dr Moriarty, the Bishop of Kerry, who denounced the same Fenians as criminals who had God's heaviest curse, 'his withering, blasting, blighting curse on them, and for whose punishment eternity is not long enough, nor hell hot enough'.

During the Black and Tan campaign these memories were dormant because it was accepted that, except for the vagaries of what was regarded as an eccentric Bishop of Cork, the official Church was on our side though in fact the Bishops assembled at Maynooth refused a request from Dail Eireann to be recognised as the legitimate Government of Ireland. The spirit of Dr Moriarty must have been stalking the corridors of Maynooth when the Pastoral Letter of October 1922 was being composed. From internal evidence the document seems to have been written in haste and under considerable emotional stress. To us who were in arms against the acceptance of the Treaty it appeared not merely intemperate in its language but vindictive in its spirit. Some of the more vehement passages in it are worth recalling.

We, the Republicans, were described as engaged in a campaign of plunder. They said that we had deliberately set out to make our Motherland a heap of ruins. By insensate blockades, we were seeking to starve the people or bring them into social stagnation. The war we were waging was a system of plunder and assassination. Our young lives, they said, were utterly spoiled by early association with cruelty and robbery, falsehood and crime. They were unable to understand how, within a few months, we had changed from being generous, kind hearted and good and became involved in a network of crime. Their hearts however, they protested, were filled with bitterest anguish on our behalf. Some of us were activated by vanity and perhaps self-deceit, by greed for land and love of loot and anarchy.

The bull 'Laudibiliter' from which have flown consequences which have done much to shape Irish history may well have prompted this passage: 'The long struggle of centuries against foreign rule and misrule has weakened respect for civil authority in the national conscience' and in the same historical vein they quote St Paul 'Let every soul be subject to the higher power' and by that, the Pastoral explains, St Paul meant the legitimate authority of the State. They decreed that we in the IRA were guilty of the gravest sins and might not be absolved in Confession nor admitted to Holy Communion.

In the first publication of the Pastoral, the Hierarchy said they had read with horror of 'the unauthorised murders recorded in the Press' but in the later versions they dropped the word 'unauthorised' and substituted the word 'many' instead. In the course of a very detailed open letter to the Archbishop of Dublin replying to the Pastoral Frank Gallagher, a leading Republican journalist, commented: "National defence becomes murder on the part of the Republican troops, but actual murder by the Free State Forces is practically abetted by the Irish Hierarchy — thus honourably has your Grace maintained the sacred impartiality of your august office".

Apart from the abusive language which we considered insulting, we regarded the Pastoral as pointless because it was based on the premise that the Staters were the legitimate Government — a premise which we did not accept. Indeed this was the issue on which we were fighting the war. In practical terms the serious part of the Pastoral was that providing for our virtual Excommunication. Considering the importance attached by all Irish Catholics to their eternal salvation this situation gave the Free Staters a considerable advantage in military morale in so far as they enjoyed the services of army chaplains to help them along the road to heaven.

This combination of the religious and secular powers in the effort to liquidate their opponents had something of the character of the Spanish Inquisition. Of that institution only Torquemada is commonly remembered but in fact he was assisted by a Council of five. It was my belief there was in Ireland a 'Torquemanda' with his 'Council of five' who initiated and supervised the implementation of the Free State policy of executions.

The Bishops were, they protested, not concerned with our politics; we were in breach of God's moral law; they had compassion for us. Like the Inquisitors they were apparently more concerned for our immortal souls than for our physical fate. They communicated this concern to the secular arm as will be seen from a speech made by

General Mulcahy in the Provisional Parliament after the execution of three teenage boys who had been taken prisoner while bearing arms near Oriel House. Mulcahy said: 'We are people who realise that man is made in the image and likeness of God and we treat men as such . . . When a man is going to his death he does get a priest'.

The official terror was well under way when Mulcahy made this statement. It had begun after the capture of Erskine Childers in early November when, as a hors d'oeuvres to his execution, four virtually unknown prisoners were executed in Dublin. As Kevin O'Higgins explained when defending these executions, the Provisional Government thought it better to begin the terror by shooting these unknown prisoners because 'if they took as their first case some man who was outstandingly active and outstandingly wicked in his activities, the unfortunate dupes throughout the country might say he was killed because he was a leader, because he was an Englishman, or because he combined with others to commit raids'.

When the Civil War ended, the official executions had accounted for seventy-seven Republicans; the 'unauthorised killings' by the Free State murder gangs, of which there were several, principally in Dublin, amounted to 153. Numerically speaking the victims of the terror were relatively few compared with similar terror campaigns in Europe before and since our Civil War. In 1871, for example, more than 20,000 Communards were massacred in Paris. But it is well to remember that our performance was no different in kind from other European terror regimes so that when we begin to feel righteous about what the Jacobins did in September 1798, Thiers in 1871, the Hungarians under Horthy in 1920, the Russians under Stalin or the Spaniards under Franco in the nineteen thirties, we should remember that proportionate to our population and resources we Irish are quite capable of matching Robespierre or Horthy or Stalin or Franco in the exercise of political repression.

It is natural that I should think that the better elements of the IRA opposed the Treaty but I doubt if we had among our leaders any with the sophistication necessary to devise counter measures to the policy of official executions. Even if we had not the ability to devise such a policy we should have had an intelligence service good enough to penetrate the inner councils of the Provisional Government; more important, we should have been able to find out who their counsellors were and eliminated them. Shooting decent men like Tom Hales would not intimidate whoever was advising the Government on the conduct of the campaign of repression.

General Mulcahy was credited (if that is the word) with initiating the executions of Mellowes, O'Connor, McKelvey and Barrett as a reprisal for the shooting of Deputy Tom Hales. We did not believe that Mulcahy would have had either the intelligence or the nerve to have devised and carried out this very effective method of preventing the killing of T.D.s and Senators. By any, except some metaphysical or occult standards, these executions were murder. We found it hard to accept that Mulcahy, pietist that he was, would have outraged his conscience unless he had some advice which would justify, for him, his action in the sight of God.

Afterwards, in the jails and camps, we discussed the matter endlessly. Some of us came to the conclusion that the execution of the four hostages was devised and urged on the Provisional Government by a powerful group of intellectuals — lawyers and academics — who inspired the Government's repressive policies. No doubt theological sanction for the grim deed was readily forthcoming. It would, of course, be possible to suggest names but it would be undesirable to do so for the same reason that the names of the men responsible for the 153 'unauthorised murders' are better left unrecorded. They were Irishmen like us; I am sure that many of them regretted their activities. Besides it is not at all unlikely, given the structure of Irish social life, that some of their children and some of our children have married so we may well have grandchildren in common. I certainly do not want my children to inherit any part of the bitterness and hatred with which I have lived so long. I am never certain that, even in my old age, my views or feelings on any aspect of Irish life are not distorted by the lesions that this hatred and bitterness has created in my mind.

The Bishops' Pastoral affected different people differently. Dowling, who was supposed to be something of an authority on Church-State relations gave me a synopsis of the bull 'Laudibiliter' (of which I had only a vague notion) going on to contend that ever since the Bishops submitted to Henry II at the Synod of Cashel in 1170, the Irish Catholic Church fully recognised the suzerainity of the English Crown over Ireland. Ewart Wilson was distressed but took the view that the Bishops had no right to deny the sacraments to any of their flock. Frank Gallagher wrote a long, detailed refutation of the Pastoral to the Archbishop of Dublin; it was a devastating reply as well as being composed in a style much more attractive than the hysterical polemics of the Pastoral.

Ernie O'Malley certainly didn't read the Pastoral nor think it worth while discussing. Paddy Caffrey, always conscious of the obscurantist role of the Church in education, produced for my edification a book called *The Ruin of Education in Ireland* by one F. Hugh O'Donnell in which the author equated the Irish Church with the Greek Orthodox Church to whom the Turks delegated the task of keeping their Greek subjects quiescent through an organisation called the 'Fanar'. 'Fanar' was the name of that quarter of Athens in what O'Donnell called 'hierocrats' lived. Caffrey's attitude to the Pastoral was that nothing better could be expected of the Hierarchy.

The Pastoral caused me no spiritual scruples; it rather amused me. Since the split in the IRA I had heard so much abuse from individual bishops and priests that I had given up going to Mass. But the few intellectuals on the anti-Treaty side took the matter seriously. Professor Arthur Clery, Dr Con Murphy and Count Plunkett appealed to the Pope against the Bishops' action in denying the sacraments to Republicans. The only response they got was a visit from Monsignor Luzio, a representative of the Vatican of indeterminate status, whose contribution to the problem could be measured by the value of a statement he made in reply to the large number of resolutions requesting his intervention as a peace maker. He said 'I will give my heart and soul to the movement and hope to be of service to the Irish people of all sorts in the interests of Peace'. Anyway by the time of his arrival the conflict was nearly over. Even the sanctimonious W. T. Cosgrave, who on a visit to Rome was said to have embarrassed the Pope with his piety, would only receive the Monsignor as a matter of courtesy.

The Pastoral had no practical effect in diminishing IRA resistance. I heard of only one prominent IRA man, who was also a leading light in one of the great Limerick Confraternities, who submitted. I knew of no member of the rank and file who did. But I knew a very great number of the rank and file who left the Church and I know of a great number of both leaders and rank and file who never went back. I remind myself that they have never been formally invited nor has the Pastoral Letter ever been withdrawn.

Neither had the Pastoral Letter any effect on the continuance of 'unauthorised murders'. But being often committed in the hot passions of conflict (though sometimes the work of psychopaths) they were to me more comprehensible than the calculated killings sanctioned by court martial. Between the two methods of repression adopted by our opponents, who had now clearly gained the upper hand, life for us who could be easily identified by our previous associates in the IRA was nerve racking. Day and night we were in a state of feral alertness. I moved about the streets as little as possible, and then only in side streets.

I had a particularly unnerving experience one afternoon when I called at his office in Ailesbury Road to find O'Malley, who always seemed to me to be in imperturbable good humour, in very bad form indeed. Fed up of being tied to the house he was obviously glad to see me because he was anxious to get out for a haircut and wanted me to come with him. He produced two .45 Webley revolvers and handed one to me. I asked where he intended to get his hair cut and was told that in his opinion the best barber in town was next to Bewley's Cafe in Westmoreland Street. I was appalled at the thought of undertaking such an excursion, mainly for my own sake because I knew that if spotted there was little chance of our surviving. O'Malley would make sure that we were not taken prisoners even if whatever gang was sent to apprehend us would want to take us alive, which was improbable. I was appalled too that the Assistant Chief of Staff should be ready to expose himself to such unnecessary risks. I should of course have refused to go but I simply hadn't the moral courage to do so lest I should be thought 'windy', which I was. To be 'windy' was to be written off.

We walked down Ailesbury Road, caught a Dalkey tram, got off at Westmoreland Street and went into the barber's saloon at the back of a tobacconist's shop. While we waited our turn my nerves were stretched to breaking point. O'Malley insisted on the full treatment; we got not merely a haircut but a singe and a shampoo as well and only just stopped short of a face massage. On the way out he bought two large Corona cigars at what seemed to me the wildly extravagant price of half a crown each. We lit the cigars in the shop before crossing the street where we had to wait some time for a Donnybrook tram. It would be difficult to devise a better method of calling attention to ourselves than by smoking large cigars on a sidewalk in the heart of the city. We were simply not dressed for the part especially as Ernie wore a conspicuously large off-white woollen cap. I got off the tram at Appian Way getting rid of my half-smoked cigar as quickly as possible and made for the comfortable refuge of one of our safe houses nearby. As I sat over a cup of tea and emerged at last from my state of shock, I could only laugh at the sheer absurdity of the whole adventure; the picture of O'Malley and myself had something of the quality of a comic strip — Mutt and Jeff! I began too to reflect on the personality of Ernie O'Malley as exemplified by the impulsive folly which allowed him to risk his life (and worse still, mine) for a haircut. He was clearly unhappy being bound to a desk dispensing circulars to what at that time were mainly non-existent units of the IRA or, where they existed, rarely sent a reply. He would have achieved true fulfilment in leading a flying column or commando unit in the field and would have been a superb field commander.

At a later stage it occurred to me that the formation of several large commando forces (say 300 men each) led by men like Ernie O'Malley, Tom Barry, Frank Aiken or Bill Quirke might have succeeded in turning the course of the war in our favour. Our morale was very low, but if we had had the wit to realise it, the morale of the Free Staters, put to the test, was no better. The capture of the towns and cities without any determined resistance on our part had served to boost their confidence. When faced by offensive action by a column led by Barry and Quirke they collapsed with little resistance in Callan, Thomastown and Mullinavat — three towns which fell to us in one day thanks to determined leadership.

O'Malley was the most complex personality I had met up to this time. Our conversations were mainly concerned with the people involved in the current conflict, the principals on both sides being well known to him. He also told me of his exploits in the country during the Tan campaign and here I seemed to detect a note of pride in his accounts of his ability to endure torture and pain. It seemed as if he actually enjoyed his experiences in such situations. He often talked about Stoics and Stoicism although he had no training in either the classics or philosophy. He had no interest in the Irish language or in the Gaelic tradition. I got the impression that he was essentially a soldier who would have been more at home in a wider field of operations than Ireland could offer. He was fascinated by the legend which was being created around T. E. Lawrence although *The Seven Pillars of Wisdom* had not yet been published. Later on, he would, I am sure, have appreciated the role of Wingate or Che Guevara despite their very different ideologies. I did not think that O'Malley was very concerned with any ideology; he was in essence a man of action with an over-riding desire to be regarded as an intellectual, accomplished in the appreciation of music, literature, languages, history and art. Unfortunately his mental equipment, in addition to an undisciplined temperament, was disproportionate to his ambitions in any of these fields.

O'Malley's office at 38 Ailesbury Road was raided by a large unit of the Free State Army early in November. He retreated to a secret room which had been incorporated in the house when it was being built to provide a refuge for the IRA leaders during the Tan campaign. Unfortunately the builder was a supporter of the Free State and a friend of Michael Collins. The raiders made straight for the secret room, opening fire before asking questions. O'Malley in typical

Scarlet Pimpernel style shot his way out and succeeded in getting free of the house only to be riddled with bullets by the soldiers posted outside. By all the laws of probability he should have been killed instantly and only survived his wounds thanks, I imagine, to his indomitable will. He was lucky that the raiding party included none of the murder gangs; he was equally lucky that the Free State medical officers had the integrity to refuse to give in to the pressure of the 'Inquisition' to certify him as fit for trial by court martial. He survived to continue to lead an unusually full and varied life.

I knew Ernie O'Malley very well after the Civil War and until he died. Our relative positions had of course changed, I being no longer his subordinate. Of all the people I met and knew — friends, acquaintances or enemies — he was the only one whom I would judge worthy of a full biography on a scale which would command universal rather than merely Irish interest. I would very much like to have been capable of writing such a biography.

I had scarcely begun working under John Dowling, our Director of Organisation, when he received an invitation from Joe McGrath, the Provisional Government's Director of Intelligence, to meet two members of the Fourth Battalion of the Dublin Brigade, who had taken the Free State side, to discuss the possibility of a truce within the Fourth Battalion area. It was agreed that Dowling could bring another man with him and both would be given a safe conduct. Dowling consulted O'Malley who thought the invitation should be accepted and decided that I should accompany Dowling as the second man on the team.

Joe McGrath, as well as being Director of Intelligence for the Free State, was also a member of the Government. He was very well known to Dowling being one of his predecessors as O/C of the Fourth Battalion. I knew nothing of McGrath except for his reputation of being one of the real believers in the 'stepping-stone' value of the Treaty and his continued belief in separatism.

The meeting took place in the house in Harold's Cross of a member of an organisation called the Neutral IRA. This consisted of IRA men who refused to take sides on the Treaty issue and devoted their energies to trying to make peace. They believed in the principle enunciated in the Gospel of St Matthew 'Every Kingdom divided against itself is brought to desolation; and every city or house divided against itself shall not stand'. Their high minded, disinterested efforts were futile because the combatants were working in accordance with a principle expressed in the same chapter of the same Gospel 'He that is not with me is against me'. The Neutral IRA were despised equally by both sides despite their generous motivation.

When we arrived at the rendezvous we found the representatives of the Staters were none other than F. X. Coughlan and one Harry Murray, a former O/C of A Company, the Fourth Battalion. I knew Murray well but not so intimately as I did Coughlan. Dowling too knew both men well but had been closer to Murray than to Coughlan. Notwithstanding the fact that I had nothing but contempt for Murray whom I regarded as a political trimmer and that John didn't specially admire Coughlan, there was no strain or formality at the meeting; the discussion, or rather conversation, was kept rather on the level of banter. Coughlan told me long afterwards that on seeing me arrive he realised at once that there was no hope that the meeting would produce the desired result. In point of fact the terms offered ruled out any likelihood of agreement. It was put to us that if we agreed to hand in our arms we could all go home without fear of harassment or discrimination in the matter of employment and that members of the Battalion in jail or internment would be released. Dowling made it clear that there was no possibility of the Free State offer being accepted but we parted on personally amicable terms making jokes about 'meeting at the barricades'. In our case this could only be a manner of speaking as we were unlikely ever to be in the position to erect barricades again.

I think we all felt glad to have even been able to talk to former comrades without spitting at one another. The momentary surcease from corroding bitterness and hatred was welcome to both sides. I couldn't bring myself to hate Coughlan. I think too that the McGrath initiative was genuinely well meant, not merely an effort to accentuate division in our ranks for propaganda purposes. McGrath had a very soft corner in his heart for the men of the Fourth Battalion. In later and less unhappy times he gave generous evidence of this trait.

I availed of the safe conduct, which covered twenty-four hours, to pay a surprise visit to my parents. I arrived as dinner was finishing and being Sunday enjoyed my share of the family joint but, when the time came to leave, my mother broke down for the first time so that in the event I was very sorry to have gone home at all. I decided then and there that further visits would only serve to distress unduly both my parents and myself and had best be postponed until the war was over. More than a year went by before I saw my parents again.

Dowling and I continued our work in the Organisation Department but there was very little real work to do. What I remember best was a prolonged correspondence with 'O/C Britain' about the state of the organisation there. The correspondence was marked by much sardonic acerbity in which art form both 'O/C Britain' and Dowling tried to out-do one another. 'O/C Britain', whom I did not know then, was one Patrick Murray, a Cork man who had a formidable record in the Tan struggle. At one stage he had gone to New York to liquidate a spy alleged to be responsible for the death of IRA men who had been captured and executed by the British. After several weeks' search in New York he finally caught up with his target getting off a street car in broad daylight. Murray fired, hit him but did not kill him; the wounded man doubled round the street car. Murray followed, shot him three times and left him to all appearances dead. But he was mistaken, Thanks to the skill of American surgeons his victim made a good recovery and presumably lived happily ever afterwards provided the memory of his infamy did not trouble him.

Working for Dowling added to my life new dimensions which I could not have anticipated; they were unconnected with the IRA. Dowling was in character, temperament, intelligence and education the antithesis of O'Malley. He had no taste for military matters; it would be impossible to think of him as leading a column into action. He had been the star pupil of St Enda's and the favourite pupil and protegé of Thomas McDonagh in the English literature faculty at University College, Dublin. He took his degree in English Literature with such distinction that he was offered a lectureship in the college. For some reason which has never been clear to me or any of his friends he decided to study dentistry. It always seemed to me that a career circumscribed by the thirty-two teeth in the human mouth offered little opportunity to develop his amazing aptitudes and interests. Despite the tensions under which we were living I found constant pleasure in listening to Dowling discoursing on subjects as diverse as Irish place names, Vasari's *Lives of the Painters*, the French Impressionists or his own excellent painting; also English poetry with particular preference for Browning, some of whose poems he often recited to me. He spoke Irish well and knew the literature too. He had a scholarly knowledge of Irish history, was familiar with the works of George Moore and Walter Pater and was particularly devoted to Robert Louis Stevenson. He could play a Mozart rondo or a Beethoven bagatelle on the piano. He had a wide repertoire of Irish songs and ballads which he sang in a pleasant tenor voice.

The only sports he actively engaged in were boxing and fishing with the wet or dry fly. He was in his time the light-weight boxing champion of UCD. He had fished every stream and river in Dublin, Meath and Kildare, could make a fly rod from raw cane or tie his own flies. He varied his fishing trips with painting landscapes in oils. Unexpectedly, he was not interested in the theatre although in later life he had two plays produced in the Abbey. He had a sceptical and sardonic mind. The ideé reçue was not for him and he found it difficult to resist the smart remark which often antagonised the victims while amusing those who were not the object of his quips. He could have matched the Renaissance ideal of the whole man except that he had no interest in money or material possessions nor had he any ambition for power or position. He had been offered by Collins personally the prestigious post of IRA Chief Liaison Officer with the British during the Truce in 1921. He refused it, to Collins' forcibly expressed annoyance.

He also suffered from the tragic flaw of being unable to see less than six sides to any question. The result was that he found it difficult to move from consideration to action in dealing with a problem. He even found some merit in the Free State stand on the Treaty. I, who by temperament could never see but one side to any problem, differed basically from him on this issue; I regarded the Provisional Government as political scoundrels, rascals and murderers supported by opportunists, gombeen men and West Britons. My threshold of tolerance was low for people or things or actions with which I disagreed. But Dowling and I got on well together, I filling the role of his intellectual chela.

Like most of our contemporaries in the Movement (now in shambles) Dowling believed Cathleen Ní Houlihan was a Queen amongst the nations and that we could well do without foreign influence but, unlike me at any rate, his chauvinism extended to a complete lack of interest in what was happening on the European or world scene — except as events affected Ireland immediately or directly. He had, like the rest of us, a deep hatred of the British Empire. I think it was the only institution in which he was unable to see any merit.

Apart from the safe houses in which we slept there were several households known to Dowling where we could visit to relax a little, drink tea and talk on matters other than the war or the political situation. We didn't have formal parties; we just dropped in of an evening. Dowling was always a welcome guest. At one such visit to Moore's of Beechwood Avenue we met Bob Brennan, the leading Republican propagandist, and Seán Lemass, afterwards Taoiseach, who was Director of Communications. The conversation turned on

259

George Moore and the Abbey Theatre. Dowling and Brennan held the floor in a witty and fascinating exchange of repartee. Bob Brennan, being more knowledgeable on the subject than Dowling, provoked him into wild assertions about the merits of Moore and Yeats, as genuine Irishmen rather than as artists. Sean Lemass was so obviously bored by the talk that he finally left the group, standing up ostentatiously to gaze gloomily out of the window. It was the first indication I had of Lemass's contempt for what he regarded as intellectuals.

But the principal gathering-place for such meetings was a flat in 19 Pembroke Road occupied by a Miss Maureen Power. Miss Power was a secondary school teacher in her middle twenties. A Tipperary woman, she was a close friend of the famous Monsignor Browne (although I don't think he had then attained the rank of Monsignor), who was a regular visitor to the flat. Monsignor Browne was a polymath and scholar of great distinction. He was regarded as one of the brightest lights of Maynooth and afterwards became President of University College, Galway. His open adherence to our side in the Civil War was a great help to our morale. Maureen was an exceptionally beautiful woman having the complexion of a colleen idealised in so many coloured illustrations of Irish life. Unlike many of the women associated with the Movement, who affected to despise current fashions, she always dressed with care and actually used some make-up which was a rare practice amongst Republican women. The net result to my inexperienced eye was very agreeable especially as Maureen was as intelligent as she was beautiful.

Visiting her flat was my first introduction to 'polite' society. Desmond Murphy, the only friend I made at St Enda's, was a constant visitor. He had developed the manners and dress of a suave man of the world. He always arrived with a gift of flowers or chocolates. I envied him the aplomb with which he presented his tribute to Maureen. Tess, Maureen's sister, was usually present when we called at the flat. She was an Arts student in UCD but was not so good looking as Maureen although she enhanced her appearance by liberal use of cosmetics. She too conformed to the latest fashions of the time.

Brendan Considine, one of my bank clerk friends in the O'Connell Street fighting who had succeeded to the post of O/C Fourth Battalion, was always present at these gatherings. Brendan had a rare measure of charm enhanced by a smooth manner, a soft voice and an elegance of dress as unusual amongst Republican men as it was amongst Republican women. It was no surprise to anyone when

Maureen fell in love with him. They became engaged to be married but she died before the marriage could take place.

For me, in my salad days, the ambiance of 19 Pembroke Road had something of the quality of the French salons about which I had read. I could easily imagine Maureen reclining on a sofa like Madame Recamier in the famous painting. Father Paddy, as we always addressed Monsignor Browne, was the 'clou' of the gathering. John Dowling was his catalyst, inducing him to discourse on art, literature and politics. Father Paddy quoted verses from Dante in Italian, from Beaudelaire in French, from Aogán O'Rahilly in Irish, as well as chunks of Rabelais in English so as to amuse us by shocking us. His mere presence as a priestly sympathiser with the Republicans assuaged any feeling of guilt I might have had as a result of abandoning my allegiance to the Church, although I could not have imagined myself going to him for confession.

As the President of a salon, Maureen Power was a powerful temptation to the male to display his mating rituals; we all did our best. My efforts, I have to admit, appeared to be of the crudest. Maureen regarded me as something of a barbarian, out of my environment. This I sensed, so that consequently I did not share the affection felt for her by the other habitués of the salon. Sharing the company of her friends did however serve to awaken my curiosity in many areas of the mind of which I was quite uninformed and for this I was grateful.

Before Christmas I got sick with quinsy which had become for me an annual ailment about this time of the year. The tenuous medical services of the IRA came to my assistance, arranging that I should go into the Stella Maris maternity home where the proprietor, who was an active Republican, nursed me through what turned out to be an unusually bad bout of sickness. The maternity home was certainly a safe refuge; despite the high temperature and delirium associated with quinsy, the illness provided a badly needed rest from the tension of my day to day existence. I suppose it was not an accident that many years afterwards my children were born in the Stella Maris, as was my first grandchild. Mrs Gaffney, the proprietor, was a kind, staunch woman, of whom there were so many associated with the IRA. Following my recovery Christmas and the New Year were spent with the ever-welcoming Wilson family after which I reported back to Dowling for duty.

* * * * *

261

Dowling thought that the Department of Organisation should make some direct contact with the country units and decided that I should begin this process by visiting Wexford. Mrs Woods was given the job of driving me there. Her husband was the proprietor of a highly profitable and successful garage and before the split their house in Donnybrook had been the meeting (often the resting) place of the Headquarters staff of the IRA. Mrs Woods was a middle-aged woman with a large family, some grown up. Her eldest son, Tony, had been captured in the Four Courts and was now in Mountjoy Prison. She was very close to Michael Collins and to Liam Mellowes. When the split occurred she was opposed to the Treaty. Being so well known her house could no longer be used as a refuge so she directed her activities into moving guns, driving IRA men around the city, carrying despatches or acting as a centre of communications.

We started for Wexford early in January, taking the route over the Featherbed mountain. I knew the Featherbed well but I had never seen it covered in deep snow nor had I ever seen hares in such great numbers; there seemed to be hundreds of them running, apparently aimlessly, over the snow. Our destination was Mount St Benedict College, Gorey, which we reached without incident. I listened to Mrs Woods' reminiscences of the personalities who had frequented her house in the happier days before the split. She was also deeply concerned with India's efforts to secure independence. From time to time Indian revolutionaries came to Dublin seeking inspiration from our activities. Mrs Woods offered them hospitality and provided them with the necessary contacts with the Movement. But her major interest appeared to be in mythological Ireland. The spirits of Dé Danann, of Mannanán Mac Lir, Lugh of the Long Arm and Midir and Étain seemed to be very real to her. This form of other-worldliness was new to me.

At Mount St Benedict we were greeted by Father Sweetman who was a member of a wealthy Catholic clan which had been active in the politics of Irish nationalism for generations. John Sweetman, a brewer, had been a member of the Directory of the United Irishmen in 1798. Father Sweetman had founded the school at Mount St Benedict to provide an alternative to Downside or Stonyhurst for the sons of wealthy upper-class Catholics whose parents regarded a public school education as a social necessity. The school was organised on the lines of an English public school but the boys were taught that their native country was Ireland rather than England although it has to be said that no great emphasis was laid on the Gaelic dimension. Unfortunately the school was short lived.

Father Sweetman had the defects of his qualities. While his strong personality, coupled with a commanding presence, attracted the respectful affection of his pupils it succeeded in antagonising many members of the local population including the local Bishop. I can only imagine the ecclesiastical intrigues and in-fighting which finally resulted in the triumph of the Bishop and the closure of the school.

Father Sweetman refused to abandon Mount St Benedict, continuing to subsist, rather frugally, on the farm attached to the school. Believing in the Sinn Féin policy of self-sufficiency he had undertaken, on a relatively large scale, the production of Irish tobacco, an enterprise which resulted in difficulties with the Revenue people. The end product was a cigarette called 'Ballyowen' which cigarette had several times the acrid strength of a 'Gauloise'. Only the most ardent Irish-Irelanders would smoke them. As there were very few Irish-Irelanders who smoked at all, because they rejected the payment of excise duty, the market for 'Ballyowen' cigarettes was limited.

I spent only a couple of days in the not particularly safe but hospitable Mount St Benedict. During that time I came to appreciate something of the character of Father Sweetman which produced boys, many of whom I afterwards knew, so different from the products of the Christian Brothers. Unlike the latter the Mount St Benedict boys had a superabundant self-confidence which manifested itself in a typical way thirty years afterwards when, on Father Sweetman's death, the Benedictine Order arranged to take the remains to Downside for burial. A group of his former pupils (no longer boys except in spirit) formed a posse, forcing the Benedictines to hand over the body for burial at Mount St Benedict.

I was collected one afternoon after dark to be taken in a battered Model T. Ford to the Brigade Headquarters in South Wexford. Slowed by the absence of a windscreen wiper and the driving rain, we were faced with a long journey over the potholed, narrow roads, skirting broken-down bridges, and arrived late at night at a village, or more accurately, a crossroads, called Dunmain about ten miles from New Ross. I was billeted in a comfortable farmhouse, provided with a large supper and had a chat with the farmer and his wife seated at a very hot anthracite fire which, I was fascinated to see, was powered by a wheel bellows. These wheel bellows were common in South Wexford. I found during my few weeks in the locality that turning them had a soothing effect on me rather like that of a lullaby on a child.

Next day I met the O/C of the Brigade, Thomas O'Sullivan.

Before I left Dublin I had learnt something about him. In his early twenties he had been Head Centre of the IRB in Wexford. His appointment as O/C of the Brigade had been manipulated by Collins in pre-Treaty days. Considerable pressure had been put on him to accept the Free State regime but he resisted all flattery, or the cajolery of proffered jobs. It was not surprising therefore that when captured in a fight with the Free Staters he should have been court martialled and sentenced to death. With inside assistance he nearly escaped from Wexford jail and was then moved to Carlow where a few days before the sentence of death was to be carried out he succeeded in escaping, again with inside assistance. Jumping from the top of the jail wall he damaged his feet so badly as to make it impossible for him to stand up, much less walk. He crawled on his hands and knees along a railway line until he came to a small house where he knocked up the owners, told them his story and asked them inform a local friendly doctor of his plight. The people of the house, fortunately, were Republican sympathisers and succeeded in fetching the doctor who then and there put O'Sullivan in his car and drove him to a convent of sympathetic nuns in South Wexford where his injuries could be treated.

As might be expected I had formed a preconceived idea of a dashing guerilla leader but this was not the kind of man who greeted me, casually I thought. Nor did his appearance inspire any great confidence. He was a tall, heavily built man with a pallid moonshaped face, who talked with a lisp and continually squinted his eyes. I felt rather disconcerted until he began to describe to me the situation in Wexford.

South of a line between New Ross and Wexford the writ of the Free State didn't run. The Staters were confined to these two towns. From time to time they made sweeps into the countryside but, the people being friendly and O'Sullivan's men being active, these sweeps had proved more costly than effective so that South Wexford was one of the few areas of the country, apart from the mountains, where armed Republicans could move around openly. One of O'Sullivan's columns had its headquarters in Dunmain. They had made a determined attempt to take New Ross but were simply not armed heavily enough. The petrol-can mine which had been so successfully adopted by Frank Aiken in Dundalk as a substitute for artillery was unknown here. I never saw it in use elsewhere and wherever I mentioned it no one seemed to be impressed by its potential. The column spent most of its time laying ambushes around New Ross for the Free State garrison but nothing came of these activities during my short visit.

O'Sullivan, on acquaintance, belied his appearance and manner. He was quick minded, knowledgeable, clear-sighted as well as being a very brave man. He knew that we, as an army, were merely holding out in the hope of making some kind of truce or settlement which would give us a chance to re-group. Fighting had virtually ceased in the adjacent Brigades of North Wexford, Carlow and Kilkenny, but he thought that resistance should be maintained as long as possible. He felt he could manage better than most because of the friendliness of the people added to the high quality of the leadership of his few remaining flying columns. The one based in the vicinity of Dunmain I got to know very well.

It was led by Malachi Sweetman, a close kinsman of Father Sweetman. Malachi had all the external qualities which I had visualized in my preconception of O'Sullivan. He was very tall, slimly built, fair haired, blue eyed with a cheerful open face. He joked continuously, expressing rather original views on all sorts of subjects. He dressed as well and as appropriately as he looked, with an expensive jacket and well cut riding breeches with polished leggings topping polished boots. Boot polish was normally in short supply amongst the IRA. With a rifle slung over his shoulder he looked like a romantic character from P. C. Wren's *Beau Geste* or *Beau Sabreur*. He was a natural leader, creating a spirit of camaraderie amongst the column members and evoking a personal loyalty to himself. In the short time that I spent with him we formed what proved to be a life long friendship.

Curiously enough, I formed similar lasting and even intimate friendships with other members of the South Wexford Brigade. Thomas O'Reilly was nominally the Intelligence Officer but in fact he was O'Sullivan's guiding light; perhaps because he so directly contrasted with him in appearance as well as in personality. A small very, very thin man, he looked like a young waif. His people were wealthy Wexford merchants who had had him educated by the Jesuits at Clongowes. After a distinguished school career he went on to Trinity College where he studied medicine. When I met him he had just taken his second examination with first class honours. In addition to his waif-like appearance his habit of wearing town clothes set off by an exceptionally large red tie added to the impression of oddity. Oddest of all was the combination of ex-Clongowes boy and an IRA man.

O'Reilly conducted all O'Sullivan's correspondence, which was not too burdensome, but also made it his business to travel all over the county establishing cells for the collection of information. O'Sullivan and O'Reilly formed a formidable partnership as well as a close and lasting personal bond despite their different backgrounds, their different positions in the IRA and their violently contrasting personal appearance. They both became doctors. O'Reilly took a first class honours degree in Trinity, then went to England where he continued his studies before returning here to found, organise and direct the National Rheumatism Clinic. O'Sullivan went to England to become absorbed in the National Health Service where he occupied one of the senior administrative posts before retiring.

It was with the column in Dunmain that I first met Aodhagán O'Rahilly who was then a mere boy (and a very turbulent one). Later he and I spent much of our adult lives working on the development of the bogs of Ireland. We are still close friends. I do not understand why it should be so but those few weeks in South Wexford are the only period of the Civil War that I look back on with pleasure. Perhaps it was because I had a personal rapport with so many of the men around Dunmain; more likely it was because the people were so hospitable as well as having the hospitality to give. They were much better off than the general run of the rural population I had met in the North Eastern counties or of those I was to meet later in the South or South West.

I imagine the way of life of the Wexford farmers in 1922 was what De Valera had in mind when, long afterwards, he formulated his ideal of 'frugal comfort'. I came across one surprising aspect of rural class consciousness there. Walking along the road with a member of the column I suggested that we stop at a nearby house to ask for a cup of tea which I badly needed. However, my companion declined to do so because the house belonged to a farm labourer; being a farmer's son, his sense of propriety prevented his seeking hospitality from a social inferior.

All over the country our men were being captured, executed or otherwise killed and our supporters arrested and interned. Disaster followed disaster during January, culminating in Liam Deasy's call from prison to our leaders to surrender. As Liam Deasy was a member of the Executive, this was a bad blow to the morale of the IRA men still in the field. My own morale was in neutral gear but even so I had no intention of opting out or of advocating such a course of action to others. While I believed the war was irrevocably lost I felt the decision to call it off was no responsibility of mine. Little faith as I had in the leaders I was prepared to do whatever they said should be done.

I was on the point of moving over to Lambert's column which

operated at the other side of the county around Wexford town when I received instructions to report to the Chief of Staff, Liam Lynch, at the house of one Seamus Lennon at Leighlinbridge in Carlow. The message was delivered verbally by a senior member of the Cumann na mBan who had come down from Dublin specifically for the purpose. It would have been unsafe to put such an instruction in writing. The lady was more than glad to be given the assignment as she was having an intense love affair with a member of the Brigade. They wanted to marry but the local priest refused to administer the Sacrament because of the Bishops' Pastoral. This was the only case of sentimental involvement I came across in the Civil War in spite of the propinquity and very free association of men and women. This particular affaire was regarded as an aberration, so that finally G.H.Q. were asked to keep the lady out of Wexford.

The summons to join Lynch came as a surprise and I wondered what he would possibly want me for; I wouldn't have thought he knew of my existence. O'Reilly was detailed by O'Sullivan to get me to the rendezvous and the usual Model T. Ford was produced, this time with the side screens broken. A few days before we left it had begun to rain heavily. It was then early in February. That year it didn't stop raining until April when I was captured, just before the end of hostilities. In that time I never had fully dried clothes or boots.

In addition to Thomas O'Reilly and the driver of the car, a Cumann na mBan girl who knew Lennon's of Leighlinbridge accompanied us. We set off after dark, later than intended, driving through a rain storm which at times reached the intensity of a monsoon. Within half an hour of starting we were thoroughly wet. The condition of the roads and the inadequacy of a hand operated windscreen wiper slowed our progress. When we got beyond Bagenalstown we were halted by floods and had to get shelter for the night.

The girl knew a nearby farmer whom she knocked up. It was now about 2 a.m. but the farmer invited us in while his wife almost automatically started making tea. This particular family was perhaps exceptional in its acceptance of a minor household invasion in the middle of the night because they were not simply sympathetic to us but were fanatically so. One of the sons of the house was interned while another was on the run. Normally the house was not 'safe' but with the flooded state of the country there was no likelihood of a raid. There were only two beds available. I was given one, O'Reilly and the driver took the other, while the girl had to make do with a chair before the fire. It would never have occurred to any of the party to have given a bed to the girl and let one of the men use the chair — the woman's place was the chair! At least she got her clothes dry.

Next morning some of the few remaining local volunteers were organised to ferry me across the flooded Barrow river leaving O'Reilly with the driver to get back to Dunmain. The girl stayed with the people of the house. Two men rowed me across the Barrow and brought me to a large house where my arrival was clearly expected. I was at once shown into the parlour where I found Liam Lynch sitting at a table surrounded by papers.

Liam was a handsome, six-foot tall man, oval-faced with a noticeably high forehead from which light brown hair was slightly receding although at this time he was only twenty-nine years old. Being short-sighted, he wore thick-lensed, gold-rimmed spectacles. Although he was generally regarded as a Corkman, he was in fact born and reared on a small farm in County Limerick. After a National School education he went to work in a hardware store in Mitchelstown. Here, on the rising tide of Irish Nationalism, he became engulfed in the activities of the Gaelic League and the GAA and, when the Volunteers were formed, he joined not merely the Volunteers but the IRB. To these two organisations he devoted the rest of his short life. It was within the confines of these organisations, their objectives, their methods, their traditions, their personalities that Liam Lynch's character developed. The formative influence exerted by the IRA and the IRB was capable of creating very strong characters but these bodies were not in themselves capable of supplying the worldly wisdom so necessary to leadership in either politics or in war (even guerilla war). Like most of the IRA leaders Liam Lynch was not only without guile, but not conscious of it in either his opponents or friends.

Liam greeted me warmly, introducing me to his companion who was working at a typewriter. This was Con Lucey, Liam's amanuensis, although he was by profession a doctor and held the title of Director of Medical Services. In addition to doing Liam's correspondence, he acted as his driver. When the preliminaries were over and we had drunk the ritual tea, Liam told me he was going to Cork 'to pull the South together' and was taking me with him as his adjutant. Even in the condition, bordering on disintegration, in which I believed the IRA to be the Chief of Staff was, in my mind, a significant figure for whom I felt great respect. Like all high priests, the occupant derives some extra quality from his office — a sort of grace of state. I was very flattered to be chosen to accompany him on whatever task he was engaged but I was still uncertain why he chose me for this assignment or what contribution he expected me to make.

He asked my opinion of the state of affairs in the country. The question surprised me as I did not think my opinion could be very valuable to the Chief of Staff, certainly not to the point of influencing his decisions.

But I did tell him that, as far as I had had the opportunity to observe at first hand, the military situation was going very badly. Nothing of course was happening north of the Border and between Dublin and the Border, except for Frank Ailen's men, the IRA had virtually ceased to exist. I told him that I thought the Dublin Brigade was so reduced in personnel as to be militarily ineffective. I related my experiences of the South Wexford men and the high opinion I formed of their quality and morale but my information was that there was nothing to be hoped for from Carlow, Kilkenny or North Wexford. I knew little about the West except that Kilroy, the O/C of the Second Western, had been captured and that Frank Barrett, O/C of the First Western, reported that his Division had been badly hit by arrests. I knew nothing about the South.

Liam discounted my pessimism. He was cheered by my account of conditions in South Wexford expressing the view that, with effort, the rest of the country could be brought to the same level of effectiveness. He refused to accept Deasy's surrender appeal and though it was a disappointment to him personally he did not think that Deasy's invitation would have much effect on the strength of IRA resistance. In this he was probably right because those who continued to be active at that stage of the war had been immunised against anything short of catastrophe. He told me he felt sure that he could restore the situation from a base in the South. He seemed to have particular confidence in Con Moloney of South Tipperary although I had seen in Dublin a copy of a letter from Moloney expressing a most pessimistic view of the situation. I pointed out, rather timidly, that we didn't seem to have any coherent plan of action either at local, Brigade or Divisional level. I might have pointed out, but didn't, that to have the Director of Medical Services acting as secretary-cum-chauffeur to the Chief of Staff was not the best evidence of good organisation.

We stayed overnight in Leighlinbridge, continuing at dusk next day on our journey south. We drove, this time in a nearly new Ford, through the night to Mooncoin on the Suir and billeted in a large house where we were obviously expected. We moved off again a couple of days later crossing the river in cots, little boats whose design must have dated from prehistoric times. I was overjoyed to see on the far bank of the river a man dressed in the uniform of the IRA.

269

It was easily distinguished from the Free State uniform by the general cut of the man's appearance and the fact that he wore an ordinary cloth cap. He had a rifle slung over his shoulder. He conducted us to a large farmhouse situated in what appeared to be a vast orchard. Again, it was clear that we were expected.

The great kitchen was shining and instead of the customary tea we were offered whiskey which was declined. For dinner we had a magnificent meal of bacon, cabbage and potatoes together with homemade cider. The cider was very tart — dry I suppose is the correct word — so sugar was added to make it more palatable to us. I thought it was great stuff and drank three pints. Invigorated by the appetising food and drink I felt quite ready to face the long journey ahead even though the rain was again pouring down as we started.

Within a mile or so I began to feel unwell. My stomach was queasy, my head dizzy and I found it difficult to focus my eyes properly. Con Lucey examind me but could find nothing wrong until it dawned on him to ask how much cider I had taken and on learning the facts he cheerfully pronounced me drunk. I had never tasted alcoholic drink before nor indeed for many years afterwards.

Our journey continued more slowly in deference to my condition. The night was spent at a house near Mothel at the foot of the Comeragh Mountains. Next day we set out to cross the mountains. It was a most unpleasant journey, a wet, windy climb over ground that was little better than a swamp. We were very tired, wet and hungry when we reached a friendly house in the Nire Valley. There we spent a night, Liam and I sharing a bed while Con Lucey shared one with a couple of children. Indeed these continued to be our sleeping arrangements during the rest of our travels together although Con had sometimes to take a mattress on the floor. Wherever we stayed overnight we were well guarded by local units although in view of the weather conditions and the difficult terrain there was little likelihood of round-ups or even forays by the Free Staters.

I had little opportunity for conversation with Liam before bedtime because we were either continuously on the march or, when we reached a billet, there were endless visits from unit commanders anxious to contact Liam to brief him on local conditions or for a general exchange of views. His reputation, in spite of all our misfortunes, was high; he was esteemed by everyone.

My relations with Liam could not have been better. I was young, strong, tireless and uncomplaining. My Dubliner's comments, often sardonic, on the habits, customs and environment of the countryman, spoken with my very pronounced accent, amused him. I think he liked having someone near him who expressed an opinion without equivocation, sometimes forcibly. The many IRA men we met on our way south were courteous and helpful in their attitude to me though a little patronising in their sympathy with my supposed difficulty in coping with the hilly, boggy country. I didn't bother to tell them that through my familiarity with the Featherbed or Djouce Mountain in Dublin I was probably more accustomed to mountain climbing than they were.

When we were undressed to our shirts — we had neither nightshirts nor pyjamas — Liam knelt down to say a decade of the Rosary. I had no Rosary beads and I made it clear to him that it would be mere hypocrisy for me to say the Rosary. It was a form of prayer I never liked and in any case by virtue of the Bishops' Pastoral I regarded myself as no longer a member of the Church. Liam remonstrated with me, emphasising the difference between the beliefs of the Roman Catholic Church and the politics of the Irish Bishops.

Before we fell asleep Liam often talked of our predicament. When he spoke of his former comrades it was with 'a countenance more in sorrow than in anger'. To him it was shocking and unintelligible how Collins, in particular, could have started a civil war to bring the nation under the sovereignty of the British Crown or how he could have accepted partition. Nor could he understand how Irishmen could behave with the sustained savagery shown by the Free Staters in shooting prisoners held as hostages or murdering IRA men. He felt that some diabolical influence had taken possession of them as much beyond their comprehension as his. It had been put to him by many of his officers that Free State soldiers, armed or unarmed, should be shot as a reprisal for executions. He would not hear of such barbarity.

He was horrified when he found that Bill Quirke of the South Tipperary Brigade had issued a proclamation to the effect that, in the event of any member of his Command being executed, an equivalent number of leading civilian Free State supporters would be shot as a reprisal. It is hardly a coincidence that no member of the South Tipperary Brigade was executed. Liam thought that shooting prisoners was immoral; he wondered how as Christians the Free Staters justified it to their own conscience. I found it difficult to understand why he was so blind to the realities of the military position in which the IRA found itself. He had developed some mental blockage which prevented him from believing that we could be beaten. To the end he indulged a persistent hope that the pre-

271

Treaty unity could be restored through the IRB. Liam built much of his hopes of our success on the acquisition of mountain guns. He told me that Michael Cremin was in England negotiating the purchase with some illicit arms dealers, that negotiations were well advanced, and that Cremin was confident in the ultimate success of the mission. I could easily understand how the possession of mountain guns would transform the situation. With these weapons, for example, the South Wexford men would have had no difficulty in taking New Ross. I knew Michael Cremin through family connections but always associated him with the Gaelic League rather than the Volunteers or the IRA. I did not share Liam's hopes of his success.

Liam sometimes talked of his home life on the family farm, regretting that family circumstances compelled him to leave the land. He seemed to regard farming as the ideal mode of life for an Irishman. Like most of the other leaders of the IRA, he gave little thought to economics. His aim in life would, I think, have been the 'frugal comfort' of which Dev. long, long afterwards, spoke so feelingly as the economic norm to which Ireland should aspire.

He had no sophistication in any field; he was a simple, uncomplicated man, believing deeply in God, the Blessed Virgin and the Saints and, loving Ireland as he did, he had dedicated his life to her under God. He felt no bitterness towards his opponents in the Provisional Government nor the Free State Army, only sadness that they had dishonoured Ireland. To the end he believed that had Collins lived events would have followed a different course.

From the Nire valley we continued, always on foot and mainly by night, till we reached the Tar River, near Newcastle. The river was in full spate but the locals thought we would have no difficulty fording it in a pony and trap. The flood was very strong and the pony stumbled several times, finally lurching so much that the trap was nearly swamped. We were more saturated than usual but succeeded in holding our places in the trap and finally got safely across. We felt very lucky not to have been drowned.

We arrived at a place called Glenaconna. In Irish Glenaconna—appropriately enough—means 'the Glen of the meeting place' (Glen na Coinneadh). It sounded to me one of the most euphonious place names I had ever come across in my journeys in rural Ireland. Over the years it still does. Maybe the lasting memory I have of it is associated with the fact that the house in which we stayed kept bee hives. We were offered at our meals as much honey as we cared to eat. I had rarely seen honey on the table at home so that I had no particular taste for it. It must have been some physiological need that made me now feel that it was the most wonderful food I had ever eaten. The Bible phrases about being 'a stranger in a strange land' and of being led into 'a land flowing with milk and honey' assumed for me a new aspect of reality.

We spent a night in Glenaconna and left very early next morning pushing on over the Knockmealdowns to Araglin. Amongst our guards and scouts was a man from Ballyporeen who recognised me from our University College days. This was Jack O'Brien, one of my steadily enlarging body of close acquaintances, a man who was to have a significant influence on my life as I was to have on his.

In Araglin Liam was in his own country. The mere fact of being back amongst his own people was a stimulant to him. He sent an urgent dispatch to Con Moloney, O/C of the Second Southern Division, whose headquarters were in the Glen of Aherlow, to come to meet him. This meant a halt of a few days in our southbound trek but it gave Liam a chance to rest and recuperate physically. Much of the time was spent studying his maps. He had with him a collection of maps of Ireland — among them a complete set of one inch maps covering the First Southern Division. He took me through the maps of the Division in detail. He knew the extent of every Brigade, Battalion and Company area as well as having an opinion — sometimes good, sometimes bad — of the officers in charge of the different units. I began to wonder whether this quite astounding and detailed knowledge of the First Southern Division acquired before the split produced in him an illusory belief in a potential which was no longer there, thus distorting his judgement of the true military situation.

Since our stay in the Nire Valley I had begun to suffer from scabies though it caused me nothing more than minor discomfort. Scabies was known as 'Republican itch'. It was widespread amongst the IRA, although very few proclaimed that they had caught it and still fewer complained about it. Equally, no one ever mentioned that they had 'crabs' or 'lice'. It was part of the mores of the time to be ashamed of disease, however minor. I told Liam about the danger of his getting the infection from me but neither he nor the Director of Medical Services, Dr Lucey, took the matter very seriously. The cure was straightforward: cleanliness and sulphur ointment. It was most difficult to keep clean in our circumstances. It was impossible to get sulphur ointment. I had to put up with my complaint on the basis of what can't be cured must be endured.

We settled into Araglin to await Con Moloney. The people of Araglin found it hard to make a living on their infertile soil. Eggs, bread, butter, tea and milk formed our daily diet. We had neither potatoes, vegetables nor meat to eat simply because they were not there to be given. Any of these would have been gladly offered to us had they been available because the people in Araglin were as friendly as any others I had encountered and hospitable to an extent really beyond their means.

Among those who presented themselves to Liam Lynch was David Kent, a man I felt honoured to meet. David Kent and his brothers had been the only men in the County of Cork who had resisted the British in 1916 and had fought it out with the troops who came to arrest them. One brother had been killed in the affair, another had been captured and executed while David had been seriously wounded. David regarded Liam Lynch as his protegé. To me he seemed to be a very old man but despite his age he insisted, rifle slung on his back, on taking his turn on guard duty over Liam. To me he seemed the personification of the men celebrated in that most poignant of patriotic ballads which touched the hearts of generations of Irishmen, perpetuating in them the separatist idea:

Adown by the glenside I met an old woman,
A-plucking young nettles, nor saw I was coming;
I listened awhile to the song she was humming—
'Glory O! Glory O to the Bold Fenian Men!'

I passed on my way, God be praised that I met her;
Be my life long or short I shall never forget her.
'We may have as good men, but we'll never have better—
'Glory O! Glory O to the Bold Fenian Men!'

We remained in Araglin for four or five days until Liam decided he could wait no longer. He had heard of peace talks taking place in West Cork and was determined to put an end to them. He decided that, if the mountain wouldn't or couldn't come to Mahomet, at least Mahomet's representative should go to the mountain. I was to be the representative, Galtee More was the mountain. Liam gave me a map, suggesting an itinerary which might vary according to the direction or advice given by the guides whom he arranged to accompany me.

My instructions were to get to Aherlow, to see Con Moloney (whom I had never met), tell him of Liam Lynch's determination to revivify IRA resistance from a base in the First Southern Division, obtain his appreciation of the military situation and report with that information to Liam in Ballingeary in West Cork. I wasn't deterred by the long trek across the mountains to Aherlow but it was by no means clear how the second and more difficult leg of the journey from Aherlow to Ballingeary would be accomplished. Liam assured me that Con Moloney would provide me with the necessary transport and gave me an address in Ballingeary where we were to meet.

I set off to retrace my steps over the Knockmealdowns through Glenaconna where I had another welcome feast of honey heaped on home made brown bread before pushing on to Ballyporeen where Jack O'Brien, my acquaintance from UCD, arranged a billet for me for the night. He and another man accompanied me on the next stage of the journey to a place called Mountain Lodge where after some difficulty a guide was found to take me over Galtee More into Aherlow and introduce me to the IRA there. We climbed over Galtee More in relatively fine weather, dropping down into Aherlow where we quickly made contact with the IRA in the person of Dan Breen whom I met for the first time. Apart from Michael Collins, Breen was the most widely known — at home and abroad — of all the IRA guerilla fighters; it was he who started the 'shooting war' in 1919 with the Solohead police ambush. Rather to my disappointment I caught up with him drinking hot port wine in a pub called The Caravanserai. I didn't like pubs and I didn't like to see an IRA man drinking — even such an odd drink as hot port wine.

Dan told me of the capture of Con Moloney in the course of one of the many sweeps the Free Staters had been mounting throughout Aherlow. It didn't take me long to realise that, far from South Tipperary being able to help Liam Lynch in his efforts 'to pull the South together', the position there had deteriorated militarily to one of mere survival of the individual senior officers.

I decided that the quicker I got back to Liam Lynch with this news the better would be his appreciation of the situation. Breen undertook to see if transport could be found for me but without success. In the meantime I met for the first time Bill Quirke, a leading officer of the South Tipperary Brigade and a member of the Executive, and enlisted his help in solving my transport problem. Bill held out hopes of being able to organise a car but none was immediately forthcoming. Nevertheless this meeting laid the foundation of a close lifelong friendship. Sean Hayes, a tall, burly farmer who reminded me of a St Bernard mountain dog was constantly in attendance on Quirke and together we wandered up and down Aherlow, looking for transport. One morning we were alerted to a round-up by the Staters. Dressing quickly we got out of the house where we were billeted and dispersed across the fields. I climbed over a hedge to find, to my terror, a file of Free State soldiers moving in extended order at the other end of the same field. I dropped into the ditch and lay there until they left, hoping that another search party was not coming immediately behind. Fortunately my hiding place was undiscovered but it was a narrow escape.

As we moved from house to house in what seemed to me an aim-less search for a car I had at least the consolation of Quirke's company. Quirke carried as many guns and bombs as a Christmas tree had baubles while Hayes had as many again. He realised we had no hope of a military victory but he had no intention of being taken prisoner. He believed that if the Staters caught him he would not be given the formality of a trial but would be shot out of hand if not tortured. In this he was probably right. But that grim speculation did not in any way affect his good spirits or his amusingly cynical comments on men and events.

Whatever house we entered, there was a special welcome for Quirke — in particular from the women. He literally radiated cheerfulness. By this time my scabies were becoming more than a mere discomfort but Quirke consoled me by showing me his leg which was peppered with boils. He told me his whole body was equally affected. After a couple of days, I came to the conclusion that transport to Ballingeary was totally out of the question. I thought it important that Lynch should know the real state of affairs in the Second Southern Division. I made up my mind that the only hope of getting to Ballingeary was to walk there. It took me eight days.

On the map it looked a formidable journey even as the crow flew. The prospects were not improved by the necessity of travelling across country mainly by night. In my decision to make the journey, apart from my sense of responsibility to Liam Lynch, I was helped to screw my courage to the sticking-place by a desire to get out of Aherlow as soon as possible. I had no wish to share Bill Quirke's probable fate.

I decided the best route to take was to retrace my steps over Galtee More through Burncourt and Glenaconna to Araglin. Quirke provided me with a guide to take me over the Galtees. From there I had no difficulty in reaching Araglin where I felt as if I had returned home, so warm was the reception. I met several of the local IRA officers with whom I discussed the problem of getting to Ballingeary. An itinerary was drawn up and I was provided with a guide for the first part of the trek as far as Kilworth. They warned me that on leaving the Araglin area I would have to be specially careful about my involvements as the population between there and West Cork was generally hostile. Republican houses were frequently raided by the Staters who were in complete control of the area. They were right. Every house I stayed in on the way was raided the next day.

Before leaving Araglin I was given a pair of thigh-length waders which fitted over my boots. They were supposed to keep me dry but were not very effective except to the extent of helping to prolong the life of my South African field boots which were already showing signs of disintegration. South African field boots were heavy boots made from some substitute leather material — compressed paper I think — for the British war-time army.

With the help of guides, I moved on from Kilworth through two villages with, to my ears, the odd sounding names of Skinawillan and Kilavullen. I crossed over the Nagle Mountains making my way down towards Donaghmore. Skirting Macroom I arrived at a place called Kilnamartra and was directed by my guide to a house where I would find accommodation for the night. It was now about 2 o'clock in the morning and raining heavily as usual. I felt all in, wet, bedraggled, miserable, suffering from the added discomfort of the scabies which was now forming sores all over my belly. In response to my knock a light appeared after some delay and the door was opened by a young woman, obviously hurriedly dressed, who regarded me suspiciously and asked what I wanted. Having, with some difficulty, convinced her of my bona fides I was given a warm welcome. She showed deep solicitude for my plight but could not avoid laughing at my near resemblance to a scarecrow.

She brightened up the fire, made me get rid of my waders, gave me tea, home made bread and boiled eggs, telling me rather apologetically, that though the house was far from safe I had no alternative but to spend the remainder of the night there. As she talked, fussing sympathetically about my sad condition, it began to dawn on me that there was something special about this household. It was in fact the home of one of the leading Republican families in Cork: O'Sullivan's of Kilnamartra. The young woman was Eileen, who had just graduated in languages at University College, Cork. She was engaged to be married to Donal Óg O'Callaghan who had succeeded Terence McSwiney as Lord Mayor of Cork city.

She was what we in Dublin would call 'a fine figure of a woman', not particularly beautiful but she had for me a quality of charm that I had not previously experienced in a woman. In happier times I got to know Eileen and Donal Og very well, spending many an evening with them. Meeting Eileen O'Sullivan was a landmark in my appreciation of women. She epitomised for me the truth of the French proverb I came across years later: 'C'est la gaieté des femmes qui dissipe la tristesse des hommes'. She insisted on providing me with a clean shirt, promising on my advice to burn the discarded one along with the waders. She got some ointment for my itch which at least acted as an emollient. She showed me to my bedroom where I slept long and deeply and more easily and comfortably than for many a day.

I stayed at O'Sullivan's until dusk when I was taken by a guide to my next stop at another safe house at Ballyvourney. I spent the night there and was delighted to hear that the people of the house, having killed a pig, would have black puddings for breakfast next morning. There were two other men on the run sleeping in the house. I was down first to breakfast to find a large plateful of puddings on the table. Not until I had eaten them all did I realise that they had been intended to be shared with the other lodgers. I wasn't being greedy but I had not seen puddings since leaving Dublin and had eaten very little meat of any kind.

We were now in Republican territory. I took off unaccompanied on the final stage of my journey to Ballingeary armed with an address where I expected to make contact with Lynch. I had only gone a couple of miles along the road when a car, full of armed men, approached. It passed me, then stopped and reversed and one of the men got out to ask who I was. I replied that I was Staff Captain Andrews on my way to join Liam Lynch. 'Jaysus' was the reply. 'Are you the man he has been expecting for days? He was beginning to think you would never turn up. He thought you had been killed or captured'. My interrogator turned out to be Tom Crofts, a leading Cork IRA man. He squashed me into the car, turned it round and drove some miles into the mountains to a place called Lackabawn.

I found Liam in a large two storey house, sitting at a table surrounded by papers and maps with Con Lucey working at his typewriter at a side table. He had a warm welcome for me. I gave him my own appreciation of the disarray in the Second Southern Division. He showed no surprise nor did my report seem in any way to upset him. He was already aware of Con Moloney's capture. I gathered from Lucey rather than from Liam that he had met the surviving members of the Divisional Council of the First Southern Division who had told him almost unanimously that there was no hope of successfully carrying on the war.

Nevertheless, Liam continued to believe in the possibility of victory and much against his will gave way to the pressure from the First Southern officers who demanded a meeting of the IRA Executive. Arrangements for a meeting to be held in Tipperary later in the month were put in hand. In the meantime Tom Barry became involved in peace negotiations initiated by Father Tom Duggan, who, himself a staunch Republican, had been a British army chaplain because he believed that souls had neither nationality nor politics. From the beginning of the civil war Father Tom, who was liked and trusted by everyone, tried to heal the split in the IRA. He was now making his last effort. He had seen Liam Lynch who made it clear that he was not willing to compromise in any way. Barry was more flexible. In a strongly worded letter, which I saw, Liam ordered him to discontinue further involvement in peace talks.

Liam, with Con Lucey and some assistance from me, continued his preparations for the meeting of the Executive. I was feeling none too well. Even though Con Lucey succeeded in getting a large box of sulphur ointment for treating the scabies I had also developed impetigo which caused the sores on my body. Although Liam knew of my condition, he expressed no objection to my sharing his bed. Oddly enough, he never seemed to have been infected by the 'Republican itch'.

Liam was not a loquacious man but at night, before we went to sleep, we would chat about the events of the day or about items in the newspapers which had developed into mere propaganda sheets for the Provisional Government. Curiously, he specially resented the term 'irregulars', by which the Staters insisted we be described. He often adverted to his belief that if we accepted the Treaty we would become a mere province of Britain. I once ventured to suggest what a misfortune it was that the country had not stood by De Valera in his rejection of the Treaty, giving him full control of the direction of affairs, supported by the unequivocal loyalty of the IRA. Liam didn't altogether agree with this view; even Document Number Two would have been too much for him willingly to accept. Liam had not been at all in favour of the IRA setting up an alternative Government; he believed that De Valera would make a compromise peace and he now opposed the holding of a meeting of the Executive for the same reason.

On another occasion I expressed the view that the burning down of the 'Big Houses' was a mistaken policy. I thought it would have been better to expropriate them because they were believed to be stuffed with treasures accumulated from all the countries of the Empire which the owners of the Big Houses or members of their families served so well. I had heard or read somewhere that much of the loot from the Winter Palace of Pekin, sacked in the Boxer Rising, had found a resting place in Ireland. Liam agreed but did not pursue the matter further.

It was while we were here on the Cork/Kerry border that we heard of the Free Stater atrocities at Countess Bridge and Ballyseedy. Liam was nauseated by the news. He seemed to live with the irradicable belief that Irish men, particularly if they had served in the pre-Truce IRA, were born without the stain of original sin. We knew the names of the Staters responsible. They were Dubliners, all formerly very active IRA men, who during the Truce had been acclaimed as heroes and whose exploits every IRA man would have been glad to emulate. It has to be said that those responsible claimed provocation because many of their men had been the victims of booby trap mines laid by the anti-Treaty forces.

Liam got a detailed report of the occurrence from Humphrey Murphy, O/C of the Kerry Number One Brigade, who came to see him a few days later. He described how our men had been tied to mines and blown to bits, how one man was blown into a tree, miraculously escaping with his life and his freedom. The events at Ballyseedy and Countess Bridge were barbarities to which there were indisputedly authentic witnesses. The country was shocked by the story despite the efforts of the newspapers to put a gloss on it. I think that at least some members of the Free State Government were taken aback; nevertheless nothing was done by way of repudiation.

One night we were awakened abruptly by the door of our bedroom being kicked open. A figure appeared with a lighted candle in one hand and in the other a sheet of paper. I was terrified by this sudden and violent intrusion. My first reaction was that the end had come at last, that we were at the mercy of the Staters. Liam recognised, more quickly than I, that the visitor was Tom Barry. He waved the piece of paper about, shouting angrily 'Lynch! Did you write this?' The paper in Barry's hand was Liam's order to withdraw from peace feelers. To the question Liam merely replied 'Yes'. There followed a tirade of abuse from Barry mainly directed at asserting the superiority of his fighting record. Barry's peroration was dramatic: 'I fought more in a week than you did in your life'. Liam simply said nothing. Having emptied himself of indignation, Barry withdrew slamming the door. I broke out laughing at this stage partly with relief, partly at the absurdity of the whole situation. Barry's dramatic entrance holding the candlestick with the lighted candle struck me as having something of the character of an Abbey Theatre farce. When

I think of it now, it still does.

The local pacificators got busy. A meeting between Liam on the one hand with, on the other, Tom Barry and Father Duggan was arranged to be held in Ballingeary. Liam, Con and I duly went to Ballingeary to find that Father Duggan and Tom Barry, accompanied by several men I did not know, had already arrived and were grouped on the opposite side of the street. The scene resembled one from a Western film when rival groups of ranchers come into some cowtown to shoot out their differences. As soon as the parties had got together, I detached myself. Remote from the problems of peace and war my mind was preoccupied with the possibility of buying sweets. I wandered around a bit before finding a small shop. The only sweets for sale were bullseyes but they were as acceptable to me as the honey of Glenaconna. No progress was made at the conference between Father Duggan and Liam Lynch. We returned to Lackabawn to find Humphrey Murphy from Kerry waiting for us.

The same afternoon we were surprised to see approaching the house a young woman fashionably dressed in city clothes. As she approached she paused for a moment to apply lipstick. In the wilderness of West Cork to be faced with such an exotic figure was as if we were seeing an apparition. The use of lipstick was a strange sight in itself; lipstick was not commonly used even in the cities, certainly not by the women of the Republican movement. This was an exceptional young woman. She was Kathleen Barry, a sister of Kevin Barry, a woman very prominent in Republican circles, working close to De Valera. It was as an emissary from him that she had come down from Dublin to discuss details of the coming meeting of the Executive. I was very glad to meet her if only to hear a Dublin accent, albeit muted.

Perhaps inspired by the courtesy he felt due to a visiting lady, Humphrey suggested that we take a trip to see some of the beauty spots of Kerry. Rather to my surprise Liam accepted the invitation. Our first stop was at the home of John Joe Rice, O/C of the Kerry Number Two Brigade, where his father, an old man, received us with a degree of courtesy that I had never experienced before. He had some rare quality of gentility (in the best sense of the word) that made a lasting impression on me.

Liam, Humphrey, Con Lucey, Kathleen Barry and myself, with the driver, mounted a jaunting car. I sat with my long legs dangling over the back of the car while I listened to Humphrey dilate on the magnificence of the Kerry scenery above Kilgarvan. I had had my fill of the countryside and in any case I thought the passing

scenery was inferior in beauty to Glendhu or Glenasmole which were
at my back door at home. Like Dr Johnson said of the Giant's
Causeway it was worth seeing but not worth going to see. I felt
miserably uncomfortable on my perch at the back of the car. As
Humphrey grew more and more rhapsodic, I was moved to interrupt
his spiel in a loud voice 'Christ! If only I could get one look at
Nelson's Pillar!' My utterance was so spontaneous, so genuinely a *cri
de coeur,* that my companions nearly fell off the sidecar laughing.

We stayed a day and a night with Humphrey who, determined to
do justice to the Kerry reputation for hospitality, had arranged what
were in the circumstances Lucullan meals. Rashers and eggs, boiled
mutton, turnips and biscuits: these delights ranked far above the
scenery in my estimation.

On returning to Lackabawn, we found that arrangements had been
made for our journey to the Executive meeting in Tipperary.
Having gathered up Liam's voluminous papers and maps we set
out one evening at dusk, by car, to a rendezvous beyond Ballingeary
where we were met by a group of officers of the First Southern as well
as a body guard who were to accompany Liam to the Executive
meeting. Con Lucey had left us at Ballingeary to return to Cork City.
A lorry had been provided to take us to our first overnight stop
at Araglin. Our feelings as the journey got under way might
justifiably have been those of men about to keep an appointment with
destiny or some such portentous assignment. We had no such
forebodings. On the contrary everyone was in good humour; there
was much banter and a certain amount of sly nudging as Tom Barry
automatically took command, less by rank than by personality.

We drove into the night and it was easy to see why Barry was
probably the best field commander in the IRA. Before approaching
any crossroads he dismounted, covering the passage of the lorry with
the body guard. The operation he was commanding wasn't
complicated, but his air of confident authority impressed me. One felt
safe with Barry in charge. Around midnight we came to a point
somewhere beyond Kilworth where it had been arranged to abandon
the lorry, continuing the journey to Araglin on foot. We disembarked near a country pub. I've always thought of the name of the
pub as 'Davey Burke's' but this name may be the product of a
blurred memory. Maybe Davey Burke never existed or I came across
the name somewhere else in my travels.

It was decided to have some refreshment before completing the
journey. Barry placed a guard around the premises before we
knocked up the proprietor. He came down with what I thought was a

very good grace but it was Seán MacSwiney, brother of Terence MacSwiney, who installed himself as barman. When it came to my turn I asked for a lemonade much to Seán's disgust because everyone else had ordered whiskey or stout; I think he suspected that there was something wrong with me. The fact that I was the only teetotaller in the group was a deep disappointment to me. So innocent was I that I still believed that only the occasional IRA man took a drink. I was surprised to see Liam drink a small whiskey because he always refused alcohol when offered in various houses we visited. I associated alcoholic drink with national degradation bearing in mind a recurrent theme from the halcyon days of Sinn Féin 'It was the drink that got us down'. I was glad to see that only one round of drinks was consumed before we resumed the journey to Araglin.

The North Cork men were expecting us and had arranged billets in different houses. As usual I stayed in the same house as Liam. While we were having a cup of tea before going to bed, I commented to the woman of the house on a flitch of bacon which was hanging from the ceiling. She told me, with great satisfaction, that the lads had commandeered a lorry load of bacon from Sir John Keane's factory at Cappoquin and had distributed it among the people of the area. It was a welcome addition to their monotonous diet which consisted almost entirely of bread, butter, eggs and tea.

I was now feeling sick and run down and apparently looked as much. Liam told me to have a rest at Araglin for a few days until he returned. He gave me a five pound note for expenses. It would have been very interesting to have been in on the Executive meeting but I was well pleased not to have to tramp again over the Knockmealdowns to Ballinamult at the foot of the Monavullagh mountains, about twenty miles away, where the meeting was to be held.

Before he left we had a long chat. In spite of all the evidence of impending defeat he had no intention of capitulating. He thought he would be able to carry the Executive with him in his determination to fight on. For some not very apparent reason he had still hopes of our making a comeback in the West, especially in Mayo. He than said something that completely knocked me off my psychological balance: namely that on his return from the Executive meeting he intended to send me to the West 'to take charge there'. I was very disconcerted by this suggestion. I was not specially modest but I just did not see myself as competent to command any army unit above the level of a Company in the Dublin Brigade. The notion of going to the West to 'take charge' was totally incomprehensible to me. I didn't even know precisely what area Liam had in mind since there were four IRA Divisions in the West. I had no knowledge of what conditions in the West were like, never having as much as crossed the Shannon. I suppose I should have been flattered that the Chief of Staff should have viewed me in these favourable terms; I always thought that he regarded me as a reliable dogsbody, agreeable and sometimes amusing. On reflection, I didn't take his remark too seriously, feeling sure that with second thoughts he would realise the absurdity of the idea or, if not, someone would surely point it out to him. I said goodbye and wished him luck as he left Araglin, accompanied by Tom Barry, Tom Crofts and Humphrey Murphy, with half a dozen men acting as his bodyguard.

When Liam left I went to bed and remained there for a few days while the kind people of the neighbourhood washed my clothes, provided me with cigarettes, sweets and even an additional supply of sulphur ointment. They tried to get me a pair of boots to replace my own which were falling apart but none could be found to fit my long feet. In addition, thanks to Sir John Keane, we had rashers for breakfast and bacon and cabbage for dinner. As a result of the improved diet and the care and attention I got from the people of Araglin I felt much better after four or five days and was looking forward with some anxiety to Liam's delayed return.

I never did, nor ever could, make adequate return to the kind people who welcomed me into their homes and fed and cared for me so generously during the Civil War. I felt and still feel guilty for doing nothing to acknowledge my debt to them apart from saying thanks when leaving. We were thoughtless young men taking, I think, too much for granted. They were grand, decent, staunch, hospitable, generous people. I am guiltily conscious of what not just I, but the separatist movement and the country at large, owes such people who, at so much sacrifice, helped to keep the embers of national feeling alight when, as we believed, British imperial interests, helped by their allies in the Provisional Government, were trying to quench them in blood.

The results of the Executive meeting were inconclusive. It was agreed to adjourn until 10 April. Liam started back for Araglin where the rearranged meeting was to take place but changed his mind. The presence of a number of members of the Executive in the Goatenbridge area became known to the Staters who saturated the area with troops and commenced a large scale round-up. Liam was killed in the course of an engagement and the other members of the Executive were forced to disperse. The events which followed Liam's death are so well documented by the historians as not to require repeating here.

Of course I was upset by Liam's death. I had become very fond of him. He was a good man, brave, strong willed, uncomplicated to the point of simplicity. He thought that all his IRA or IRB colleagues were as highly motivated as he was. He had been more than kind to me. He had the religious faith of an Irish Catholic countryman. God and the saints were real to him. He regarded them as allies of the Irish Republic to which he had dedicated his life. He had had little opportunity to acquire a broad knowledge of men or affairs, being only twenty-nine years of age when he died. By this time I had long since lost my faith not merely in the Church but even in the comfortable myth that we Irish were the salt of the earth.

With Liam Lynch's death I knew the end of the Civil War had come. Only his iron will had kept it going for the last few months. After his death the members of the Executive scattered over the hills. Austin Stack, Frank Barrett of Clare, Sean Gaynor of North Tipperary, Dan Breen of South Tipperary, and Humphrey Murphy of Kerry arrived with several other Commandants in Araglin having successfully got through the cordon of Staters. Austin Stack, who was billeted in a nearby house, sent word to me to call on him.

I had never met Austin Stack although I had often seen him in the Dáil or at public meetings. I was mildly curious as to why he should want to see me. When I presented myself he was sitting at a table working on some documents and appeared to be in a nervous, agitated state. Stack, I gathered, had heard about me from Liam and I seemed to detect in him a feeling of surprise as if he had been expecting a different sort of person. To him I must have looked immature. He told me he thought the time had come to call off the fighting. He had prepared a statement for publication to this end. He gave me the statement to read and asked my opinion of it. As I read I suggested a few verbal alterations here and there. I think he regarded my suggestions as criticisms whereas they were only intended to improve the syntax and spelling. I told him I agreed that further military action by the IRA was futile but that I was not sure how best to call a halt.

Stack replied that he proposed to call a meeting of any members of the Executive as well as any IRA officers who were still in the Araglin area to request them to add their signatures to the document which he then would issue. With very considerable diffidence I suggested that neither he nor the officers mentioned had any authority to act in this way; such an appeal issued under such auspices would have no effect except further to confuse and demoralise the men in the field if this was possible. Low as morale was it was certain that such an appeal would at best get a limited response.

I told Stack that I thought it improbable that any of the officers concerned would be willing to sign the statement but in any case I personally could not agree to do so because I was far too junior in rank to be publicly dictating IRA policy in a matter of such importance. Stack had no difficulty in agreeing about my juniority. He felt he had made a mistake in consulting me, being evidently under a misunderstanding of my status as adjutant to Liam Lynch. He neither liked nor valued my views. Obviously I had not established a rapport with Austin Stack. At the same time I felt sorry for him. By temperament I was always anxious to be given responsibility in matters however trivial. Seeing the agonising effect Stack's sense of responsibility was producing on him, I was very glad that I was not in his shoes.

Stack called a meeting which was attended by Frank Barrett, Sean Gaynor, Dan Breen as well as several officers whose names I don't recall; they were mainly Tipperary men. About ten of us gathered to hear Stack's statement presented for approval and signature. All those present, with the exception of Dan Breen, agreed with Stack that it was neither politic nor sensible to carry on the war. Breen made a dramatic, highly emotional speech, though rather out of context, the nub of which was that he would never surrender. No one of the group was willing to go along with Stack's proposal; all thought it would be better to leave the decision to call a halt to hostilities to the Executive which had been reconvened for 20 April.

We received information that the Staters were planning a round up of the Araglin area. In the meantime we had decided to move across the Knockmealdown mountains towards the Comeraghs in the search for greater security. When the raiding party did arrive the only success they had was to recapture the remains of Sir John Keane's flitches of bacon which they took back to restore to their owner. By this time I had cured myself of the worst of the scabies and impetigo while rest, good food and cleanliness had fully restored my physical condition so that I didn't mind the idea of another long mountain trek.

The group, about twelve of us including guides, got as far as the Clogheen/Cappoquin main road which we crossed without incident. In a state of near exhaustion we dragged ourselves to the side of a ravine which borders the road. Darkness was falling when a Free State armoured car arrived on the scene opening machine gun fire on s just as we had reached the top of the ravine. We took whatever cover was possible, waiting until it was fully dark before regrouping. We took shelter in a nearby house where Breen, with the Tipperary men, decided to press on to their home base in Aherlow. Austin Stack, Frank Barrett, Sean Gaynor and myself decided to stay put intending to make our way along the foot of the Comeraghs towards Mullinahone in the vicinity of which the adjourned Executive meeting was to be held.

As we were close to the famous Cistercian Monastery of Mount Melleray we thought of invoking the well known hospitality of the monks but our guides advised against it as the place was far from being immune from raids. Next day scouts brought news of the round-up being resumed by the Staters. We were in the middle of the area of the sweep. We moved our billets several times, travelling at night. We eventually reached a place called Crow Hill, where we were lodged in a house in which a dug-out had been constructed in a hay barn. It wasn't long before we had to use it.

Very early in the morning scouts warned that Free State troops were approaching. We got into the dugout which was formed from a hay-stack hollowed out in the centre. It was barely capable of holding the four of us even when squashed closely together and we could not stand upright. It was painfully uncomfortable for want of movement and air. Our discomfort was compounded by the problems of urinating or refraining from coughing. After hiding for an hour in this fetid hole Stack, who was feeling sick, could stand it no longer. In comparison with the rest of us he was an old man, not in very good physical condition. It was not surprising that he decided to get back to the farm house and take his chances.

My own inclination was to follow suit but I decided to stay a little longer. Nothing happened for about half an hour after Stack left; then we heard footsteps in the barn, followed by the probing of the hay with a bayonet which grazed Frank Barrett's eye. We held our breath until the probing stopped and the footsteps receded. Finally on the point of suffocation and unable to endure confinement any longer all three of us emerged only to learn that the troops had arrived immediately after Stack had reached the house. He was recognised and taken prisoner whereupon the raiders departed without searching the house much less the barn. Stack's arrest was a sufficient reward for them for that day's work. What we thought was a solider's bayonet was actually the farmer removing hay with a fork for his stock. It hadn't occurred to the farmer to tell us when the troops had gone because, he said, they might come back.

The Free State propaganda machine made great play with the

arrest of Austin Stack, particularly with the 'stop the war' document which we had refused to sign but which was found in his wallet.

In the early evening we moved again, this time to an unusually comfortable house where there was considerable disagreement between us whether to spend the night there or push on towards the Nire Valley which might be outside the round-up area. By this time we were very weary, very dispirited and very wet. We were on the run in the most literal sense being hunted as animals are hunted from lair to lair. Our minds were emptied of all thoughts of the coming Executive meeting, of the future of the IRA, of the future of Ireland or of any future but our own. We were preoccupied with the sole problem of survival.

My boots had finally disintegrated, kept together only by tying the soles to the uppers with twine. The decent people of the house were pressing in their invitation to stay and it was easy to persuade ourselves that this was the best course. The inevitable happened. Next morning we were awakened only to find the place completely surrounded by Staters. We put on our boots and coats (the only things taken off when going to bed) and dashed out of the house to be met with a burst of rifle fire. We scattered but only got as far as the perimeter of the yard when the troops met us almost face to face. We were prisoners. I was minus the sole of one boot.

The captain in charge of the operation came forward to ask our names and where we came from. I'm not sure what we expected, but I was surprised to find no hostility in his demeanour. He was a young, tall, good looking man with a pronounced West Cork accent. We each gave false names but when I told him my name was O'Keeffe from Glenaugh in South Tipperary he laughed saying an accent like mine didn't come from Tipperary. I had to concede the point and amended my story by giving my Uncle's name of Paddy Moran from Summerhill.

He led us to a lorry standing on a nearby bohereen. He said that I obviously needed new boots but, being a Sunday morning, this might prove difficult. He also said that he had a feeling that he had seen me before. This might well have been when I was taking over the barracks from the British in West Cork but I decided to make no comment at the time. Our bedraggled appearance must have evoked some sympathy in him or perhaps he guessed that Barrett and Gaynor constituted a significant capture.

His troops, who seemed to be West Cork men, were quite civil to us. I certainly did not expect that the Captain would go the trouble of searching for a pair of boots for me. He directed the lorry into the little village of Ballinamult and found a shop that sold boots. He knocked up the owners and explained what was wanted. I was fortunate enough to get a pair of heavy boots, size tēn and a half. I suppose the Provisional Government paid for them one way or another.

We resumed our journey, arriving in the afternoon at Lismore Castle where we were confined to one room with two beds and a mattress with blankets laid on the floor. Later the Captain brought us a day old *Cork Examiner* to read as well as cigarettes and matches and we were given a meal. Writing materials were supplied to enable us to write to our families and the Captain undertook to see that our letters were posted. I wrote to an aunt by marriage; the others wrote to relatives with names different from their own.

We had time now to reflect on what was going to happen to us. It was almost certain that the IRA Executive would order a cessation of hostilities but we didn't know whether it would take the form of an unconditional surrender or just a unilateral cease fire. We might be tried and executed or sentenced to long terms of imprisonment. We thought it unlikely that we would merely be interned. The mild treatment we had so far received was very unexpected.

Tired as we were we found it hard to sleep because apart from our own anxieties about the future almost continuous volleys of rifle fire could be heard coming from different parts of the quiet castle all through the night. Vainly, we thought the Staters had fallen out amongst themselves. Next morning after a good breakfast the Captain ordered us to pack up as he was taking us to Fermoy army barracks. None of us had anything to pack except a razor, shaving sticks, shaving brush and comb which we were carrying in our pockets. As the Captain (whose name we never learned) parted company with us I told him that he had seen me before and where. He was pleased to have so well remembered a face. It is a common human vanity to think that 'I never forget a face'.

We arrived at Fermoy where the friendly Captain handed us over to a surly Commandant who asked for our names and addresses. This time we disclosed our real names. He expressed no surprise nor did he pursue the interrogation, nor were we searched. We asked if we might have a bath and a shave, to which he replied disagreeably that he was not running a hotel. We were glad to see the last of him. A junior officer with a guard of soldiers conducted us to a large room where three mattresses were laid out on the floor. During the two days of our stay in Fermoy we saw only the guards who brought our meals or conducted us to the latrines except for one visit from a group of senior Free State officers, headed by General David Reynolds, who came to the door of our room, looked in for a minute or two and departed without a word.

We were next brought by lorry to Cork Female Jail which was now being used as a prison for Republicans; there were, of course, no females about. Several hundred IRA prisoners were housed there but we were kept away from the main body in a remote part of the jail. Again, we were not 'processed' but were placed together in one cell which had three mattresses on the floor. We didn't meet the Governor whose name, if I remember rightly, was Commandant Vaughan, an old IRA man from north Cork.

A captain of the guard called on us. He informed us, rather apologetically, that by order from HQ we were not to be allowed to associate with the other prisoners and that special arrangements would be made for us to exercise. He asked if there was anything we wanted. Barrett and Gaynor had each a few pounds but I had nothing apart from the five pounds given me by Liam Lynch which I was determined not to part with except in an emergency. We asked the officer to get us some cigarettes, matches and chocolates and if possible some reading matter. He promised to try to locate a few books and magazines and that arrangements would be made to have the *Cork Examiner* and *Evening Echo* sent to us every day. He said that the Commandant had instructed him to have our food sent daily from the officers' mess.

The general attitude of the Free Staters we came in contact with, apart from those in Fermoy, was so different from what we expected as to astonish us. We began to wonder if we were cast in the role of a goose being fattened for Christmas dinner or more likely that of the condemned prisoner who is allowed to order anything he likes before execution. We didn't know if the good treatment was official policy or just decency on the part of the Governor and his staff. In fact, it was due to the Governor. I saw him in the distance a few times but never knowingly met him either then or since. I hope he is alive and reads this some day.

We knew that by this time the Executive had met or was in session. We looked forward to news of it with anxious interest but in our isolation there was no possibility of even hearing rumours of what was happening. We hadn't long to wait for on 27 April, just a week after we arrived in Cork Jail, De Valera and Frank Aiken ordered a 'cease fire'.

We were very relieved at this announcement as it minimised the risk of being taken out and shot, which was our main fear. Sean

Gaynor and I had no one to consider except ourselves. Frank Barrett had the additional worry of being a young married man starting to raise a family. I felt very sorry for his evident anxieties. The cease fire made no immediate difference to our living conditions which, but for being continuously confined to one another's company, were as good as could be expected. Apart from boredom it was easy enough to get on one another's nerves under conditions of such propinquity. The Governor sent us in a few books of the Nat Gould variety and we were glad enough to have them.

Soon, without anything being said, our cell door was left open all day. In no time we had visits from other prisoners — most of them Cork men, none of whom I knew, although some, like the Free State Captain who arrested us, remembered me from taking over the West Cork barracks or from having met or seen me with Liam Lynch. Little by little we merged with the rest of the prisoners, ultimately being able to occupy separate cells, a great relief to all three of us.

I was readily accepted by my fellow prisoners on the plane of an active IRA man; I was one of themselves. Indeed, not for the first time, I found I had a certain status rating, a 'rub-off' from my association with Liam Lynch. Otherwise I found that they regarded me, in the friendliest possible way, as an oddity. To them I was the original Dublin 'Jackeen'. Most of us were very young men so that our childhood, boyhood and early adulthood were still very close to us. As the men from Cork city talked amongst themselves of the places where they played and swam and shopped, their teachers and their friends, I realised that our frame of reference had little in common. The men from the rural areas were even more remote from my experiences of growing up in Dublin.

Some of them were quite fanatical on the subject of Gaelic football or hurling. They vehemently discussed the relative merits of the Barrs or Glen Rovers, teams of which I had never heard. My dislike of both Gaelic football and hurling, and the fact that I was a devotee of soccer, didn't help towards establishing common ground. The only athletic interest we shared was an enthusiasm for handball and a dislike for Rugby football in which the followers of the game were included.

None of them had been prisoners for very long and now that the ceasefire had been announced it was generally believed that they would not be held much longer. They all seemed to have jobs or farms to go back to when released. They were a light-hearted crowd, amusing themselves with banter and practical jokes which often developed into rough-housing. They didn't share my resentment and bitterness towards the Free Staters. They frequently expressed regret at the death of Collins and, like Liam Lynch, were convinced that things would have been different had he lived.

Among the few Kerry prisoners the feeling was quite different. They regarded the Staters as traitors or murderers. They had no particular admiration or regret for Collins. The fall of Cork to the Free Staters reflected no credit on the Cork IRA units and in the guerilla phase of the war they put up less resistance than might have been expected. I felt that the Cork IRA suffered from a sense of collective guilt for the death of Collins. The civilian population of Cork was predominantly pro-Treaty which made it difficult for guerillas to operate. There were relatively few Free State atrocities in Cork nor much harassment of the civil population although, even in Cork, there was widespread indiscriminate chivvying of Republican sympathisers.

In Kerry the position was very different. The majority of the people were anti-Treaty. The Kerry IRA put up stronger and more successful resistance to the Staters than anywhere else in the country. They were finally crushed by troops drawn specially from the 'tough' men of the Dublin and Northern units who emulated the methods of Cromwell or the Yeos of 1798. Prisoners were sometimes not taken or, if taken, were murdered in custody. They were beaten or flogged. Civilians were ill treated, their houses constantly raided, their movements constantly impeded or disrupted. In March Charles Daly, a very well known, distinguished Kerryman, and two companions, who had earlier been sent to Donegal to form part of the proposed Army of the North, were captured and executed at Drumboe in County Donegal. These executions created particular bitterness being regarded by us as coming into the same category as the executions of Mellows, O'Connor, McKelvey and Barrett in that they were intended as a reprisal for the Kerry resistance with some element of personal vengeance as well.

My fellow prisoners in Cork seemed to be fascinated by my accent which then carried even more of the vowels, consonants and multi-syllables of Summerhill than it does now. I was constantly being teased about my pronounciation of words like book, school, or zoo. To their ears, my version sounded like 'buke', 'skule', and 'azoo'. To me, their accents were equally odd, sometimes unintelligible.

I became friendly with Jim Hurley, a leading West Cork IRA man, later on a Cork County hurler and an academic in University College, Cork. Our friendship began with our common interest in handball. We played in an improvised alley in the prison yard. I had quite a 'tip' about myself as a handballer. During the last month of my stay in Cork Female Jail I played a few games every morning with Jim Hurley but never once succeeded in beating him.

The time passed, if not agreeably, painlessly enough. My mother sent me a complete outfit of clothes including boots, several shirts, a coat and trousers and leggings; I was about the best dressed prisoner in the jail. From time to time, Barret, Gaynor and I gathered to discuss the political situation outside or as much as we read about it in the Cork papers. At this stage so loose was the prison discipline that a newsboy from the streets came in morning and evening to sell us the *Examiner* or *Echo*. Cork jail was really a detention centre rather than a permanent internment camp. It reminded me of Arbour Hill rather than the Rath Camp.

De Valera now had complete direction of the Republican Movement. He did his utmost to arrive at some sort of compromise settlement with the Free State Government. These overtures invariably foundered on the question of the oath of allegiance to the British Crown. It appeared to us that the Free State authorities were determined to humiliate us. They ignored the 'ceasefire' and continued the arrest and execution of IRA activists into May. The Public Safety Act was passed to enable them to perpetuate this policy as well as to keep thousands of prisoners in jail without trial. Even after the executions ceased the power to resume them was retained as an ever present threat to our immunity. They behaved as what in reality they were, successful dictators heavily backed by the British Government.

I had long since changed my mind on the virtues of a military dictatorship because I had ceased to believe that the IRA leadership would have had the capacity to give the country a stable administration. I was now learning what it was like to have one's liberty placed at the mercy of a dictatorship. In spite of the humane, even generous treatment extended to us in Cork, we were nevertheless prisoners with no assured prospects of being released. Although I wrote home at least every week, receiving parcels and magazines by return, I was hankering after home and my parents. I was also hankering after Dublin. I had never been away from the city for so long. To be in Dublin gave me a feeling of confidence and security; I felt surrounded by friends, by familiar buildings and streets. The pavement was where I belonged. To be exiled was in itself a heavy punishment.

After about two months in Cork a group of about fifty of us were told one morning to pack up. Barrett and Gaynor were not included. We were paraded in the exercise yard where there was a unit of Free State troops waiting to take us in charge. To my embarrassment the officer in charge turned out to be a member of my old 'E' Company of the Fourth Dublin Battalion. He and I had been close friends. He was the one I have referred to earlier as the 'Bricriu' of the Company.

He had always been a source of great amusement to me and even many long arguments during the early days of the Treaty debates had not affected our friendship. When he saw me among the prisoners he detached himself from his men and advanced on me beaming, with outstretched hand. Succinctly I told him what he could do with himself but he refused to be insulted. I knew that he was really glad to see me and wished me no harm; nevertheless I didn't want to have any personal relations with any Free Stater and I told him so. He still refused to be insulted, indulging in a lot of the banter and codology which I had found comical in the past. Finally my resistance collapsed and I broke into laughter. From him I learned we were being transferred to an internment camp—he wasn't sure which but thought it was the Curragh. His job was merely to put us on the train at Cork Station. We were driven to the station in lorries and as I was getting into a carriage a sergeant handed me a carton of 500 cigarettes which he said was a gift from the Commandant.

At Newbridge Station we disembarked to find that we were to be interned in the local barracks. Newbridge had been the headquarters of the fashionable British cavalry regiments in Ireland. It was there that King Edward VII, as Prince of Wales, had lost his virginity. It was an enormous place with wide parade grounds, many stables with saddle rooms attached, a spacious sports field, a hospital, kitchens and canteens. The extensive barrack blocks were three stories high. The Free State authorities had converted the complex into the largest internment camp in the country and it already held nearly two and a half thousand prisoners. On arrival we were looked over by the Camp Governor and his staff. It did not take long to realise that their attitude to us was very different from the humane behaviour of their counterparts in Cork Female Jail. As we were 'processed' into internment, we found them to be a brusque, bullying lot.

We were allocated a number and a billet before being let loose into the compound. My number was 2571 and I was assigned a billet in one of the barrack blocks. We were immediately surrounded by friends — mine being, of course, Dubliners — who assured us that it was unnecessary to pay any attention to the billet allocation. Some very old friends of mine whisked me off to share their quarters, army hut number 60, which housed about thirty Dublin men mainly from the Four Courts garrison. It was a great pleasure to be once again amongst so many colleagues and acquaintances.

By the time I had been fed and settled in I knew that relations between the prisoners and the Camp authorities were very bad. A few weeks earlier following the discovery of a tunnel some of the prisoners had been beaten by the guard and others, caught more or less in the act of escape, had been taken to the 'glasshouse' in the Curragh where they were very roughly treated before being returned to Newbridge. Parcels and letters were stopped though they had been resumed just before we arrived. The prisoners had been given a bad time by parties of Staters who raided their huts or dormitories, upsetting the furniture and scattering their belongings. It was the kind of upheaval that invariably occurs in internment camps when escapes, whether successful or otherwise, are attempted. The prisoners' O/C, Tom McMahon, with the entire prisoners' Camp Council, had been removed to Mountjoy Jail. The prisoners had not got around to choosing a new O/C and the consequent lack of discipline tended to aggravate the general discontent which was never far from the surface in any internment camp at that time.

My new companions in Hut 60 had been interned, first in Mountjoy and then in Newbridge, for a long time. They were hungry for news of their friends and of outside events. I was just as anxious to hear of their experiences, particularly details of what had happened in Mountjoy on the morning of 8 December 1922, when the infamous reprisal executions took place.

I spent my early days in Newbridge touring the camp, meeting at every turn acquaintances from all over the country. It began to dawn on me what an enormous number of people I had got to know and what large areas of Ireland I had travelled since the beginning of the Civil War. Again I noticed, to my surprise, that my mere association with Liam Lynch had conferred on me a minor distinction. Often I was asked about his last days; often I had to correct the impression that I was actually with him when he was killed.

I met an old friend, Jack Callanan, the second of the bank clerks who had been with me in the O'Connell Street fighting in Dublin. Jack had been with me in the Tramway Office when I was wounded. He was a rugby football fan, so enthusiastic that he succeeded in forming several rugby teams in the camp. However, soccer seemed to be the most popular game played there, pointing up the predominance of the Dublin internees. Gaelic was played too but to a much lesser extent.

These aspects of camp life turned my mind to the many contrasts between conditions in Newbridge and life as I remembered it in the Rath camp under the British regime. In the Rath camp rugby or soccer would not have been tolerated by the prisoners. The high morale which existed in the Rath had disappeared to be supplanted by the disenchantment of defeat. The future of the nation had no meaning for us. We were waiting more or less stoically to be released. Even release was not looked forward to with much enthusiasm because most of the prisoners had no special future to look forward to. Escape, the great stimulus to the morale of internment camps in any country in any time, was rarely mooted.

The other customary prison occupations were scarcely practised. Many of the men neglected their appearance, didn't shave, didn't take baths. The prevailing atmosphere of the camp was like that of a mediaeval monastery in the grip of accidie. This attitude of mind did not obtain among our group in Hut 60 thanks largely to Paddy Rigney, one of the few members of the Active Service Unit of the Dublin Brigade who took the anti-Treaty side. He was a natural leader, a disciplinarian with an almost passionate interest in the cleanliness and order of our hut. Once a week the hut was swabbed out with Jeyes' Fluid, beds were properly made every day, fatigues were fulfilled. We all knew one another well; here we had common terms of reference.

There was no library. Making macramé bags or beating coins into finger rings was unknown. The occupants of our hut were divided into messes of four or five people. Each mess shared parcels together. My mess included Jack Plunkett, one of the surviving sons of Count Plunkett, whose brother, Joseph, had been executed by the British in 1916. Another member was Andy McDonald who had been in charge of transport in the Four Courts. He was one of the prisoners who had been in the 'glasshouse' in the Curragh. The fourth member of the mess was Bobby Byrne whom I had known since childhood. We were a compatible quartet.

The physical conditions in the camp were as good as one could reasonably expect. The food was the same as that given to our guards which meant that, unlike the British food in the Rath, the butter, meat and vegetables were of a high quality. We had beds instead of bed boards, as many blankets as we wanted as well as sheets. After the upheaval which followed the attempt to escape, the Staters interfered minimally with our daily routine.

The will to escape had gone. Interest in the Irish language was at a discount; nobody spoke it and nobody learned it. Cathleen Ní

Houlihan was something of a joke. The fact is that a considerable number of the prisoners should not have been interned at all; they had no convictions nor any involvement in the Republican movement.

Jim Moloney, who was the senior officer and who before his capture had been Director of Communications, was appointed Camp O/C. He appointed me Camp Adjutant and an officer of the Dublin Brigade named Luke Masterson as Camp Quartermaster. Masterson's chief function was to act as liaison officer with the Free State authorities. Jim Moloney was by profession a pharmacist from Tipperary town. He was amongst the finest characters I had met in the Movement (although by this time the word had faded from our vocabulary) and was widely read and informed. Modest, though not retiring, I thought he never appreciated his own worth. He had more than his share of common sense. With the help of the more responsible men in the different billets he re-established discipline, seeing to it that the necessary fatigues, such as washing out billets weekly and clearing litter from the compound, were carried out.

As Camp Adjutant, I became the repository for the prisoners' complaints: something had been stolen, someone's bed was defective, a man wanted a change of billet, some huts were not getting their fair share of the food rations. I did not expect that I would also be asked to give advice on personal problems which had nothing to do with camp life. Men came to me to ask permission to 'sign the form' in order to obtain their release. I had to explain that neither I nor anyone in the camp had the authority to allow them to sign the form. It meant that the signatory undertook to recognise the Free State Government set up by the British as the legitimate Government of the country. The Civil War was fought to deny that claim and there was a strict IRA order forbidding prisoners to seek release on these terms. Still the men insisted on telling me their tales of woe and asking my advice. Some had parents who were in poor financial circumstances and it was possible to do something for them by referring the case to the Prisoners' Dependants' Fund. There was little I could do to help a couple of men who had 'got a girl into trouble' to use the euphemism of the day. Nor could I do much to console one who had received an anonymous letter to the effect that his wife was carrying on with another man, nor yet another whose wife had run away in his absence.

My days were largely filled with listening to such problems. At the end of the day I was tired, often emotionally drained from having been brought so closely in contact with so much human misery. It wasn't that I was unaware of indigence, seduction or marital

297

infidelity. I had always been aware of indigence; living in Summerhill or Terenure it was inescapable. But cases of seduction, common enough though they were, were merely hinted at, never discussed openly. Once, in Terenure, a terrible tragedy occurred as a result of marital infidelity but while everyone talked about the case its real cause was never mentioned. My experiences as father confessor had at least the advantage of helping to hasten my maturity.

I was always very relieved when lock-up came and I could relax with my friends in Hut 60. In the evenings we usually gathered round one another's beds to chat. The principal topic of conversation was the Civil War. We talked about our dead comrades, of happenings in other prisons, of personalities on our side or of the iniquities of the Staters with particular reference to those we knew personally. We talked about why we lost the war and of the odious prospect of having to live our lives under the Free State regime. Our nightly conversations had the inevitable effect of continuously recharging the batteries of hate.

We read little except the daily papers which, having become propagandist sheets for the Free State, had little interest for anyone except those of us who studied the 'Births' Deaths and Marriages' column or sports results. I noticed that my brother Paddy won the Dublin schools' all-round athletic championship and wrote to congratulate him. He replied making an incomprehensible reference to his 'experience'. Later I found out that, still a schoolboy, he had been taken off the pitch at Croke Park while playing hurling by two CID men. They took him to Collins Barracks where he was held for two days before F. X. Coughlan, who was visiting the Barracks by chance, discovered him and arranged for his immediate release, sending him home in an Army tender.

I still got the *New Statesman* and *The Observer*. I found the book reviews in the *New Statesman* entertaining. I made mental book lists and all sorts of resolutions to read them when I got out. *The Observer* kept me informed, reasonably objectively, of world affairs, particularly the happenings in Russia and in Turkey where I followed with great interest the career of Kemal Pasha Attaturk, mainly because he was twisting the British Lion's tail.

I became very close to Jack Plunkett. He was a quiet-spoken reserved man, almost a recluse. His principal interests were mechanical engineering, especially the internal combustion engine, and Thomistic philosophy. I loathed anything to do with machines, even bicycles, but I was quite curious about philosophical matters in a wide but ill-informed way. I was delighted to listen to Jack discourse on the Summa Theologica of which I had never before heard. Jack's faith was unshaken by the Bishop's Pastoral; the Summa provided him with much justification for taking that position. I'm afraid I found the Angelic Doctor too subtle or too logical for my badly trained mind to recognise the force of his arguments as expounded by Jack.

For a young man, without responsibilities, eating well (with the addition of parcels, eating almost luxuriously) and enjoying the company of agreeable companions as I did in Hut 60, I did not feel too badly when it became apparent that we could not hope for early release. Life in the internment camp was fairly diversified. Apart from the three codes of football — Gaelic, Rugby and Soccer — concerts and theatrical shows were organised.

'Drag' was always a popular feature of the theatricals; there were some extraordinarily good female impersonators. It was perhaps not surprising that 'drag' was so popular amongst so many men deprived of female company. 'Bad language' was quite common, being sometimes brought to the level of a fine art. It was a form of catharsis and possibly indicative of repressed sexuality. Dirty stories were rare and homosexuality unknown.

The general acceptance of bad language was also a symptom of falling morale; such language would not have been endured in the Rath Camp. There it would have been associated with the British Army. On the other hand, sex was rarely discussed; too many of the men had been at some stage of their lives Christian Brothers' boys. Any adventures they may have had in ditches or hay barns in the country or city alleys or tenement hall-ways were kept to themselves.

From time to time boxing tournaments were organised. At one of these I encountered my aeronautical friend, 'the Deacon', still living in his 'Walter Mitty' world, this time as a champion light-weight boxer. The poor man's fantasy was dissipated when, with some reluctance, he was persuaded to get into the ring with a semi-professional boxer called Stouty. After the first round Stouty realised he was dealing with a tyro. He prolonged the fight for the three stipulated rounds, much to the cruel amusement of the spectators. But the Deacon was in no way abashed.

The prospect of release did not seem improved by the Government's decision to hold a General Election in the autumn. Misled by its massive, highly competent propaganda machine we assumed that the Government would be returned by a huge majority, especially as there were 12,000 IRA men in jail who would have been the most active election workers for Sinn Féin, the anti-Treaty party. But the Government itself, no less than us, had been misled by its own propaganda. To its dismay, it got only 39% of the votes; we got 27.6% while the rest was distributed amongst Labour, the Farmers' Party and Independents.

Furthermore, it was far from being a free election. In every constituency we had a few brave, usually elderly, active supporters who were neither on the run nor interned and who fought the election in the face of intimidation. To quote from *The Irish Republic,* Dorothy MacArdle's definitive book: 'Police, military and intelligence agents were used to dislocate the election work of Sinn Féin. Election offices were raided; literature was seized at the printing works or removed from speakers' cars; boys engaged in bill-posting were beaten; a parcel of Sinn Fein seals for ballot boxes were stolen from a messenger; many chairmen and speakers were arrested . . .'

The 27.6% of the voters who supported us, when added to the potential votes of the Nationalists in the Six Counties, constitute roughly one third of the Irish people. I see this figure as representing the permanently irreducible minimum number of separatists who did not accept then, do not accept now, nor will accept in the future anything less than complete national independence. It is a segment of the population sufficiently large to ensure that, so long as the British occupy any part of this island, normal political conditions cannot prevail.

De Valera appeared at an election meeting in Ennis before an immensely enthusiastic crowd but before he could speak a squad of soldiers with fixed bayonets moved in on the platform to arrest him. He was kept in prison for nearly a year. At that point he again became the unquestionably accepted leader of Irish Republicanism. The first step was taken to bring the fight against the Treaty from a military on to a political plane.

We were surprised by the outcome of the election and were encouraged to hope that it might hasten our release. The Treatyites, under the party name of Cumann na nGael, may have been dismayed by the result but their high-powered propaganda represented it as an overwhelming endorsement for their draconian policies. At the same time they sat back to enjoy the spoils. Patronage was liberally dispensed while the social activities of a bourgeois elite — dances, balls, garden parties, bridge parties, dinner parties and receptions — were fully reported in the columns of the newspapers.

It was a frequently expressed regret in these circles that the

Governor General, Mr Timothy Healy, the arch scamp of Irish politics who had been more or less forced on the Free State Government by Lord Beaverbrook, was not as hospitable as he might have been. Their regard for him was not increased by a quip he made on the lack of *savoir vivre* shown by the Free State Generals. 'What would you expect' he said, 'considering their mothers were "generals" (a colloquial version of the term "general servant" at that time) too'. The capers of the Free State establishment were alien, even distasteful to many of its supporters; to us they were laughable.

Conditions in all the prisons and internment centres were not as endurable as they were in Newbridge. In Mountjoy the position was especially bad, some very brutal treatment being handed out to the prisoners. In October over four hundred men went on hunger strike there. An order of the day was issued by Aiken, now Chief of Staff, to all IRA men and civilian sympathisers asking for support for the Mountjoy hunger strikers. Whatever the intention, it was interpreted in the internment camps as an invitation to support the Mountjoy prisoners by joining the hunger strike and in Newbridge over two thousand decided to do so. Within days men found they couldn't endure the lack of food and abandoned the hunger strike in increasing numbers until one day, after about a week had passed, a mass hysteria swept the camp. The cookhouse with its very abundant stock of food was raided by prisoners transformed into an uncontrollable mob. It was a most unedifying and humiliating sight.

Some men persevered but day by day more dropped out. After fourteen days Jack Plunkett and I decided that the whole effort was futile and was creating division and personal animosities in the camp. We decided to come off the strike. Fourteen days without food, like my earlier experience in Mountjoy, left me with no disabilities, real or imaginary, beyond the discomfort of hunger which became much less after a few days. We lived on tobacco and cigarettes and 'hunger strike soup'. I didn't have to stay in bed. I walked round the compound as usual. In the beginning men came to ask my permission to discontinue the strike. I explained a dozen times that taking part in a hunger strike was a matter of individual decision, that there was no question of compulsion, that there was no disgrace in giving up. Unfortunately men felt that in abandoning the strike they were guilty of weakness. Human nature being what it is, they resented those who continued to hold out.

Of the two thousand men who started the strike there were about thirty still refusing to take food at the end of a month. One of these, Denis Barry of Cork, became very ill. I approached the prison chaplain to request his attendance on Barry but was met by a blast of abuse against Republicans in general supported by quotations from the Bishops' Pastoral. He was particularly scathing about the men who were prolonging the hunger strike to the point of committing suicide; they had put themselves outside the Church. I wasn't backward in matching abuse by abuse, telling him how lucky men should feel no longer to be accountable to him or associated with the Church which he represented.

We parted on very bad terms and refused to recognise one another whenever afterwards we met in the compound. Nevertheless I felt he had not completely ignored my protest because Denis Barry was almost immediately removed to the Curragh Hospital where he died after a few days still refusing to take food. I would be surprised if he did not die in the arms of the Church as I think it unlikely that many priests faced with this situation were prepared to see terms of the Bishops' Pastoral through to the ultimate conclusion.

I too had a deep sense of guilt about the whole affair. I think I was the only man in the camp who had previously taken part in a hunger strike. I knew the inevitable consequences of a prolonged mass action of this nature. I should have had the moral courage to refuse to take part in it. Within the camp I had become a man of some consequence. My example, had I had the moral courage to follow my convictions, might have prevented the demoralisation as well as the recriminations which followed the collapse of the strike.

Some of the men simply refused to give in. They carried on for over forty days reacting to the prolonged fast in very different ways. Some suffered from hallucinations, some were just wasted from hunger, some were apparently unaffected physically or mentally. I saw Dan Breen's brother, 'Sparky', walking around after forty days without food smoking a clay pipe. On the initiative of some prisoners in Kilmainham the strike was called off at the end of November. We were spared much embarrassment in Newbridge when almost at once on the conclusion of the hunger strike regular releases were again resumed. I doubt whether mass hunger strikes, under whatever provocation, will ever again take place in Ireland.

The rate of release accelerated until, nearing Christmas, we were reduced in numbers to five or six hundred. My mother wrote proposing to send me a Christmas hamper by car if I hadn't been released before Christmas Eve but I declined the offer in emphatic terms. I told her what she should have known: that I never liked Christmas nor could I see why on one day in the year it was necessary to change one's eating habits.

On Christmas Eve I was called to the Governor's office. He gave me no hearty Christmas welcome. He told me that apparently I had some high up friend in Dublin who wanted me released for Christmas and that I was free to go home that day if I signed 'this' — in other words the detestable form acknowledging my allegiance to the State. I felt genuinely insulted and reacted accordingly. I suspected that my 'friend' in Dublin was F. X. Coughlan and this he confirmed. I then told the Governor that he, with the help of F. X. Coughlan, could dispose of the form in a certain well known Dublin manner. He replied very angrily that I could rot in jail as far as he was concerned.

I returned to the now almost deserted compound. Jack Callanan and nearly all my friends from Hut 60, except Jack Plunkett and his brother George, had been released. Bert Earle who had been discharged from Gormanstown some time previously sent me books to read. Jack Callanan deluged me with cigarettes. More cigarettes and chocolates came from other friends of mine who had just been released. But with all that we spent rather a miserable Christmas. All the life had gone out of the camp. We were just waiting to go home.

But our time had not yet come. The barrack blocks were cleared out and the remaining prisoners concentrated in the huts. Jack Plunkett and I managed to stick together. We got billets in Hut 40. Our fellow prisoners were mainly Midlanders. More releases occurred after Christmas. Early in January we were herded together and marched to an internment centre on the Curragh — Tintown number 2 — where I became prisoner number 876 although in fact it contained only five or six hundred prisoners in all, the residue from several internment camps which had been closed.

Jack Plunkett and I succeeded in staying together in the same Hut in adjacent beds. We had barely settled in when releases recommenced but only on a sporadic basis. One day four prisoners would be released, another day only one. The result of this policy meant that we couldn't settle down to any reasonable routine; every day we expected our turn would come. We became tense and restless: 'hope deferred maketh the heart sick'. The one way to relieve boredom was to read. Thanks to Earle I was well supplied with reading matter and there were always a few books to be borrowed around the camp so that my lapsed reading habits could now be resumed. The weather was so bad that it was nearly impossible to leave the hut. There was nothing much else to do except read or chat.

Jack and I spent most of our time together, sometimes talking about St Thomas Aquinas' distinction between faith and reason, sometimes about the saints and scholars of the early Christian

Church. It would be more correct to say that Jack talked while I listened with, sometimes sceptical, interest. We talked about more recent Irish history and indulged in many arid discussions about the might-have-beens of 1916. Jack held strong views on this subject blaming Eoin MacNeill for depriving the 1916 men of any chance of success. We fought the Civil War over and over again and speculated on a rumour of a mutiny in the Free State Army. So we passed the time until April, when an officer of the guard came to the hut, called my name and told me to pack up as I was being released. I left Jack the five pound note which Liam Lynch had given to me.

I took nothing with me except my shaving gear. I was brought to the office, given a rail ticket to Dublin, told the time of the train and sent on my way to the local station. On arriving at Kingsbridge, I hadn't a single coin to pay my tram fare. I asked the tram conductor to let me travel free to Capel Street Bridge. Learning my predicament, he readily agreed.

I went down Capel Street to my father's office where I found him 'on the perch' conducting a jewellery sale. I intended to wait until he had finished but on seeing me he interrupted the sale. He was emotionally overwhelmed by my unexpected arrival. He insisted on giving me a fiver when I only wanted my tram fare home to Terenure. He gave me that too.

As I got off the tram at Terenure, the first person I met was my brother. He had grown into a tall handsome young man since I last saw him more than a year before. He insisted on preceding me to break the shock of my unexpected appearance to my mother. I had arrived back to the warmth and security of my home.

The Civil War was over for me. I had survived. I was nearly twenty-three years of age, unimpaired in health but with a mind ineffaceably scarred by bitterness. I believed the Free Staters had reduced the status of the nation to that of a materialistic province of Britain, still in part occupied by British troops, governed by what appeared to us Republicans a clique of Castle Catholics. It was not the Ireland we visualised, nor was it the Ireland we Republicans were willing to accept although we had no idea as to how we could alter the situation.

But despite much disenchantment, I was more firmly convinced than ever of the validity of Wolfe Tone's 'Theory': 'To subvert the tyranny of our execrable Government, to break the connection with England, the never-failing source of all our political evils and to assert the independence of my country — these were my objects'.

304

Epilogue

It took a few days to convince my mother that my health was not permanently damaged by being on the run and in jail. This period of cosseting was not unwelcome; it gave me the opportunity for recollection and reflection.

Europe was in turmoil, suffering the disastrous consequences of the Treaty of Versailles. This was the time of the beginning of the rise of the dictators. Lenin died, to be succeeded by Stalin and the consolidation of the Bolshevik revolution. Attaturk was installed as dictator of Turkey and Mussolini was fastening his hold on Italy. Hitler's first bid for power in the 'putch' at Munich had failed but the failure was merely temporary. I watched all this with intense interest, always hoping that some misfortune would undermine the British Empire. But in the early 1920s this seemed a remote possibility.

However, international events excited little interest in Ireland. Even the coming to power of the first Labour Government in Britain with the inept Ramsey McDonald as Prime Minister passed without much notice. To us Republicans it was a matter of indifference what brand of government was in power in Britain — Conservative, Liberal or Labour — we could not hope for complete freedom unless some form of force majeure compelled the British to abandon their hold on the country. We believed in the maxim 'England's difficulty is Ireland's opportunity'.

We were convinced that even if the English people or the majority of the House of Commons wanted to get rid of their Irish problem, the Establishment, particularly the War Office, would not allow it to happen. That seemed to us a great pity because we felt no animosity to the English people; we knew the majority of them had been thoroughly ashamed of the Black and Tans and wished us well. If only they would get out and leave us alone we could be very good neighbours.

In 1924, as I began to take up the threads of my life, nothing had changed under the new political regime except, as was commonly said at the time, the pillar boxes had been painted green. Metaphorically that was true. The Dáil adopted the rules and regulations of Westminster. The Civil Service was developed exactly on the British model, the laws as they stood were adopted holus bolus, the procedures and practices of the courts were much the same as they had always been. The most noticeable difference was the evidence of bi-lingualism in public signs and notices.

In rural Ireland the Gardai looked different from the Royal Irish Constabulary and were unarmed but in Dublin there was not much difference in appearance between the Dublin Metropolitan Police and the new force.

The physical damage caused by the Civil War, which was anyway not very great, had been or was being repaired. The real damage to the nation was the intense bitterness and hatreds created by the split. The nation suffered a psychological wound which was largely unhealed until the second World War when the whole people rallied behind the policy of Neutrality. Even then, the psyches of many of the participants in the Civil War were never healed: it was a burden many carried all their lives.

To every action there is an equal and opposite reaction and our hatred of the Free Staters was balanced for us by that marvellous spirit of comradeship, loyalty and friendship which only shared experiences can bring about. I found this aspect of the Republican Movement particularly rewarding; it was my good fortune to have met hundreds of worthwhile people from all over the country in my travels and in the jails and camps. Also, I had got an opportunity to know the topography and the customs of the countryside outside Dublin which was unusual for a Dublin man with my background. I used to boast that I could cash a cheque in any part of Ireland if I had had a cheque book.

But we Republicans did not have cheque books, not necessarily because we had no money but rather because we regarded a cheque book as an undesirable status symbol just as we regarded plus fours, white flannels, dinner jackets, white ties, morning coats and above all, silk hats, as political symbols. Our attitude to sartorial usage was in fact a distinguishing mark between us and the Free Staters.

The newspapers published a photograph of the Government of the day standing in line, dressed in frock coats, striped trousers, lavender waistcoats, silk hats and carrying umbrellas. They were indistinguishable from the chorus line of a musical show called 'The

Byng Boys' which was running in London at the time. If that didn't seem to us absurd enough, a photograph appeared in the papers showing the President of the Executive Council, W. T. Cosgrave, in the Court Dress in which he attended some function at Buckingham Palace. His silver buckled shoes, silk stockings, velvet knee breeches, lace shirt and velvet jacket looked painfully ridiculous.

These fancy dress extravaganzas were peculiarly offensive to us confirming our belief that the Free Staters had accepted for the country the status of a British province in which they would adopt and operate the social structure and manners of the former Ascendancy.

The sense of Liberty, Fraternity, Equality had always been a potent element in the mores of Sinn Fein and the IRA. A particular characteristic of the egalitarianism of the Movement was the universal use of Christian names. Irrespective of the positions of responsibility they held, men were addressed by their Christian names. There was one exception. Nobody called Eamonn De Valera anything but 'Mister' De Valera, 'Sir' or, if one was reasonably close to him, 'Chief'. It is said that Harry Boland, his companion on his American trips, called him Ned. No one has disclosed how his Limerick family addressed him.

Except for birth and death, everything happens in Ireland on a smaller scale than in almost any other nation. I could look back on my young life without any cause for complaint and say with truth that, small as the country was, I had tasted many of the possibilities of the human condition even if only in homoeopathic-like doses. I had had a happy childhood in Summerhill and Terenure, school days which I thoroughly enjoyed, accumulated friendships — the most gratifying feature of my life. I had had a fair share of adventures and emotional experiences. Hunger striking, street fighting, escaping from jail, being wounded, tramping the country under arms, all added up to help my maturation. So too did the fears I endured in the basement cell of Arbour Hill jail. I had exercised some authority and taken some responsibility. I found that I liked exercising authority and welcomed responsibility. I had learned some of the lore of the river along the Dodder and of trees and birds in Shaw's Wood. I knew Dublin city life well, with its slums, its bustle, its characters and its sardonic humour.

I was less interested in my future than in my past. Thanks to the feeling of security provided by my ever-indulgent parents. I had no fears for the future. I had made up my mind to go back to College in the autumn and was toying with the idea of doing Agricultural

Science because agriculture seemed to be the best prospect for earning a living. I had no defined personal ambition but I felt that the leisure of university life would give me the opportunity to participate in the re-building of the shattered Republican Movement.

I could not then foresee that the country which meant so much to me was going to afford me a life as full, varied and satisfying as any Irishman living in Ireland could hope for.

INDEX

309

310